Lamar



# SAS® Programming III: Advanced Programming Techniques

## Course Notes

*SAS® Programming III: Advanced Techniques Course Notes* was developed by Susan Farmer and Jane Stroupe. Editing and production support was provided by the Curriculum Development and Support Department.



The Institute is a private company devoted to the support and further development of its software and related services.

**SAS® Programming III: Advanced Techniques Course Notes**



---

Book code 58019, course code PROG3, prepared date 17Jul00.

# Table of Contents

# Course Description

This course builds on the concepts presented in the SAS® Programming II: Manipulating Data with the DATA Step course. This course focuses on

- reading different forms of data
- writing and creating data
- investigating data with the COMPARE, CONTENTS and DATASETS procedures
- summarizing data with the SUMMARY and SQL procedures
- combining summary data and detail data
- presenting data.

Managing data structures and data values is also discussed.

## To learn more...

A full curriculum of general and statistical instructor-based training is available at any of the Institute's training facilities. Institute instructors can also provide on-site training.

For information on other courses in the curriculum, contact the Professional Services Division at 1-919-677-8000, then press 1-7321, or send email to saspsd@vm.sas.com. You can also find this information on the Web at www.sas.com/training/ as well as in the Training Course Catalog.

For a list of other SAS books that relate to the topics covered in this Course Notes, USA customers can contact our Book Sales Department at 1-800-727-3228 or send email to sasbook@sas.com. Customers outside the USA, please contact your local SAS Institute office.

Also, see the Publications Catalog on the Web at www.sas.com/pubs for a complete list of books and a convenient order form.

# Prerequisites

Before attending this course, you should have completed the SAS® Programming II: Manipulating Data with the DATA Step course, or its Version 6 equivalent, SAS® Programming. You should have at least nine months of experience writing SAS programs.

Specifically, you should be able to

- understand file structures and write system commands to create and access files
- understand programming logic concepts and error messages in the SAS log
- understand the compilation and execution process of the DATA step
- use different kinds of input to create SAS data sets from external files
- read and write different types of data (including simple access of relational databases)
- create and use SAS date values and use SAS functions to perform data manipulation and transformations
- read, concatenate, merge, match-merge, and interleave SAS data sets by using the SET, MERGE, and BY statements appropriately
- create multiple output data sets
- use array processing and DO loops to process data iteratively
- create default and HTML list reports, summary reports, and exceptions reports.

# General Conventions

This section explains the various conventions used in presenting text, SAS language syntax, and examples in this book.

## Typographical Conventions

You will see several type styles in this book. This list explains the meaning of each style:

| | |
|---|---|
| UPPERCASE ROMAN | is used for SAS statements, variable names, and other SAS language elements when they appear in the text. |
| *italic* | identifies terms or concepts that are defined in text. Italic is also used for book titles when they are referenced in text, as well as for various syntax and mathematical elements. |
| **bold** | is used for emphasis within text. |
| `monospace` | is used for examples of SAS programming statements and for SAS character strings. Monospace is also used to refer to field names in windows, information in fields, and user-supplied information. |
| **select** | indicates selectable items in windows and menus. This book also uses icons to represent selectable items. |

## Syntax Conventions

The general forms of SAS statements and commands shown in this book include only that part of the syntax actually taught in the course. For complete syntax, see the appropriate SAS reference guide.

**PROC CHART** DATA= *SAS-data-set;*<br>
    **HBAR** | **VBAR** *chart-variables* </ *options*>;<br>
**RUN**;

This is an example of how SAS syntax is shown in text:

- **PROC** and **CHART** are in uppercase bold because they are SAS keywords.
- DATA= is in uppercase to indicate that it must be spelled as shown.
- *SAS-data-set* is in italic because it represents a value that you supply. In this case, the value must be the name of a SAS data set.
- **HBAR** and **VBAR** are in uppercase bold because they are SAS keywords. They are separated by a vertical bar to indicate they are mutually exclusive; you can choose one or the other.
- *chart-variables* is in italic because it represents a value or values that you supply.
- </ *options*> represents optional syntax specific to the HBAR and VBAR statements. The angle brackets enclose the slash as well as *options* because if no options are specified you do not include the slash.
- **RUN** is in uppercase bold because it is a SAS keyword.

# Chapter 1

# 1.1 Introduction

## General Business Scenario

International Airlines has several data files that need to be manipulated so that they can create reports.

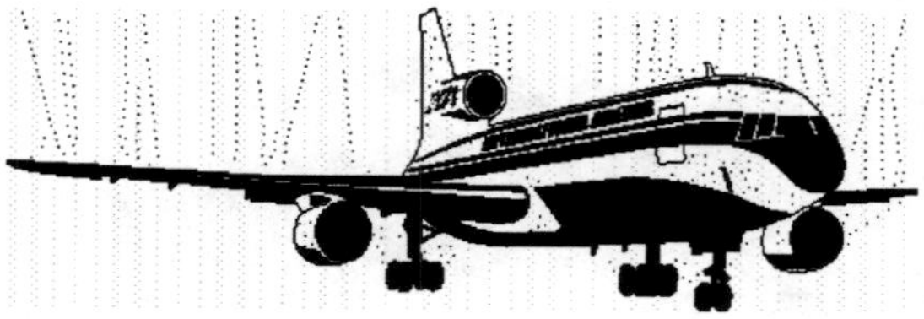

3

## General Business Scenario

Our to-do list includes

- converting various raw data file structures to SAS data sets

```
xxxxxyy123
xxxxxyy456
xxxxxyy789
```

| CharVar1 | CharVar2 | Num |
|---|---|---|
| xxxxx | yy | 123 |
| xxxxx | yy | 456 |
| xxxxx | yy | 789 |

*continued...*

4

## General Business Scenario

- appending both raw data files and SAS data sets to create a single SAS data set

*continued...*

5

## General Business Scenario

- creating a data view so that the data is always up to date

*continued...*

6

## General Business Scenario

- creating random samples for the marketing department to use for various analysis

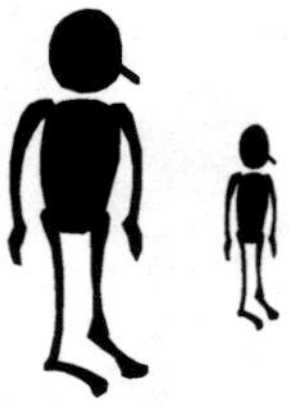

- creating versions of SAS data sets

*continued...*

7

## General Business Scenario

- merging
  - ❒ three SAS data sets without common by variables
  - ❒ a summary data set with a detail data set
  - ❒ a small data set with a large data set

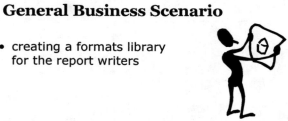

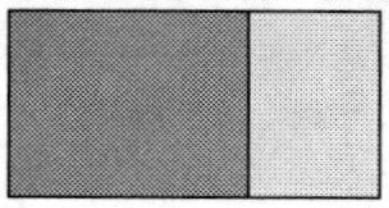

*continued...*

8

## General Business Scenario

- creating a formats library for the report writers

- preparing data for data entry applications and modifications of data in place.

9

# 1.2 Determining File Structures

## Objectives

- Investigate raw data file structures.
- Assign a libref.
- Concatenate libraries.
- Reference the physical filename of a SAS data set in a procedure.
- View the descriptor portion of a SAS data set.

11

...

## Business Scenario

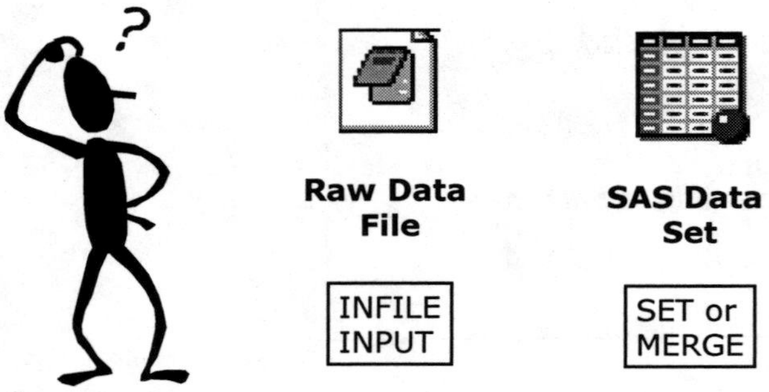


12

## Business Scenario

**Raw Data File**

Investigate the file structure to determine if we need

- INFILE statement options
- INFORMATS.

13

## Business Scenario

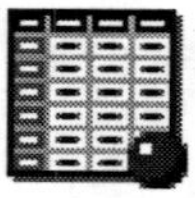

**SAS Data Set**

Investigate the descriptor portion of the data to determine

- VARIABLE names
- number of OBSERVATIONS
- SORT order of the data values
- available INDEXES.

14

PROC CONTENTS

## Raw Data Files

You can use the FSLIST procedure to view the values of a raw data file.

General form of the PROC FSLIST statement:

```
PROC FSLIST FILE = file-specification;
RUN;
```

15

The FILEREF= option is an alias to the FILE= option.

In addition to viewing the values of the raw data file, you need to obtain the file layout for the fields in the raw data file.

PROC FSLIST is part of base SAS in Version 8.

## Viewing the Structure of a Raw Data File

c01s2d1

```
proc fslist file = 'multirow.dat';
run;
```

Output

```
FSLIST: C:\Program Files\SAS Institute\SAS\V8\multirow.dat
IA00100 03JAN2000 11 24 144
$17,600 $26,160 $76,464
IA00101 03JAN2000 13 29 162
$20,800 $31,610 $86,022
IA00100 04JAN2000 13 25 144
$20,800 $27,250 $76,464
IA00101 04JAN2000 14 25 126
$22,400 $27,250 $66,906
IA00100 05JAN2000 11 26 134
$17,600 $28,340 $71,154
IA00101 05JAN2000 11 27 123
$17,600 $29,430 $65,313
IA00100 06JAN2000 11 25 144
$17,600 $27,250 $76,464
IA00101 06JAN2000 12 28 128
$19,200 $30,520 $67,968
IA00100 07JAN2000 11 26 148
$17,600 $28,340 $78,588
IA00101 07JAN2000 14 29 160
$22,400 $31,610 $84,960
IA00100 08JAN2000 12 28 162
$19,200 $30,520 $86,022
IA00101 08JAN2000 11 26 160
$17,600 $28,340 $84,960
```

## Assigning a Libref

For SAS data sets, use a LIBNAME statement to assign a libref.

General form of the LIBNAME statement:

**LIBNAME** *libref* *'SAS-data-library'*;

17

### Reference Information

SAS uses internal sets of instructions called *engines* to provide transparent access to data stored in a wide variety of forms.

Engines

- open files, perform I/O, and close files
- create and maintain the directory of SAS data libraries
- provide access to data sets in SAS data libraries using native engines such as V6 or V8
- provide access to other software vendor's files such as Oracle or DB2 as if they are SAS data sets. (The Oracle and DB2 engines are part of the SAS/ACCESS products.)

You can assign an engine in a LIBNAME statement.

**LIBNAME** *libref <engine>* '*SAS-data-library*';

## Referencing the Physical Filename of a SAS Data Set

Instead of using *libref.SAS-data-set*, you can use the physical filename of a SAS data set.

**Windows:**

```
proc print data = 'c:\AircraftData\airplanes';
run;
```

**Unix:**

```
proc print data = 'users/AircraftData/airplanes';
run;
```

**OS/390**

```
proc print data = 'userid.aircraft(airplanes)';
run;
```

For OS/390, 'userid.aircraft' is the SAS data library.

OpenVMS example:

```
proc print data = 'disk:[aircraft]airplanes';
run;
```

## Library Concatenation

You can specify two or more libraries on the LIBNAME statement.

General form of the LIBNAME statement:

**LIBNAME** *libref* ('*data-lib1*'...'*data-libn*');
**LIBNAME** *libref* (*libref1*...*librefn*);

19

You can use both SAS data library names and librefs in a library concatenation.

## Concatenating Libraries

```
Libname local 'c:\mydata';
libname oradata oracle userid = abc
                       password = xyz;
libname server 'u:\public\prog3';
libname alldata (local oradata server);
```

20

The following example shows how to use both SAS data library names and librefs in a library concatenation.

```
libname oradata oracle userid = abc password = xyz;
libname airline V8 ('c:\newdata' 'u:\commondata' oradata);
```

Any of the names not in quotes are logical names that have been previously assigned.

An engine assignment and options apply to libraries specified with physical names, not those specified with a logical name. In this example, the V8 engine applies only to 'c:\newdata' and 'u:\commondata'.

If a *libref* or path does exist when it was assigned, it is removed from the concatenation, and a warning message appears in the Log window.

## Benefits of Concatenating Libraries

You can

- mix engine types.
- simplify your programming tasks.

21

## Search Path for Concatenated Libraries

| When a file is open for... | The file used is.... |
|---|---|
| INPUT/UPDATE | First file found |
| DELETE/RENAME | First file found |
| OUTPUT | First library found |

| Listing created by | The file reported is.... |
|---|---|
| PROC CONTENTS | First file found |
| PROC DATASETS | First file found |
| EXPLORER window | First file found |

22

## SAS Data Sets

After you assign a libref, you can view the structure of a SAS data set using the

- CONTENTS procedure
- DATASETS procedure
- Properties window in the SAS Explorer.

23

## SAS Data Sets

General form of the PROC CONTENTS statement:

**PROC CONTENTS** DATA = *SAS-data-set*
*<VARNUM>*;
**RUN**;

General form of the PROC DATASETS statement:

**PROC DATASETS** LIBRARY = *libref;*
CONTENTS DATA = *SAS-data-set <VARNUM>*;
**RUN**;

24

| | |
|---|---|
| VARNUM option | prints a list of the variables by their position in the data set. |

## Viewing the Structure of a SAS Data Set

c01s2d2

Example 1

Program

```
proc contents data = ia.Revenue varnum;
   title 'Contents of a SAS Data Set';
run;
```

Output

```
                          Contents of a SAS data set

                             The CONTENTS Procedure

Data Set Name: IA.REVENUE                            Observations:          1744
Member Type:   DATA                                  Variables:                7
Engine:        V8                                    Indexes:                  0
Created:       13:17 Thursday, June 22, 2000         Observation Length:      48
Last Modified: 13:17 Thursday, June 22, 2000         Deleted Observations:     0
Protection:                                          Compressed:              NO
Data Set Type:                                       Sorted:                  NO
Label:


               -----Engine/Host Dependent Information-----

        Data Set Page Size:          4096
        Number of Data Set Pages:    22
        First Data Page:             1
        Max Obs per Page:            84
        Obs in First Data Page:      48
        Number of Data Set Repairs:  0
        File Name:                   d:\prog 3 test\revenue.sas7bdat
        Release Created:             8.0101M0
        Host Created:                WIN_NT


                -----Variables Ordered by Position-----

                #    Variable              Type    Len
                ------------------------------------------
                1    Origin                Char      3
                2    Destination           Char      3
                3    FlightIDNumber        Char      7
                4    FlightDate            Num       8
                5    RevenueFirstClass     Num       8
                6    RevenueBusiness       Num       8
                7    RevenueEconomy        Num       8
```

Example 2 (Self-Study)

```
proc datasets lib = ia;
   contents data = Revenue varnum;
   title 'Contents of a SAS Data Set';
run;
```

QUIT; /* CAUSES PROC DATASETS TO QUIT RUNNING */

Example 3 (Self-Study)

To open the Properties Windows,

1. activate the Explorer Window.
2. double-click on the Libraries icon.
3. double-click on the IA library.
4. click on the SAS data set IA.REVENUE.
5. right-click and select **<u>Properties</u>** from the pop-up menu.

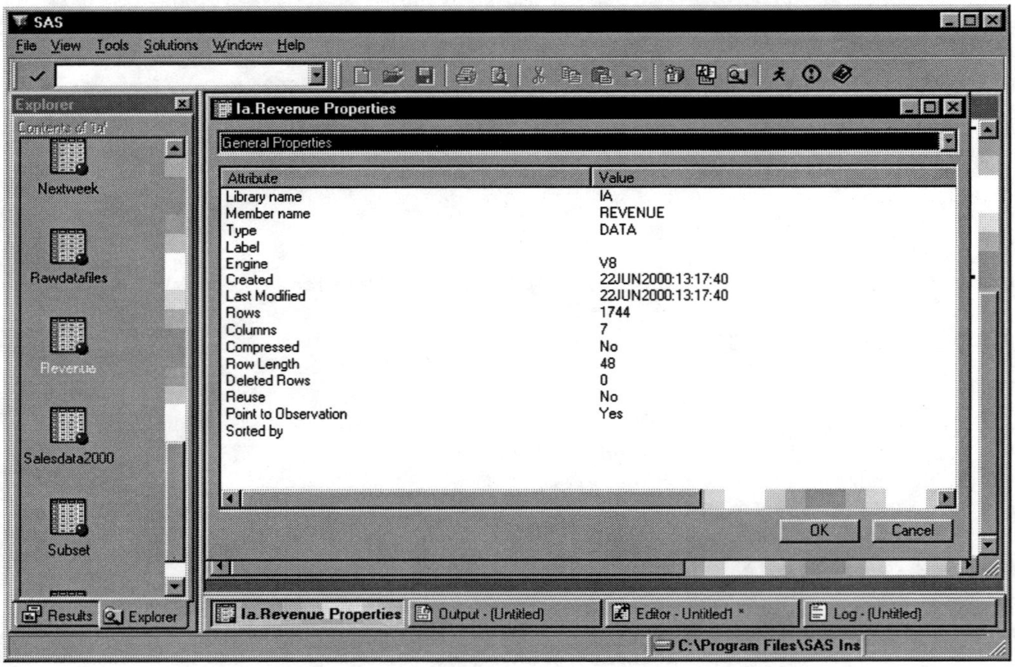


✎ You can view the General Properties, the Engine/Host Information, the Columns, and Indexes.

## Exercises

The SAS data libraries are in the following default locations:

| Operating System | Location |
|---|---|
| OS/390 | `userid.prog3.sasdata` |
| Windows | `C:\workshop\winsas\prog3` |
| UNIX | `/userid/prog3` |

If your data sets are not in one of the defaults, the location is

______________________________________________.

1. Look at the data values in the Employee_Data SAS data set in the SAS data library. Use the physical file name in PROC PRINT to create a simple listing report.
2. Look at the descriptor portion of the same SAS data set using PROC DATASETS or PROC CONTENTS.

# 1.3 Compiling and Executing the DATA Step

## Objectives

- Investigate what happens at DATA step compilation.
- Investigate what happens at DATA step execution.

28

## Submitting a DATA Step

A DATA step is processed in two phases

- compilation
- execution.

29

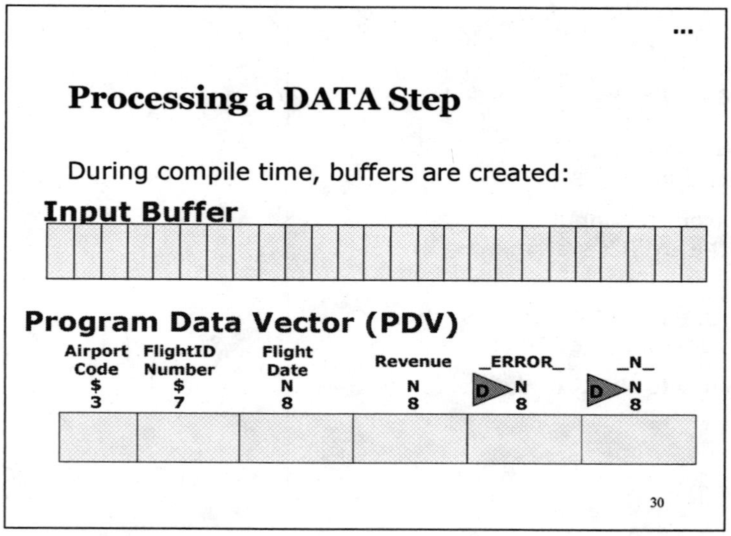


ALL VARIABLES DEFINED BEFORE FIRST RECORD READ

When the DATA step reads SAS data sets, no input buffer is created.

When the DATA step processes, SAS creates the automatic variables, _ERROR_ and _N_ in the PDV.

_ERROR_ signals the occurrence of an error in the data during an execution of the DATA step

- equals 1 when a data error is encountered
- equals 0 when no data error is encountered.

_N_ counts the number of times the DATA step has begun executing.

The PDV can contain other automatic variables such as *first.by-variable* and *last.by-variable.*

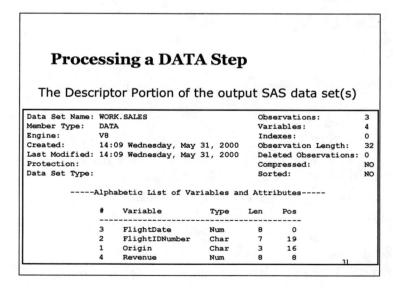

## Processing a DATA Step

The Descriptor Portion of the output SAS data set(s)

```
Data Set Name: WORK.SALES                          Observations:         3
Member Type:   DATA                                Variables:            4
Engine:        V8                                  Indexes:              0
Created:       14:09 Wednesday, May 31, 2000       Observation Length:   32
Last Modified: 14:09 Wednesday, May 31, 2000       Deleted Observations: 0
Protection:                                        Compressed:           NO
Data Set Type:                                     Sorted:               NO

        -----Alphabetic List of Variables and Attributes-----

            #    Variable          Type    Len    Pos
            ------------------------------------------
            3    FlightDate        Num       8      0
            2    FlightIDNumber    Char      7     19
            1    Origin            Char      3     16
            4    Revenue           Num       8      8
```

31

### Processing a DATA Step

By default, at execution time SAS

- reads the data from the input source identified with the INFILE statement or the SET statement
- modifies the data using statements such as assignment statements
- writes the data out to the SAS data sets listed on the DATA statement.

32

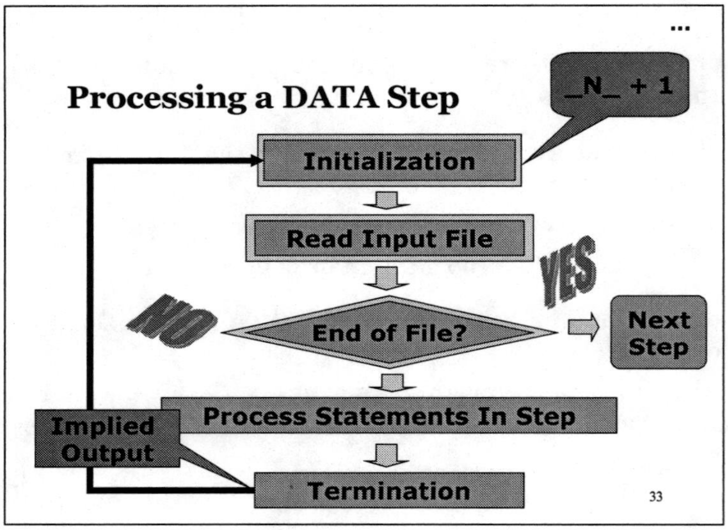


At execution time,

1. variables in the PDV are initialized to missing before each execution of the DATA step.
2. each statement is executed sequentially.
3. the INPUT, SET, or MERGE statement reads the next record from the file identified by the INFILE statement in the case of raw data or the SAS data set identified by the SET or MERGE statement.
4. other statements can then modify the current observation.
5. the values in the PDV are written to the SAS data set(s) at the bottom of the DATA step.
6. program flow returns to the top of the step.
7. the step is executed until the end-of-file marker is reached in the input file.

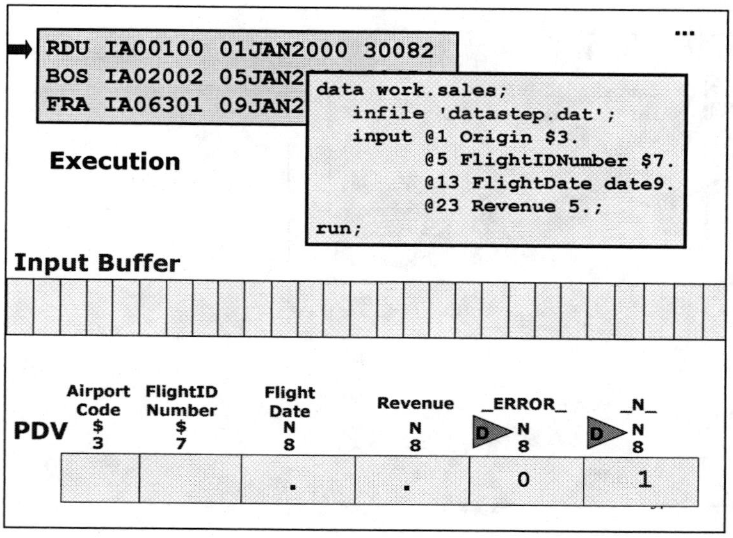


Since _ERROR_ and _N_ are automatic variables, they have a DROP flag in the PDV.

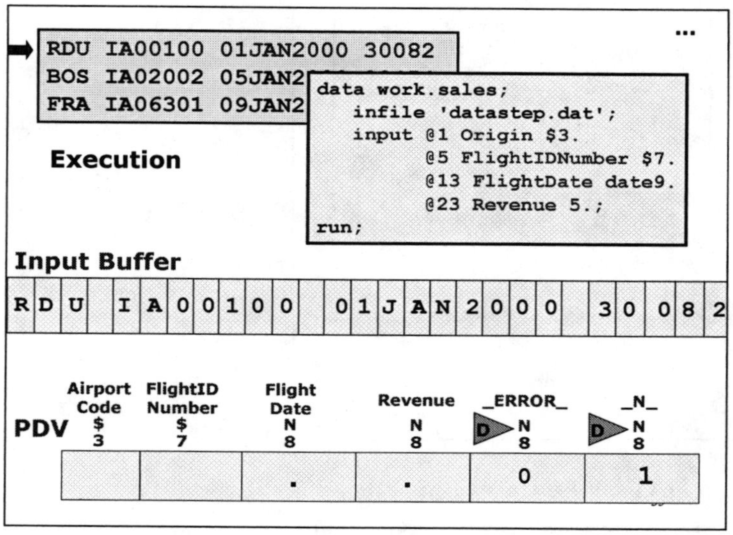


DON'T NEED RETAIN TO KEEP THE LAST RECORD IF DATA COMES FROM A SAS DATA STEP

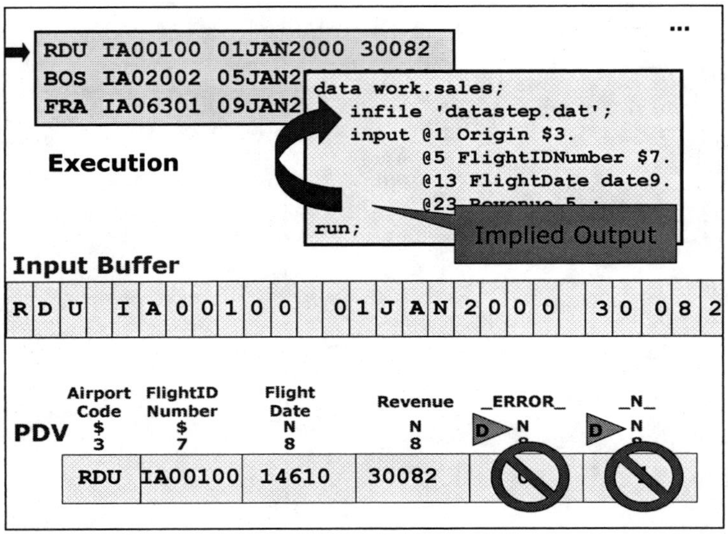


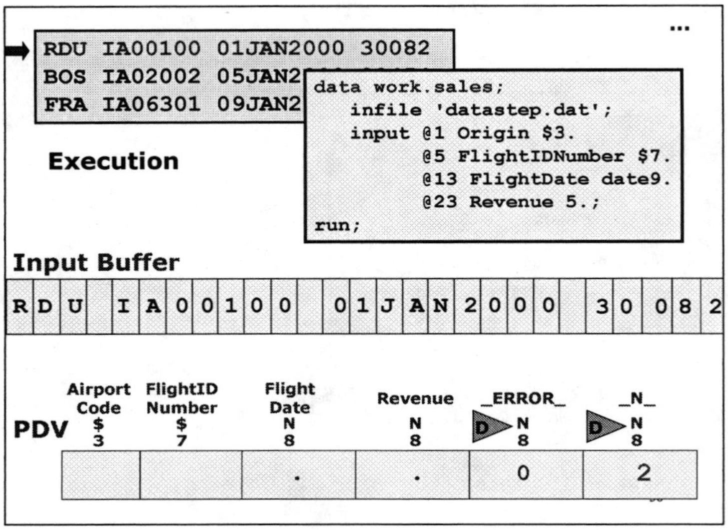


At the beginning of each DATA step iteration:

- new variables that are not retained are reinitialized to missing
- _N_ increments by 1
- _ERROR_ is reset to 0

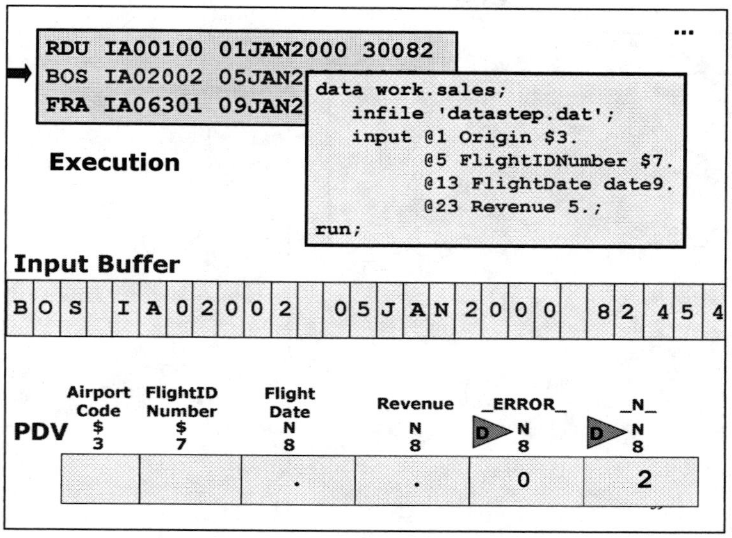


The next record is loaded into the input buffer.

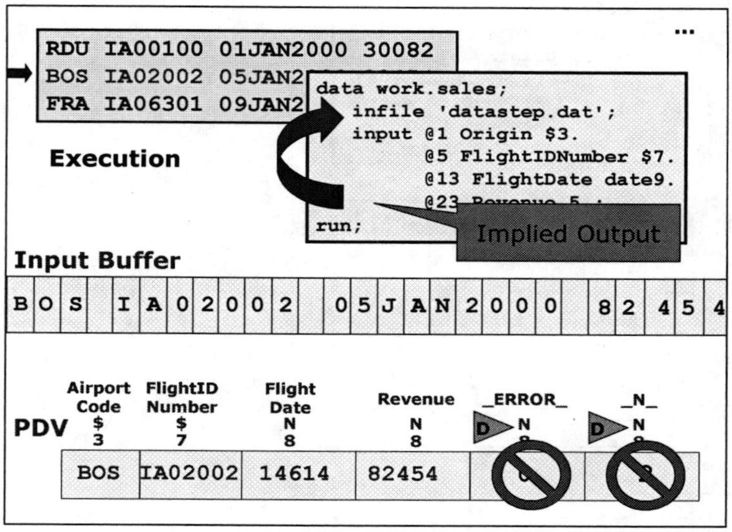

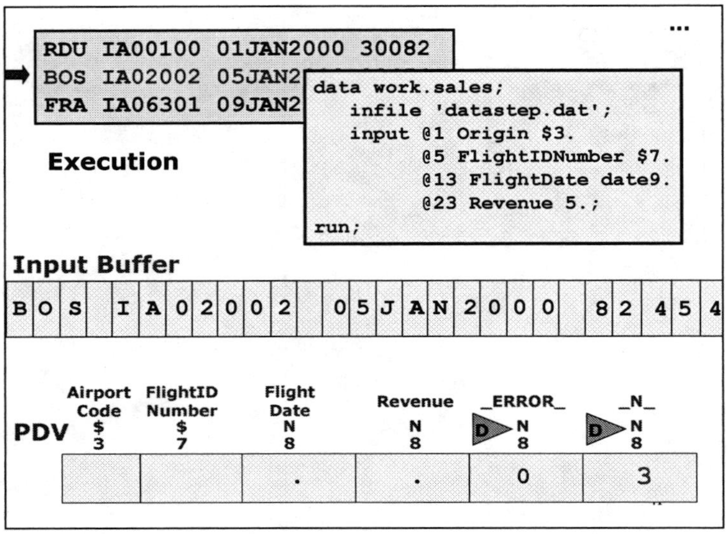
...
RDU IA00100 01JAN2000 30082
BOS IA02002 05JAN2
FRA IA06301 09JAN2
data work.sales;
infile 'datastep.dat';
input @1 Origin $3.
@5 FlightIDNumber $7.
@13 FlightDate date9.
@23 Revenue 5.;
run;
Execution
Input Buffer
B O S I A 0 2 0 0 2 0 5 J A N 2 0 0 0 8 2 4 5 4
PDV
Airport Code $ 3
FlightID Number $ 7
Flight Date N 8
Revenue N 8
_ERROR_ N 8
_N_ N 8
.
.
0
3

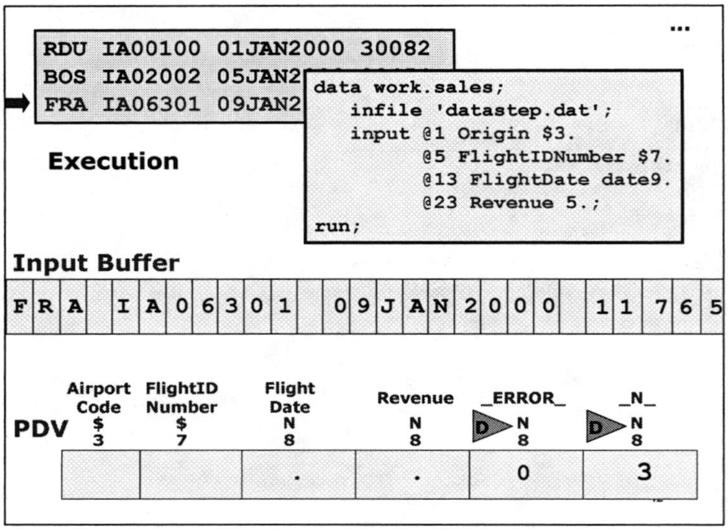
...
RDU IA00100 01JAN2000 30082
BOS IA02002 05JAN2
FRA IA06301 09JAN2
data work.sales;
infile 'datastep.dat';
input @1 Origin $3.
@5 FlightIDNumber $7.
@13 FlightDate date9.
@23 Revenue 5.;
run;
Execution
Input Buffer
F R A I A 0 6 3 0 1 0 9 J A N 2 0 0 0 1 1 7 6 5
PDV
Airport Code $ 3
FlightID Number $ 7
Flight Date N 8
Revenue N 8
_ERROR_ N 8
_N_ N 8
.
.
0
3

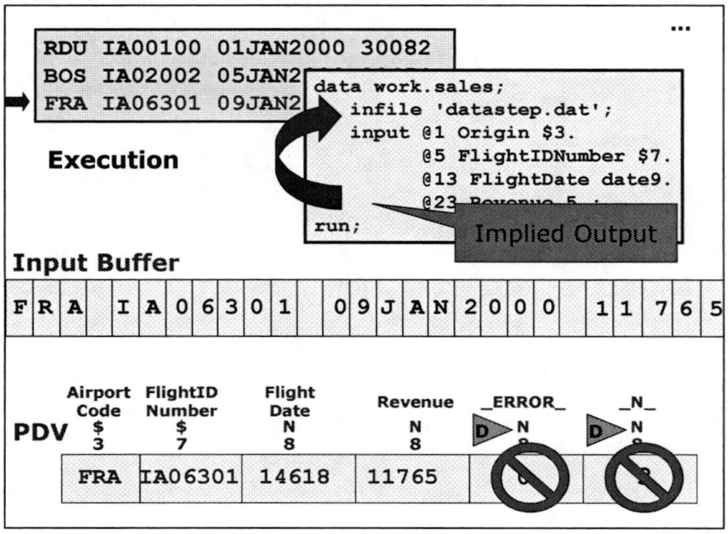
...
RDU IA00100 01JAN2000 30082
BOS IA02002 05JAN2
FRA IA06301 09JAN2
data work.sales;
infile 'datastep.dat';
input @1 Origin $3.
@5 FlightIDNumber $7.
@13 FlightDate date9.
run;
Implied Output
Execution
Input Buffer
F R A I A 0 6 3 0 1 0 9 J A N 2 0 0 0 1 1 7 6 5
PDV
Airport Code $ 3
FlightID Number $ 7
Flight Date N 8
Revenue N 8
_ERROR_ N
_N_ N
FRA
IA06301
14618
11765

## Resulting Data Set

| Airport Code | FlightID Number | Flight Date | Revenue |
|---|---|---|---|
| RDU | IA00100 | 01JAN2000 | 30082 |
| BOS | IA02002 | 05JAN2000 | 82454 |
| FRA | IA06301 | 09JAN2000 | 11765 |

44

## 1.4 Chapter Summary

You can use the FSLIST procedure to view the values of a raw data file.

> **PROC FSLIST** FILE = *file-specification*;
> **RUN**;

For SAS data sets, use a LIBNAME statement to assign a *LIBREF*.

General form of the LIBNAME statement:

> **LIBNAME** *libref 'SAS-data-library'*;

You can specify the physical filename of a SAS data set in a procedure.

> **PROC** *procedure-name* DATA = *'path.datasetname'*;
> **RUN**;

You can specify two or more libraries on the LIBNAME statement.

General form of the LIBNAME statement:

> **LIBNAME** *libref ('data-lib1'...'data-libn')*;
> **LIBNAME** *libref (libref1...librefn)*;

Search Path for Concatenated Libraries

| **When a file is open for...** | **The file used is....** |
|---|---|
| INPUT/UPDATE | First file found |
| DELETE/RENAME | First file found |
| OUTPUT | First library found |

| Listing created by | The file reported is.... |
|---|---|
| PROC CONTENTS | First file found |
| PROC DATASETS | First file found |
| EXPLORER window | First file found |

To view the structure of a SAS data set, use

- the CONTENTS procedure

```
PROC CONTENTS DATA = SAS-data-set
                     <VARNUM>;
RUN;
```

- the DATASETS procedure

```
PROC DATASETS LIBRARY = libref;
   CONTENTS DATA = SAS-data-set <VARNUM>;
RUN;
```

- the Properties window in the SAS Explorer.

To open the Properties Windows,

1. activate the Explorer Window.
2. double-click on the Libraries icon.
3. double-click on the IA library.
4. click on the SAS data set IA.SALESDATA2000.
5. right-click and select **Properties** from the pop-up menu.

A DATA step is processed in two phases.

SAS

- compilation
- execution.

During COMPILE time, buffers are created:

- Input Buffer
- Program Data Vector
- Descriptor Portion

By default, at execution time SAS

- reads the data from the input source identified with the INFILE statement or the SET statement
- modifies the data using statements such as assignment statements
- writes the data out to the SAS data sets listed on the DATA statement.

Entire Program

```
/********* c01s2d1 *******************/

/*************************************/
/*    View the records in a          */
/*     raw data file.                */
/*************************************/

proc fslist file = 'multirow.dat';
run;




/********* c01s2d2 *******************/

/*************************************/
/*    View the contents of a         */
/*     SAS data set.                 */
/*************************************/

proc contents data = ia.Revenue varnum;
   title 'Contents of a SAS Data Set';
run;


/*************************************/
/* Self Study                        */
/*************************************/
proc datasets lib = ia;
   contents data = Revenue;
   title 'Contents of a SAS Data Set';
run;
```

# 1.5 Solutions to Exercises

1. Look at the data values in the Employee_Data SAS data set in the SAS data library. Use the physical file name in PROC PRINT to create a simple listing report.

The solutions to these may vary.

Windows

```
proc print data = 'c:\workshop\winsas\prog3\Employee_Data';
run;
```

UNIX

```
proc print data = '/users/prog3/Employee_Data';
run;
```

OS/390

```
proc print data = 'userid.prog3(Employee_Data)';
run;
```

2. Look at the descriptor portion of the same SAS data set using PROC DATASETS or PROC CONTENTS.

```
proc contents data = 'name-of-the-physical-file-here';
run;

proc datasets lib = ia;
      contents Employee_Data;
run;
quit;
```

# Chapter 2

# 2.1 Introduction

## General Business Scenario

International Airlines has raw data files containing information about revenue for airfare and cargo for two weeks. The people who create reports from SAS data sets need to have the data concatenated into one SAS data.

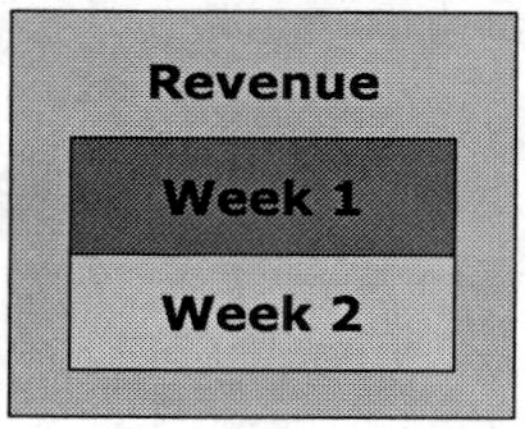


3

## General Business Scenario

When we look at the file layout of the raw data files, we discover that

- one file contains data for the first week of January and has multiple rows per observation

```
IA00100 03JAN2000 11 24 144
$17,600 $26,160 $76,464
IA00101 03JAN2000 13 29 162
$20,800 $31,610 $86,022
IA00100 04JAN2000 13 25 144
$20,800 $27,250 $76,464
```

4

## General Business Scenario

- after the first week the file structure changed. In these files, each record contains the same columns, but for the USA rows the fields are formatted differently.

```
USA  IA00100  10JAN2000  11  26  128  ...
IA00201  01-10-2000 13  25  140  ...
IA00200  01-10-2000 13  28  144  ...
USA  IA00300  10JAN2000  11  26  153  ...
```

5

## Organize the Tasks:

- Create a SAS data file from the raw data with multiple rows per observation.
- Create a SAS data file from the raw data with different formats.
- Create a SAS data view from the raw data with different formats.
- Concatenate the data.
- Copy the data file into a permanent library and rename it.

6

# 2.2 Multiple Records per Observation

## Objectives

- Determine that a raw data file contains multiple records per observation.
- Create a SAS data set from a raw data file containing multiple records for each observation in the SAS data set.

8

## Business Scenario

The first raw data file contains records for the first week of January and has multiple rows of raw data for each observation of SAS data.

```
IA00100 03JAN2000 11 24 144  } One SAS
$17,600 $26,160 $76,464      } Observation
IA00101 03JAN2000 13 29 162
$20,800 $31,610 $86,022
IA00100 04JAN2000 13 25 144
$20,800 $27,250 $76,464
```

9

## Business Scenario

We need to create a SAS data set from the raw data file.

**work.FirstWeek**

| Flight IDNumber | Flight Date | Revenue First Class | Revenue Business | Revenue Economy |
|---|---|---|---|---|
| IA00100 | 14612 | 17600 | 26160 | 76464 |
| IA00101 | 14612 | 20800 | 31610 | 86022 |
| IA00100 | 14613 | 20800 | 27250 | 76464 |

10

## Organize the Tasks:

- **Create a SAS data file from the raw data with multiple rows per observation.**
- Create a SAS data file from the raw data with different formats.
- Create a SAS data view from the raw data with different formats.
- Concatenate the data.
- Copy the data file into a permanent library and rename it.

11

### Using the INPUT Statement

```
data work.FirstWeek;
   infile 'multirow.dat';
   input FlightIDNumber $
         FlightDate : date9.;
   input RevenueFirstclass : comma7.
      RevenueBusiness : comma7.
      RevenueEconomy : comma7.;
run;
```

12

Each INPUT statement reloads the input buffer with the next record.

The colon (:) format modifier is used with list input style to allow for the use of an informat.

### Using the Relative Line Pointer Control (/ )

```
data work.FirstWeek;
   infile 'multirow.dat';
   input FlightIDNumber $
         FlightDate : date9. /
         RevenueFirstclass : comma7.
         RevenueBusiness : comma7.
         RevenueEconomy : comma7.;
run;
```

13

The relative line pointer control (/) loads the next record into the input buffer and positions the column pointer in column one. It can be used to skip records.

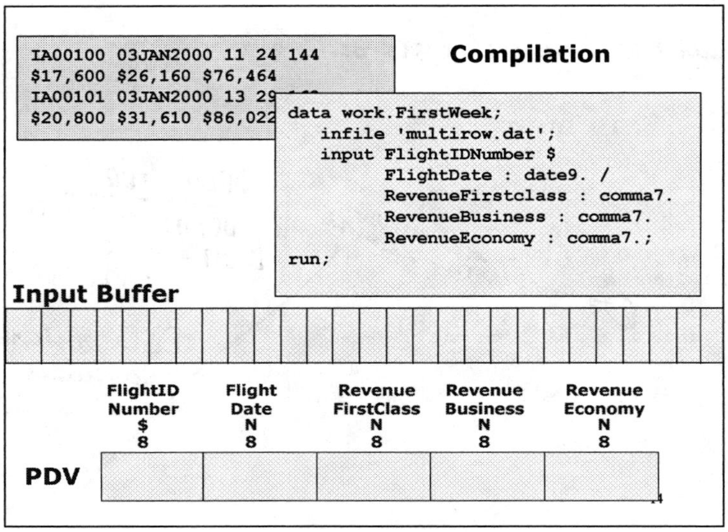
IA00100 03JAN2000 11 24 144
$17,600 $26,160 $76,464
IA00101 03JAN2000 13 29
$20,800 $31,610 $86,022
Compilation
data work.FirstWeek;
infile 'multirow.dat';
input FlightIDNumber $
FlightDate : date9. /
RevenueFirstclass : comma7.
RevenueBusiness : comma7.
RevenueEconomy : comma7.;
run;
Input Buffer
FlightID Number $ 8
Flight Date N 8
Revenue FirstClass N 8
Revenue Business N 8
Revenue Economy N 8
PDV

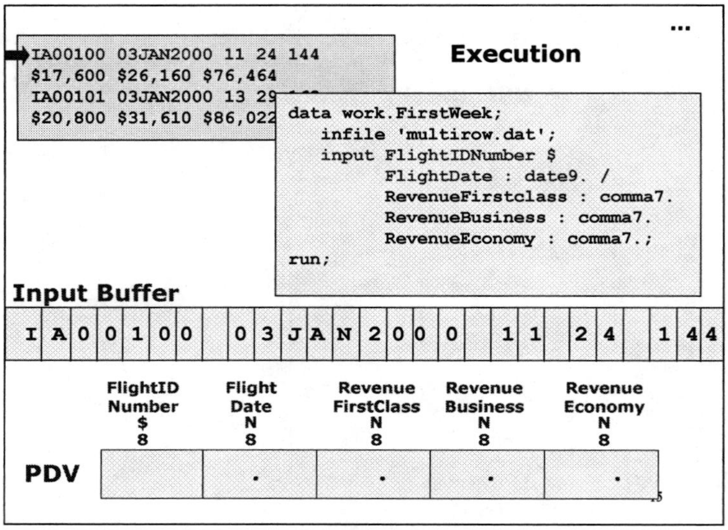
...
IA00100 03JAN2000 11 24 144
$17,600 $26,160 $76,464
IA00101 03JAN2000 13 29
$20,800 $31,610 $86,022
Execution
data work.FirstWeek;
infile 'multirow.dat';
input FlightIDNumber $
FlightDate : date9. /
RevenueFirstclass : comma7.
RevenueBusiness : comma7.
RevenueEconomy : comma7.;
run;
Input Buffer
I A 0 0 1 0 0 0 3 J A N 2 0 0 0 1 1 2 4 1 4 4
FlightID Number $ 8
Flight Date N 8
Revenue FirstClass N 8
Revenue Business N 8
Revenue Economy N 8
PDV
. . . .

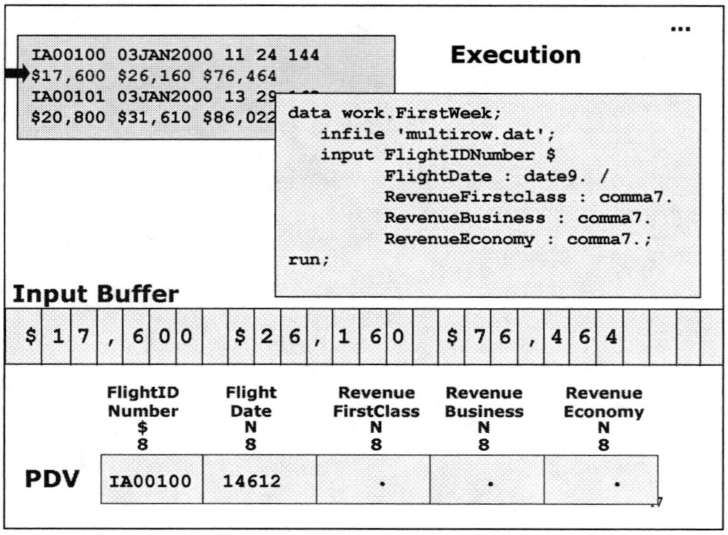
...
IA00100 03JAN2000 11 24 144
$17,600 $26,160 $76,464
IA00101 03JAN2000 13 29
$20,800 $31,610 $86,022
Execution
data work.FirstWeek;
infile 'multirow.dat';
input FlightIDNumber $
FlightDate : date9. /
RevenueFirstclass : comma7.
RevenueBusiness : comma7.
RevenueEconomy : comma7.;
run;
Input Buffer
$ 1 7 , 6 0 0 $ 2 6 , 1 6 0 $ 7 6 , 4 6 4
FlightID Number $ 8
Flight Date N 8
Revenue FirstClass N 8
Revenue Business N 8
Revenue Economy N 8
PDV
IA00100 14612 . . .

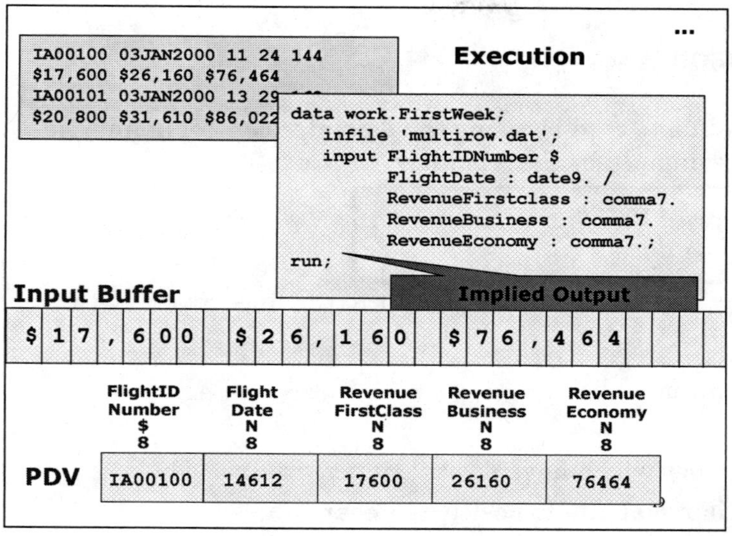
...
IA00100 03JAN2000 11 24 144
$17,600 $26,160 $76,464
IA00101 03JAN2000 13 29
$20,800 $31,610 $86,022
Execution
data work.FirstWeek;
infile 'multirow.dat';
input FlightIDNumber $
FlightDate : date9. /
RevenueFirstclass : comma7.
RevenueBusiness : comma7.
RevenueEconomy : comma7.;
run;
Implied Output
Input Buffer
$ 1 7 , 6 0 0 $ 2 6 , 1 6 0 $ 7 6 , 4 6 4
FlightID Number $ 8
Flight Date N 8
Revenue FirstClass N 8
Revenue Business N 8
Revenue Economy N 8
PDV
IA00100
14612
17600
26160
76464

## Reference Information

You can specify which line to read by using the # pointer control in any INPUT statement. The default for the # pointer control is 1.

**INPUT** *#n1 variable(s) #n2 variable(s)...*
*#nn variable(s);*

where *#n1, #n2, ..., #nn* move the pointer to the lines given by the values of *#n1, #n2, ..., #nn.*

*#n1, #n2, ..., #nn* must be

- positive integers
- numeric variables which have positive integer values
- expressions that evaluate to positive integer values.

For example, all of these DATA steps are equivalent.

```
data newdataset;
   infile 'raw-data-file';
   input firstvariable;
   input;
   input secondvariable;
run;

data newdataset;
   infile 'raw-data-file';
   input firstvariable // secondvariable;
run;

data newdataset;
   infile 'raw-data-file';
   input #1 firstvariable #3 secondvariable;
run;
```

## Multiple Records per Observation

c02s2d1

The first raw data file contains records for the first week of January and has multiple rows of raw data for each observation of SAS data. We need to convert the data into a SAS data set.

Partial Listing of Raw Data File

```
IA00100 03JAN2000 11 24 144
$17,600 $26,160 $76,464
IA00101 03JAN2000 13 29 162
$20,800 $31,610 $86,022
IA00100 04JAN2000 13 25 144
$20,800 $27,250 $76,464
IA00101 04JAN2000 14 25 126
$22,400 $27,250 $66,906
IA00100 05JAN2000 11 26 134
$17,600 $28,340 $71,154
IA00101 05JAN2000 11 27 123
$17,600 $29,430 $65,313
IA00100 06JAN2000 11 25 144
$17,600 $27,250 $76,464
IA00101 06JAN2000 12 28 128
$19,200 $30,520 $67,968
IA00100 07JAN2000 11 26 148
$17,600 $28,340 $78,588
IA00101 07JAN2000 14 29 160
$22,400 $31,610 $84,960
IA00100 08JAN2000 12 28 162
$19,200 $30,520 $86,022
IA00101 08JAN2000 11 26 160
$17,600 $28,340 $84,960
IA00100 09JAN2000 11 29 126
```

Program:

```
data work.FirstWeek;
   infile 'multirow.dat';
   input FlightIDNumber $
         FlightDate : date9. /
         RevenueFirstclass : comma7.
         RevenueBusiness : comma7.
         RevenueEconomy : comma7.;
run;

proc print data = work.FirstWeek (obs = 15);
   title 'Reading Multiple Rows per Observation';
run;
```

### Output

Reading Multiple Rows per Observation

| Obs | Flight IDNumber | Flight Date | Revenue Firstclass | Revenue Business | Revenue Economy |
|---|---|---|---|---|---|
| 1 | IA00100 | 14612 | 17600 | 26160 | 76464 |
| 2 | IA00101 | 14612 | 20800 | 31610 | 86022 |
| 3 | IA00100 | 14613 | 20800 | 27250 | 76464 |
| 4 | IA00101 | 14613 | 22400 | 27250 | 66906 |
| 5 | IA00100 | 14614 | 17600 | 28340 | 71154 |
| 6 | IA00101 | 14614 | 17600 | 29430 | 65313 |
| 7 | IA00100 | 14615 | 17600 | 27250 | 76464 |
| 8 | IA00101 | 14615 | 19200 | 30520 | 67968 |
| 9 | IA00100 | 14616 | 17600 | 28340 | 78588 |
| 10 | IA00101 | 14616 | 22400 | 31610 | 84960 |
| 11 | IA00100 | 14617 | 19200 | 30520 | 86022 |
| 12 | IA00101 | 14617 | 17600 | 28340 | 84960 |
| 13 | IA00100 | 14618 | 17600 | 31610 | 66906 |
| 14 | IA00101 | 14618 | 17600 | 28340 | 81243 |
| 15 | IA00201 | 14612 | 17600 | 27250 | 82305 |

## Exercises

1. Use the EmpMulti raw data file to create a SAS data set.

| Operating System | File Name |
|---|---|
| OS/390 | .prog3.rawdata(EmpMulti) |
| Windows | EmpMulti.dat |
| Unix | EmpMulti.dat |

- Use PROC FSLIST to view the structure of the raw data file.
- Create a SAS data set named EmployeeC2. Place it in a permanent SAS data library.
- Examine the values in the data set as well as the descriptor portion.
- Save the program containing the DATA step used to create EmployeeC2.

The EmpMulti raw data file has two rows per employee. The record layout is as follows:

| Line Number | Start Column | Description | Width |
|---|---|---|---|
| 1 | 1 | Employee Id | 6 |
| 1 | 8 | Employee's Last Name | 32 |
| 1 | 41 | Employee's Extension | 8 |
| 1 | 50 | Employee's Location | 25 |
| 2 | 8 | Employee's Division | 30 |
| 2 | 39 | Date Hired (ex. 19OCT1989) | 9 |
| 2 | 49 | Employee's Job Code | 6 |
| 2 | 56 | Employee's Current Salary (ex. $80,000) | 10 |

COLUMN empid $ 1-6

FORMAT @1 empid $6.

LIST @1 empid $

# 2.3 Mixed Record Types

## Objectives

- Determine that a raw data file contains mixed record types.
- Create a SAS data set from a raw data file containing mixed record types.

23

## Business Scenario

The second raw data file and all subsequent raw data files contain records that have different data structures.

```
USA  IA00100  10JAN2000  11  26  128  $17,600  ...
IA00201  01-10-2000 13  25  140  $20.800 $27.250 ...
IA00200  01-10-2000 13  28  144  $20.800 $30.520 ...
USA  IA00300  10JAN2000  11  26  153  $19,371 ...
USA  IA00301  10JAN2000  13  28  147  $22,893 ...
IA00400  01-10-2000 11  25  149  $19.371 $30.025 ...
```

24

The USA records have dates that need to be read using the DATE9. informat and revenue figures that need to be read using the COMMA7. informat.

The other records have dates that need to be read using the MMDDYY10. informat and revenue figures that need to be read using the COMMAX7. informat.

## Business Scenario

We need to create a SAS data set from the raw data file with a consistent format and structure for each row.

| Revenue Flight IDNumber | FlightDate | First Class | Revenue Business | Revenue Economy |
|---|---|---|---|---|
| IA00100 | 01-10-2000 | $17,600 | $28,340 | $67,968 |
| IA00201 | 01-10-2000 | $20,800 | $27,250 | $74,340 |
| IA00200 | 01-10-2000 | $20,800 | $30,520 | $76,464 |

25

## Organize the Tasks

- Create a SAS data file from the raw data with multiple rows per observation.
- **Create a SAS data file from the raw data with different formats.**
- Create a SAS data view from the raw data with different formats.
- Concatenate the data.
- Copy the data file into a permanent library and rename it.

26

## Undesirable Results

```
data ia.NextWeek (drop = country);
   infile 'diffrows.dat';
   input @1 country $3.;
   if country = 'USA' then
      input  @6 FlightIDNumber $7.
             @15 FlightDate date9.
             @39 RevenueFirstClass comma7.
             @48 RevenueBusiness comma7.
             @57 RevenueEconomy comma7.;
```

*continued...* 27

## Undesirable Results

```
   else
       input @1 FlightIDNumber $
            @10 FlightDate mmddyy10.
            @34 RevenueFirstClass commax7.
            @42 RevenueBusiness commax7.
            @50 RevenueEconomy commax7.;
 run;
```

28

The default INPUT creates undesirable results.

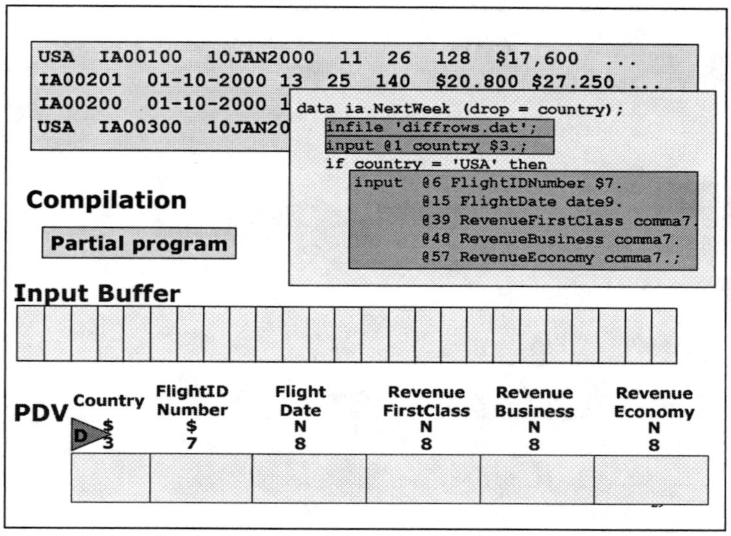


During compilation, an input buffer and a program data vector (PDV) are created.

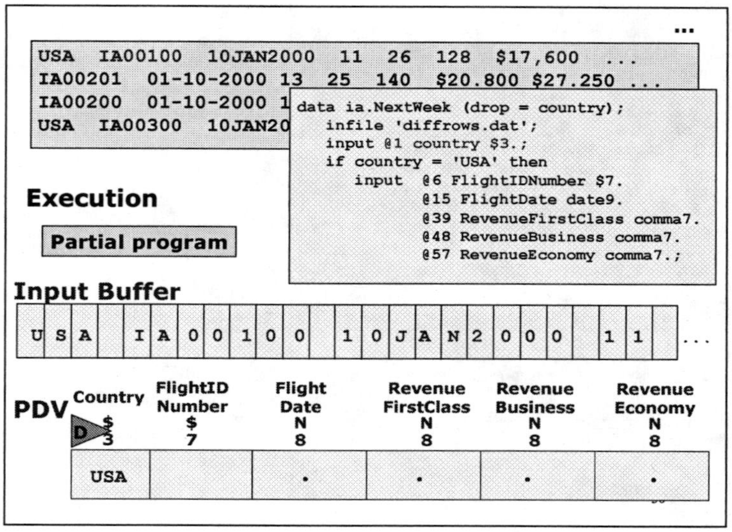


At execution,

1. the PDV is initialized to missing
2. values are read into the PDV using the INPUT statement.

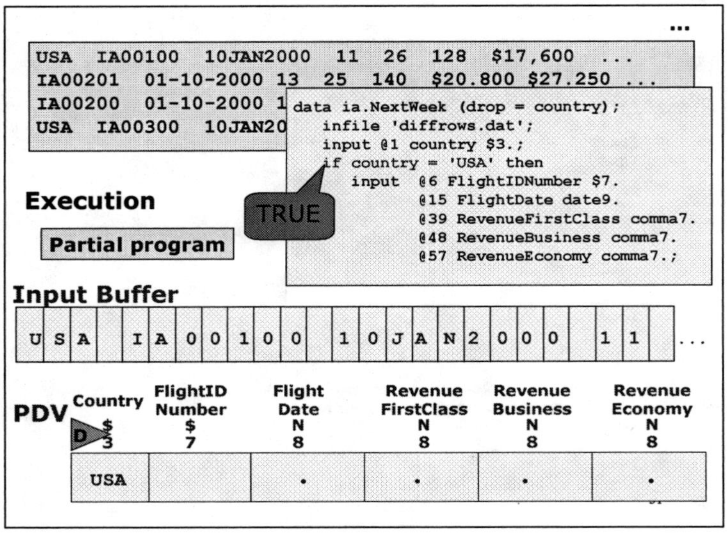


Because the IF statement is true, SAS processes the INPUT statement.

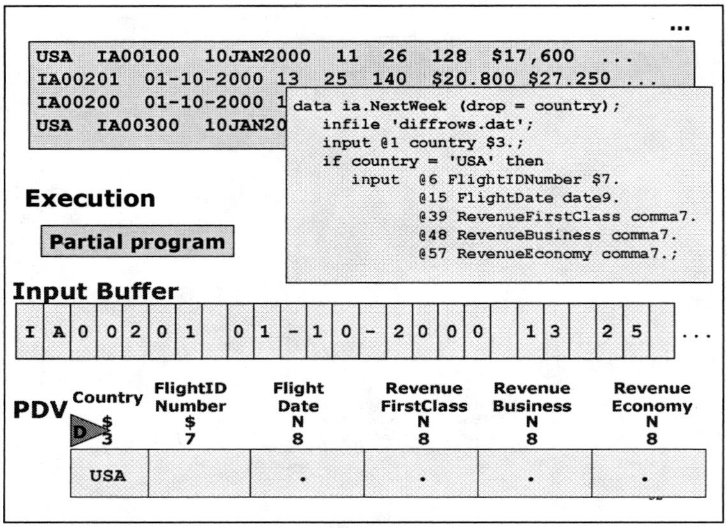


Because there is an INPUT statement, SAS loads the input buffer with the next record.

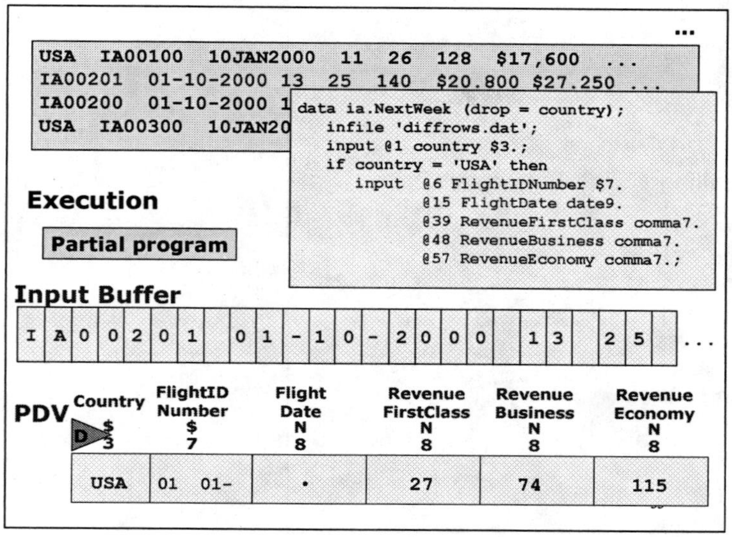


The values in the input buffer do not have the correct form for the informats; therefore, the values are incorrect.

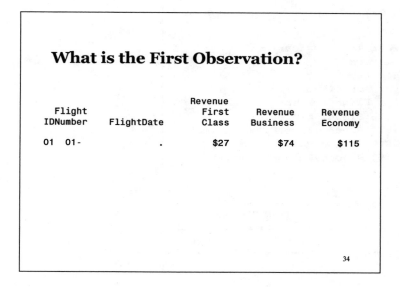

## What is the First Observation?

| Flight IDNumber | FlightDate | Revenue First Class | Revenue Business | Revenue Economy |
|---|---|---|---|---|
| 01 01- | . | $27 | $74 | $115 |

34

## What to Do?

You can use the trailing @ line-hold specifier to hold the

- current data line in the input buffer for another INPUT statement to process
- column pointer at its present location in that data line.

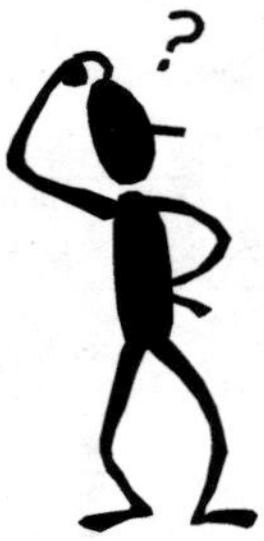

35

## Using the INPUT Statement with @

```
data ia.NextWeek (drop = country);
   infile 'diffrows.dat';
   input @1 country $3. @;
   if country = 'USA' then
      input  @6 FlightIDNumber $7.
             @15 FlightDate date9.
             @39 RevenueFirstClass comma7.
             @48 RevenueBusiness comma7.
             @57 RevenueEconomy comma7.;
```

*continued...* 36

## Using the INPUT Statement with @

```
   else
       input @1 FlightIDNumber $
            @10 FlightDate mmddyy10.
            @34 RevenueFirstClass commax7.
            @42 RevenueBusiness commax7.
            @50 RevenueEconomy commax7.;
run;
```

37

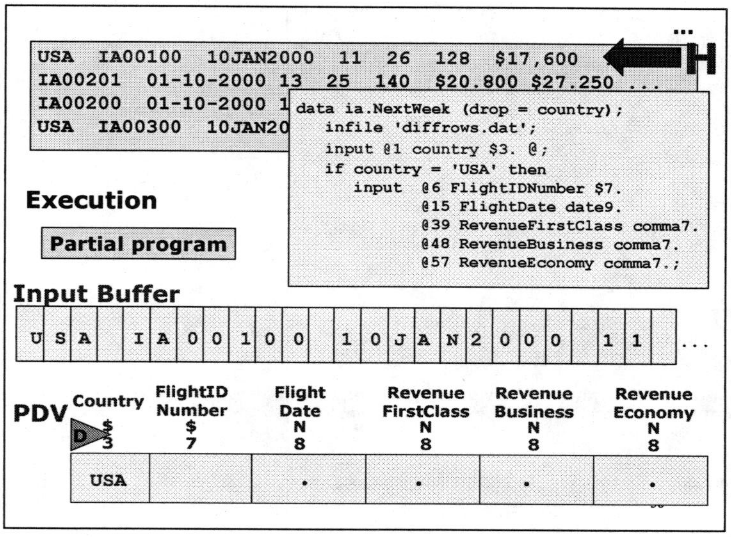
...
USA IA00100 10JAN2000 11 26 128 $17,600
IA00201 01-10-2000 13 25 140 $20.800 $27.250 ...
IA00200 01-10-2000 1
USA IA00300 10JAN20
H
data ia.NextWeek (drop = country);
infile 'diffrows.dat';
input @1 country $3. @;
if country = 'USA' then
input @6 FlightIDNumber $7.
@15 FlightDate date9.
@39 RevenueFirstClass comma7.
@48 RevenueBusiness comma7.
@57 RevenueEconomy comma7.;
Execution
Partial program
Input Buffer
U S A I A 0 0 1 0 0 1 0 J A N 2 0 0 0 1 1 ...
PDV
Country $ 3
D
FlightID Number $ 7
Flight Date N 8
Revenue FirstClass N 8
Revenue Business N 8
Revenue Economy N 8
USA . . . .

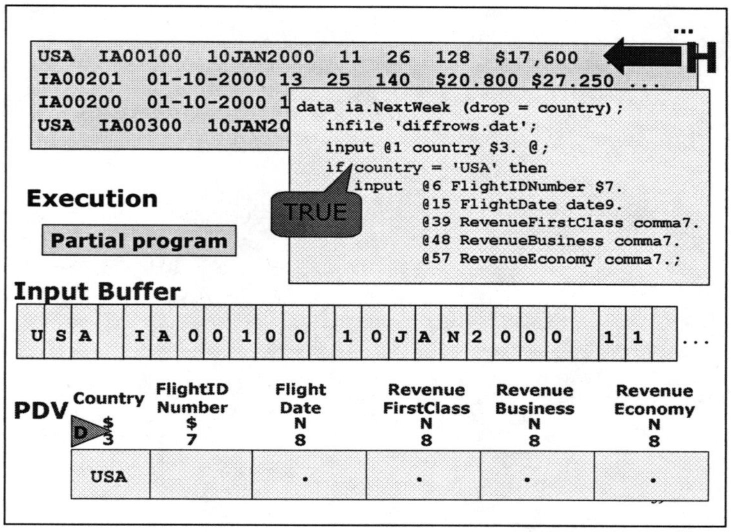
...
USA IA00100 10JAN2000 11 26 128 $17,600
IA00201 01-10-2000 13 25 140 $20.800 $27.250 ...
IA00200 01-10-2000 1
USA IA00300 10JAN20
H
data ia.NextWeek (drop = country);
infile 'diffrows.dat';
input @1 country $3. @;
if country = 'USA' then
input @6 FlightIDNumber $7.
@15 FlightDate date9.
@39 RevenueFirstClass comma7.
@48 RevenueBusiness comma7.
@57 RevenueEconomy comma7.;
TRUE
Execution
Partial program
Input Buffer
U S A I A 0 0 1 0 0 1 0 J A N 2 0 0 0 1 1 ...
PDV
Country $ 3
D
FlightID Number $ 7
Flight Date N 8
Revenue FirstClass N 8
Revenue Business N 8
Revenue Economy N 8
USA . . . .

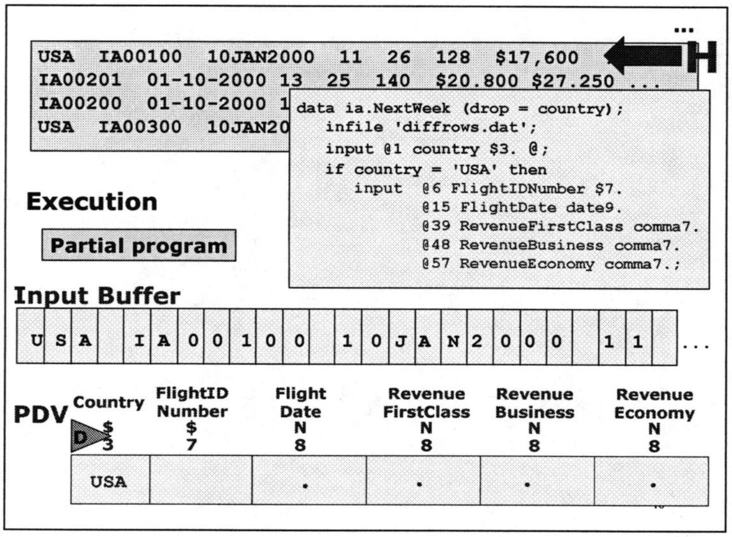
...
USA IA00100 10JAN2000 11 26 128 $17,600
IA00201 01-10-2000 13 25 140 $20.800 $27.250 ...
IA00200 01-10-2000 1
USA IA00300 10JAN20
H
data ia.NextWeek (drop = country);
infile 'diffrows.dat';
input @1 country $3. @;
if country = 'USA' then
input @6 FlightIDNumber $7.
@15 FlightDate date9.
@39 RevenueFirstClass comma7.
@48 RevenueBusiness comma7.
@57 RevenueEconomy comma7.;
Execution
Partial program
Input Buffer
U S A I A 0 0 1 0 0 1 0 J A N 2 0 0 0 1 1 ...
PDV
Country $ 3
D
FlightID Number $ 7
Flight Date N 8
Revenue FirstClass N 8
Revenue Business N 8
Revenue Economy N 8
USA . . . .

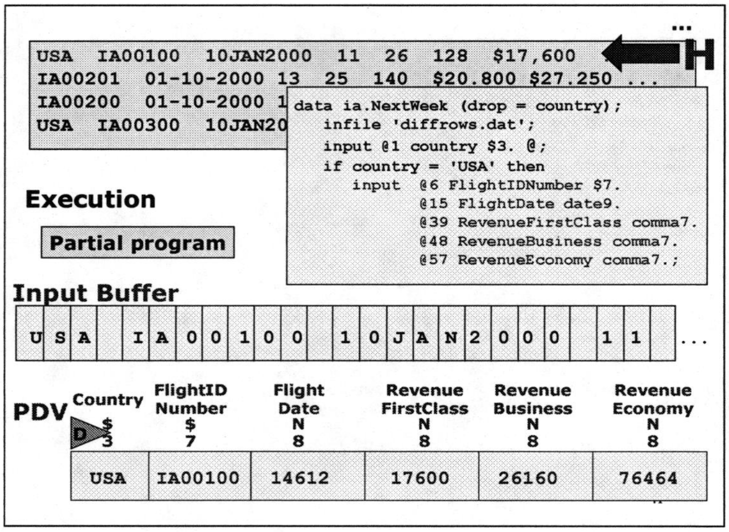
...
USA IA00100 10JAN2000 11 26 128 $17,600
IA00201 01-10-2000 13 25 140 $20.800 $27.250 ...
IA00200 01-10-2000 1
USA IA00300 10JAN20
H
data ia.NextWeek (drop = country);
infile 'diffrows.dat';
input @1 country $3. @;
if country = 'USA' then
input @6 FlightIDNumber $7.
@15 FlightDate date9.
@39 RevenueFirstClass comma7.
@48 RevenueBusiness comma7.
@57 RevenueEconomy comma7.;
Execution
Partial program
Input Buffer
U S A I A 0 0 1 0 0 1 0 J A N 2 0 0 0 1 1 ...
PDV
Country $ 3
FlightID Number $ 7
Flight Date N 8
Revenue FirstClass N 8
Revenue Business N 8
Revenue Economy N 8
D
USA
IA00100
14612
17600
26160
76464

## Mixed Record Types

c02s3d1

The second raw data file, and all subsequent raw data files, contains records that have different data structures. The rows for the United States have dates in the date9. structure and the revenue figures in the form of $17,600. The other records have dates in the mmddyy10. structure and the revenues in the form of $27.250.

Partial Listing of Raw Data File

```
USA IA00100 10JAN2000 11 26 128 $17,600 $28,340 $67,968 $121030
IA00201 01-10-2000 13 25 140 $20.800 $27.250 $74.340 $114.660
IA00200 01-10-2000 13 28 144 $20.800 $30.520 $76.464 $111.230
USA IA00300 10JAN2000 11 26 153 $19,371 $31,226 $89,505 $119880
USA IA00301 10JAN2000 13 28 147 $22,893 $33,628 $85,995 $120960
IA00400 01-10-2000 11 25 149 $19.371 $30.025 $87.165 $122.580
IA00401 01-10-2000 13 30 146 $22.893 $36.030 $85.410 $120.420
USA IA02900 10JAN2000 13 30 159 $12,844 $20,190 $52,152 $63,840
USA IA02901 10JAN2000 13 29 142 $12,844 $19,517 $46,576 $69,312
USA IA03000 10JAN2000 14 30 134 $13,832 $20,190 $43,952 $71,136
```

Program

```
data ia.NextWeek (drop = country);
   infile 'diffrows.dat';
   input @1 country $3. @;
   if country = 'USA' then
      input  @6 FlightIDNumber $7.
            @15 FlightDate date9.
            @39 RevenueFirstClass comma7.
            @48 RevenueBusiness comma7.
            @57 RevenueEconomy comma7.;
   end;
   else
      input  @1 FlightIDNumber $7.
            @10 FlightDate mmddyy10.
            @34 RevenueFirstClass commax7.
            @42 RevenueBusiness commax7.
            @50 RevenueEconomy commax7.;
run;
```

```
proc print data = ia.NextWeek (obs = 15);
   format FlightDate mmddyyd10. RevenueFirstClass
          RevenueBusiness RevenueEconomy dollar8.;
   title 'Reading Mixed Record Types';
run;
```

Output

Reading Mixed Record Types

| Obs | Flight IDNumber | FlightDate | Revenue First Class | Revenue Business | Revenue Economy |
|---|---|---|---|---|---|
| 1 | IA00100 | 01-10-2000 | $17,600 | $28,340 | $67,968 |
| 2 | IA00201 | 01-10-2000 | $20,800 | $27,250 | $74,340 |
| 3 | IA00200 | 01-10-2000 | $20,800 | $30,520 | $76,464 |
| 4 | IA00300 | 01-10-2000 | $19,371 | $31,226 | $89,505 |
| 5 | IA00301 | 01-10-2000 | $22,893 | $33,628 | $85,995 |
| 6 | IA00400 | 01-10-2000 | $19,371 | $30,025 | $87,165 |
| 7 | IA00401 | 01-10-2000 | $22,893 | $36,030 | $85,410 |
| 8 | IA02900 | 01-10-2000 | $12,844 | $20,190 | $52,152 |
| 9 | IA02901 | 01-10-2000 | $12,844 | $19,517 | $46,576 |
| 10 | IA03000 | 01-10-2000 | $13,832 | $20,190 | $43,952 |
| 11 | IA03001 | 01-10-2000 | $10,868 | $20,190 | $44,936 |
| 12 | IA03300 | 01-10-2000 | $17,268 | $25,480 | $69,642 |
| 13 | IA03301 | 01-10-2000 | $15,829 | $27,440 | $62,964 |
| 14 | IA03400 | 01-10-2000 | $20,146 | $27,440 | $66,303 |
| 15 | IA03401 | 01-10-2000 | $20,146 | $28,420 | $76,797 |

## Exercises

**2.** Use the Airports raw data file to create a SAS data set. The raw data file has mixed record types. If the first 3 columns (TYPE field) are NR2, there is no second geographical region. If the TYPE field is R2, there is a second geographical region.

The raw data file is comma delimited. Name the new SAS data set AirportsC2.

The record layout is as follows:

| Description | Width |
|---|---|
| Type of Field | 3 |
| Airport Code | 3 |
| Airport City | 30 |
| Second Geographical Region (ex. State, Province, etc.) | 20 |
| Airport Country | 15 |

A sample of the raw data file is below:

```
R2,ABB,Abingdon,England,United Kingdom
NR2,ABD,Abadan,Iran
R2,ABE,Allentown,PA,USA
NR2,ABF,Abaiang,Kiribati
R2,ABG,Abingoon,Queensland,Australia
R2,ABH,Alpha,Queensland,Australia
R2,ABI,Abilene,TX,USA
NR2,ABJ,Abidjan,Ivory Coast
NR2,ABK,Kabri Dar,Ethiopia
R2,ABL,Ambler,AK,USA
R2,ABM,Cape York,Queensland,Australia
NR2,ABN,Albina,Suriname
NR2,ABO,Aboisso,Ivory Coast
NR2,ABP,Atkamba,Papua New Guine
R2,ABQ,Albuquerque,NM,USA
```

# 2.4 Creating a DATA Step View

## Objectives

- Investigate types of SAS data sets.
- Create and use DATA step views.
- Determine the advantages of DATA step views.
- Examine guidelines for using DATA step views.

45

## Business Scenario

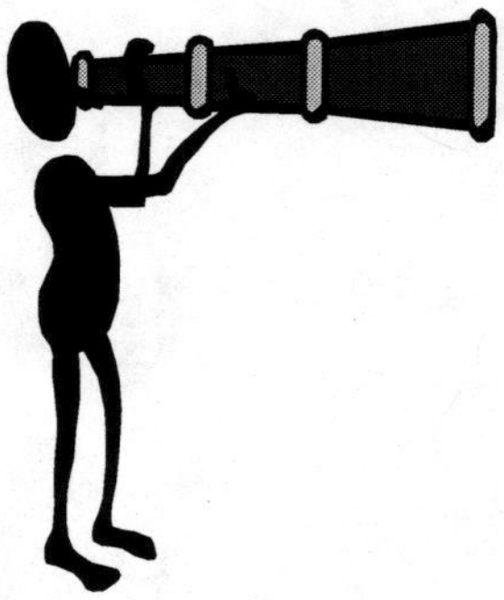

Since there are several raw data files created with this structure, we can create a DATA step view from the raw data instead of a SAS data file.

46

## Organize the Tasks

- Create a SAS data file from the raw data with multiple rows per observation.
- Create a SAS data file from the raw data with different formats.
- **Create a SAS data view from the raw data with different formats.**
- Concatenate the data.
- Copy the data file into a permanent library and rename it.

47

...

## SAS Data Sets

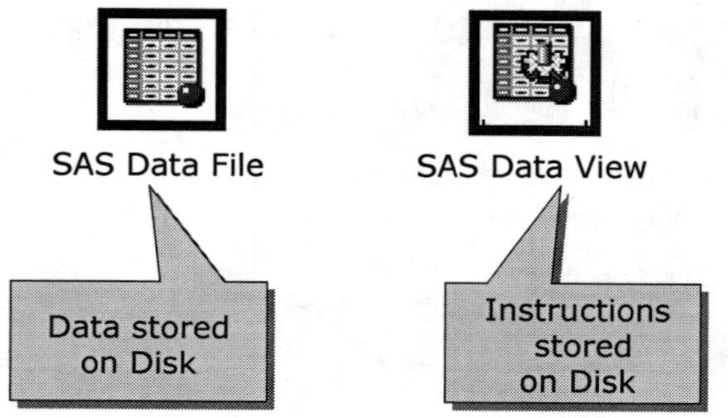


48

| A DATA Step File | A DATA Step View |
|---|---|
| Is a SAS file with a member type of DATA | Is a SAS file with a member type of VIEW |
| Enables read or write capabilities | Is read only |
| Contains data and a descriptor portion that are stored on disk | Contains no data |
| | Contains a partially compiled DATA step |

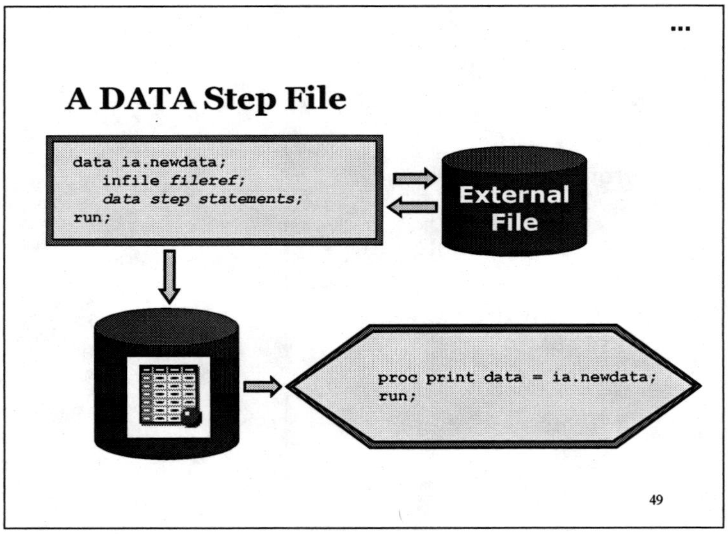


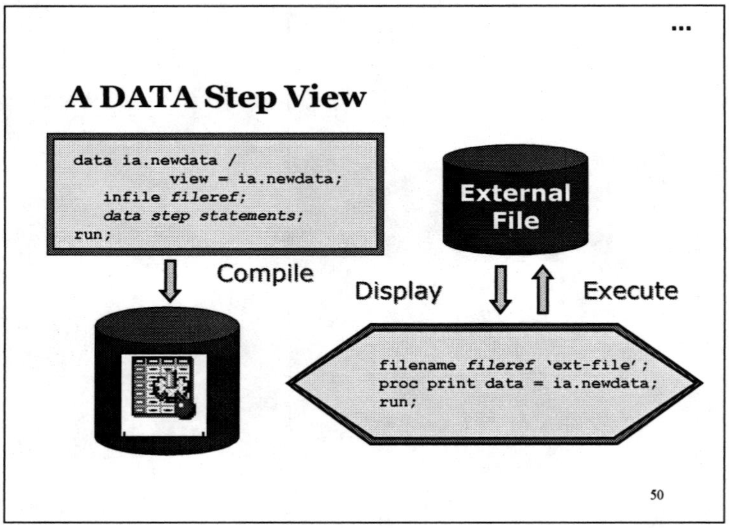


You cannot have a SAS data file and a SAS data view with the same member name in the same SAS data library.

## DATA Statement with VIEW= Option Syntax

General form of the DATA statement with VIEW= option:

**DATA** *data-set-name* / VIEW=*view-name* ;
INFILE fileref;
INPUT *variable(s);*
**RUN;**

view-name specifies a view that the DATA step uses to store the input DATA step view. The *view-name* must match one of the data set names.

51

The name of a DATA view must be different from the name of a DATA file.

You can use the DESCRIBE statement to retrieve program source code from a DATA step view. SAS writes the source statements to the SAS log.

General form of the DESCRIBE statement:

**DATA VIEW =** *view-name;*
**DESCRIBE;**
**RUN;**

## FILENAME Statement Syntax

**FILENAME** *fileref <device-type> 'external-file' <host-options>*;

*fileref*

is any SAS name that is 8 characters or less.

*'external-file'*

is the physical name of an external file. The physical name is the name that is recognized by the operating environment.

52

A FILENAME statement associates a *fileref* with a physical external file.

## Creating a DATA Step View

c02s4d1

Example 1

Since there are several raw data files created with this structure, we can create a DATA step view from the raw data instead of a SAS data file.

Program:

```
data ia.NewWeek (drop = country) / view = ia.NewWeek;
   infile differ;
   input @1 country $3. @;
   if country = 'USA' then
      input   @6 FlightIDNumber $7.
             @15 FlightDate date9.
             @39 RevenueFirstClass comma7.
             @48 RevenueBusiness comma7.
             @57 RevenueEconomy comma7.;
   else
      input  @1 FlightIDNumber $7.
            @10 FlightDate mmddyy10.
            @34 RevenueFirstClass commax7.
            @42 RevenueBusiness commax7.
            @50 RevenueEconomy commax7.;
run;


filename differ 'diffrows.dat';

proc print data = ia.NewWeek (obs = 15);
   format FlightDate mmddyyd10. RevenueFirstClass
          RevenueBusiness RevenueEconomy dollar8.;
   title 'Creating a DATA Step View';
run;
```

Output

Creating a DATA Step View

| Obs | Flight IDNumber | FlightDate | Revenue First Class | Revenue Business | Revenue Economy |
|---|---|---|---|---|---|
| 1 | IA00100 | 01-10-2000 | $17,600 | $28,340 | $67,968 |
| 2 | IA00201 | 01-10-2000 | $20,800 | $27,250 | $74,340 |
| 3 | IA00200 | 01-10-2000 | $20,800 | $30,520 | $76,464 |
| 4 | IA00300 | 01-10-2000 | $19,371 | $31,226 | $89,505 |
| 5 | IA00301 | 01-10-2000 | $22,893 | $33,628 | $85,995 |
| 6 | IA00400 | 01-10-2000 | $19,371 | $30,025 | $87,165 |
| 7 | IA00401 | 01-10-2000 | $22,893 | $36,030 | $85,410 |
| 8 | IA02900 | 01-10-2000 | $12,844 | $20,190 | $52,152 |
| 9 | IA02901 | 01-10-2000 | $12,844 | $19,517 | $46,576 |
| 10 | IA03000 | 01-10-2000 | $13,832 | $20,190 | $43,952 |
| 11 | IA03001 | 01-10-2000 | $10,868 | $20,190 | $44,936 |
| 12 | IA03300 | 01-10-2000 | $17,268 | $25,480 | $69,642 |
| 13 | IA03301 | 01-10-2000 | $15,829 | $27,440 | $62,964 |
| 14 | IA03400 | 01-10-2000 | $20,146 | $27,440 | $66,303 |
| 15 | IA03401 | 01-10-2000 | $20,146 | $28,420 | $76,797 |

Example 2

```
data view = ia.NewWeek;
   describe;
run;
```

Log

```
1     data view = ia.NewWeek;
2        describe;
3     run;

NOTE: DATA step view IA.NEWWEEK is defined as:

data ia.NewWeek (drop = country) / view = ia.NewWeek;
   infile differ truncover;
   input @1 country $3. @;
   if country = 'USA' then
      input @6 FlightIDNumber $7. @15 FlightDate date9. @39  RevenueFirstClass
comma7. @48
            RevenueBusiness comma7. @57 RevenueEconomy comma7.;
   else
      input @1 FlightIDNumber $7. @10 FlightDate mmddyy10. @34
RevenueFirstClass commax7. @42
            RevenueBusiness commax7. @50 RevenueEconomy commax7.;
run;
```

## Advantages of DATA Step Views

You can use DATA step views to

- combine data from multiple sources
- hide complex code from users
- access the most current data in changing files
- avoid storing a copy of a large data file.

54

## Guidelines for Creating and Using Views

- If data is used many times in one program, it is more efficient to create and reference a SAS data file than a view.
- Expect a degradation in performance when using a SAS data view with a procedure that requires multiple passes through the data.
- Avoid creating views on files whose structures often change.

55

## Reference Information

### Creating a VIEW and a FILE

Only one view can be created in a DATA step.

In addition to the view name, you can specify other data set names in the DATA statement. The data sets are not created until the view is processed.

For example,

```
data ia.NewWeek (drop = country)
     work.USA / view = ia.NewWeek;
   infile differ;
   input @1 country $3. @;
   if country = 'USA' then do;
      input   @6 FlightIDNumber $7.
             @15 FlightDate date9.
             @39 RevenueFirstClass comma7.
             @48 RevenueBusiness comma7.
             @57 RevenueEconomy comma7.
       output; /*outputs to both ia.NewWeek and work.USA*/
   end;
   else do;
      input  @1 FlightIDNumber $7.
            @10 FlightDate mmddyy10.
            @34 RevenueFirstClass commax7.
            @42 RevenueBusiness commax7.
            @50 RevenueEconomy commax7.;
      output ia.NewWeek; /*outputs only to ia.NewWeek*/
   end;
run;
```

### Using Macro Variables

Because SAS macro variables are resolved during compilation, any macro variables used in a DATA step view are resolved when the view is created.

You can use the SYMGET function to postpone macro resolution until the view is executed.

For example,

```
data ia.NewWeek (drop = country) / view = ia.NewWeek;
   infile differ;
   input @1 country $3. @;
   if country = 'USA' then
      input   @6 FlightIDNumber $7.
             @15 FlightDate date9.
             @39 RevenueFirstClass comma7.
             @48 RevenueBusiness comma7.
             @57 RevenueEconomy comma7.
   else
```

```
        input  @1 FlightIDNumber $7.
               @10 FlightDate mmddyy10.
               @34 RevenueFirstClass commax7.
               @42 RevenueBusiness commax7.
               @50 RevenueEconomy commax7.;
     if FlightDate = symget('ThisDate');
run;
```

Use the %LET statement to provide a value for the macro variable THISDATE.

```
%let ThisDate = '12JAN2000'd;
proc print data = ia.NewWeek;
run;
```

## Exercises

3. Use the **NewEmps** raw data file to create a SAS data view. The raw data file has 2 rows for each employee. Name the data view NewEmployeesC2. Place it in a permanent SAS data library.

   Remember to use a fileref instead of the physical file name.

   The record layout is the same as Section 2.

# 2.5 Appending Data

## Objectives

- Append two data sets.

58

...

## Business Scenario

We need to append these two SAS data sets together.

- work.FirstWeek
- ia.NewWeek

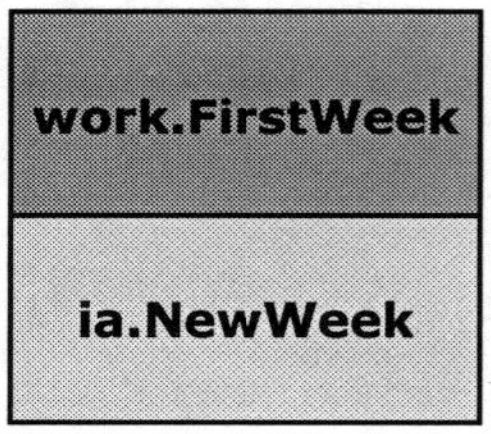


59

## Organize the Tasks:

- Create a SAS data file from the raw data with multiple rows per observation.
- Create a SAS data file from the raw data with different formats.
- Create a SAS data view from the raw data with different formats.
- **Concatenate the data.**
- Copy the data file into a permanent library and rename it.

61

## Using the APPEND Procedure

You can use PROC APPEND to concatenate two SAS data sets.

General form of the APPEND procedure:

```
PROC APPEND BASE = SAS-data-set
            DATA = SAS-data-set
            <FORCE>;
```

62

The FORCE options enables PROC APPEND to concatenate two SAS data sets that have different descriptor portions.

## Reference Information

The FORCE option enables PROC APPEND to concatenate the data sets even though there may be variables in the DATA= data set that either do not exist in the BASE data set or have different attributes than BASE= variables.

The FORCE option may cause loss of data due to truncation.

For example,

The data set ia.MoreData has the eleven variables:

Partial PROC CONTENTS Output

-----Alphabetic List of Variables and Attributes-----

| # | Variable | Type | Len | Pos | Label |
|---|---|---|---|---|---|
| 10 | AirportCity | Char | 50 | 62 | City Where Airport is Located |
| 11 | AirportName | Char | 50 | 112 | Airport Name |
| 5 | Destination | Char | 3 | 59 | Airport Code |
| 2 | FlightDate | Num | 8 | 0 | |
| 1 | FlightIDNumber | Char | 8 | 48 | |
| 4 | Origin | Char | 3 | 56 | |
| 9 | Profit | Num | 8 | 40 | |
| 7 | RevenueBusiness | Num | 8 | 24 | |
| 8 | RevenueEconomy | Num | 8 | 32 | |
| 6 | RevenueFirstClass | Num | 8 | 16 | |
| 3 | TotalExpenses | Num | 8 | 8 | |

The data set ia.PartData has the four variables:

Partial PROC CONTENTS Output

-----Alphabetic List of Variables and Attributes-----

| # | Variable | Type | Len | Pos |
|---|---|---|---|---|
| 2 | FlightDate | Num | 8 | 0 |
| 1 | FlightIDNumber | Char | 8 | 16 |
| 4 | Origin | Char | 3 | 24 |
| 3 | TotalExpenses | Num | 8 | 8 |

The following code results in the data set ia.MoreData having eleven variables.

```
proc append base = ia.MoreData data = ia.PartData force;
run;

proc print data = ia.MoreData;
run;
```

Partial Log

```
25   proc append base = ia.MoreData data = ia.PartData force;
26   run;

NOTE: Appending IA.PARTDATA to IA.MOREDATA.
WARNING: Variable Destination was not found on DATA file.
WARNING: Variable RevenueFirstClass was not found on DATA file.
WARNING: Variable RevenueBusiness was not found on DATA file.
WARNING: Variable RevenueEconomy was not found on DATA file.
WARNING: Variable Profit was not found on DATA file.
WARNING: Variable AirportCity was not found on DATA file.
WARNING: Variable AirportName was not found on DATA file.
NOTE: There were 25 observations read from the data set IA.PARTDATA.
NOTE: 25 observations added.
NOTE: The data set IA.MOREDATA has 15 observations and 11 variables.
NOTE: PROCEDURE APPEND used:
      real time           0.44 seconds
      cpu time            0.10 seconds
```

Output

| Obs | Flight IDNumber | Flight Date | Total Expenses | Origin | Destination | Revenue First Class | Revenue Business |
|---|---|---|---|---|---|---|---|
| 1 | IA03300 | 14580 | 76562 | RDU | ANC | 18707 | 22540 |
| 2 | IA03300 | 14581 | 75105 | RDU | ANC | 15829 | 29400 |
| 3 | IA03300 | 14582 | 20233 | RDU | ANC | 20146 | 29400 |
| 4 | IA03300 | 14583 | 115370 | RDU | ANC | 17268 | 24500 |
| 5 | IA03300 | 14584 | 75484 | RDU | ANC | 15829 | 24500 |
| 6 | IA03300 | 14585 | 13531 | RDU | ANC | 18707 | 23520 |
| 7 | IA03300 | 14586 | 51365 | RDU | ANC | 20146 | 25480 |
| 8 | IA03300 | 14587 | 87475 | RDU | ANC | 15829 | 29400 |
| 9 | IA03300 | 14588 | 47752 | RDU | ANC | 17268 | 29400 |
| 10 | IA03300 | 14589 | 53091 | RDU | ANC | 17268 | 29400 |
| 11 | IA03300 | 14580 | 76562 | RDU | | . | . |
| 12 | IA03300 | 14581 | 75105 | RDU | | . | . |
| 13 | IA03300 | 14582 | 20233 | RDU | | . | . |
| 14 | IA03300 | 14583 | 115370 | RDU | | . | . |
| 15 | IA03300 | 14584 | 75484 | RDU | | . | . |

| Obs | Revenue Economy | Profit | AirportCity | AirportName |
|---|---|---|---|---|
| 1 | 62010 | 26695 | Anchorage, AK | Anchorage International Airport |
| 2 | 66303 | 36427 | Anchorage, AK | Anchorage International Airport |
| 3 | 77751 | 107064 | Anchorage, AK | Anchorage International Airport |
| 4 | 76797 | 3195 | Anchorage, AK | Anchorage International Airport |
| 5 | 69165 | 34010 | Anchorage, AK | Anchorage International Airport |
| 6 | 74412 | 103108 | Anchorage, AK | Anchorage International Airport |
| 7 | 59148 | 53409 | Anchorage, AK | Anchorage International Airport |
| 8 | 69165 | 26919 | Anchorage, AK | Anchorage International Airport |
| 9 | 70119 | 69035 | Anchorage, AK | Anchorage International Airport |
| 10 | 64872 | 58449 | Anchorage, AK | Anchorage International Airport |
| 11 | . | . | | |
| 12 | . | . | | |
| 13 | . | . | | |
| 14 | . | . | | |
| 15 | . | . | | |

The following code results in the data set ia.PartData having four variables.

```
proc append base = ia.PartData data = ia.MoreData force;
run;

proc print data = ia.PartData;
run;
```

Partial Log

```
59   proc append base = ia.PartData data = ia.MoreData force;
60   run;

NOTE: Appending IA.MOREDATA to IA.PARTDATA.
WARNING: Variable Destination was not found on BASE file.
WARNING: Variable RevenueFirstClass was not found on BASE file.
WARNING: Variable RevenueBusiness was not found on BASE file.
WARNING: Variable RevenueEconomy was not found on BASE file.
WARNING: Variable Profit was not found on BASE file.
WARNING: Variable AirportCity was not found on BASE file.
WARNING: Variable AirportName was not found on BASE file.
NOTE: FORCE is specified, so dropping/truncating will occur.
NOTE: There were 10 observations read from the data set IA.MOREDATA.
NOTE: 10 observations added.
NOTE: The data set IA.PARTDATA has 15 observations and 4 variables.
NOTE: PROCEDURE APPEND used:
      real time           0.09 seconds
      cpu time            0.09 seconds
```

Output

| Obs | Flight IDNumber | Flight Date | Total Expenses | Origin |
|---|---|---|---|---|
| 1 | IA03300 | 14580 | 76562 | RDU |
| 2 | IA03300 | 14581 | 75105 | RDU |
| 3 | IA03300 | 14582 | 20233 | RDU |
| 4 | IA03300 | 14583 | 115370 | RDU |
| 5 | IA03300 | 14584 | 75484 | RDU |
| 6 | IA03300 | 14580 | 76562 | RDU |
| 7 | IA03300 | 14581 | 75105 | RDU |
| 8 | IA03300 | 14582 | 20233 | RDU |
| 9 | IA03300 | 14583 | 115370 | RDU |
| 10 | IA03300 | 14584 | 75484 | RDU |
| 11 | IA03300 | 14585 | 13531 | RDU |
| 12 | IA03300 | 14586 | 51365 | RDU |
| 13 | IA03300 | 14587 | 87475 | RDU |
| 14 | IA03300 | 14588 | 47752 | RDU |
| 15 | IA03300 | 14589 | 53091 | RDU |

## Appending Data

c02s5d1

We need to append only two SAS data sets together. PROC APPEND is the most efficient technique to use.

Program:

```
proc print data = work.FirstWeek (firstobs = 3161);
   title 'Last Rows of Work.FirstWeek';
run;
```

Last Rows of Work.FirstWeek

| Obs | Flight IDNumber | Flight Date | Revenue Firstclass | Revenue Business | Revenue Economy |
|---|---|---|---|---|---|
| 3161 | IA11200 | 14616 | 40337 | 43410 | 138180 |
| 3162 | IA11201 | 14616 | 38214 | 49198 | 125490 |
| 3163 | IA11200 | 14617 | 33968 | 40516 | 134655 |
| 3164 | IA11201 | 14617 | 36091 | 40516 | 129015 |
| 3165 | IA11200 | 14618 | 38214 | 46304 | 131835 |
| 3166 | IA11201 | 14618 | 40337 | 43410 | 132540 |

```
filename differ 'diffrows.dat';

proc append base = work.FirstWeek
            data = ia.NewWeek;
run;
```

```
proc print data = work.FirstWeek
         (firstobs = 3160 obs = 3170);
   title 'Appended Data';
run;
```

Output

Appended Data

| Obs | Flight IDNumber | Flight Date | Revenue Firstclass | Revenue Business | Revenue Economy | |
|---|---|---|---|---|---|---|
| 3160 | IA11201 | 14615 | 36091 | 40516 | 121965 | work.FirstWeek |
| 3161 | IA11200 | 14616 | 40337 | 43410 | 138180 | |
| 3162 | IA11201 | 14616 | 38214 | 49198 | 125490 | |
| 3163 | IA11200 | 14617 | 33968 | 40516 | 134655 | |
| 3164 | IA11201 | 14617 | 36091 | 40516 | 129015 | |
| 3165 | IA11200 | 14618 | 38214 | 46304 | 131835 | |
| 3166 | IA11201 | 14618 | 40337 | 43410 | 132540 | |
| 3167 | IA00100 | 14619 | 17600 | 28340 | 67968 | work.NewWeek |
| 3168 | IA00201 | 14619 | 20800 | 27250 | 74340 | |
| 3169 | IA00200 | 14619 | 20800 | 30520 | 76464 | |
| 3170 | IA00300 | 14619 | 19371 | 31226 | 89505 | |

## Exercises

4. Append the NewEmployeesC2 SAS data view, created in a previous exercise, to the EmployeeC2 permanent SAS data set. EmployeeC2 was also created in a previous exercise.

   The raw data file used in NewEmployeeC2 is named NewEmps.

# 2.6 Managing SAS Data Sets

## Objectives

- Copy a SAS data set from one data library to another.
- Rename a SAS data set.

66

## Business Scenario

There are problems with the work.FirstWeek data set:

- it is temporary
- it has an inaccurate name.

Solutions include:

- copying to permanent library
- renaming the data set.

67

## Organize the Tasks

- Create a SAS data file from the raw data with multiple rows per observation.
- Create a SAS data file from the raw data with different formats.
- Create a SAS data view from the raw data with different formats.
- Concatenate the data.
- **Copy the data file into a permanent library and rename it.**

68

## Using the DATASETS Procedure

With PROC DATASETS, you can

- copy SAS files from one SAS library to another
- rename SAS files
- delete SAS files
- manipulate passwords on SAS files
- modify attributes of SAS data sets and variables within the data sets.

69

## PROC DATASETS Syntax

General form of DATASETS procedure:

```
PROC DATASETS <LIBRARY=libref>;
   CHANGE old-SAS-data-set-name =
            new-SAS-data-set-name;
   COPY  IN=libref  OUT=libref;
      EXCLUDE memberlist;
      SELECT memberlist;
   DELETE memberlist;
RUN;
QUIT;
```

70

This is not an exclusive list of the PROC DATASETS syntax. For more documentation, see the SAS Online Doc or the SAS Procedures Guide.

## Managing SAS Data Sets

c02s6d1

Now that the process is working, we realize that we have created the first data set as a temporary one and have given it a name that does not represent the fact that this file eventually contains data from other weeks than just the first. Rather than rerun all the programs, we can just copy the temporary file to a permanent library and rename it.

Program:

```
proc datasets lib = ia nolist;
   copy in = work out = ia;
      select FirstWeek;
   change FirstWeek = YearToDate;
run;
quit;
```

In subsequent weeks, we can use PROC APPEND to append the current week's data to the ia.YearToDate data without submitting any data steps.

```
filename differ2 'diffrows2.dat';

proc append base = ia.YearToDate
            data = ia.NewWeek;
run;
```

# 2.7 Chapter Summary

You can read multiple records from a raw data file by using

- multiple input statements
- the relative line pointer control (/).

You can use the trailing @ line-hold specifier to hold the

- current data line in the input buffer for another INPUT statement to process
- column pointer at its present location in that data line.

A DATA step view is a partially compiled DATA step and is stored in a SAS file with a member type of VIEW. The DATA step view can be used as a SAS data set in DATA and PROC steps with the limitation that it is read-only. The DATA step is executed only when the view is used; therefore, no data values are stored in the view. The data values are extracted at run time.

General form for creating a DATA step view:

```
DATA data-set-name / VIEW=view-name ;
  DATA step statements;
RUN;
```

You can use DATA step views to access the most current data in changing files, pull together data from multiple sources, and avoid storing a SAS copy of data. DATA step views do, however, require more resources to process than their data file counterparts.

You can use PROC APPEND to concatenate two SAS data sets.

```
PROC APPEND BASE = SAS-data-set
            DATA = SAS-data-set
            <FORCE>;
```

You can use PROC DATASETS to

- copy SAS files from one SAS library to another
- rename SAS files
- delete SAS files
- manipulate passwords on SAS files
- modify attributes of SAS data sets and variables within the data sets.

General form for PROC DATASETS

**PROC DATASETS** <LIBRARY=*libref*>;
   CHANGE oldname=newname;
   COPY IN=*libref* OUT=*libref*;
      EXCLUDE *memberlist*;
      SELECT *memberlist*;
   DELETE *memberlist*;
RUN;
QUIT;

Entire Program

```
/********* c02s2d1 ******************/

/************************************/
/*    Create a SAS data set from    */
/*    a raw data file with multiple */
/*    rows for each observation of  */
/*    SAS data.                     */
/************************************/


data work.FirstWeek;
   infile 'multirow.dat';
   input FlightIDNumber $
         FlightDate : date9. /
         RevenueFirstclass : comma7.
         RevenueBusiness : comma7.
         RevenueEconomy : comma7.;
run;

proc print data = work.FirstWeek (obs = 15);
   title 'Reading Multiple Rows per Observation';
run;



/********* c02s3d1 ******************/

/************************************/
/*    Create a SAS data set from    */
/*    a raw data file with mixed    */
/*    record types.                 */
/************************************/


data ia.NextWeek (drop = country);
   infile 'diffrows.dat';
   input @1 country $3. @;
   if country = 'USA' then
      input  @6 FlightIDNumber $7.
            @15 FlightDate date9.
            @39 RevenueFirstClass comma7.
            @48 RevenueBusiness comma7.
            @57 RevenueEconomy comma7.;
   else
      input  @1 FlightIDNumber $7.
            @10 FlightDate mmddyy10.
            @34 RevenueFirstClass commax7.
            @42 RevenueBusiness commax7.
            @50 RevenueEconomy commax7.;
run;
```

```
proc print data = ia.NextWeek (obs = 15);
   format FlightDate mmddyyd10. RevenueFirstClass
          RevenueBusiness RevenueEconomy dollar8.;
   title 'Reading Mixed Record Types';
run;
```

```
/********* c02s4d1 ******************/

/*************************************/
/*    Create a SAS data view from    */
/*    a raw data file with mixed     */
/*    record types.                  */
/*************************************/


data ia.NewWeek (drop = country) / view = ia.NewWeek;
   infile differ;
   input @1 country $3. @;
   if country = 'USA' then
      input   @6 FlightIDNumber $7.
             @15 FlightDate date9.
             @39 RevenueFirstClass comma7.
             @48 RevenueBusiness comma7.
             @57 RevenueEconomy comma7.;
   else
      input  @1 FlightIDNumber $7.
            @10 FlightDate mmddyy10.
            @34 RevenueFirstClass commax7.
            @42 RevenueBusiness commax7.
            @50 RevenueEconomy commax7.;
run;


filename differ 'diffrows.dat';

proc print data = ia.NewWeek (obs = 15);
   format FlightDate mmddyyd10. RevenueFirstClass
          RevenueBusiness RevenueEconomy dollar8.;
   title 'Creating a DATA Step View';
run;


data view = ia.NewWeek;
   describe;
run;
```

```
/********* c02s5d1 ******************/

/*************************************/
/*    Append work.FirstWeek and      */
/*    ia.NewWeek.                    */
/*************************************/

proc print data = work.FirstWeek (firstobs = 3161);
   title 'Last Five Rows of Work.FirstWeek';
run;


filename differ 'diffrows.dat';

proc append base = work.FirstWeek
            data = ia.NewWeek;
run;

proc print data = work.FirstWeek
                  (firstobs = 3160 obs = 3170);
   title 'Appended Data';
run;


/********* c02s6d1 ******************/

/*************************************/
/*    Copy the FirstWeek data set    */
/*    from the WORK library to the   */
/*    IA library and rename it.      */
/*************************************/

proc datasets lib = ia nolist;
   copy in = work out = ia;
      select FirstWeek;
   change FirstWeek = YearToDate;
run;
quit;

/*************************************/
/*  In subsequent weeks, we can use  */
/*  PROC APPEND to append the current */
/*  week's data to the IA.YearToDate */
/*  data without submitting any data */
/*  steps.                           */
/*************************************/

filename differ2 'diffrows2.dat';

proc append base = ia.YearToDate
            data = ia.NewWeek;
run;
```

# 2.8 Solutions to Exercises

1. **Use the EmpMulti raw data file to create a SAS data set.**
   - Use PROC FSLIST to view the structure of the raw data file.
   - Create a SAS data set named EmployeeC2. Place it in a permanent SAS data library.
   - Examine the values in the data set as well as the descriptor portion.
   - Save the program containing the DATA step used to create EmployeeC2.

```
data ia.EmployeeC2;
   infile 'EmpMulti.dat';
   input @1  EmpID $6.
          @8  LastName $32. @41 Phone $8.
         @50 Location $25. /
          @8  Division $30.
         @39 HireDate date9.
         @49 JobCode $6.
         @56 Salary dollar10.;
run;
```

2. **Use the Airports raw data file to create a SAS data set.**

   The raw data file has mixed record types. If the first 3 columns (TYPE field) are NR2, there is no second geographical region. If the TYPE field is R2, there is a second geographical region.

   The raw data file is comma delimited. Name the new SAS data set AirportsC2.

```
data work.AirportsC2;
   length code $ 3 city $ 30 GeoReg2 $ 20 country $ 15;
   infile 'Airports2.dat' dsd;
   input type $ @;
   if type='R2' then input  code $ city $ GeoReg2 $
                            country $;
   else input code $ city $ country $;
run;
```

**3. Use the NewEmps raw data file to create a SAS data view.**

The raw data file has 2 rows for each employee. Name the data view NewEmployeesC2. Place it in a permanent SAS data library.

Remember to use a fileref instead of the physical file name.

The record layout is the same as Section 2.

```
data ia.NewEmployeesC2/view=ia.NewEmployeesC2;
   infile Empdat;
   input @1  EmpID $6.
          @8  LastName $32.
         @41 Phone $8.
         @50 Location $25. /
          @8  Division $30.
         @39 HireDate date9.
         @49 JobCode $6.
         @56 Salary dollar10.;
run;
```

**4. Append the NewEmployeesC2 SAS data view, created in a previous exercise, to the EmployeeC2 permanent SAS data set.** EmployeeC2 was also created in a previous exercise.

The raw data file used in NewEmployeeC2 is named NewEmps.

```
filename empdat 'NewEmps.dat';

proc append base = ia.EmployeeC2
            data = ia.NewEmployeesC2;
run;
```

# Chapter 3

# 3.1 Introduction

...

## General Business Scenario

International Airlines has six raw data files containing the same type of information about fares. We must concatenate the raw data files into one SAS data set that the marketing department can use for several applications.

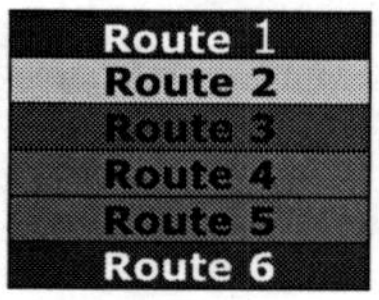


3

...

## General Business Scenario

One application compares fares from International Airlines to those from Super Economy Fly Us, which has only one fare per class for all routes.

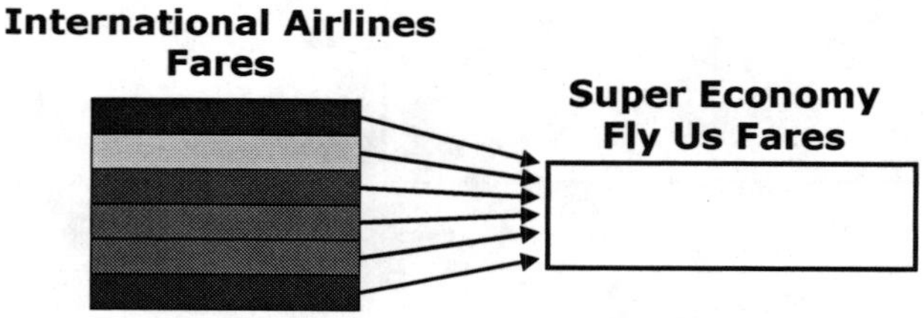


4

...

## General Business Scenario

The final application samples the data to select 7 to 10 observations, systematically and randomly, to allow for more detailed comparisons.

**International Airlines Fares**

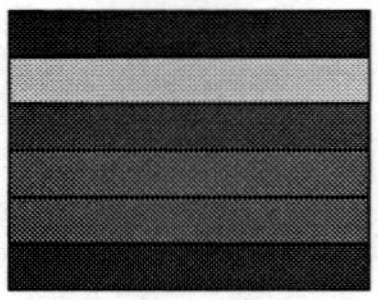

**Random Sample**

5

## Organize the Tasks:

- Create a SAS data file by concatenating 6 raw data files.
- Compare the fares by using an array.
- Systematically and randomly sample the data.

6

# 3.2 Reading Multiple Raw Data Files

## Objectives

- Create a SAS data set from multiple raw data files.

8

## Business Scenario

International Airlines has six raw data files containing information for six routes.

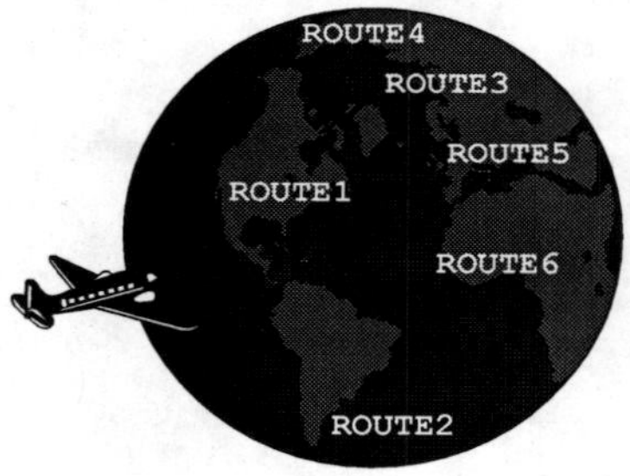


9

## Business Scenario

We need to create a SAS data set from the raw data files.

Route1 Raw Data File Sample

```
0000002LHRRDU 389316001090 531    2
0000004FRARDU 428817611201 585    3
0000043LHRCDG  223   91   62   30    0
0000044CDGLHR  223   91   62   30    0
0000045LHRGLA  347  142   97   47    0
0000046GLALHR  347  142   97   47    0
```

10

## Business Scenario

The file layout for this raw data file:

| Description | Type | Comments |
|---|---|---|
| Route ID Number | C | 1 – 7 |
| Origin | C | 8 - 10 |
| Destination | C | 11 – 13 |
| Distance | N | 14 – 18 |
| Fare for First Class | N | 19 – 22 |
| Fare for Business Class | N | 23 – 26 |
| Fare for Economy Class | N | 27 – 30 |
| Cargo Cost | N | 31 - 35 |

11

## Organize the Tasks

- **Create a SAS data file by concatenating 6 raw data files.**
- Compare the fares by using an array.
- Systematically and randomly sample the data.

12

## Reading Multiple Raw Data Files

To read multiple raw data files, you can use

- multiple INFILE statements if you want the files to remain open in order to change which file is being read
- the FILEVAR= option to define a variable that causes the INFILE statement to close the current input file and open a new one when the variable changes values.

13

Use multiple INFILE statements when you want to read a record from one raw data file, a record from the second raw data file, a record from the third raw data file, etc. (similar to an interleave).

Use the FILEVAR= option when you want to concatenate multiple raw data files.

The value of a FILEVAR= variable is a character string that contains the physical filename of the raw data file to be read.

## INFILE Statement with FILEVAR= Option

General form of the FILEVAR= variable option:

**INFILE** *file-specification* FILEVAR=*variable;*

FILEVAR=*variable*

names a variable whose change in value causes the INFILE statement to close the current input file and open a new one. When the next INPUT statement executes, it reads from the new file that the FILEVAR= variable specifies. Like automatic variables, this variable is not written to the data set.

14

## INFILE Statement with END= Option

General form of the END= variable option:

```
INFILE file-specification END=variable;
```

The END= option names a variable that SAS sets to

0 when the current input data record is not the last in the input file

1 when SAS processes the last data record.

15

The END= variable is not written to the SAS data set.

## DATALINES Statement

General form of the DATALINES statement:

```
DATALINES;
```

Use the DATALINES statement with an INPUT statement to read data that you enter directly in the program, rather than data stored in an external file.

16

The CARDS statement is equivalent to the DATALINES statement.

```
data ia.AllFareInformation;
   length readit $200; ①
   input readit $;  ②
   infile in ③ filevar = readit ④ end = last ⑤;
   do while(last = 0); ⑥
      input  @1 RouteIDNumber $7.  @8 Origin $3.
             @11 Destination $3.   @14 Distance 5.
             @19 FareFirstclass 4. @23 FareBusiness 4.
             @27 FareEconomy 4.    @31 FareCargo 5.;
      output; ⑦
   end;
   datalines; ⑧
   'route1.dat' ⑨
   'route2.dat'
   'route3.dat'
   'route4.dat'
   'route5.dat'
   'route6.dat'
      ;
run;
```

❶ Creates a temporary variable READIT that holds the value used by the FILEVAR= option. The values for READIT are read from the first INPUT statement.

❷ The INPUT statement reads a value from the in stream data identified by the DATALINES statement.

❸ IN is a placeholder, not an actual filename or a *fileref* that has been previously assigned to a file. SAS uses this placeholder for reporting processing information to the SAS log. The placeholder (IN) is an arbitrary word; however, it must be eight characters or fewer, begin with an alpha characters or underscore, followed with alphanumeric characters or underscores.

❹ Specifies the value for the FILEVAR= variable. The INFILE statement closes the current file and opens a new one if the value of READIT has changed when the INFILE statement executes.

❺ LAST is the arbitrary variable name created by the END= option. LAST is a temporary variable.

❻ The DO WHILE loop checks the value of the variable LAST at the top of the loop; therefore, the INPUT statement reads from the currently open INPUT file. Use a DO WHILE loop, not a DO UNTIL loop. The DO UNTIL loop is not appropriate in this example because the DO UNTIL stops the DATA step execution if any file is empty..

❼ The OUTPUT statement writes the contents of the Program Data Vector to create an observation in the SAS data set. The OUTPUT statement is required in this DATA step. Without the OUTPUT statement, the data set IA.FARECOMPARE contains only six observations, one per external file.

❽ The DATALINES statement identifies the instream data to the INPUT statement at ❷.

❾ The files 'Route1.dat', 'Route2.dat', 'Route3 .dat', 'Route4.dat', 'Route5.dat', and 'Route6.dat' are the names of the raw data files to be read.

## Reading Multiple Raw Data Files

c03s2d1

Rather than creating six SAS data sets, one from each of the raw data files, we can create a single SAS data set and concatenate the raw data files as we create the SAS file.

Program

```
data ia.AllFareInformation;
   length readit $200;
   input readit $;
   infile in filevar = readit end = last;
   do while(last = 0);
      input  @1 RouteIDNumber $7.
             @8 Origin $3.
            @11 Destination $3.
            @14 Distance 5.
            @19 FareFirstclass 4.
            @23 FareBusiness 4.
            @27 FareEconomy 4.
            @31 FareCargo 5.;
      output;
   end;
   datalines;
'route1.dat'
'route2.dat'
'route3.dat'
'route4.dat'
'route5.dat'
'route6.dat'
      ;
run;


proc print data = ia.AllFareInformation(obs = 10) noobs;
   title 'All Fares from Six Raw Data Files';
run;
```

## Output

All Fares from Six Raw Data Files

| Route IDNumber | Origin | Destination | Distance | Fare Firstclass | Fare Business | Fare Economy | Fare Cargo |
|---|---|---|---|---|---|---|---|
| 0000001 | RDU | LHR | 3893 | 1600 | 1090 | 531 | 2 |
| 0000003 | RDU | FRA | 4288 | 1761 | 1201 | 585 | 3 |
| 0000005 | RDU | JFK | 428 | 176 | 120 | 58 | 0 |
| 0000006 | JFK | RDU | 428 | 176 | 120 | 58 | 0 |
| 0000007 | RDU | SFO | 2419 | 993 | 677 | 330 | 2 |
| 0000008 | SFO | RDU | 2419 | 993 | 677 | 330 | 2 |
| 0000009 | RDU | LAX | 2255 | 926 | 631 | 307 | 1 |
| 0000010 | LAX | RDU | 2255 | 926 | 631 | 307 | 1 |
| 0000011 | RDU | ORD | 645 | 265 | 181 | 88 | 0 |
| 0000012 | ORD | RDU | 645 | 265 | 181 | 88 | 0 |

## Log

```
/********* c03s2d1 *******************/

/**************************************/
/*    Create a SAS data set from      */
/*    multiple raw data files.        */
/**************************************/


data ia.AllFareInformation;
   length readit $200;
   input readit $;
   infile in filevar = readit end = last;
   do while(last = 0);
      input  @1 RouteIDNumber $7.
             @8 Origin $3.
            @11 Destination $3.
            @14 Distance 5.
            @19 FareFirstclass 4.
            @23 FareBusiness 4.
            @27 FareEconomy 4.
            @31 FareCargo 5.;
      output;
   end;
   datalines;

NOTE: The infile IN is:
      File Name=C:\workshop\winsas\prog3\route1.dat,
      RECFM=V,LRECL=256

NOTE: The infile IN is:
      File Name=C:\workshop\winsas\prog3\route2.dat,
      RECFM=V,LRECL=256

NOTE: The infile IN is:
      File Name=C:\workshop\winsas\prog3\route3.dat,
      RECFM=V,LRECL=256
```

```
NOTE: The infile IN is:
      File Name=C:\workshop\winsas\prog3\route4.dat,
      RECFM=V,LRECL=256

NOTE: The infile IN is:
      File Name=C:\workshop\winsas\prog3\route5.dat,
      RECFM=V,LRECL=256

NOTE: The infile IN is:
      File Name=C:\workshop\winsas\prog3\route6.dat,
      RECFM=V,LRECL=256

NOTE: 301 records were read from the infile IN.
      The minimum record length was 35.
      The maximum record length was 35.
NOTE: 49 records were read from the infile IN.
      The minimum record length was 35.
      The maximum record length was 35.
NOTE: 245 records were read from the infile IN.
      The minimum record length was 35.
      The maximum record length was 35.
NOTE: 105 records were read from the infile IN.
      The minimum record length was 35.
      The maximum record length was 35.
NOTE: 35 records were read from the infile IN.
      The minimum record length was 35.
      The maximum record length was 35.
NOTE: 49 records were read from the infile IN.
      The minimum record length was 35.
      The maximum record length was 35.
NOTE: The data set IA.ALLFAREINFORMATION has 784 observations and 8 variables.
NOTE: DATA statement used:
      real time           1.87 seconds
      cpu time            0.62 seconds


31        ;
32    run;
33
34
35    proc print data = ia.AllFareInformation (obs = 10) noobs;
36       title 'All Fares from Six Raw Data Files';
37    run;

NOTE: There were 10 observations read from the data set IA.ALLFAREINFORMATION.
NOTE: PROCEDURE PRINT used:
      real time           1.21 seconds
      cpu time            0.31 seconds
```

## Reference Information

In addition to using the DATALINES statement to identify the names of the raw data files, you can read the raw data file names from a SAS data set or from a raw data file.

### Storing the Raw Data File Names in a SAS Data Set

If raw data files that are to be read are in the SAS data set ia.RawDataFiles, you can use the following code.

IA.RAWDATAFILES

| Obs | readit |
|---|---|
| 1 | route1.dat |
| 2 | route2.dat |
| 3 | route3.dat |
| 4 | route4.dat |
| 5 | route5.dat |
| 6 | route6.dat |

```
data ia.AllFareInformation;
   set ia.RawDataFiles;
   infile in filevar = readit end = last;
   do while(last = 0)
      input  @1 RouteIDNumber $7.
             @8 Origin $3.
            @11 Destination $3.
            @14 Distance 5.
            @19 FareFirstclass 4.
            @23 FareBusiness 4.
            @27 FareEconomy 4.
            @31 FareCargo 5.;
      output;
   end;
run;
```

### Storing the Raw Data File Names in an External File

If the raw data files to be read are in the external file RawDataFiles.dat, you can use the following code.

RAWDATAFILES.DAT

```
route1.dat
route2.dat
route3.dat
route4.dat
route5.dat
route6.dat
```

```
data ia.AllFareInformation;
   infile 'RawDataFiles.dat';
   input readit $ 10.;
   infile in filevar = readit end = last;
   do while(last = 0)
      input  @1 RouteIDNumber $7.
             @8 Origin $3.
            @11 Destination $3.
            @14 Distance 5.
            @19 FareFirstclass 4.
            @23 FareBusiness 4.
            @27 FareEconomy 4.
            @31 FareCargo 5.;
      output;
   end;
run;
```

## Exercises

1. Each company division has a raw data file with an identical file structure containing employee information. In a single DATA step, create a SAS data set named IA.AllDivisions by concatenating the following raw data files.

| File Names |
|---|
| AptOp. |
| CorpOp |
| CorpPlan |
| FinIT |
| FltOP |
| HRFac |
| SM |

By default, the location of these files is:

| Operating System | Location |
|---|---|
| OS/390 | userid.prog3.rawdata |
| WIN | c:\workshop\winsas\prog3 |
| UNIX | /userid/prog3 |

If your external files are not in the default location, they are located in

The record layout of all the files is as follows:

| Start Column | Description | Width |
|---|---|---|
| 1 | Employee ID | 6 |
| 8 | Employee Last Name | 32 |
| 41 | Employee Phone Number | 8 |
| 50 | Employee Location | 25 |
| 76 | Employee Division | 30 |

# 3.3 Using Arrays to Create New Variables

## Objectives

- Use an array to reference existing variables.
- Use an array to reference new variables.
- Use an array to reference constants.

21

## Business Scenario

We need to compare our fares to those from Super Economy Fly Us, an airline that charges a fixed fare for each class of service as well as for cargo.

Super Economy Fly Us Rates

| | |
|---|---|
| First Class | $1000 |
| Business Class | $500 |
| Economy Class | $100 |
| Pound of Cargo | $1 |

22

## Business Scenario

International Airline Rates

**ia. AllRouteInformation**

| Route IDNumber | … | FareFirst Class | Fare Business | Fare Economy | Fare Cargo |
|---|---|---|---|---|---|
| 0000001 | ... | 1600 | 1090 | 531 | 2 |
| 0000003 | ... | 1761 | 1201 | 585 | 3 |
| 0000005 | ... | 176 | 120 | 58 | 0 |

23

## Organize the Tasks

- Create a SAS data file by concatenating 6 raw data files.
- **Compare the fares by using an array.**
- Systematically and randomly sample the data.

24

## Using an Array to Create New Variables

An *array* is a way to refer to a group of variables in one observation with a single name.

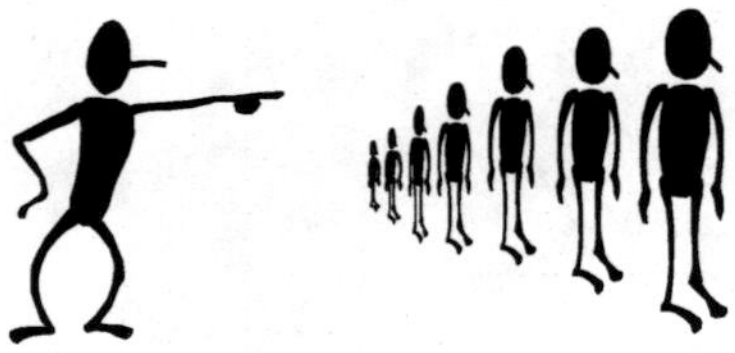

25

An array references all character or all numeric variables.

## Using Arrays to Create New Variables

Think of an array as being an alias for

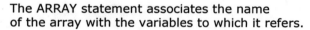

- existing variables
- new variables
- temporary variables.

The ARRAY statement associates the name of the array with the variables to which it refers.

26

Each variable of the array is

- called an *element*
- identified by an index value that represents the position of the element in the array.

Array names

- cannot be used in LABEL, FORMAT, DROP, KEEP, or LENGTH statements
- exist only for the duration of the DATA step
- can be a maximum of 32 characters.

...

## Using an ARRAY Statement to Reference Existing Variables

The ARRAY statement that references existing variables is

**ARRAY** *ArrayName{n} <$ length> elements*;

Dimensions     Existing Variables

Example:

```
array ours{4} FareFirstClass FareBusiness
              FareEconomy FareCargo;
```

27

## Reference Information

The general form of the ARRAY statement:

**ARRAY** *array-name{dimensions} $ length elements (initial values)*;

| | |
|---|---|
| *array-name* | a valid SAS name up to 32 characters in length. |
| *dimensions* | specifies the number of elements in the array. |
| *$* | indicates that the array references character variables. |
| *length* | defines a length for new variables. The default is 8. |
| *elements* | specifies the variables to which the array refers. |
| *initial values* | gives initial values for the corresponding elements. |

The ARRAY statement
- must be used to define an array before the array name can be referenced
- creates variables if they do not already exist in the PDV
- is not executable.

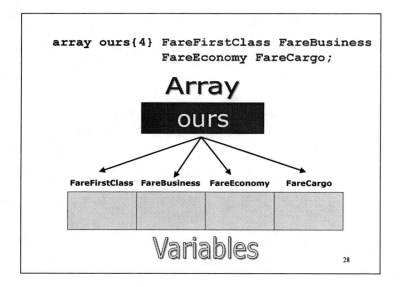

```
array ours{4} FareFirstClass FareBusiness
              FareEconomy FareCargo;
```

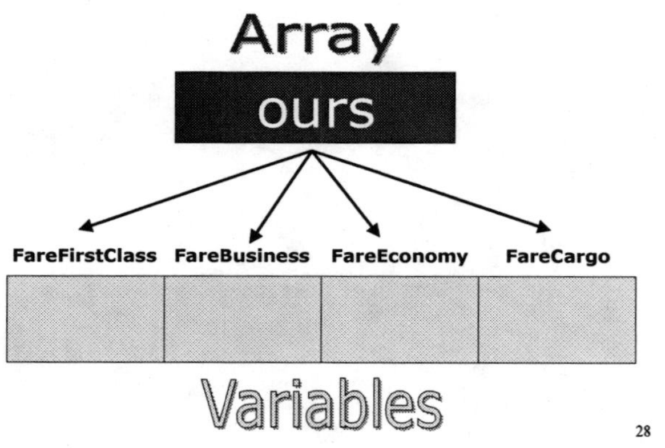

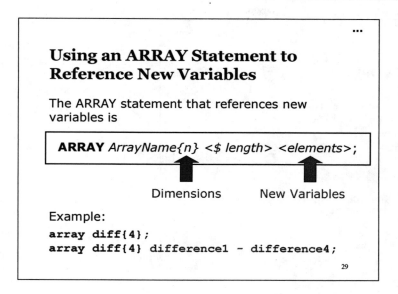

## Using an ARRAY Statement to Reference New Variables

The ARRAY statement that references new variables is

**ARRAY** *ArrayName{n}* <*$ length*> <*elements*>;

Dimensions    New Variables

Example:

```
array diff{4};
array diff{4} difference1 - difference4;
```

29

```
array diff{4};
```

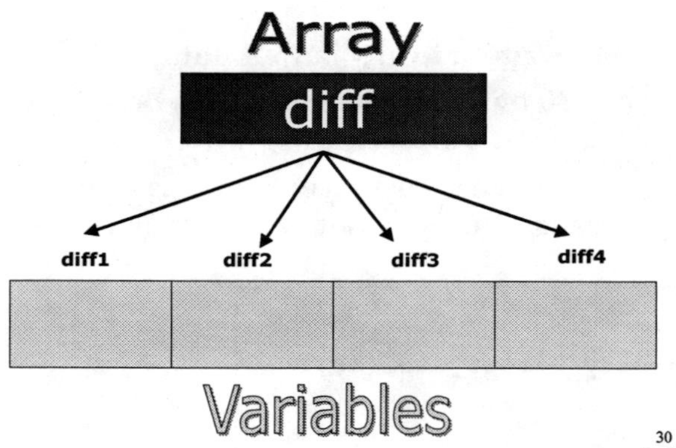


30

...

## Using an Array to Create Temporary Variables

The ARRAY statement that references temporary variables containing constants is

**ARRAY** *ArrayName{n} _TEMPORARY_ (a1, a2, ...an)*;

Dimensions Keyword Initial Values

Example:

```
array theirs{4} _temporary_ (1000,500,100,1);
```

31

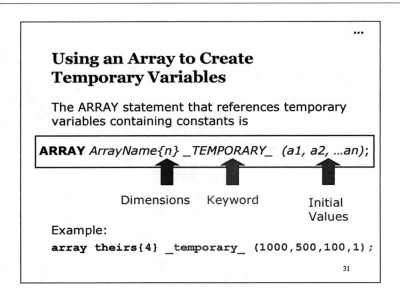

Since the constants are needed only for the duration of DATA step execution, you can use the keyword _TEMPORARY_ instead of specifying variable names and assign the initial values to the temporary array elements.

Advantages of Temporary Arrays

- Elements of the array are not written to any output data set.
- Each element requires about 40 bytes less memory than do DATA step variables that are used as array elements.
- Elements are always in contiguous buffer space, resulting in faster retrieval of values. Variables may, or may not, be contiguous.

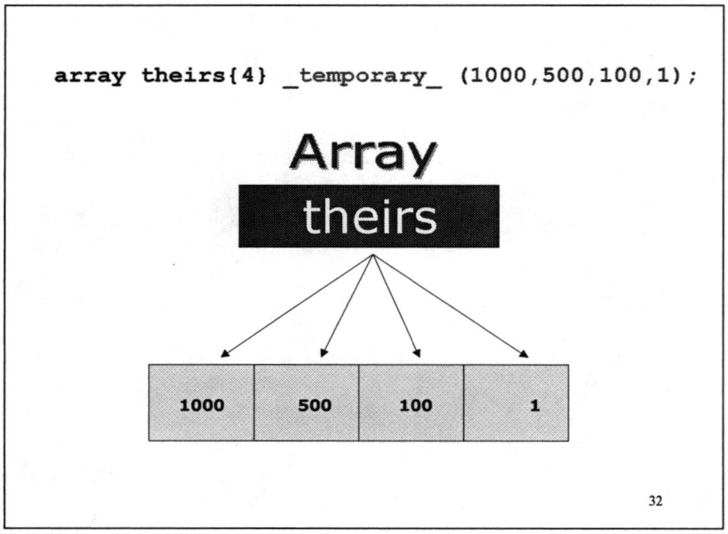

## Using Arrays

```
data ia.FareCompare(drop = i);
   array theirs{4} _temporary_ (1000,500,100,1);
   array diff{4};
   array ours{4} FareFirstclass
                 FareBusiness
                 FareEconomy
                 FareCargo;
   set ia.AllFareInformation(drop = distance);
   do i = 1 to 4;
      diff{i} = ours{i} - theirs{i};
   end;
run;
```

33

...

```
data ia.FareCompare(drop = i);
   array theirs{4} _temporary_  (1000,500,100,1);
   array diff{4};
   array ours{4} FareFirstclass FareBusiness
                 FareEconomy FareCargo;
   set ia.AllFareInformation (drop = distance);
   do i = 1 to 4;
      diff{i} = ours{i} - theirs{i};
   end;
run;
```

**Compilation**

theirs →

| | | | |
|---|---|---|---|
| 1000 | 500 | 100 | 1 |

34

The ARRAY statement to create the array reference THEIRS is compiled.

Since the array THEIRS uses the _TEMPORARY_ keyword, the array does not reference existing data set variables, nor does it create new variables.

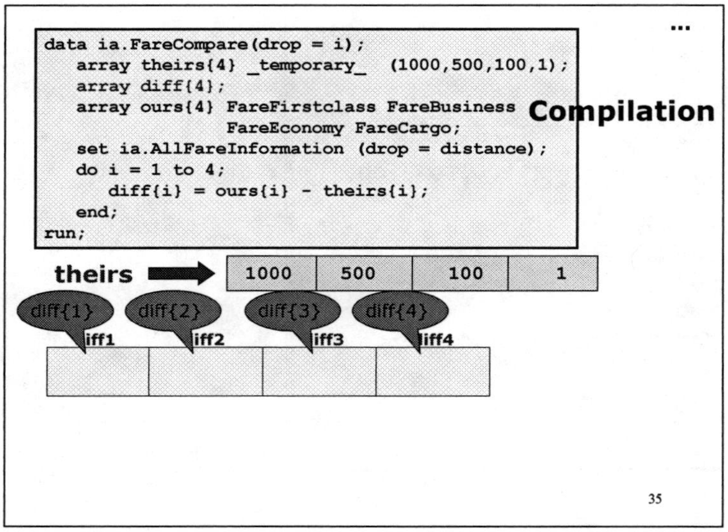


The ARRAY statement to create the array reference DIFF is compiled.

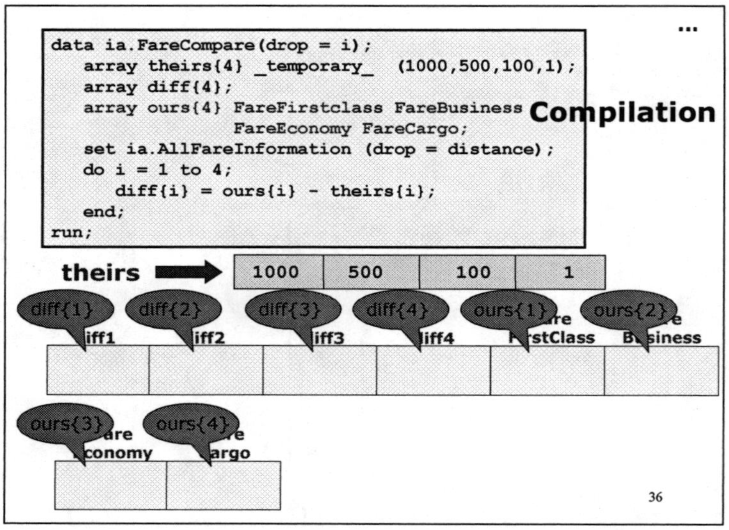


The ARRAY statement to create the array reference OURS is compiled.

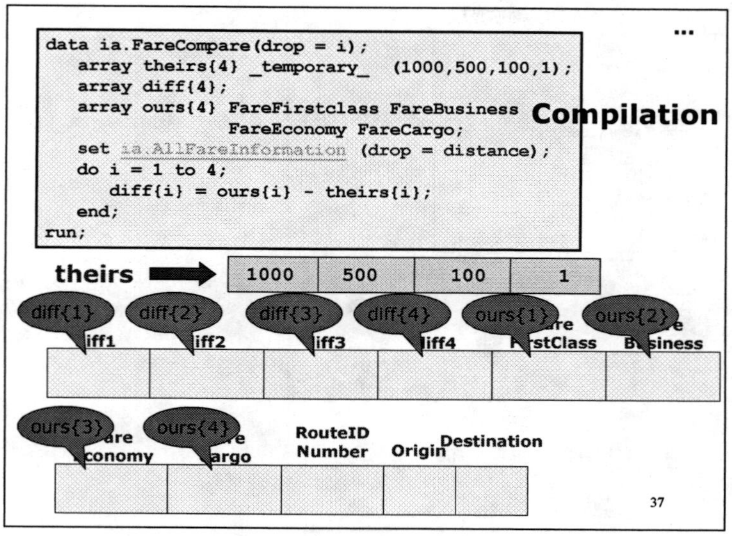


The SET statement is compiled.

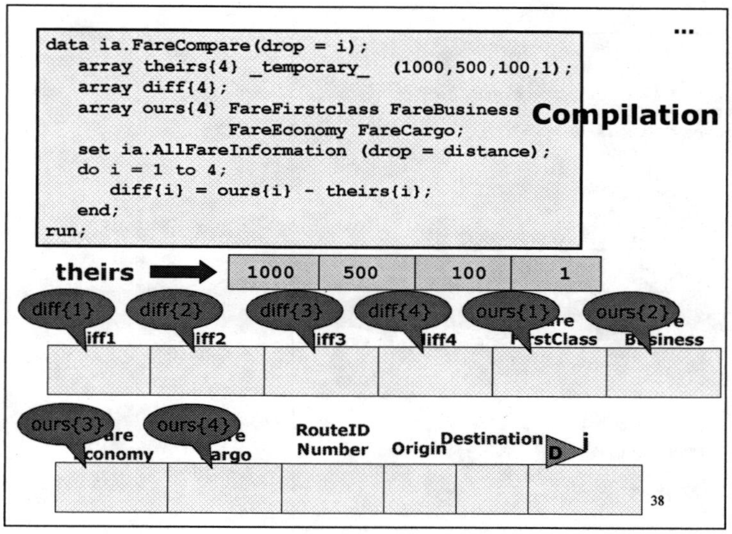


The DO statement is compiled.

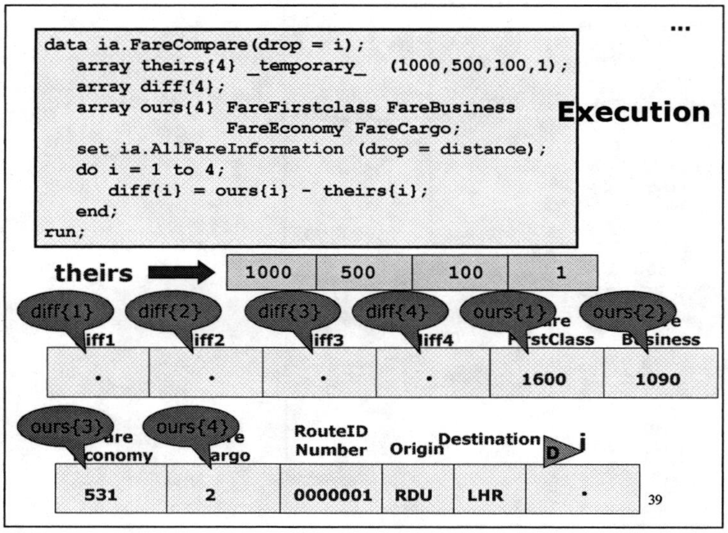


The SET statement is executed.

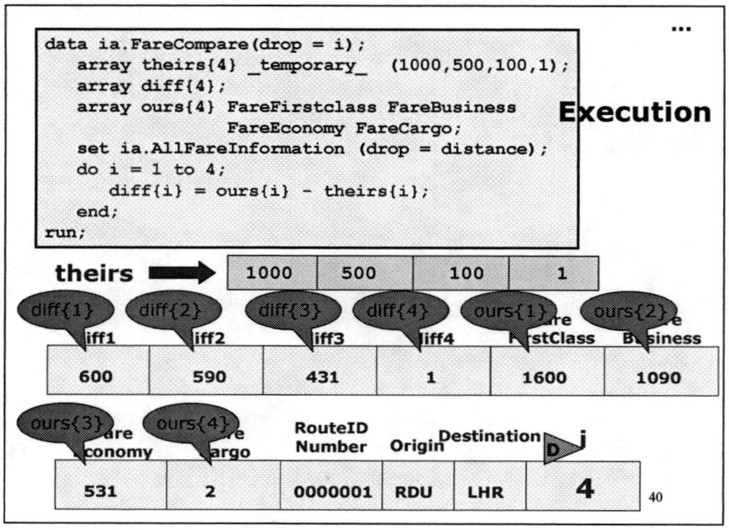


The DO loop is executed four times. At the bottom of the DO loop, the variable I is incremented by 1.

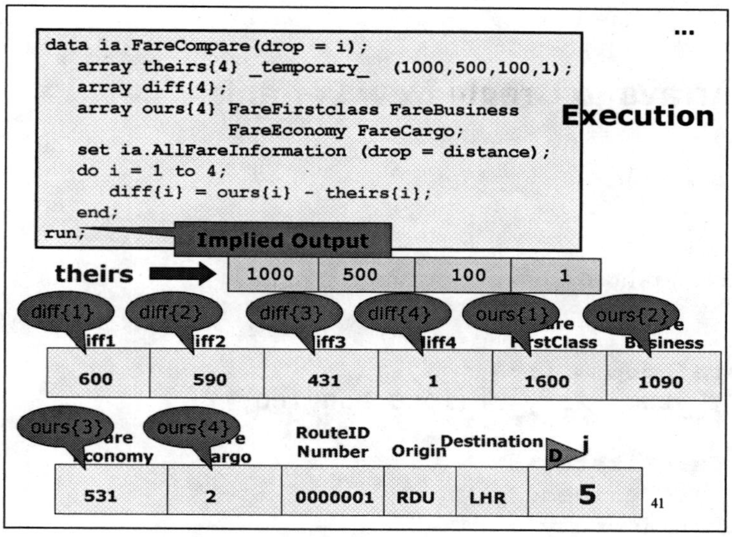


When I = 5, execution of the DO loop stops. At the bottom of the DATA step, the first observation is output.

## Using Arrays to Create New Variables

c03s3d1

Let us compare our fares to those from Super Economy Fly Us.

Program

```
data ia.FareCompare(drop = i);
   array theirs{4} _temporary_  (1000,500,100,1);
   array diff{4};
   array ours{4} FareFirstclass
                 FareBusiness
                 FareEconomy
                 FareCargo;
   set ia.AllFareInformation(drop = distance);
   do i = 1 to 4;
      diff{i} = ours{i} - theirs{i};
   end;
run;


proc print data = ia.FareCompare(obs = 10) heading = h;
   title 'Comparison of International Airlines Fares';
   title2 'With those of Super Economy You Fly Us';
run;
```

By default, PROC PRINT fits as many variables on a row as possible. For some reports, putting the variable names vertically on the page enables all of the variables in the report to fit on one row. The HEADING = *h* PROC PRINT option prints the variable names horizontally rather than vertically.

Output

Comparison of International Airlines Fares
With those of Super Economy You Fly Us

| Obs | diff1 | diff2 | diff3 | diff4 | Fare Firstclass | Fare Business |
|---|---|---|---|---|---|---|
| 1 | 600 | 590 | 431 | 1 | 1600 | 1090 |
| 2 | 761 | 701 | 485 | 2 | 1761 | 1201 |
| 3 | -824 | -380 | -42 | -1 | 176 | 120 |
| 4 | -824 | -380 | -42 | -1 | 176 | 120 |
| 5 | -7 | 177 | 230 | 1 | 993 | 677 |
| 6 | -7 | 177 | 230 | 1 | 993 | 677 |
| 7 | -74 | 131 | 207 | 0 | 926 | 631 |
| 8 | -74 | 131 | 207 | 0 | 926 | 631 |
| 9 | -735 | -319 | -12 | -1 | 265 | 181 |
| 10 | -735 | -319 | -12 | -1 | 265 | 181 |

| Obs | Fare Economy | Fare Cargo | Route IDNumber | Origin | Destination |
|---|---|---|---|---|---|
| 1 | 531 | 2 | 0000001 | RDU | LHR |
| 2 | 585 | 3 | 0000003 | RDU | FRA |
| 3 | 58 | 0 | 0000005 | RDU | JFK |
| 4 | 58 | 0 | 0000006 | JFK | RDU |
| 5 | 330 | 2 | 0000007 | RDU | SFO |
| 6 | 330 | 2 | 0000008 | SFO | RDU |
| 7 | 307 | 1 | 0000009 | RDU | LAX |
| 8 | 307 | 1 | 0000010 | LAX | RDU |
| 9 | 88 | 0 | 0000011 | RDU | ORD |
| 10 | 88 | 0 | 0000012 | ORD | RDU |

## Exercises

2. Create a temporary SAS data set named ProjectedSalaries from the SAS data set named IA.EmployeeC2. Use arrays to calculate the salaries for each employee for the next 10 years based upon estimated percentage cost of living adjustment.

   The projected percentage increases for the next 10 years starting with the current year are:

   .05, .045, .055, .05, .06, .04, .05, .055, .045, .06

   Remember the salaries progressively increase. The percentages above should be calculated on the newest calculated salary, not repeatedly on this year's salary.

# 3.4 Creating a Sample Data Set

## Objectives

- Create a systematic sample containing seven observations.
- Create a systematic sample containing an unknown number of observations.
- Create a random sample with replacement.
- Create a random sample without replacement.

45

...

## Business Scenario

We need to create several random samples to use for various reports.

| Obs | diff1 | diff2 | diff3 | diff4 | Fare Firstclass | Fare Business |
|---|---|---|---|---|---|---|
| 1 | 600 | 590 | 431 | 1 | 1600 | 1090 |
| ➡ 2 | 761 | 701 | 485 | 2 | 1761 | 1201 |
| 3 | -824 | -380 | -42 | -1 | 176 | 120 |
| 4 | -824 | -380 | -42 | -1 | 176 | 120 |
| 5 | -7 | 177 | 230 | 1 | 993 | 677 |
| 6 | -7 | 177 | 230 | 1 | 993 | 677 |
| ➡ 7 | -74 | 131 | 207 | 0 | 926 | 631 |
| 8 | -74 | 131 | 207 | 0 | 926 | 631 |
| 9 | -735 | -319 | -12 | -1 | 265 | 181 |
| ➡ 10 | -735 | -319 | -12 | -1 | 265 | 181 |

46

## Organize the Tasks

- Create a SAS data file by concatenating 6 raw data files.
- Compare the fares by using an array.
- **Systematically and randomly sample the data.**

47

## Using the POINT= Option

To create a sample, use the POINT= option on the SET statement.

General form of the POINT= option:

**SET** *data-set-name* POINT = *point-variable*;

*point-variable*

- names a temporary numeric variable that contains the observation number of the observation to read
- must be given a value before the execution of the SET statement.

48

The POINT= variable must be an integer greater than 0 and less than or equal to the number of observations in the SAS data set.

## Using the STOP Statement

The POINT= option

- uses direct-access read mode
- does not detect the end-of-file.

To prevent the DATA step from looping continuously, use the STOP statement.

```
STOP;
```

49

## Creating a Systematic Sample

We need to select a seven-observation subset by reading every hundredth observation from observation number 100 to observation number 700.

```
data ia.subset;
   do pickit=100 to 700 by 100; ①
      set ia.FareCompare point = pickit; ②
      output; ③
   end;
   stop; ④
run;
```

50

❶ The DO loop assigns a value to the variable PICKIT.

❷ PICKIT is assigned a value before it is used by the POINT= option to select an observation from the SAS data set.

❸ The OUTPUT statement writes the values in the PDV to the SAS data set.

❹ The STOP statement stops the DATA step from continuing to execute after the seven observations are selected. Without a STOP statement, the DATA step gets into an infinite loop.

## Creating a Systematic Sample with Seven Observations

c03s4d1

Program

```
data ia.subset;
   do pickit = 100 to 700 by 100;
      set ia.FareCompare point = pickit;
      output;
    end;
    stop;
run;

proc print data = ia.subset heading = h;
   title 'Creating a Systematic Sample of 7 Observations';
run;
```

Output

Creating a Systematic Sample of 7 Observations

| Obs | diff1 | diff2 | diff3 | diff4 | Fare Firstclass | Fare Business |
|---|---|---|---|---|---|---|
| 1 | 392 | 448 | 362 | 1 | 1392 | 948 |
| 2 | 235 | 341 | 310 | 1 | 1235 | 841 |
| 3 | 389 | 447 | 361 | 1 | 1389 | 947 |
| 4 | -789 | -356 | -30 | -1 | 211 | 144 |
| 5 | -894 | -429 | -65 | -1 | 106 | 71 |
| 6 | -257 | 7 | 147 | 0 | 743 | 507 |
| 7 | 2185 | 1671 | 958 | 4 | 3185 | 2171 |

| Obs | Fare Economy | Fare Cargo | Route IDNumber | Origin | Destination |
|---|---|---|---|---|---|
| 1 | 462 | 2 | 0000016 | SEA | RDU |
| 2 | 410 | 2 | 0000030 | HNL | SFO |
| 3 | 461 | 2 | 0000054 | LAX | RDU |
| 4 | 70 | 0 | 0000057 | FRA | CPH |
| 5 | 35 | 0 | 0000050 | BRU | LHR |
| 6 | 247 | 1 | 0000094 | SIN | CCU |
| 7 | 1058 | 5 | 0000111 | HND | SFO |

## Creating a Systematic Sample with an Unknown Number of Observations

You can use the NOBS= option on the SET statement to determine how many observations there are in a SAS data set.

**SET** *SAS-data-set* NOBS = *variable*;

The NOBS= option creates a temporary variable whose value is

- the number of observations in the input data set(s)
- assigned a value during compilation.

52

## Creating a Systematic Sample with an Unknown Number of Observations

We need to select a subset by reading every hundredth observation from observation number 100 to the end of the SAS data set.

```
data ia.subset;
   do pickit = 100 to totobs by 100; ②
      set ia.FareCompare point = pickit
                        nobs = totobs; ①
      output;
   end;
   stop;
run;
```

53

❶ The NOBS= variable-name creates a temporary variable that contains the number of observations in the input data file. During compilation, SAS reads the descriptor portion of the data file and assigns the value of the NOBS= variable.

❷ You can refer to the NOBS variable in executable statements that come before the SET statement.

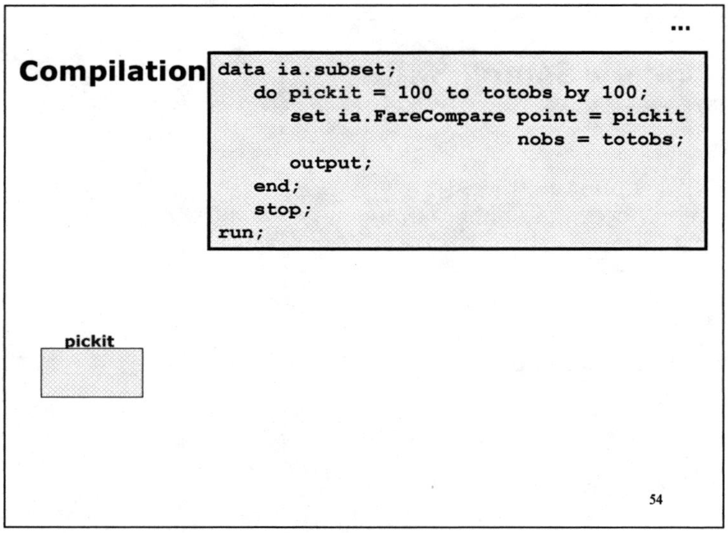
...
Compilation
data ia.subset;
do pickit = 100 to totobs by 100;
set ia.FareCompare point = pickit
nobs = totobs;
output;
end;
stop;
run;
pickit
54

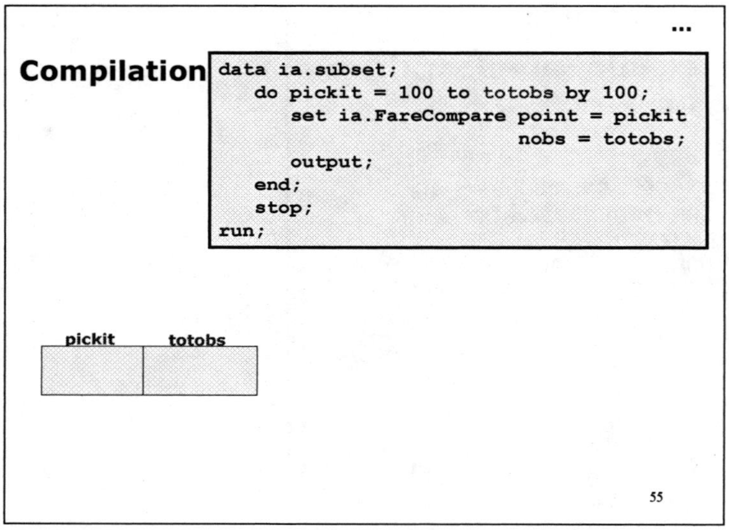
...
Compilation
data ia.subset;
do pickit = 100 to totobs by 100;
set ia.FareCompare point = pickit
nobs = totobs;
output;
end;
stop;
run;
pickit
totobs
55

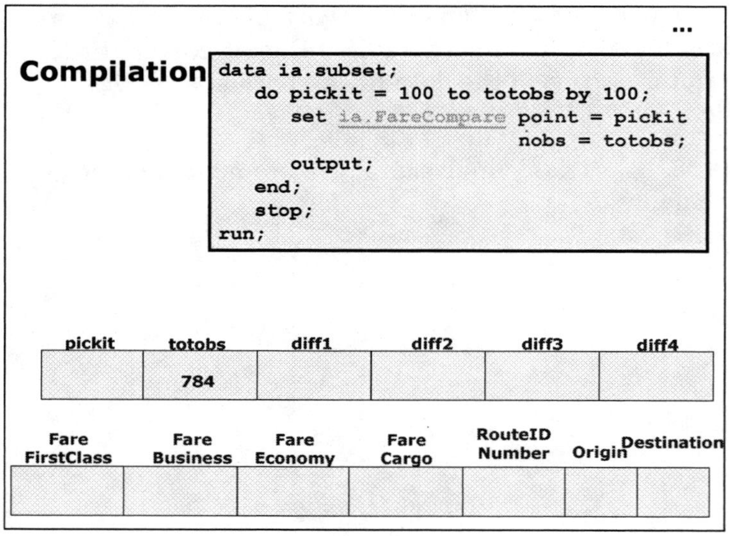
...
Compilation
data ia.subset;
do pickit = 100 to totobs by 100;
set ia.FareCompare point = pickit
nobs = totobs;
output;
end;
stop;
run;
pickit
totobs
diff1
diff2
diff3
diff4
784
Fare FirstClass
Fare Business
Fare Economy
Fare Cargo
RouteID Number
Origin
Destination

...

**Execution**

```
data ia.subset;
   do pickit = 100 to totobs by 100;
      set ia.FareCompare point = pickit
                         nobs = totobs;
      output;
   end;
   stop;
run;
```

| pickit | totobs | diff1 | diff2 | diff3 | diff4 |
|---|---|---|---|---|---|
| 100 | 784 | . | . | . | . |

| Fare FirstClass | Fare Business | Fare Economy | Fare Cargo | RouteID Number | Origin | Destination |
|---|---|---|---|---|---|---|
| . | . | . | . | | | |

...

**Execution**

```
data ia.subset;
   do pickit = 100 to totobs by 100;
      set ia.FareCompare point = pickit
                         nobs = totobs;
      output;
   end;
   stop;
run;
```

| pickit | totobs | diff1 | diff2 | diff3 | diff4 |
|---|---|---|---|---|---|
| 100 | 784 | 392 | 448 | 362 | 1 |

| Fare FirstClass | Fare Business | Fare Economy | Fare Cargo | RouteID Number | Origin | Destination |
|---|---|---|---|---|---|---|
| 1392 | 948 | 462 | 2 | 0000016 | SEA | RDU |

...

**Execution**

```
data ia.subset;
   do pickit = 100 to totobs by 100;
      set ia.FareCompare point = pickit
                         nobs = totobs;
      output;
   end;
   stop;
run;
```

Explicit Output

| pickit | totobs | diff1 | diff2 | diff3 | diff4 |
|---|---|---|---|---|---|
| 100 | 784 | 392 | 448 | 362 | 1 |

| Fare FirstClass | Fare Business | Fare Economy | Fare Cargo | RouteID Number | Origin | Destination |
|---|---|---|---|---|---|---|
| 1392 | 948 | 462 | 2 | 0000016 | SEA | RDU |

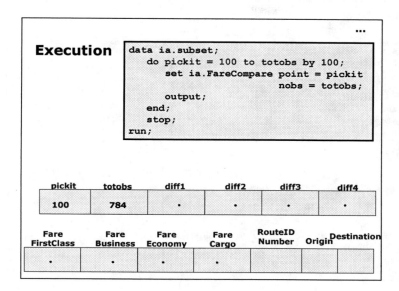

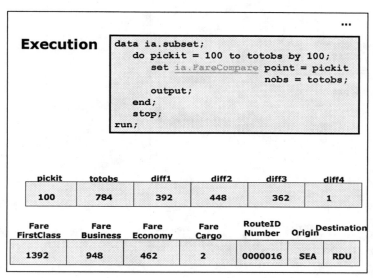

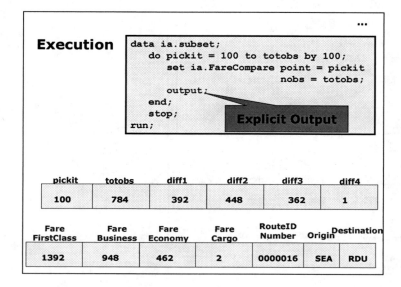

...

**Execution**

```
data ia.subset;
   do pickit = 100 to totobs by 100;
      set ia.FareCompare point = pickit
                         nobs = totobs;
      output;
   end;
   stop;
```

pickit = 200

| pickit | totobs | diff1 | diff2 | diff3 | diff4 |
|---|---|---|---|---|---|
| 200 | 784 | 392 | 448 | 362 | 1 |

| Fare FirstClass | Fare Business | Fare Economy | Fare Cargo | RouteID Number | Origin | Destination |
|---|---|---|---|---|---|---|
| 1392 | 948 | 462 | 2 | 0000016 | SEA | RDU |

...

**Execution**

```
data ia.subset;
   do pickit = 100 to totobs by 100;
      set ia.FareCompare point = pickit
                         nobs = totobs;
      output;
   end;
   stop;
run;
```

| pickit | totobs | diff1 | diff2 | diff3 | diff4 |
|---|---|---|---|---|---|
| 200 | 784 | 235 | 341 | 310 | 1 |

| Fare FirstClass | Fare Business | Fare Economy | Fare Cargo | RouteID Number | Origin | Destination |
|---|---|---|---|---|---|---|
| 1235 | 841 | 410 | 2 | 0000030 | HNL | SFO |

...

**Execution**

```
data ia.subset;
   do pickit = 100 to totobs by 100;
      set ia.FareCompare point = pickit
                         nobs = totobs;
      output;
   end;
   stop;
run;
```

Explicit Output

| pickit | totobs | diff1 | diff2 | diff3 | diff4 |
|---|---|---|---|---|---|
| 200 | 784 | 235 | 341 | 310 | 1 |

| Fare FirstClass | Fare Business | Fare Economy | Fare Cargo | RouteID Number | Origin | Destination |
|---|---|---|---|---|---|---|
| 1235 | 841 | 410 | 2 | 0000030 | HNL | SFO |

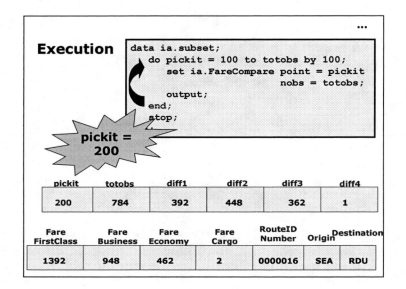

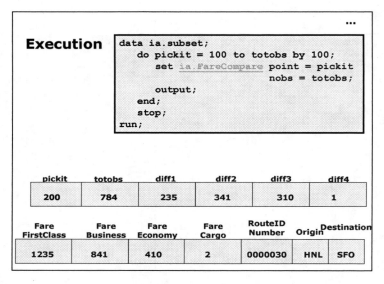

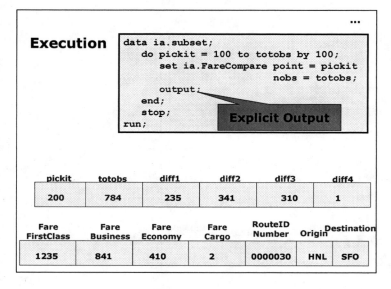

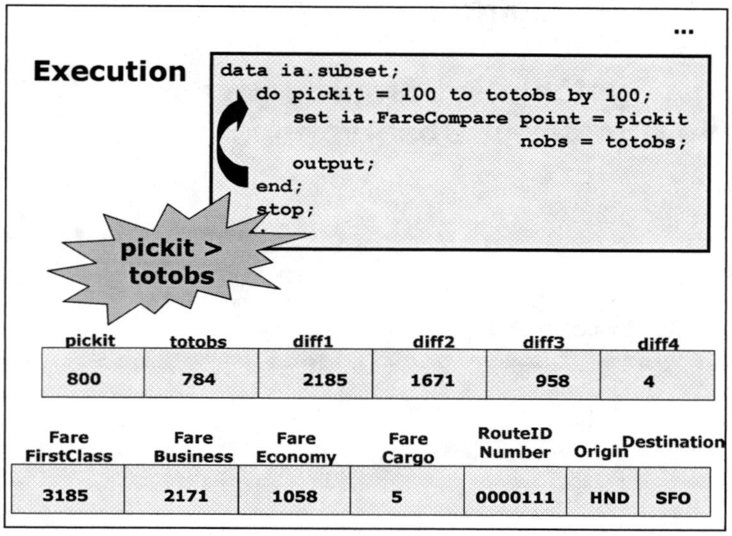
...
Execution
data ia.subset;
do pickit = 100 to totobs by 100;
set ia.FareCompare point = pickit
nobs = totobs;
output;
end;
stop;
pickit > totobs
pickit totobs diff1 diff2 diff3 diff4
800 784 2185 1671 958 4
Fare FirstClass Fare Business Fare Economy Fare Cargo RouteID Number Origin Destination
3185 2171 1058 5 0000111 HND SFO

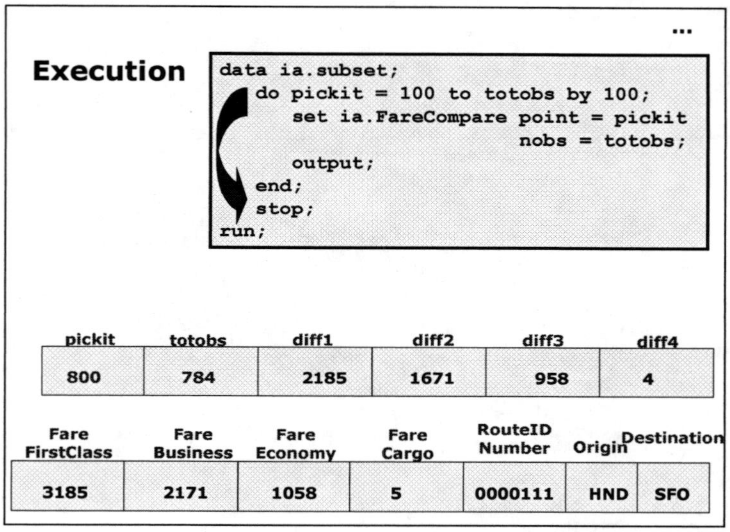
...
Execution
data ia.subset;
do pickit = 100 to totobs by 100;
set ia.FareCompare point = pickit
nobs = totobs;
output;
end;
stop;
run;
pickit totobs diff1 diff2 diff3 diff4
800 784 2185 1671 958 4
Fare FirstClass Fare Business Fare Economy Fare Cargo RouteID Number Origin Destination
3185 2171 1058 5 0000111 HND SFO

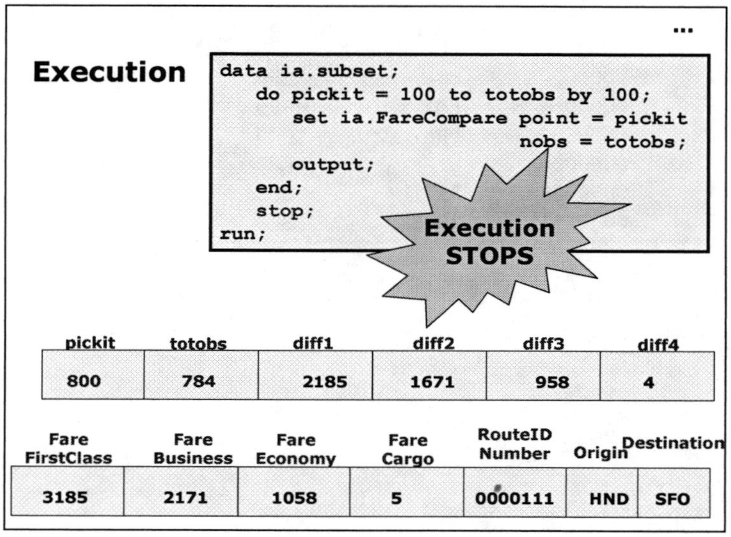
...
Execution
data ia.subset;
do pickit = 100 to totobs by 100;
set ia.FareCompare point = pickit
nobs = totobs;
output;
end;
stop;
run;
Execution STOPS
pickit totobs diff1 diff2 diff3 diff4
800 784 2185 1671 958 4
Fare FirstClass Fare Business Fare Economy Fare Cargo RouteID Number Origin Destination
3185 2171 1058 5 0000111 HND SFO

## Creating a Systematic Sample with an Unknown Number of Observations

c03s4d2

Program

```
data ia.subset;
   do pickit = 100 to totobs by 100;
      set ia.FareCompare point = pickit nobs = totobs;
      output;
   end;
   stop;
run;

proc print data = ia.subset heading = h;
   title 'A Systematic Sample of Fares';
run;
```

Output

A Systematic Sample of Fares

| Obs | diff1 | diff2 | diff3 | diff4 | Fare Firstclass | Fare Business |
|---|---|---|---|---|---|---|
| 1 | 392 | 448 | 362 | 1 | 1392 | 948 |
| 2 | 235 | 341 | 310 | 1 | 1235 | 841 |
| 3 | 389 | 447 | 361 | 1 | 1389 | 947 |
| 4 | -789 | -356 | -30 | -1 | 211 | 144 |
| 5 | -894 | -429 | -65 | -1 | 106 | 71 |
| 6 | -257 | 7 | 147 | 0 | 743 | 507 |
| 7 | 2185 | 1671 | 958 | 4 | 3185 | 2171 |

| Obs | Fare Economy | Fare Cargo | Route IDNumber | Origin | Destination |
|---|---|---|---|---|---|
| 1 | 462 | 2 | 0000016 | SEA | RDU |
| 2 | 410 | 2 | 0000030 | HNL | SFO |
| 3 | 461 | 2 | 0000054 | LAX | RDU |
| 4 | 70 | 0 | 0000057 | FRA | CPH |
| 5 | 35 | 0 | 0000050 | BRU | LHR |
| 6 | 247 | 1 | 0000094 | SIN | CCU |
| 7 | 1058 | 5 | 0000111 | HND | SFO |

## Creating a Random Sample

There are several random number functions to generate random numbers from various distributions.

General form of the RANUNI function:

```
RANUNI(seed)
```

67

## Using the RANUNI Function

The RANUNI function returns a number between 0 and 1 (non-inclusive) generated from a uniform distribution.

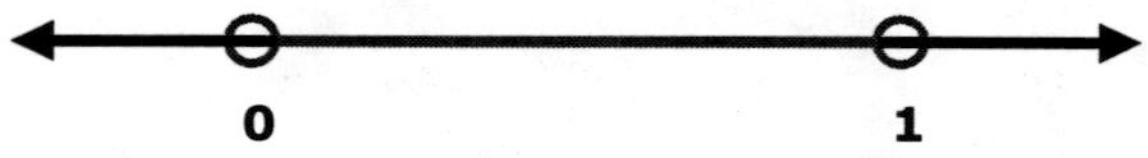


**ranuni(0)**

68

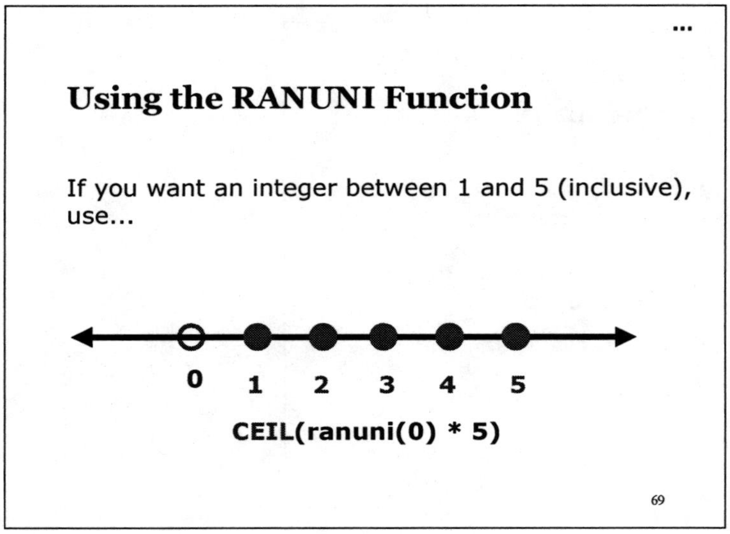


The CEIL function returns the smallest integer that is greater than or equal to the argument.

## Creating a Random Sample

c03s4d3

Example 1

Program

Create a random sample with replacement. A sample with replacement can contain duplicate observations because an observation could be selected more than one time.

```
data ia.subset (drop = i sampsize);
   sampsize = 10;
   do i = 1 to sampsize;
      pickit = ceil(ranuni(0)*totobs);
      set ia.FareCompare point = pickit nobs = totobs;
      output;
   end;
   stop;
run;

proc print data = ia.subset heading = h;
   title 'A Random Sample with Replacement';
run;
```

## Output

A Random Sample with Replacement

| Obs | diff1 | diff2 | diff3 | diff4 | Fare Firstclass | Fare Business |
|---|---|---|---|---|---|---|
| 1 | 2495 | 1882 | 1061 | 4 | 3495 | 2382 |
| 2 | -893 | -427 | -64 | -1 | 107 | 73 |
| 3 | 2328 | 1768 | 1005 | 4 | 3328 | 2268 |
| 4 | 389 | 447 | 361 | 1 | 1389 | 947 |
| 5 | -841 | -391 | -47 | -1 | 159 | 109 |
| 6 | 1159 | 970 | 616 | 2 | 2159 | 1470 |
| 7 | 480 | 508 | 391 | 1 | 1480 | 1008 |
| 8 | -905 | -435 | -68 | -1 | 95 | 65 |
| 9 | 218 | 330 | 304 | 1 | 1218 | 830 |
| 10 | -711 | -303 | -4 | -1 | 289 | 197 |

| Obs | Fare Economy | Fare Cargo | Route IDNumber | Origin | Destination |
|---|---|---|---|---|---|
| 1 | 1161 | 5 | 0000084 | JNB | LHR |
| 2 | 36 | 0 | 0000014 | IAD | RDU |
| 3 | 1105 | 5 | 0000083 | LHR | JNB |
| 4 | 461 | 2 | 0000054 | LAX | RDU |
| 5 | 53 | 0 | 0000107 | WLG | AKL |
| 6 | 716 | 3 | 0000034 | ANC | RDU |
| 7 | 491 | 2 | 0000082 | JED | LHR |
| 8 | 32 | 0 | 0000013 | RDU | IAD |
| 9 | 404 | 2 | 0000016 | SEA | RDU |
| 10 | 96 | 0 | 0000041 | RDU | PWM |

Example 2 (Self-Study)

Create a random sample without replacement. A sample without replacement cannot contain duplicate observations because after an observation is output to IA.SUBSET, programmatically it can not be selected again.

```
data ia.subset(drop = obsleft sampsize);
   sampsize = 10;
   obsleft = totobs;
   do while(sampsize > 0);
      pickit + 1;
      if ranuni(0) < sampsize/obsleft then
         do;
            set ia.FareCompare point = pickit
                               nobs = totobs;
            output;
            sampsize = sampsize - 1;
         end;
      obsleft = obsleft - 1;
   end;
   stop;
run;

proc print data = ia.subset heading = h;
   title 'A Random Sample without Replacement';
run;
```

### Output

A Random Sample without Replacement

| Obs | diff1 | diff2 | diff3 | diff4 | Fare Firstclass | Fare Business |
|---|---|---|---|---|---|---|
| 1 | 1139 | 958 | 611 | 2 | 2139 | 1458 |
| 2 | -767 | -342 | -23 | -1 | 233 | 158 |
| 3 | 799 | 725 | 496 | 2 | 1799 | 1225 |
| 4 | -431 | -112 | 89 | 0 | 569 | 388 |
| 5 | -904 | -436 | -68 | -1 | 96 | 64 |
| 6 | 1633 | 1294 | 775 | 3 | 2633 | 1794 |
| 7 | 1578 | 1257 | 756 | 3 | 2578 | 1757 |
| 8 | -620 | -241 | 25 | 0 | 380 | 259 |
| 9 | -160 | 73 | 179 | 0 | 840 | 573 |
| 10 | 473 | 504 | 389 | 1 | 1473 | 1004 |

| Obs | Fare Economy | Fare Cargo | Route IDNumber | Origin | Destination |
|---|---|---|---|---|---|
| 1 | 711 | 3 | 0000003 | RDU | FRA |
| 2 | 77 | 0 | 0000026 | IND | RDU |
| 3 | 596 | 3 | 0000033 | RDU | ANC |
| 4 | 189 | 1 | 0000079 | LHR | HEL |
| 5 | 32 | 0 | 0000050 | BRU | LHR |
| 6 | 875 | 4 | 0000083 | LHR | JNB |
| 7 | 856 | 4 | 0000111 | HND | SFO |
| 8 | 125 | 1 | 0000091 | DEL | CCU |
| 9 | 279 | 1 | 0000094 | SIN | CCU |
| 10 | 489 | 2 | 0000089 | JRS | DEL |

## Exercises

3. Generate a random sample with replacement of 50 employees from IA.EmployeeC2 to analyze their current salaries.

   If the current salary is over $50,000, then place the employee's information in the WORK.OVER50 SAS data set.

   If the current salary is $50,000 or less, then place the employee's information in the WORK.LTorEQ50 SAS data set.

## 3.5 Chapter Summary

To read multiple raw data files, you can use

- multiple INFILE statements if you want the files to remain open in order to change which file is being read.
- the FILEVAR= option to define a variable that causes the INFILE statement to close the current input file and open a new one when the variable changes values.

General form for the FILEVAR=variable option

> **INFILE** file-specification FILEVAR=*variable*;

You can use the END= option to name a variable that SAS sets to 1 when the current input data record is the last in the input file and to 0 when SAS processes the last data record.

General form for the END=*variable*

> **INFILE** file-specification END=*variable*;

Use the DATALINES statement with an INPUT statement to read data that you enter directly in the program, rather than data stored in an external file.

> **DATALINES;**

You can use an ARRAY to refer to multiple numeric or character variables with one reference. All the variables must be of the same type.

The general form of the ARRAY statement:

> **ARRAY** array-name{dimensions} $ length
> elements (initial values);

| | |
|---|---|
| *array-name* | a valid SAS name up to 32 characters in length |
| *dimensions* | specifies the number of elements in the array |
| *$* | indicates that the array references character variables |
| *length* | defines a length for new variables. The default is 8 |
| *elements* | specifies the variables to which the array refers |
| *initial values* | gives initial values for the corresponding elements |

The ARRAY statement

- must be used to define an array before the array name can be referenced
- creates variables if they do not already exist in the PDV
- is not executable.

You can use the POINT= SET statement option to create a sample.

| |
|---|
| **SET** data-set-name POINT = point-variable; |

*point-variable*

- names a temporary numeric variable that contains the observation number of the observation to read
- must be given a value before the execution of the SET statement.

To prevent the DATA step from looping continuously, use the STOP statement.

| |
|---|
| **STOP**; |

You can use the NOBS= SET statement option to determine how many observations there are in a SAS data set.

| |
|---|
| **SET** *SAS-data-set* NOBS=*variable*; |

You can use the RANUNI function to select a random sample.

General form of the RANUNI function:

| |
|---|
| RANUNI(*seed*) |

The RANUNI function returns a number between 0 and 1 generated from a uniform distribution.

Entire Program

```
/********* c03s2d1 ******************/

/***********************************/
/*    Create a SAS data set from      */
/*    multiple raw data files.        */
/***********************************/

data ia.AllFareInformation;
   length readit $200;
   input readit $;
   infile in filevar = readit end = last;
   do while(last = 0);
      input  @1 RouteIDNumber $7.
             @8 Origin $3.
            @11 Destination $3.
            @14 Distance 5.
            @19 FareFirstclass 4.
            @23 FareBusiness 4.
            @27 FareEconomy 4.
            @31 FareCargo 5.;
      output;
   end;
   datalines;
'route1.dat'
'route2.dat'
'route3.dat'
'route4.dat'
'route5.dat'
'route6.dat'
     ;
run;

proc print data = ia.AllFareInformation(obs = 10) noobs;
   title 'All Fares from Six Raw Data Files';
run;
```

```
/********* c03s3d1 ******************/

/************************************/
/*    Use an array to create new    */
/*    variables.                    */
/************************************/

data ia.FareCompare(drop = i);
   array theirs{4} _temporary_  (1000,500,100,1);
   array diff{4};
   array ours{4} FareFirstclass
                 FareBusiness
                 FareEconomy
                 FareCargo;
   set ia.AllFareInformation(drop = distance);
   do i = 1 to 4;
      diff{i} = ours{i} - theirs{i};
   end;
run;

proc print data = ia.FareCompare(obs = 10) heading = h;
   title 'Comparison of International Airlines Fares';
   title2 'With those of Super Economy You Fly Us';
run;
```

```
/********* c03s4d1 ******************/

/*************************************/
/*    Create a systematic sample     */
/*    containing 7 observations.     */
/*************************************/

data work.subset;
   do pickit = 100 to 700 by 100;
      set ia.FareCompare point = pickit;
      output;
    end;
    stop;
run;

proc print data = work.subset heading = h;
   title 'Creating a Systematic Sample of 7 Observations';
run;
```

```
/********* c03s4d2 ******************/

/*************************************/
/*    Create a systematic sample     */
/*    containing an unknown number   */
/*    of observations.               */
/*************************************/

data work.subset;
   do pickit = 100 to totobs by 100;
      set ia.FareCompare point = pickit nobs = totobs;
      output;
   end;
   stop;
run;

proc print data = work.subset heading = h;
   title 'A Systematic Sample of Fares';
run;
```

```
/********* c03s4d3 ******************/
/********* Example 1 ****************/

/*************************************/
/*    Create a random sample         */
/*    with replacement.              */
/*************************************/

data work.subset(drop = i sampsize);
   sampsize = 10;
   do i = 1 to sampsize;
      pickit = ceil(ranuni(0)*totobs);
      set ia.FareCompare point = pickit nobs = totobs;
      output;
    end;
    stop;
run;

proc print data = work.subset heading = h;
   title 'A Random Sample with Replacement';
run;
```

```
/********* c03s4d3 ******************/
/********* Example 2 ****************/
/********* Self Study ***************/

/************************************/
/*    Create a random sample        */
/*    without replacement.          */
/************************************/

data ia.subset(drop = obsleft sampsize);
   sampsize = 10;
   obsleft = totobs;
   do while(sampsize > 0);
      pickit + 1;
      if ranuni(0) < sampsize/obsleft then
         do;
            set ia.FareCompare point = pickit
                               nobs = totobs;
            output;
            sampsize = sampsize - 1;
         end;
      obsleft = obsleft - 1;
   end;
   stop;
run;

proc print data = ia.subset heading = h;
   title 'A Random Sample without Replacement';
run;
```

# 3.6 Solutions to Exercises

1. Each company division has a raw data file with an identical file structure containing employee information. In a single DATA step, create a SAS data set named IA.AllDivisions by concatenating the following raw data files.

| File Names |
|---|
| AptOp |
| CorpOp |
| CorpPlan |
| FinIT |
| FltOP |
| HRFac |
| SM |

By default, the location of these files is

| Operating System | Location |
|---|---|
| OS/390 | userid.prog3.rawdata |
| WIN | c:\workshop\winsas\prog3 |
| UNIX | /userid/prog3 |

If your external files are not in the default location, they are located in

_______________________________________________

The record layout of all the files is as follows:

| Start Column | Description | Width |
|---|---|---|
| 1 | Employee ID | 6 |
| 8 | Employee Last Name | 32 |
| 41 | Employee Phone Number | 8 |
| 50 | Employee Location | 25 |
| 76 | Employee Division | 30 |

```
data ia.AllDivisons;
   length readit $200;
   input readit $;
   infile in filevar = readit end = last;
   do while(last = 0);
      input  @1 empid $6.
           @8 LastName $32.
          @41 Phone $8.
          @50 Location $25.
          @76 Division $30.;
      output;
   end;
datalines;
'AptOP.dat'
'CorpOP.dat'
'CorpPlan.dat'
'FinIT.dat'
'FltOP.dat'
'HRFac.dat'
'SM.dat'
;
run;
```

2. Create a temporary SAS data set named ProjectedSalaries from the SAS data set named IA.EmployeeC2. Use arrays to calculate the salaries for each employee for the next 10 years based upon estimated percentage cost of living adjustment.

   The projected percentage increases for the next 10 years starting with the current year are:

   .05, .045, .055, .05, .06, .04, .05, .055, .045, .06

   Remember the salaries progressively increase. The percentages above should be calculated on the newest calculated salary, not repeatedly on this year's salary.

```
data work.ProjectedSalaries(drop = i);
   set ia.EmployeeC2;
   array increase{10} _temporary_
         (.05,.045,.055,.05,.06,.04,.05,.055,.045,.06);
   array newsals{10};
   newsals{1} = salary*(1 + increase{1});
   do i = 2 to 10;
      newsals{i}=newsals{i - 1} * (1 + increase{i});
   end;
   format newsals1 - newsals10 dollar12.2;
run;
```

**Alternate Solution:**

```
data work.rojectedSalaries(drop = i);
   set ia.EmployeeC2;
   array increase{10} _temporary_
         (.05,.045,.055,.05,.06,.04,.05,.055,.045,.06);
   array newsals{10};
   tempsal = salary;
   do i = 1 to 10;
   newsals{i} = tempsal + (tempsal * increase{i});
   tempsal = newsals{i};
   end;
   format newsals1 - newsals10 dollar12.2;
run;
```

**3.** Generate a random sample with replacement of 50 employees from IA.EmployeeC2 to analyze their current salaries.

If the current salary is over $50,000, then place the employee's information in the WORK.OVER50 SAS data set.

If the current salary is $50,000 or less, then place the employee's information in the WORK.LTorEQ50 SAS data set.

```
data work.Over50 work.LTorEQ50;
   sampsize=50;
   do i=1 to sampsize;
      pickit=ceil(ranuni(0)*totobs);
         set ia.EmployeeC2 point=pickit nobs=totobs;
         if salary > 50000 then output Over50;
         else output LTorEQ50;
   end;
   stop;
run;
```

# Chapter 4

# 4.1 Introduction

## General Business Scenario

International Airlines has two raw data files:

one contains information about revenue

```
Destination
FlightDate
FlightIDNumber
Origin
RevenueBusiness
RevenueEconomy
RevenueFirstClass
```

the second contains information about expenses.

```
FlightDate
FlightIDNumber
TotalExpenses
```

3

## General Business Scenario

They also have a SAS data set that contains names and cities for the destinations.

**ia.AirportData**

```
AirportCity
AirportCode
AirportCountry
AirportName
```

4

## General Business Scenario

The people who create reports from SAS data sets need to have all the data merged into one SAS data set.

When we look at the file layout of the raw data files, we discover that

- one file has header records and detail records (hierarchical)
- the other contains one row of raw data that needs to be several rows of SAS data.

5

## General Business Scenario

To complicate matters,

- the three files do not have a common variable, though there is a common variable in two pairs of data sets
- the data set created by the merge is not in the form that the report writers need.

6

## Organize the Tasks:

- Create a SAS data file from the hierarchical file.
- Create a SAS data file from the raw data containing multiple observations per row.
- Merge or join two of the SAS data sets.
- Merge or join the result with the third data set.
- Transpose the resulting data set.

7

# 4.2 Reading Hierarchical Files

## Objectives

- Create a SAS data set from a raw data file that has header records and detail records.

9

...

## Business Scenario

The first raw data file has data in hierarchical form.

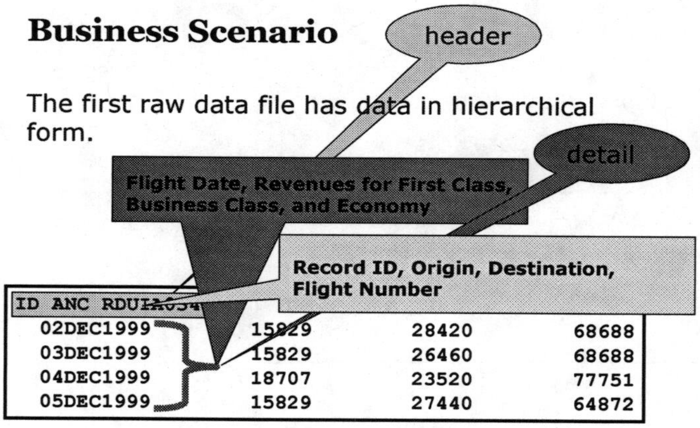


10

## Business Scenario

We need to create a SAS data set from the raw data file.

| Origin | Destination | Flight IDNumber | Flight Date | Revenue First Class | Revenue Business | Revenue Economy |
|---|---|---|---|---|---|---|
| ANC | RDU | IA03400 | 14580 | 15829 | 28420 | 68688 |
| ANC | RDU | IA03400 | 14581 | 15829 | 26460 | 68688 |
| ANC | RDU | IA03400 | 14582 | 18707 | 23520 | 77751 |
| ANC | RDU | IA03400 | 14583 | 15829 | 27440 | 64872 |
| ANC | RDU | IA03400 | 14584 | 17268 | 27440 | 67257 |

11

## Organize the Tasks

- **Create a SAS data file from the hierarchical file.**
- Create a SAS data file from the raw data containing multiple observations per row.
- Merge or join two of the SAS data sets.
- Merge or join the result with the third data set.
- Transpose the resulting data set.

12

## RETAIN Statement

The RETAIN statement causes a variable that is created by an INPUT or assignment statement to retain its value from one iteration of the DATA step to the next.

General form of the RETAIN statement:

```
RETAIN variable-1 <initial value>
       ... variable-n <initial value>;
```

13

If you do not specify an argument, the RETAIN statement causes the values of all variables that are created with INPUT or assignment statements to be retained from one iteration of the DATA step to the next.

## Reading Hierarchical Files

```
data ia.revenue(drop = type);
   retain Origin Destination FlightIDNumber;
   infile 'hiery.dat';
   input type $2. @;
   if type = 'ID' then
     input @4 Origin $3.
           @8 Destination $3.
           @11 FlightIDNumber $7.;
   else
      do;
        input @3 FlightDate date9.
              @13 RevenueFirstClass 6.
              @25 RevenueBusiness 6.
              @35 RevenueEconomy 6. ;
        output;
      end;
run;
```

14

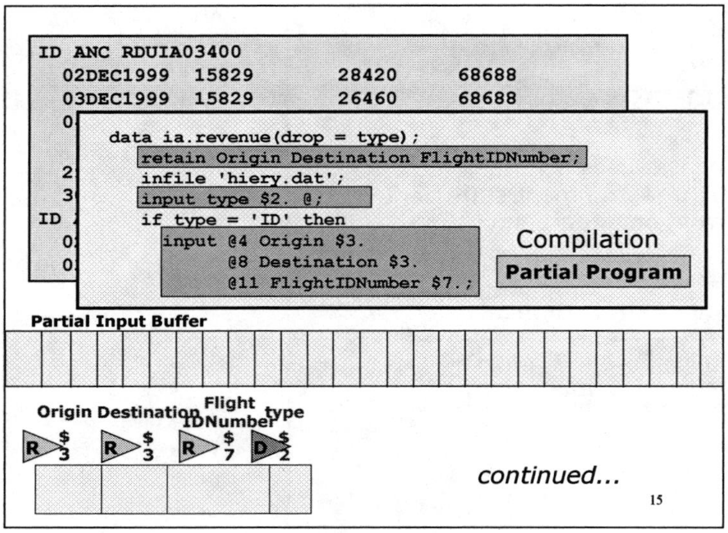
ID ANC RDUIA03400
02DEC1999 15829 28420 68688
03DEC1999 15829 26460 68688
data ia.revenue(drop = type);
retain Origin Destination FlightIDNumber;
infile 'hiery.dat';
input type $2. @;
if type = 'ID' then
input @4 Origin $3.
@8 Destination $3.
@11 FlightIDNumber $7.;
Compilation
Partial Program
Partial Input Buffer
Origin Destination Flight IDNumber type
R $ 3 R $ 3 R $ 7 D $ 2
continued...
15

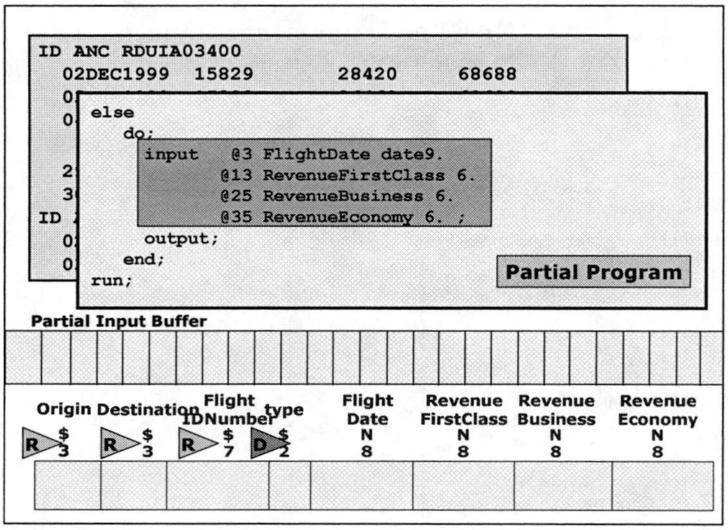
ID ANC RDUIA03400
02DEC1999 15829 28420 68688
else
do;
input @3 FlightDate date9.
@13 RevenueFirstClass 6.
@25 RevenueBusiness 6.
@35 RevenueEconomy 6. ;
output;
end;
run;
Partial Program
Partial Input Buffer
Origin Destination Flight IDNumber type Flight Date Revenue FirstClass Revenue Business Revenue Economy
R $ 3 R $ 3 R $ 7 D $ 2 N 8 N 8 N 8 N 8

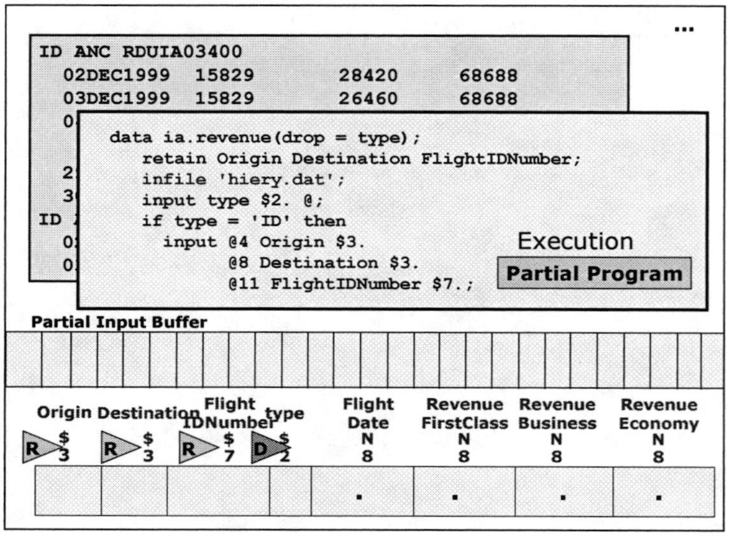
...
ID ANC RDUIA03400
02DEC1999 15829 28420 68688
03DEC1999 15829 26460 68688
data ia.revenue(drop = type);
retain Origin Destination FlightIDNumber;
infile 'hiery.dat';
input type $2. @;
if type = 'ID' then
input @4 Origin $3.
@8 Destination $3.
@11 FlightIDNumber $7.;
Execution
Partial Program
Partial Input Buffer
Origin Destination Flight IDNumber type Flight Date Revenue FirstClass Revenue Business Revenue Economy
R $ 3 R $ 3 R $ 7 D $ 2 N 8 N 8 N 8 N 8
. . . .

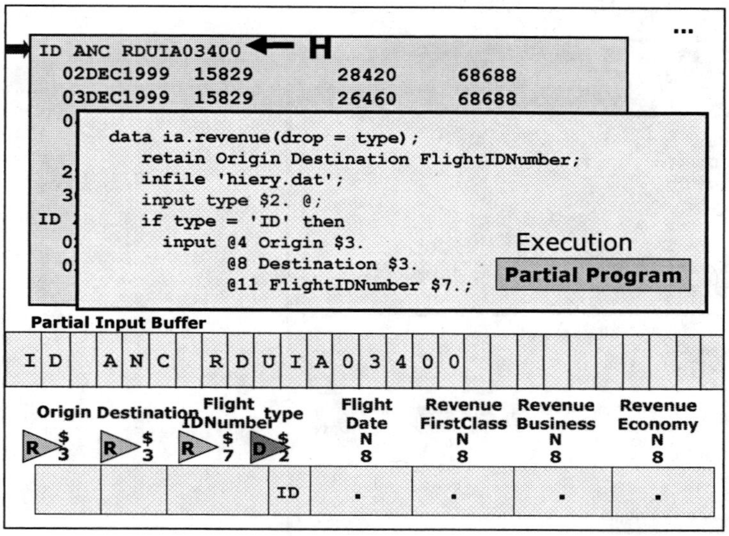
ID ANC RDUIA03400
H
02DEC1999 15829 28420 68688
03DEC1999 15829 26460 68688
data ia.revenue(drop = type);
retain Origin Destination FlightIDNumber;
infile 'hiery.dat';
input type $2. @;
if type = 'ID' then
input @4 Origin $3.
@8 Destination $3.
@11 FlightIDNumber $7.;
Execution
Partial Program
Partial Input Buffer
I D A N C R D U I A 0 3 4 0 0
Origin Destination Flight IDNumber type Flight Date Revenue FirstClass Revenue Business Revenue Economy
ID . . . .

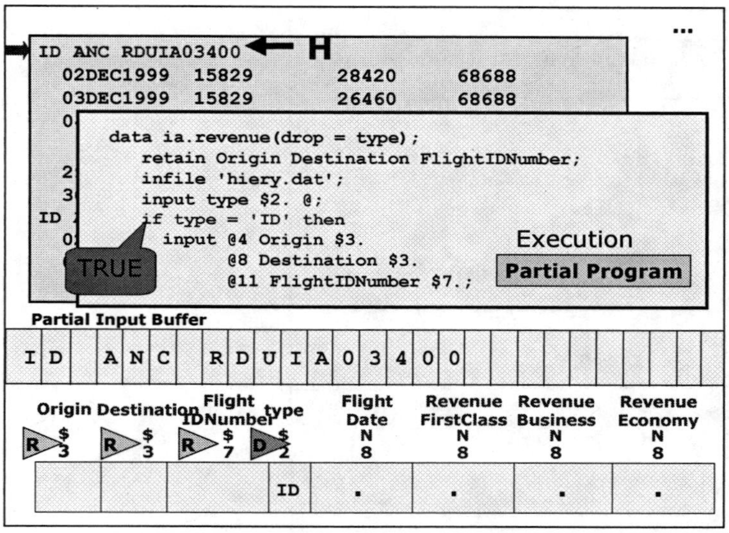
ID ANC RDUIA03400
H
02DEC1999 15829 28420 68688
03DEC1999 15829 26460 68688
data ia.revenue(drop = type);
retain Origin Destination FlightIDNumber;
infile 'hiery.dat';
input type $2. @;
if type = 'ID' then
input @4 Origin $3.
@8 Destination $3.
@11 FlightIDNumber $7.;
TRUE
Execution
Partial Program
Partial Input Buffer
I D A N C R D U I A 0 3 4 0 0
Origin Destination Flight IDNumber type Flight Date Revenue FirstClass Revenue Business Revenue Economy
ID . . . .

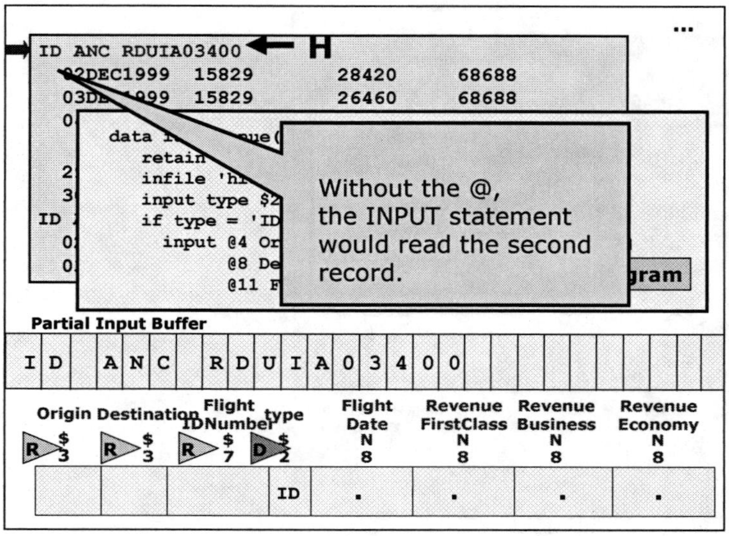
ID ANC RDUIA03400
H
Without the @,
the INPUT statement
would read the second
record.
Partial Input Buffer
I D A N C R D U I A 0 3 4 0 0
Origin Destination Flight IDNumber type Flight Date Revenue FirstClass Revenue Business Revenue Economy
ID . . . .

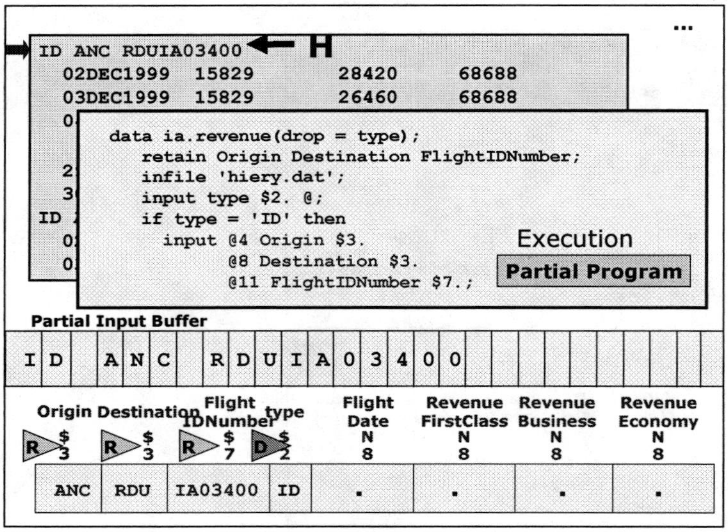
ID ANC RDUIA03400
02DEC1999 15829 28420 68688
03DEC1999 15829 26460 68688
H
data ia.revenue(drop = type);
retain Origin Destination FlightIDNumber;
infile 'hiery.dat';
input type $2. @;
if type = 'ID' then
input @4 Origin $3.
@8 Destination $3.
@11 FlightIDNumber $7.;
Execution
Partial Program
Partial Input Buffer
I D A N C R D U I A 0 3 4 0 0
Origin Destination FlightIDNumber type Flight Date Revenue FirstClass Revenue Business Revenue Economy
ANC RDU IA03400 ID . . . .

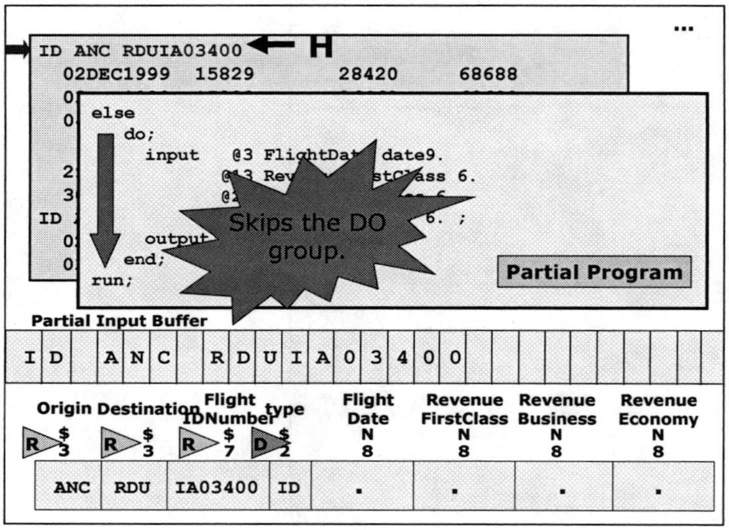
ID ANC RDUIA03400
02DEC1999 15829 28420 68688
H
else
do;
input @3 FlightDate date9.
output
end;
run;
Skips the DO group.
Partial Program
Partial Input Buffer
I D A N C R D U I A 0 3 4 0 0
Origin Destination FlightIDNumber type Flight Date Revenue FirstClass Revenue Business Revenue Economy
ANC RDU IA03400 ID . . . .

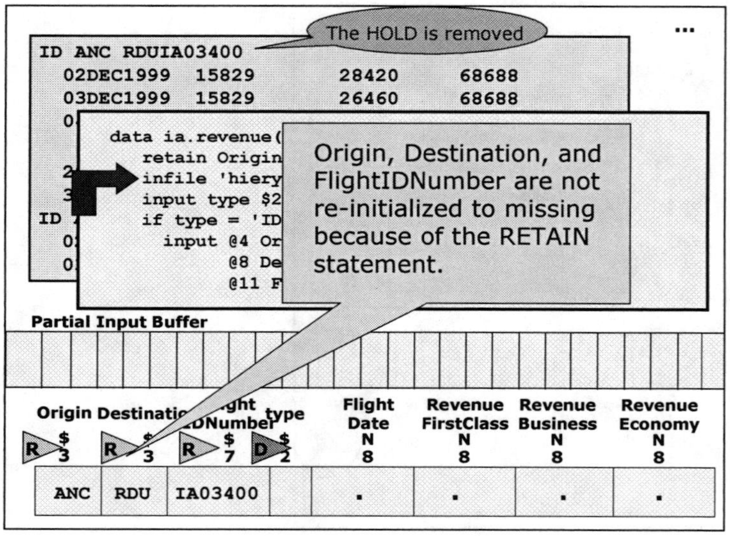
The HOLD is removed
ID ANC RDUIA03400
02DEC1999 15829 28420 68688
03DEC1999 15829 26460 68688
Origin, Destination, and FlightIDNumber are not re-initialized to missing because of the RETAIN statement.
Partial Input Buffer
Flight Date Revenue FirstClass Revenue Business Revenue Economy
ANC RDU IA03400 . . . .

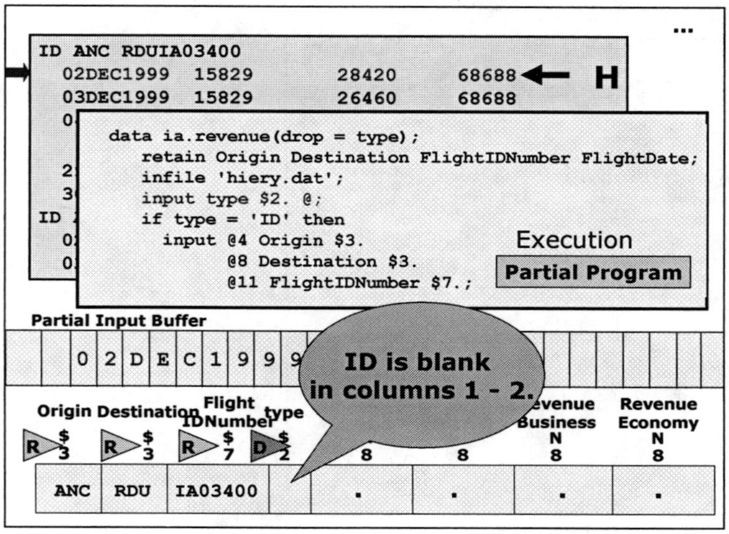

...
ID ANC RDUIA03400
02DEC1999 15829 28420 68688
03DEC1999 15829 26460 68688
H
data ia.revenue(drop = type);
retain Origin Destination FlightIDNumber FlightDate;
infile 'hiery.dat';
input type $2. @;
if type = 'ID' then
input @4 Origin $3.
@8 Destination $3.
@11 FlightIDNumber $7.;
Execution
Partial Program
Partial Input Buffer
0 2 D E C 1 9 9 9
ID is blank in columns 1 - 2.
Origin Destination FlightIDNumber type
Revenue Business
Revenue Economy
ANC RDU IA03400


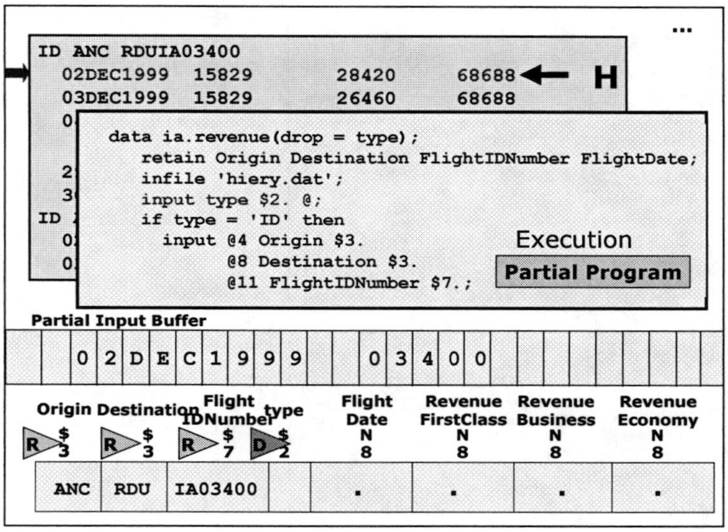

...
ID ANC RDUIA03400
02DEC1999 15829 28420 68688
03DEC1999 15829 26460 68688
H
data ia.revenue(drop = type);
retain Origin Destination FlightIDNumber FlightDate;
infile 'hiery.dat';
input type $2. @;
if type = 'ID' then
input @4 Origin $3.
@8 Destination $3.
@11 FlightIDNumber $7.;
Execution
Partial Program
Partial Input Buffer
0 2 D E C 1 9 9 9 0 3 4 0 0
Origin Destination FlightIDNumber type
Flight Date
Revenue FirstClass
Revenue Business
Revenue Economy
ANC RDU IA03400


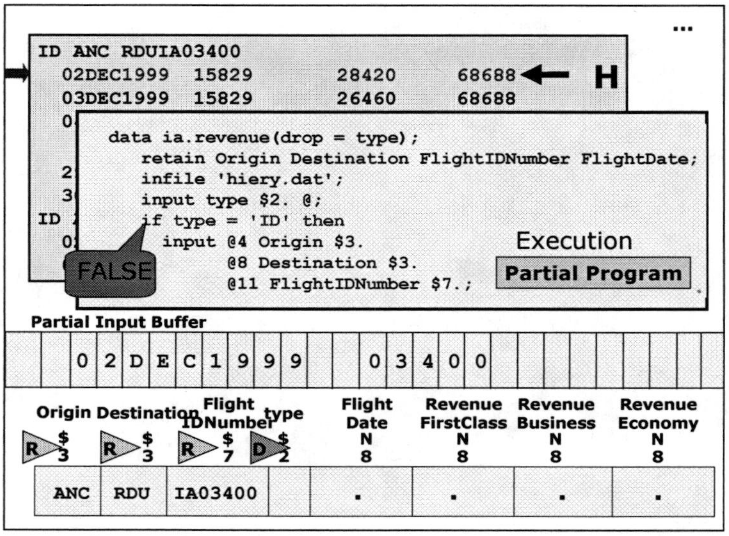

...
ID ANC RDUIA03400
02DEC1999 15829 28420 68688
03DEC1999 15829 26460 68688
H
data ia.revenue(drop = type);
retain Origin Destination FlightIDNumber FlightDate;
infile 'hiery.dat';
input type $2. @;
if type = 'ID' then
input @4 Origin $3.
@8 Destination $3.
@11 FlightIDNumber $7.;
FALSE
Execution
Partial Program
Partial Input Buffer
0 2 D E C 1 9 9 9 0 3 4 0 0
Origin Destination FlightIDNumber type
Flight Date
Revenue FirstClass
Revenue Business
Revenue Economy
ANC RDU IA03400

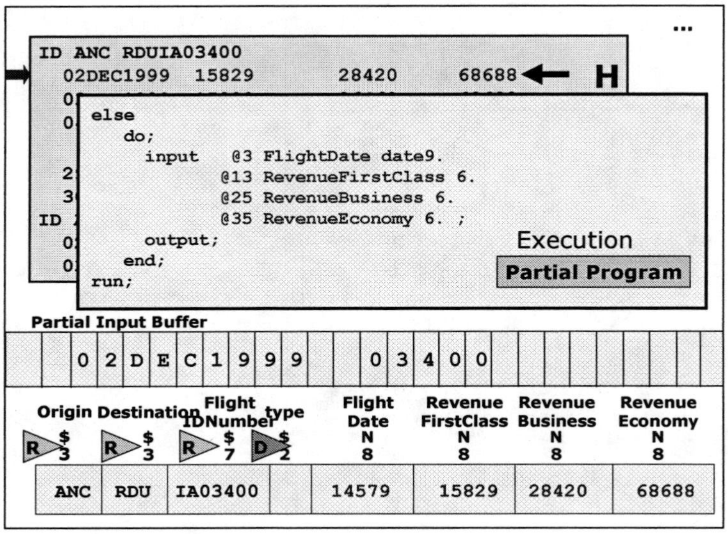
ID ANC RDUIA03400
02DEC1999 15829 28420 68688
H
else
do;
input @3 FlightDate date9.
@13 RevenueFirstClass 6.
@25 RevenueBusiness 6.
@35 RevenueEconomy 6. ;
output;
end;
run;
Execution
Partial Program
Partial Input Buffer
0 2 D E C 1 9 9 9 0 3 4 0 0
Origin Destination Flight IDNumber type Flight Date Revenue FirstClass Revenue Business Revenue Economy
ANC RDU IA03400 14579 15829 28420 68688

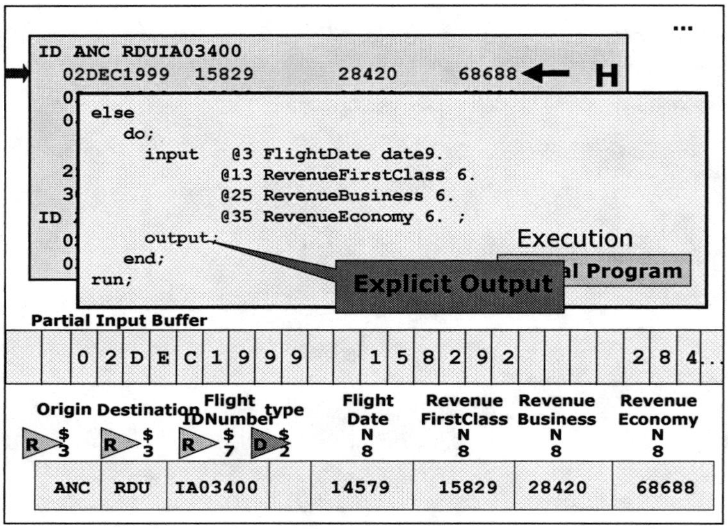
ID ANC RDUIA03400
02DEC1999 15829 28420 68688
H
else
do;
input @3 FlightDate date9.
@13 RevenueFirstClass 6.
@25 RevenueBusiness 6.
@35 RevenueEconomy 6. ;
output;
end;
run;
Execution
Explicit Output
Partial Input Buffer
0 2 D E C 1 9 9 9 1 5 8 2 9 2 2 8 4...
Origin Destination Flight IDNumber type Flight Date Revenue FirstClass Revenue Business Revenue Economy
ANC RDU IA03400 14579 15829 28420 68688

## Reading Hierarchical Files

c04s2d1

Program

```
data ia.revenue(drop = type);
   retain Origin Destination FlightIDNumber FlightDate;
   infile 'hiery.dat';
   input type $2. @;
   if type = 'ID' then
     input  @4 Origin $3.
            @8 Destination $3.
           @11 FlightIDNumber $7.;
   else
      do;
         input  @3 FlightDate date9.
               @13 RevenueFirstClass 6.
               @25 RevenueBusiness 6.
               @35 RevenueEconomy 6. ;
        output;
      end;
run;

proc print data = ia.revenue (obs = 10) noobs;
   title 'Revenue Data';
run;
```

Output

Revenue Data

| Origin | Destination | Flight IDNumber | Flight Date | First Class | Revenue Business | Revenue Economy |
|---|---|---|---|---|---|---|
| ANC | RDU | IA03400 | 14580 | 15829 | 28420 | 68688 |
| ANC | RDU | IA03400 | 14581 | 15829 | 26460 | 68688 |
| ANC | RDU | IA03400 | 14582 | 18707 | 23520 | 77751 |
| ANC | RDU | IA03400 | 14583 | 15829 | 27440 | 64872 |
| ANC | RDU | IA03400 | 14584 | 17268 | 27440 | 67257 |
| ANC | RDU | IA03400 | 14585 | 15829 | 26460 | 66303 |
| ANC | RDU | IA03400 | 14586 | 20146 | 24500 | 59148 |
| ANC | RDU | IA03400 | 14587 | 20146 | 27440 | 65826 |
| ANC | RDU | IA03400 | 14588 | 15829 | 26460 | 65826 |
| ANC | RDU | IA03400 | 14589 | 20146 | 28420 | 58671 |

## Exercises

1. Create a SAS data set named work.Dependents from the hierarchical file Dependnt. The employee's ID number serves as the header record. All employee ID numbers start with E followed by a digit.

   One too many records follow with the information about the employee's dependents. The dependent record is free-formatted with the dependent's last name, first name, and dependent type (S=spouse C=Child).

   A sample of the file is as follows:

   DEPENDNT.DAT

```
E00179
ROBERTS SANDRA S
E00356
FULKERSON DAVID C
FULKERSON MICHAEL C
FULKERSON ALICE C
FULKERSON AMY C
FULKERSON JORN C
E00533
MILLS DINA C
MILLS GREG C
```

Work.Dependents should have the following structure.

Partial Output

| Obs | EmpID | LastName | FirstName | relation |
|---|---|---|---|---|
| 1 | E00179 | ROBERTS | SANDRA | S |
| 2 | E00356 | FULKERSON | DAVID | C |
| 3 | E00356 | FULKERSON | MICHAEL | C |
| 4 | E00356 | FULKERSON | ALICE | C |
| 5 | E00356 | FULKERSON | AMY | C |
| 6 | E00356 | FULKERSON | JORN | C |
| 7 | E00533 | MILLS | DINA | C |
| 8 | E00533 | MILLS | GREG | C |

# 4.3 Reading Repeated Fields

## Objectives

- Create a SAS data set from a raw data file containing repeated fields.

33

## Business Scenario

The second raw data file has repeated fields in one row.

```
IA03400 01DEC1999 30082 IA03400 02DEC1999 89155 IA03400 03DEC1999 ...
IA03400 05DEC1999 82454 IA03400 06DEC1999 85174 IA03400 07DEC1999 ...
IA03400 09DEC1999 11765 IA03400 10DEC1999 95976 IA03400 11DEC1999 ...
IA03400 13DEC1999 113726 IA03400 14DEC1999 39599 IA03400 15DEC1999...
IA03400 17DEC1999 36100 IA03400 18DEC1999 35789 IA03400 19DEC1999 ...
IA03400 21DEC1999 18333 IA03400 22DEC1999 81326 IA03400 23DEC1999 ...
IA03400 25DEC1999 46648 IA03400 26DEC1999 66800 IA03400 27DEC1999 ...
```

34

## Business Scenario

We need to create a SAS data set from the raw data file.

| Flight IDNumber | Flight Date | Total Expenses |
|---|---|---|
| IA03400 | 14579 | 30082 |
| IA03400 | 14580 | 89155 |
| IA03400 | 14581 | 22008 |
| IA03400 | 14582 | 71609 |
| IA03400 | 14583 | 82454 |

35

## Organize the Tasks

- Create a SAS data file from the hierarchical file.
- **Create a SAS data file from the raw data containing multiple observations per row.**
- Merge or join two of the SAS data sets.
- Merge the or join result with the third data set.
- Transpose the resulting data set.

36

## Reading Repeated Fields

```
data ia.expenses;
   infile 'repeat.dat';
   input FlightIDNumber $
         FlightDate : date9.
         TotalExpenses @@;
run;
```

37

## Using @@

You can use the double trailing @ line-hold specifier to hold the

- current data line in the input buffer for another INPUT statement to process
- current data line in the input buffer across executions of the DATA step
- column pointer at its present location in that data line.

38

## Using @@

When you use the double trailing @,

- execution of a subsequent INPUT statement without @@ turns off the holding effect of @@
- a new record is loaded into the input buffer if the end-of-record is encountered on the current record.

39

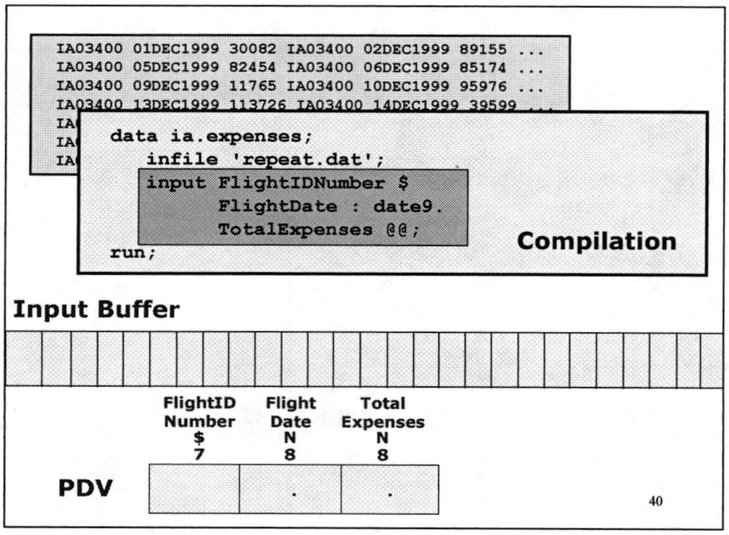

IA03400 01DEC1999 30082 IA03400 02DEC1999 89155 ...
IA03400 05DEC1999 82454 IA03400 06DEC1999 85174 ...
IA03400 09DEC1999 11765 IA03400 10DEC1999 95976 ...
IA03400 13DEC1999 113726 IA03400 14DEC1999 39599 ...
data ia.expenses;
infile 'repeat.dat';
input FlightIDNumber $
FlightDate : date9.
TotalExpenses @@;
run;
Compilation
Input Buffer
FlightID Number $ 7
Flight Date N 8
Total Expenses N 8
PDV
.
.
40


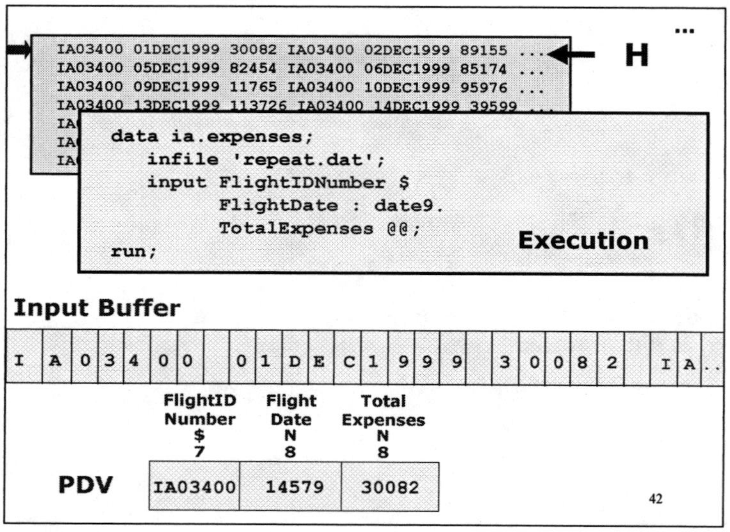

...
IA03400 01DEC1999 30082 IA03400 02DEC1999 89155 ...
H
IA03400 05DEC1999 82454 IA03400 06DEC1999 85174 ...
IA03400 09DEC1999 11765 IA03400 10DEC1999 95976 ...
IA03400 13DEC1999 113726 IA03400 14DEC1999 39599 ...
data ia.expenses;
infile 'repeat.dat';
input FlightIDNumber $
FlightDate : date9.
TotalExpenses @@;
run;
Execution
Input Buffer
I A 0 3 4 0 0 0 1 D E C 1 9 9 9 3 0 0 8 2 I A..
FlightID Number $ 7
Flight Date N 8
Total Expenses N 8
PDV
IA03400
14579
30082
42


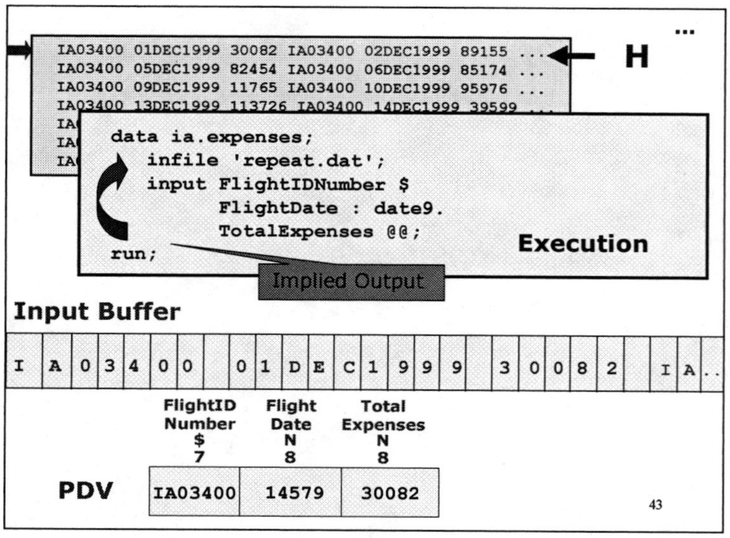

...
IA03400 01DEC1999 30082 IA03400 02DEC1999 89155 ...
H
IA03400 05DEC1999 82454 IA03400 06DEC1999 85174 ...
IA03400 09DEC1999 11765 IA03400 10DEC1999 95976 ...
IA03400 13DEC1999 113726 IA03400 14DEC1999 39599 ...
data ia.expenses;
infile 'repeat.dat';
input FlightIDNumber $
FlightDate : date9.
TotalExpenses @@;
run;
Execution
Implied Output
Input Buffer
I A 0 3 4 0 0 0 1 D E C 1 9 9 9 3 0 0 8 2 I A..
FlightID Number $ 7
Flight Date N 8
Total Expenses N 8
PDV
IA03400
14579
30082
43

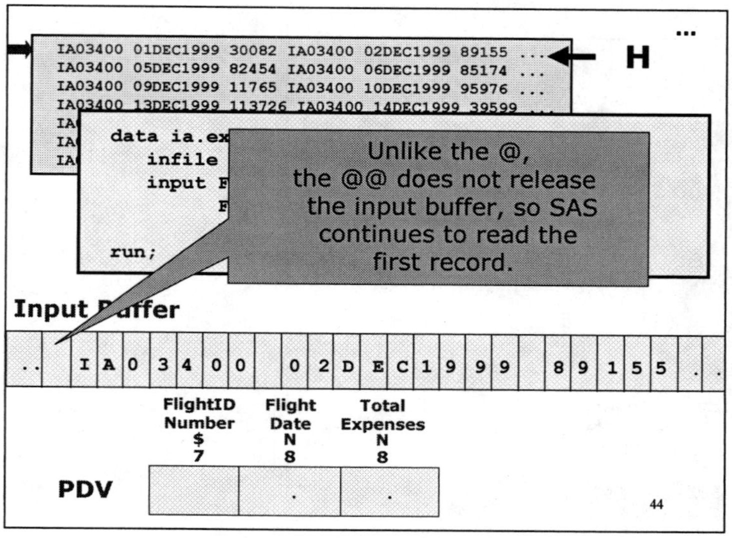
IA03400 01DEC1999 30082 IA03400 02DEC1999 89155 ...
IA03400 05DEC1999 82454 IA03400 06DEC1999 85174 ...
IA03400 09DEC1999 11765 IA03400 10DEC1999 95976 ...
H
Unlike the @, the @@ does not release the input buffer, so SAS continues to read the first record.
run;
Input Buffer
.. I A 0 3 4 0 0 0 2 D E C 1 9 9 9 8 9 1 5 5 . .
FlightID Number $ 7
Flight Date N 8
Total Expenses N 8
PDV
44

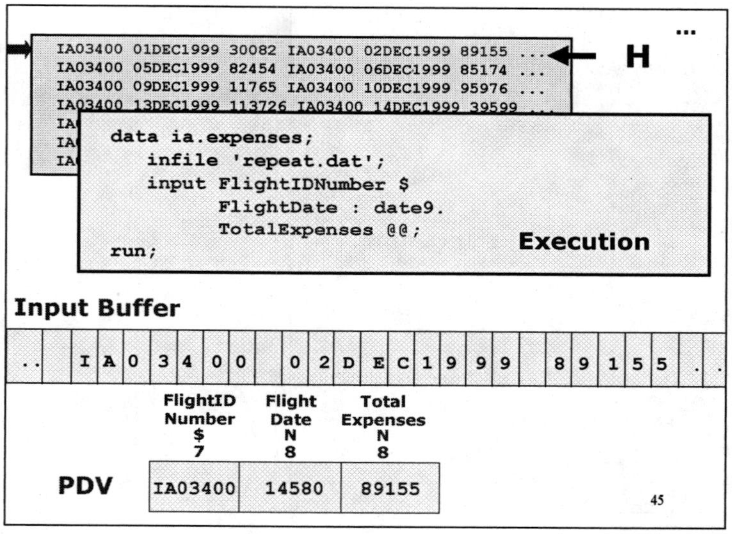
IA03400 01DEC1999 30082 IA03400 02DEC1999 89155 ...
IA03400 05DEC1999 82454 IA03400 06DEC1999 85174 ...
IA03400 09DEC1999 11765 IA03400 10DEC1999 95976 ...
H
data ia.expenses;
infile 'repeat.dat';
input FlightIDNumber $
FlightDate : date9.
TotalExpenses @@;
run;
Execution
Input Buffer
.. I A 0 3 4 0 0 0 2 D E C 1 9 9 9 8 9 1 5 5 . .
FlightID Number $ 7
Flight Date N 8
Total Expenses N 8
PDV
IA03400 14580 89155
45

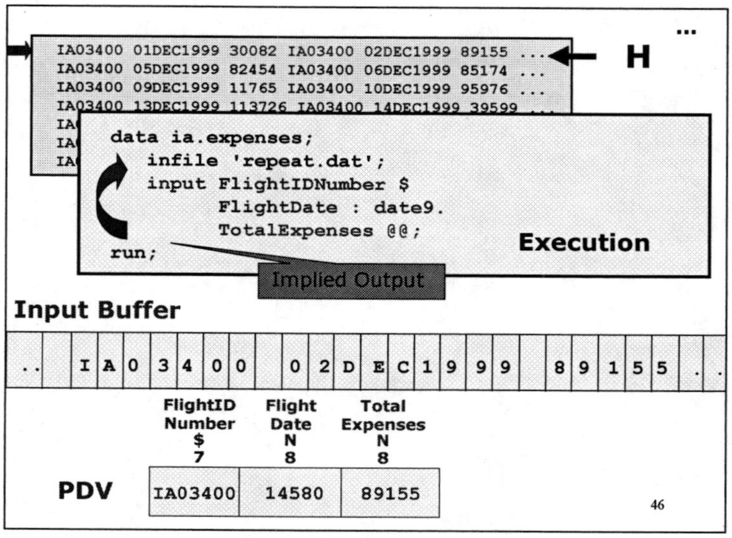
IA03400 01DEC1999 30082 IA03400 02DEC1999 89155 ...
IA03400 05DEC1999 82454 IA03400 06DEC1999 85174 ...
IA03400 09DEC1999 11765 IA03400 10DEC1999 95976 ...
H
data ia.expenses;
infile 'repeat.dat';
input FlightIDNumber $
FlightDate : date9.
TotalExpenses @@;
run;
Execution
Implied Output
Input Buffer
.. I A 0 3 4 0 0 0 2 D E C 1 9 9 9 8 9 1 5 5 . .
FlightID Number $ 7
Flight Date N 8
Total Expenses N 8
PDV
IA03400 14580 89155
46

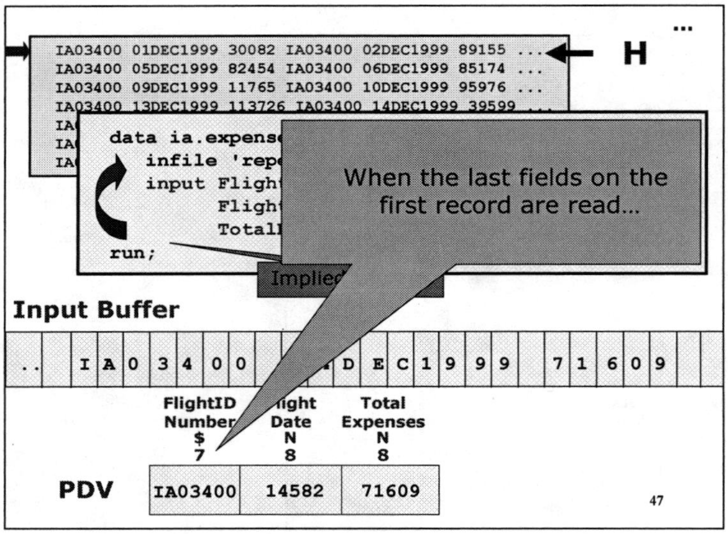
...
IA03400 01DEC1999 30082 IA03400 02DEC1999 89155 ...
IA03400 05DEC1999 82454 IA03400 06DEC1999 85174 ...
IA03400 09DEC1999 11765 IA03400 10DEC1999 95976 ...
IA03400 13DEC1999 113726 IA03400 14DEC1999 39599 ...
H
data ia.expens
infile 'rep
input Fligh
Fligh
Total
run;
When the last fields on the first record are read...
Implied
Input Buffer
FlightID Number $ 7
Date N 8
Total Expenses N 8
PDV
IA03400
14582
71609
47

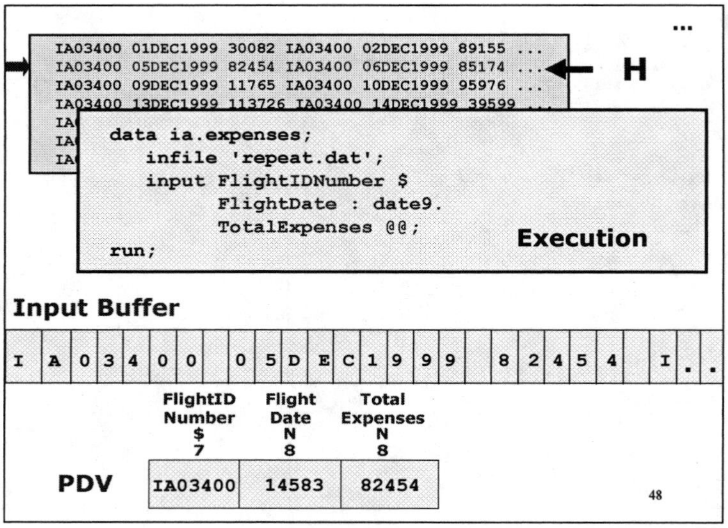
...
IA03400 01DEC1999 30082 IA03400 02DEC1999 89155 ...
IA03400 05DEC1999 82454 IA03400 06DEC1999 85174 ...
IA03400 09DEC1999 11765 IA03400 10DEC1999 95976 ...
IA03400 13DEC1999 113726 IA03400 14DEC1999 39599 ...
H
data ia.expenses;
infile 'repeat.dat';
input FlightIDNumber $
FlightDate : date9.
TotalExpenses @@;
run;
Execution
Input Buffer
I A 0 3 4 0 0 0 5 D E C 1 9 9 9 8 2 4 5 4 I . .
FlightID Number $ 7
Flight Date N 8
Total Expenses N 8
PDV
IA03400
14583
82454
48

## Double Trailing @@

The double trailing @@

- works like the trailing @ except it also holds the data line in the input buffer across executions of the DATA step
- typically is used to read multiple SAS observations from a single data line
- should not be used with the @ pointer control, column input, or the MISSOVER option.

49

## Reading Repeated Fields

c04s3d1

```
data ia.Expenses;
   infile 'repeat.dat';
   input FlightIDNumber $
         FlightDate : date9.
         TotalExpenses @@;
run;

proc print data = ia.Expenses(obs = 10);
   title 'Expenses Data';
run;
```

Expenses Data

| Obs | Flight IDNumber | Flight Date | Total Expenses |
|---|---|---|---|
| 1 | IA03400 | 14579 | 30082 |
| 2 | IA03400 | 14580 | 89155 |
| 3 | IA03400 | 14581 | 22008 |
| 4 | IA03400 | 14582 | 71609 |
| 5 | IA03400 | 14583 | 82454 |
| 6 | IA03400 | 14584 | 85174 |
| 7 | IA03400 | 14585 | 107526 |
| 8 | IA03400 | 14586 | 80020 |
| 9 | IA03400 | 14587 | 11765 |
| 10 | IA03400 | 14588 | 95976 |

## Exercises

2. Create a SAS data set named work.Commissions from the commissn raw data file. From one row of data create several SAS observations.

   Here is a sample of the raw data:

```
E00002   2704.07 E00002   2705.43 E00002   2706.78 E00002   2708.14
E00002   2709.50 E00002   2710.85 E00002   2712.21 E00003   2030.15
E00003   12036.18 E00003  12042.21 E00003  12048.24 E00003  12054.27
E00004   4218.99 E00005   1900.95 E00005   1901.91 E00005   1902.86
E00005   1903.82 E00005   1904.77 E00005   1905.73 E00005   1906.68
E00005   1907.64 E00005   1908.59 E00007   2904.37 E00007   2905.83
```

   Here is a sample of the resulting SAS data set:

| Obs | EmpID | amount1 |
|---|---|---|
| 1 | E00002 | 2704.07 |
| 2 | E00002 | 2705.43 |
| 3 | E00002 | 2706.78 |
| 4 | E00002 | 2708.14 |
| 5 | E00002 | 2709.50 |
| 6 | E00002 | 2710.85 |
| 7 | E00002 | 2712.21 |
| 8 | E00003 | 12030.15 |
| 9 | E00003 | 12036.18 |
| 10 | E00003 | 12042.21 |

# 4.4 Merging Three Data Sets

## Objectives

- Merge three SAS data sets using the DATA step with a MERGE statement.
- Join three SAS data sets using PROC SQL.
- Investigate the differences between the DATA step MERGE and PROC SQL.

53

...

## Business Scenario

We need to merge the previous two SAS data sets with a third one; however, the three SAS data sets do not have a common BY variable.

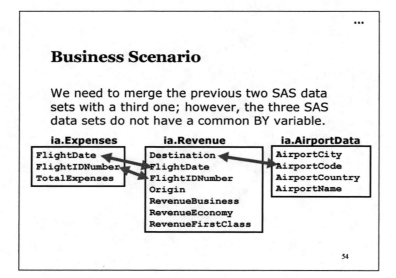

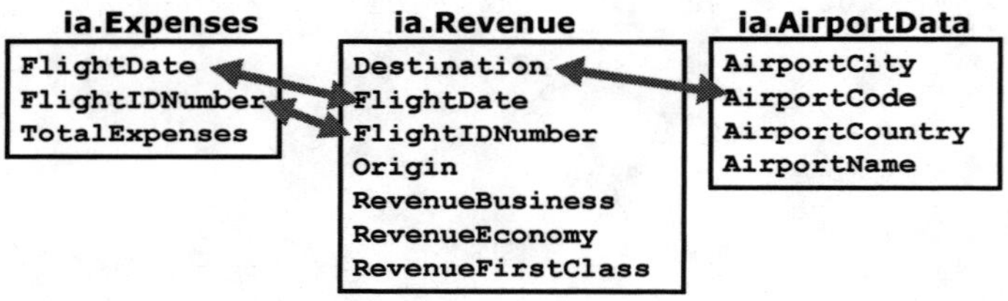


54

## Business Scenario

The result of the match merge is

| Flight IDNumber | Flight Date | Total Expenses | Origin | Destination |
|---|---|---|---|---|
| IA03300 | 14580 | 76562 | RDU | ANC |
| IA03300 | 14581 | 75105 | RDU | ANC |
| IA03300 | 14582 | 20233 | RDU | ANC |
| IA03300 | 14583 | 115370 | RDU | ANC |
| IA03300 | 14584 | 75484 | RDU | ANC |

| Revenue First Class | Revenue Business | Revenue Economy | Profit |
|---|---|---|---|
| 18707 | 22540 | 62010 | 26695 |
| 15829 | 29400 | 66303 | 36427 |
| 20146 | 29400 | 77751 | 107064 |
| 17268 | 24500 | 76797 | 3195 |
| 15829 | 24500 | 69165 | 34010 |

55

## Organize the Tasks:

- Create a SAS data file from the hierarchical file.
- Create a SAS data file from the raw data containing multiple observations per row.
- **Merge or join two of the SAS data sets.**
- **Merge or join the result with the third data set.**
- Transpose the resulting data set.

56

## Methods for the Match Merge

You can perform a match merge with

- the DATA step with the MERGE statement and a BY statement.
- the PROC SQL join.

57

## DATA Step Merge

```
DATA data-set-name;
   MERGE data-set-1 ...data-set-n;
   BY by-variable-1...by-variable-n;
RUN;
```

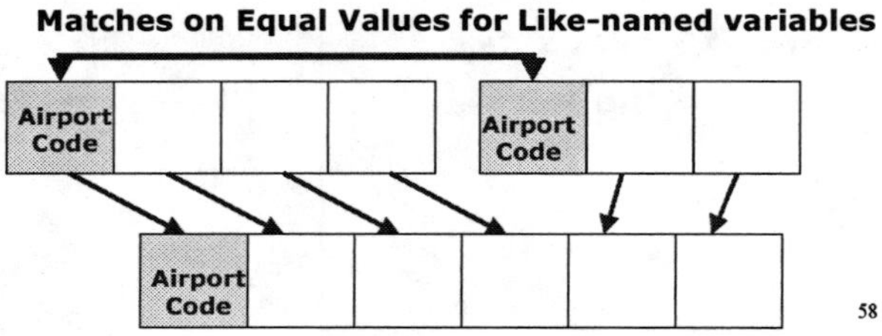


58

## Advantages of DATA Step Merges

- Multiple values can be returned.
- There is no limit to the size of the table, other than disk space.
- Multiple BY variables enable lookups that depend on more than one variable.
- Multiple data sets can be used to provide access to different tables.

59

## Disadvantages of DATA Step Merges

- Data sets must be sorted by or indexed based on the BY variable(s).
- An exact match on the key value(s) must be found.
- The BY variable(s) must be present in all data sets.

60

## Using the DATA Step to Perform a Match Merge

c04s4d1

```
proc sort data = ia.expenses out = work.expenses;
   by FlightIDNumber FlightDate;
run;

proc sort data = ia.revenue out = work.revenue;
   by FlightIDNumber FlightDate;
run;

data work.expenses_revenue;
   merge work.expenses(in = e) work.revenue(in = r);
   by FlightIDNumber FlightDate;
   if e and r;
   Profit = sum(RevenueFirstClass, RevenueBusiness,
                RevenueEconomy, - TotalExpenses);
run;

proc sort data = work.expenses_revenue;
     by Destination;
run;

data ia.AllData;
   merge work.expenses_revenue(in = exp) ia.AirportData
         (rename = (AirportCode = Destination)
          keep = AirportCity AirportName AirportCode);
   by Destination;
   if exp;
run;

proc print data = ia.AllData(obs = 10);
   title 'Result of Merging Three Data Sets';
   format FlightDate date9.;
run;
```

## Output

Result of Merging Three Data Sets

| Obs | Flight IDNumber | Flight Date | Total Expenses | Origin | Destination | Revenue First Class | Revenue Business |
|---|---|---|---|---|---|---|---|
| 1 | IA03300 | 02DEC1999 | 76562 | RDU | ANC | 18707 | 22540 |
| 2 | IA03300 | 03DEC1999 | 75105 | RDU | ANC | 15829 | 29400 |
| 3 | IA03300 | 04DEC1999 | 20233 | RDU | ANC | 20146 | 29400 |
| 4 | IA03300 | 05DEC1999 | 115370 | RDU | ANC | 17268 | 24500 |
| 5 | IA03300 | 06DEC1999 | 75484 | RDU | ANC | 15829 | 24500 |
| 6 | IA03300 | 07DEC1999 | 13531 | RDU | ANC | 18707 | 23520 |
| 7 | IA03300 | 08DEC1999 | 51365 | RDU | ANC | 20146 | 25480 |
| 8 | IA03300 | 09DEC1999 | 87475 | RDU | ANC | 15829 | 29400 |
| 9 | IA03300 | 10DEC1999 | 47752 | RDU | ANC | 17268 | 29400 |
| 10 | IA03300 | 11DEC1999 | 53091 | RDU | ANC | 17268 | 29400 |

| Obs | Revenue Economy | Profit | AirportCity | AirportName |
|---|---|---|---|---|
| 1 | 62010 | 26695 | Anchorage, AK | Anchorage International Airport |
| 2 | 66303 | 36427 | Anchorage, AK | Anchorage International Airport |
| 3 | 77751 | 107064 | Anchorage, AK | Anchorage International Airport |
| 4 | 76797 | 3195 | Anchorage, AK | Anchorage International Airport |
| 5 | 69165 | 34010 | Anchorage, AK | Anchorage International Airport |
| 6 | 74412 | 103108 | Anchorage, AK | Anchorage International Airport |
| 7 | 59148 | 53409 | Anchorage, AK | Anchorage International Airport |
| 8 | 69165 | 26919 | Anchorage, AK | Anchorage International Airport |
| 9 | 70119 | 69035 | Anchorage, AK | Anchorage International Airport |
| 10 | 64872 | 58449 | Anchorage, AK | Anchorage International Airport |

## PROC SQL

General form of the SQL procedure:

```
PROC SQL;
  CREATE TABLE SAS-data-set AS
    SELECT column-1, column-2,… ,column-n
      FROM table-1, table-2,…,table-n
      WHERE joining criteria;
```

62

CAN CREATE A VIEW W/ PROC SQL.

## Advantages of PROC SQL Joins

- Multiple data sets can be joined without having common variables in all data sets.
- Data sets do not have to be sorted or indexed.
- You can create data sets (tables), views, or query reports.
- PROC SQL follows ANSI standard language definitions, so that you can use knowledge gained from other implementations.

63

## Disadvantages of PROC SQL Joins

- The maximum number of tables that can be joined at one time is thirty-two with an inner join.
- PROC SQL requires more resources than the DATA step with the MERGE statement for simple joins.

64

## Using PROC SQL Join to Perform a Match Merge

c04s4d2

```
proc sql;
   create table ia.AllDataSQL as
      select revenue.FlightIDNumber,
             revenue.FlightDate,
             expenses.TotalExpenses, revenue.Origin,
             revenue.Destination,
             revenue.revenueFirstClass,
             revenue.revenueBusiness,
             revenue.revenueEconomy,
             sum(revenue.RevenueFirstClass,
                 revenue.RevenueBusiness,
                 revenue.RevenueEconomy,
                 - TotalExpenses) as profit,
             AirportData.AirportCity,
             AirportData.AirportName
          from work.expenses, work.revenue, ia.AirportData
          where
                expenses.FlightIDNumber =
                revenue.FlightIDNumber
          and expenses.FlightDate = revenue.FlightDate
          and AirportData.AirportCode = revenue.Destination
          order by revenue.Destination,
                   revenue.FlightIDNumber,
                   revenue.FlightDate;


proc print data = ia.AllData(obs = 10);
   title 'Result of Joining Three Data Sets';
   format FlightDate date9.;
run;
```

Output

Result of Joining Three Data Sets

| Obs | Flight IDNumber | Flight Date | Total Expenses | Origin | Destination | Revenue First Class | Revenue Business |
|---|---|---|---|---|---|---|---|
| 1 | IA00100 | 02DEC1999 | 58907 | RDU | LHR | 19200 | 31610 |
| 2 | IA00100 | 03DEC1999 | 108543 | RDU | LHR | 17600 | 25070 |
| 3 | IA00100 | 04DEC1999 | 21963 | RDU | LHR | 17600 | 28340 |
| 4 | IA00100 | 05DEC1999 | 31517 | RDU | LHR | 17600 | 32700 |
| 5 | IA00100 | 06DEC1999 | 105682 | RDU | LHR | 22400 | 29430 |
| 6 | IA00100 | 07DEC1999 | 66992 | RDU | LHR | 22400 | 29430 |
| 7 | IA00100 | 08DEC1999 | 92873 | RDU | LHR | 20800 | 27250 |
| 8 | IA00100 | 09DEC1999 | 59560 | RDU | LHR | 22400 | 32700 |
| 9 | IA00100 | 10DEC1999 | 41096 | RDU | LHR | 20800 | 32700 |
| 10 | IA00100 | 11DEC1999 | 10272 | RDU | LHR | 22400 | 29430 |

| Obs | Revenue Economy | profit | AirportCity | AirportName |
|---|---|---|---|---|
| 1 | 79650 | 71553 | London, England | Heathrow Airport |
| 2 | 80181 | 14308 | London, England | Heathrow Airport |
| 3 | 84960 | 108937 | London, England | Heathrow Airport |
| 4 | 72216 | 90999 | London, England | Heathrow Airport |
| 5 | 74871 | 21019 | London, England | Heathrow Airport |
| 6 | 84960 | 69798 | London, England | Heathrow Airport |
| 7 | 82305 | 37482 | London, England | Heathrow Airport |
| 8 | 84429 | 79969 | London, England | Heathrow Airport |
| 9 | 67968 | 80372 | London, England | Heathrow Airport |
| 10 | 78588 | 120146 | London, England | Heathrow Airport |

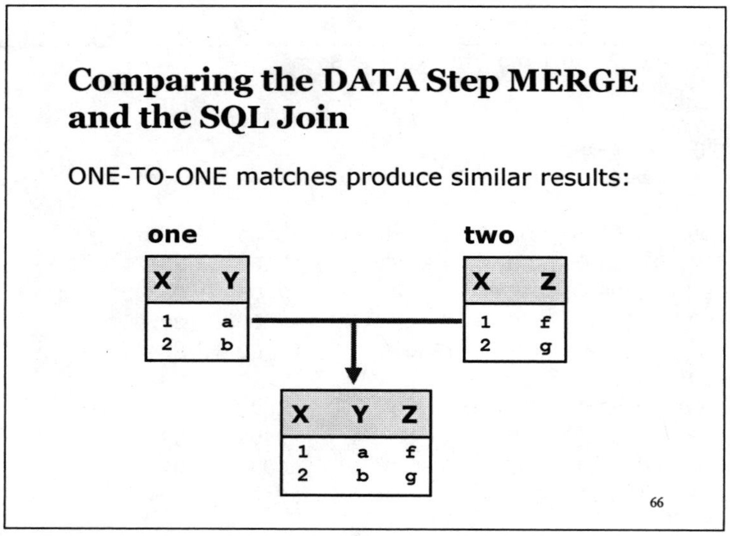


The DATA step syntax:

```
data three;
   merge one two;
   by x;
run;
```

The PROC SQL syntax:

```
proc sql;
   select one.x, one.y, two.z
      from one,two
      where one.x = two.x;
quit;
```

## Comparing the DATA Step MERGE and the SQL Join

ONE-TO-MANY matches produce similar results:

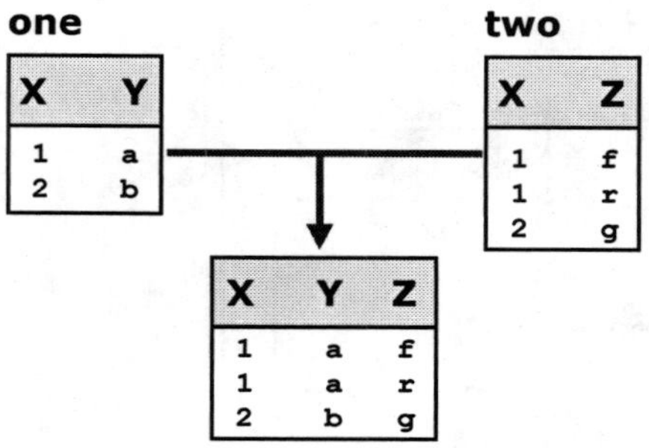


67

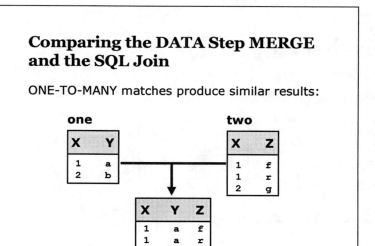

The DATA step syntax:

```
data three;
   merge one two;
   by x;
run;
```

The PROC SQL syntax:

```
proc sql;
   select one.x, one.y, two.z
      from one,two
      where one.x = two.x;
quit;
```

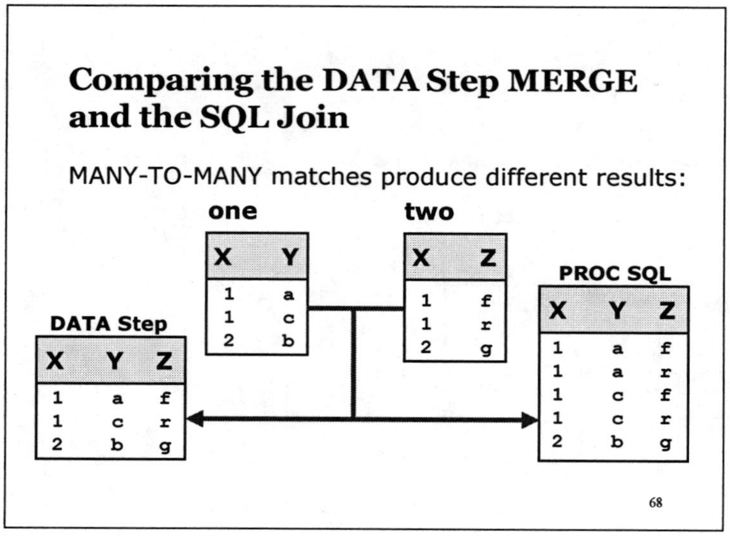


The DATA step syntax:

```
data three;
   merge one two;
   by x;
run;
```

The PROC SQL syntax:

```
proc sql;
   select one.x, one.y, two.z
      from one,two
      where one.x = two.x;
quit;
```

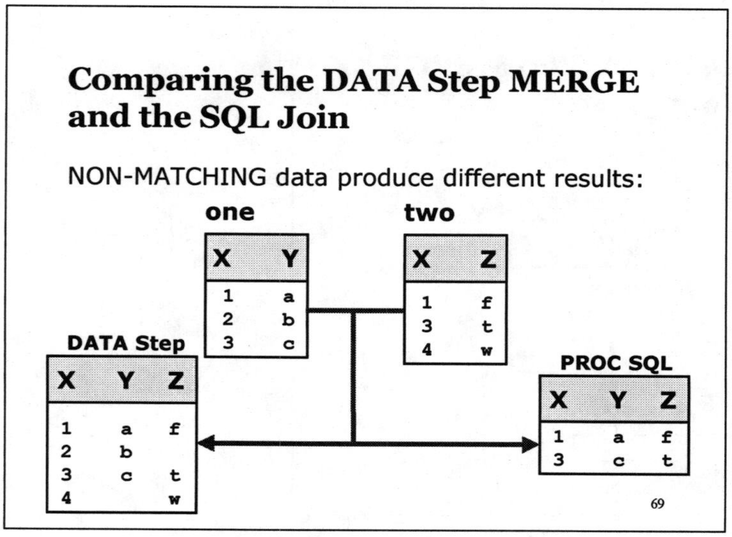


The DATA step syntax:

```
data three;
   merge one two;
   by x;
run;
```

The PROC SQL syntax:

```
proc sql;
   select one.x, one.y, two.z
      from one,two
      where one.x = two.x;
quit;
```

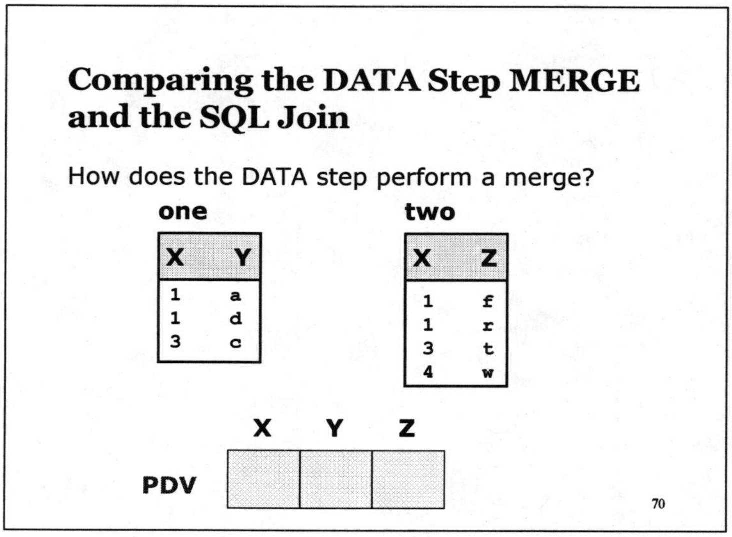


The DATA step MERGE processes sequentially.

## Comparing the DATA Step MERGE and the SQL Join

How does the DATA step perform a merge?

**one**

| X | Y |
|---|---|
| 1 | a |
| 1 | d |
| 3 | c |

**two**

| X | Z |
|---|---|
| 1 | f |
| 1 | r |
| 3 | t |
| 4 | w |

**PDV**

| X | Y | Z |
|---|---|---|
| 1 | a | f |

71

## Comparing the DATA Step MERGE and the SQL Join

How does the DATA step perform a merge?

**one**

| X | Y |
|---|---|
| 1 | a |
| 1 | d |
| 3 | c |

**two**

| X | Z |
|---|---|
| 1 | f |
| 1 | r |
| 3 | t |
| 4 | w |

**PDV**

| X | Y | Z |
|---|---|---|
| 1 | d | r |

72

## Comparing the DATA Step MERGE and the SQL Join

How does the DATA step perform a merge?

**one**

| X | Y |
|---|---|
| 1 | a |
| 1 | d |
| 3 | c |

**two**

| X | Z |
|---|---|
| 1 | f |
| 1 | r |
| 3 | t |
| 4 | w |

**PDV**

| X | Y | Z |
|---|---|---|
| 3 | c | t |

73

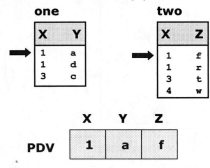

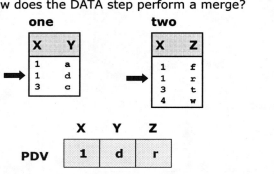

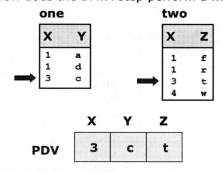

## Comparing the DATA Step MERGE and the SQL Join

How does the DATA step perform a merge?

**one**

| X | Y |
|---|---|
| 1 | a |
| 1 | d |
| 3 | c |

EOF

**two**

| X | Z |
|---|---|
| 1 | f |
| 1 | r |
| 3 | t |
| 4 | w |

**PDV**

| X | Y | Z |
|---|---|---|
| 4 | | w |

74

## Comparing the DATA Step MERGE and the SQL Join

How does the DATA step perform a merge?

**one**

| X | Y |
|---|---|
| 1 | a |
| 1 | d |
| 3 | c |

**three**

| X | Y | Z |
|---|---|---|
| 1 | a | f |
| 1 | d | r |
| 3 | c | t |
| 4 | | w |

**two**

| X | Z |
|---|---|
| 1 | f |
| 1 | r |
| 3 | t |
| 4 | w |

**Both the matches and the non-matches on X remain.**

75

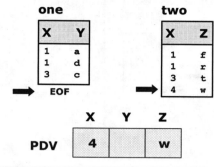

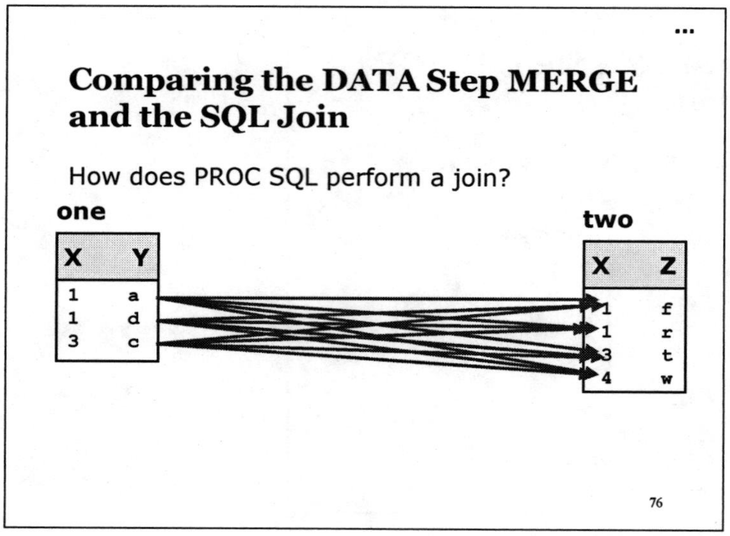


PROC SQL processes by creating a Cartesian Product.

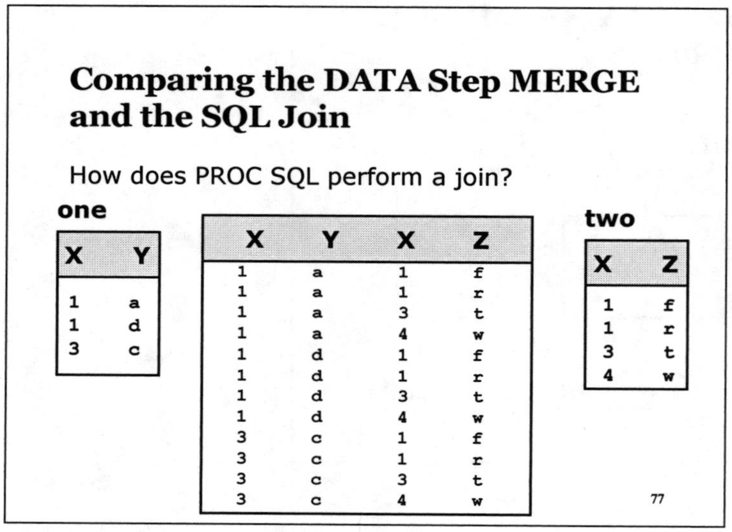


Conceptually, PROC SQL creates the result set pictured here. There are optimization routines that make the process efficient.

## Comparing the DATA Step MERGE and the SQL Join

How does PROC SQL perform a join?

**one**

| X | Y |
|---|---|
| 1 | a |
| 1 | d |
| 3 | c |

| X | Y | X | Z |
|---|---|---|---|
| 1 | a | 1 | f |
| 1 | a | 1 | r |
| ~~1~~ | ~~a~~ | ~~3~~ | ~~t~~ |
| ~~1~~ | ~~a~~ | ~~4~~ | ~~w~~ |
| 1 | d | 1 | f |
| 1 | d | 1 | r |
| ~~1~~ | ~~d~~ | ~~3~~ | ~~t~~ |
| ~~1~~ | ~~d~~ | ~~4~~ | ~~w~~ |
| ~~3~~ | ~~c~~ | ~~1~~ | ~~f~~ |
| ~~3~~ | ~~c~~ | ~~1~~ | ~~r~~ |
| 3 | c | 3 | t |
| ~~3~~ | ~~c~~ | ~~4~~ | ~~w~~ |

**two**

| X | Z |
|---|---|
| 1 | f |
| 1 | r |
| 3 | t |
| 4 | w |

78

The non-matches on X are eliminated.

## Comparing the DATA Step MERGE and the SQL Join

How does PROC SQL perform a join?

**one**

| X | Y |
|---|---|
| 1 | a |
| 1 | d |
| 3 | c |

**three**

| X | Y | Z |
|---|---|---|
| 1 | a | f |
| 1 | a | r |
| 1 | d | f |
| 1 | d | r |
| 3 | c | t |

**two**

| X | Z |
|---|---|
| 1 | f |
| 1 | r |
| 3 | t |
| 4 | w |

**Only the matches on X remain.**

79

## Exercises

**3.** Using PROC SQL, join IA.Employee_Data, IA.Job_Code_Data, and IA.NewSals to create a report that displays:

```
Employee ID
Employee Job Code
Job Code Description
Current Salary
New Salary
```

There is not a common variable to all 3 SAS data sets. Use PROC CONTENTS or PROC DATASETS to determine the columns on which to join the rows.

**4.** Repeat the same task using the DATA step MERGE statement to merge all three data sets.

# 4.5 Transposing Data

## Objectives

- Use PROC TRANSPOSE to transpose a SAS data set.
- Use the DATA step with an array to rotate a SAS data set.

82

## Business Scenario

This is the report we need to create.

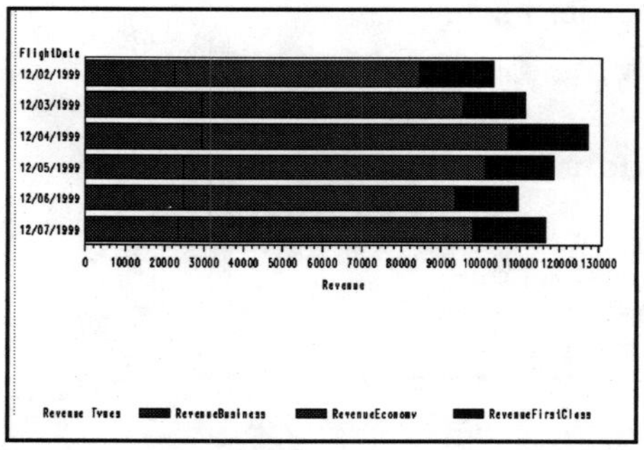


83

## Business Scenario

Variables in the data set IA.AllData

```
FlightIDNumber
FlightDate
TotalExpenses
Origin
Destination
RevenueFirstClass
RevenueBusiness
RevenueEconomy
Profit
AirportCity
AirportRevenueType
```

There is no
variable
REVENUE

85

## Organize the Tasks:

- Create a SAS data file from the hierarchical file.
- Create a SAS data file from the raw data containing multiple observations per row.
- Merge or join two of the SAS data sets.
- Merge or join the result with the third data set.
- **Transpose the resulting data set.**

86

## Methods for Transposing

To transpose data use

- the TRANSPOSE procedure
- an ARRAY in a DATA step.

87

## Using PROC TRANSPOSE

General form of the TRANSPOSE procedure:

```
PROC TRANSPOSE <DATA=input-data-set>
               <OUT=output-data-set>
               <NAME = variable-name>;
   BY <DESCENDING> variable-1
      <...<DESCENDING> variable-n>;
   ID variable;
   IDLABEL variable;
   VAR variable(s);
RUN;
```

88

NAME = *variable name*

specifies the name for the new variable in the output data set that contains the name of the existing variable being transposed to create the current observation.

## PROC TRANSPOSE

| To | Use |
|---|---|
| transpose each BY group | **BY** Statement |
| specify a variable whose values name the transposed variables | **ID** Statement |
| create labels for the transposed variables | **IDLABEL** Statement |
| list the variables to transpose | **VAR** Statement |

89

## Transposing Data with PROC TRANSPOSE

c04s5d1

```
proc sort data = ia.AllData;
   by FlightIDNumber FlightDate;
run;

proc transpose data = work.AllData
                           (keep = FlightDate
                                   FlightIDNumber
                                   RevenueFirstClass
                                   RevenueEconomy
                                   RevenueBusiness)
               out = ia.AllDataTrans
                     (rename = (col1 = Revenue))
               name = RevenueType;
   by FlightIDNumber FlightDate;
   var RevenueFirstClass RevenueEconomy RevenueBusiness;
run;

proc print data = ia.AllDataTrans(obs = 10);
   title 'Data Transposed';
   format FlightDate mmddyy10.;
run;
```

Data Transposed

| Obs | Flight IDNumber | FlightDate | RevenueType | Revenue |
|---|---|---|---|---|
| 1 | IA00100 | 12/02/1999 | RevenueFirstClass | 19200 |
| 2 | IA00100 | 12/02/1999 | RevenueEconomy | 79650 |
| 3 | IA00100 | 12/02/1999 | RevenueBusiness | 31610 |
| 4 | IA00100 | 12/03/1999 | RevenueFirstClass | 17600 |
| 5 | IA00100 | 12/03/1999 | RevenueEconomy | 80181 |
| 6 | IA00100 | 12/03/1999 | RevenueBusiness | 25070 |
| 7 | IA00100 | 12/04/1999 | RevenueFirstClass | 17600 |
| 8 | IA00100 | 12/04/1999 | RevenueEconomy | 84960 |
| 9 | IA00100 | 12/04/1999 | RevenueBusiness | 28340 |
| 10 | IA00100 | 12/05/1999 | RevenueFirstClass | 17600 |

## Using an Array to Rotate Data

You can use an array in a DATA step to rotate the data.

```
data ia.AllDataTrans(keep = FlightDate Revenue RevenueType);
   array Rev{3} RevenueFirstClass
                RevenueBusiness
                RevenueEconomy;
   set ia.alldata(keep = FlightDate RevenueFirstClass
                         RevenueEconomy RevenueBusiness);
   do i = 1 to 3;
      revenue = Rev{i};
      if i = 1 then RevenueType = 'RevenueFirstClass';
      else if i = 2 then RevenueType = 'RevenueBusiness';
      else RevenueType = 'RevenueEconomy';
      output;
   end;
run;
```

## Reference Information

In the DO loop, you can use the DIM function to return the number of array elements.

For example,

```
do i = 1 to dim(Rev);
   statements;
end;
```

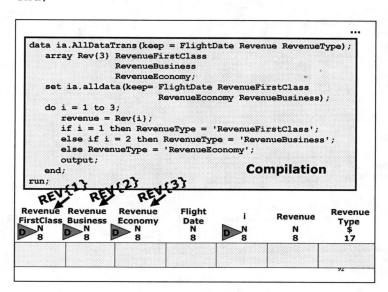

...

```
data ia.AllDataTrans(keep = FlightDate Revenue RevenueType);
   array Rev{3} RevenueFirstClass
                RevenueBusiness
                RevenueEconomy;
   set ia.alldata(keep= FlightDate RevenueFirstClass
                        RevenueEconomy RevenueBusiness);
   do i = 1 to 3;
      revenue = Rev{i};
      if i = 1 then RevenueType = 'RevenueFirstClass';
      else if i = 2 then RevenueType = 'RevenueBusiness';
      else RevenueType = 'RevenueEconomy';
      output;
   end;
run;
```

**Compilation**

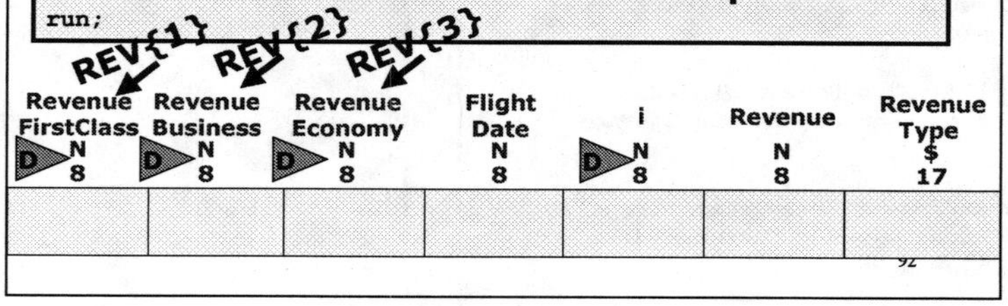

```
data ia.AllDataTrans(keep = FlightDate Revenue RevenueType);
   array Rev{3} RevenueFirstClass
                RevenueBusiness
                RevenueEconomy;
   set ia.alldata(keep= FlightDate RevenueFirstClass
                        RevenueEconomy RevenueBusiness);
   do i = 1 to 3;
      revenue = Rev{i};
      if i = 1 then RevenueType = 'RevenueFirstClass';
      else if i = 2 then RevenueType = 'RevenueBusiness';
      else RevenueType = 'RevenueEconomy';
      output;
   end;
run;
```

**Execution**

| REV{1} | REV{2} | REV{3} | | | | |
|---|---|---|---|---|---|---|
| Revenue FirstClass D N 8 | Revenue Business D N 8 | Revenue Economy D N 8 | Flight Date N 8 | i D N 8 | Revenue N 8 | Revenue Type $ 17 |
| 18707 | 22540 | 62010 | 14580 | | | |

```
data ia.AllDataTrans(keep = FlightDate Revenue RevenueType);
   array Rev{3} RevenueFirstClass
                RevenueBusiness
                RevenueEconomy;
   set ia.alldata(keep= FlightDate RevenueFirstClass
                        RevenueEconomy RevenueBusiness);
   do i = 1 to 3;
      revenue = Rev{i};
      if i = 1 then RevenueType = 'RevenueFirstClass';
      else if i = 2 then RevenueType = 'RevenueBusiness';
      else RevenueType = 'RevenueEconomy';
      output;
   end;
run;
```

**Execution**

| REV{1} | REV{2} | REV{3} | | | | |
|---|---|---|---|---|---|---|
| Revenue FirstClass D N 8 | Revenue Business D N 8 | Revenue Economy D N 8 | Flight Date N 8 | i D N 8 | Revenue N 8 | Revenue Type $ 17 |
| 18707 | 22540 | 62010 | 14580 | 1 | | |

```
data ia.AllDataTrans(keep = FlightDate Revenue RevenueType);
   array Rev{3} RevenueFirstClass
                RevenueBusiness
                RevenueEconomy;
   set ia.alldata(keep= FlightDate RevenueFirstClass
                        RevenueEconomy RevenueBusiness);
   do i = 1 to 3;
      revenue = Rev{i};
      if i = 1 then RevenueType = 'RevenueFirstClass';
      else if i = 2 then RevenueType = 'RevenueBusiness';
      else RevenueType = 'RevenueEconomy';
      output;
   end;
run;
```

**Execution**

| REV{1} | REV{2} | REV{3} | | | | |
|---|---|---|---|---|---|---|
| Revenue FirstClass D N 8 | Revenue Business D N 8 | Revenue Economy D N 8 | Flight Date N 8 | i D N 8 | Revenue N 8 | Revenue Type $ 17 |
| 18707 | 22540 | 62010 | 14580 | 1 | 18707 | |

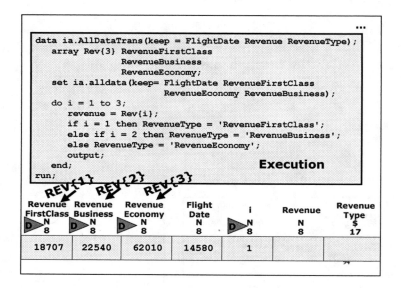

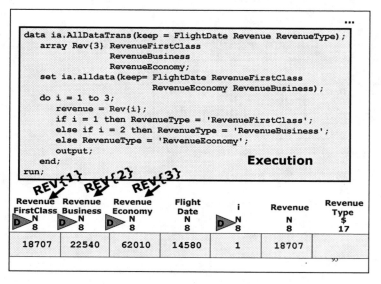

...

```
data ia.AllDataTrans(keep = FlightDate Revenue RevenueType);
   array Rev{3} RevenueFirstClass
                RevenueBusiness
                RevenueEconomy;
   set ia.alldata(keep= FlightDate RevenueFirstClass
                        RevenueEconomy RevenueBusiness);
   do i = 1 to 3;
      revenue = Rev{i};
      if i = 1 then RevenueType = 'RevenueFirstClass';
      else if i = 2 then RevenueType = 'RevenueBusiness';
      else RevenueType = 'RevenueEconomy';
      output;
   end;
run;
```

**Execution**

REV{1} REV{2} REV{3}

| Revenue FirstClass D N 8 | Revenue Business D N 8 | Revenue Economy D N 8 | Flight Date N 8 | i D N 8 | Revenue N 8 | Revenue Type $ 17 |
|---|---|---|---|---|---|---|
| 18707 | 22540 | 62010 | 14580 | 1 | 18707 | RevenueFirstClass |

...

```
data ia.AllDataTrans(keep = FlightDate Revenue RevenueType);
   array Rev{3} RevenueFirstClass
                RevenueBusiness
                RevenueEconomy;
   set ia.alldata(keep= FlightDate RevenueFirstClass
                        RevenueEconomy RevenueBusiness);
   do i = 1 to 3;
      revenue = Rev{i};
      if i = 1 then RevenueType = 'RevenueFirstClass';
      else if i = 2 then RevenueType = 'RevenueBusiness';
      else RevenueType = 'RevenueEconomy';
      output;
   end;
run;
```

**Execution**

REV{1} REV{2} REV{3}

| Revenue FirstClass D N 8 | Revenue Business D N 8 | Revenue Economy D N 8 | Flight Date N 8 | i D N 8 | Revenue N 8 | Revenue Type $ 17 |
|---|---|---|---|---|---|---|
| 18707 | 22540 | 62010 | 14580 | 1 | 18707 | RevenueFirstClass |

...

```
data ia.AllDataTrans(keep = FlightDate Revenue RevenueType);
   array Rev{3} RevenueFirstClass
                RevenueBusiness
                RevenueEconomy;
   set ia.alldata(keep= FlightDate RevenueFirstClass
                        RevenueEconomy RevenueBusiness);
   do i = 1 to 3;
      revenue = Rev{i};
      if i = 1 then RevenueType = 'RevenueFirstClass';
      else if i = 2 then RevenueType = 'RevenueBusiness';
      else RevenueType = 'RevenueEconomy';
      output;
   end;
run;
```

**Execution**

REV{1} REV{2} REV{3}

| Revenue FirstClass D N 8 | Revenue Business D N 8 | Revenue Economy D N 8 | Flight Date N 8 | i D N 8 | Revenue N 8 | Revenue Type $ 17 |
|---|---|---|---|---|---|---|
| 18707 | 22540 | 62010 | 14580 | 2 | 18707 | RevenueFirstClass |

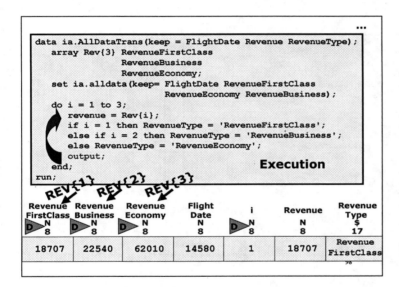

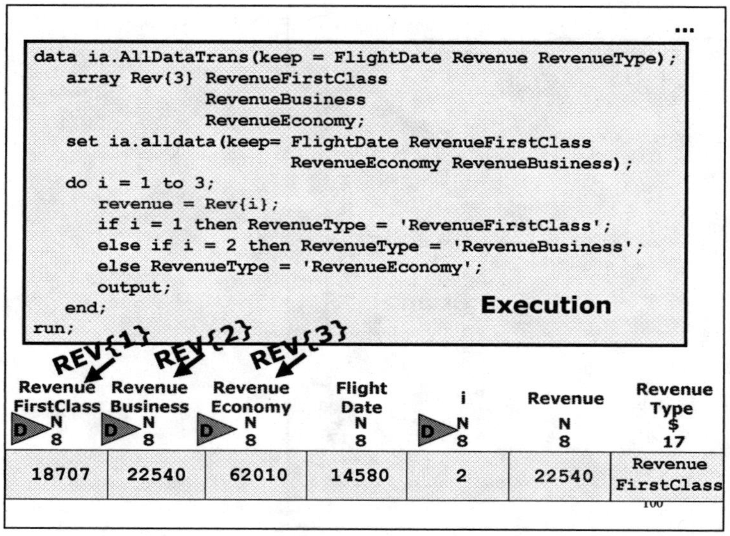
data ia.AllDataTrans(keep = FlightDate Revenue RevenueType);
array Rev{3} RevenueFirstClass
RevenueBusiness
RevenueEconomy;
set ia.alldata(keep= FlightDate RevenueFirstClass
RevenueEconomy RevenueBusiness);
do i = 1 to 3;
revenue = Rev{i};
if i = 1 then RevenueType = 'RevenueFirstClass';
else if i = 2 then RevenueType = 'RevenueBusiness';
else RevenueType = 'RevenueEconomy';
output;
end;
run;
Execution
REV{1}
REV{2}
REV{3}
Revenue FirstClass N 8
Revenue Business N 8
Revenue Economy N 8
Flight Date N 8
i N 8
Revenue N 8
Revenue Type $ 17
18707
22540
62010
14580
2
22540
Revenue FirstClass

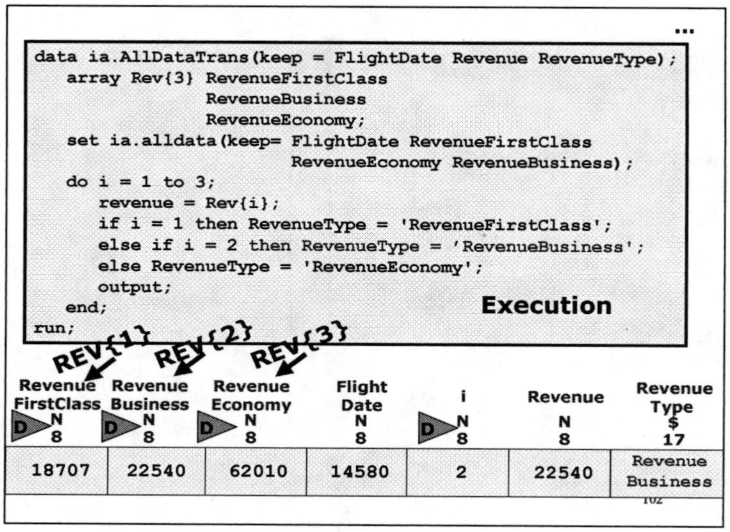
data ia.AllDataTrans(keep = FlightDate Revenue RevenueType);
array Rev{3} RevenueFirstClass
RevenueBusiness
RevenueEconomy;
set ia.alldata(keep= FlightDate RevenueFirstClass
RevenueEconomy RevenueBusiness);
do i = 1 to 3;
revenue = Rev{i};
if i = 1 then RevenueType = 'RevenueFirstClass';
else if i = 2 then RevenueType = 'RevenueBusiness';
else RevenueType = 'RevenueEconomy';
output;
end;
run;
Execution
REV{1}
REV{2}
REV{3}
Revenue FirstClass N 8
Revenue Business N 8
Revenue Economy N 8
Flight Date N 8
i N 8
Revenue N 8
Revenue Type $ 17
18707
22540
62010
14580
2
22540
Revenue Business

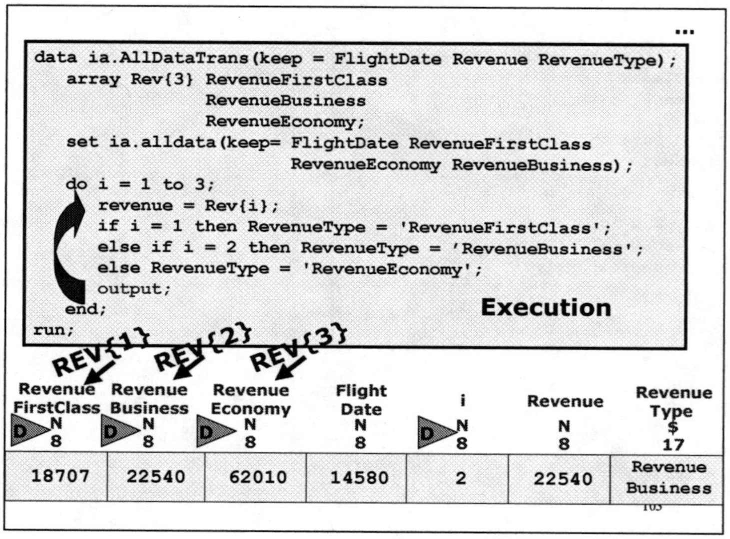
data ia.AllDataTrans(keep = FlightDate Revenue RevenueType);
array Rev{3} RevenueFirstClass
RevenueBusiness
RevenueEconomy;
set ia.alldata(keep= FlightDate RevenueFirstClass
RevenueEconomy RevenueBusiness);
do i = 1 to 3;
revenue = Rev{i};
if i = 1 then RevenueType = 'RevenueFirstClass';
else if i = 2 then RevenueType = 'RevenueBusiness';
else RevenueType = 'RevenueEconomy';
output;
end;
run;
Execution
REV{1}
REV{2}
REV{3}
Revenue FirstClass N 8
Revenue Business N 8
Revenue Economy N 8
Flight Date N 8
i N 8
Revenue N 8
Revenue Type $ 17
18707
22540
62010
14580
2
22540
Revenue Business

...

```
data ia.AllDataTrans(keep = FlightDate Revenue RevenueType);
   array Rev{3} RevenueFirstClass
                RevenueBusiness
                RevenueEconomy;
   set ia.alldata(keep= FlightDate RevenueFirstClass
                        RevenueEconomy RevenueBusiness);
   do i = 1 to 3;
      revenue = Rev{i};
      if i = 1 then RevenueType = 'RevenueFirstClass';
      else if i = 2 then RevenueType = 'RevenueBusiness';
      else RevenueType = 'RevenueEconomy';
      output;
   end;
run;
```

**Execution**

REV{1} REV{2} REV{3}

| Revenue FirstClass D N 8 | Revenue Business D N 8 | Revenue Economy D N 8 | Flight Date N 8 | i D N 8 | Revenue N 8 | Revenue Type $ 17 |
|---|---|---|---|---|---|---|
| 18707 | 22540 | 62010 | 14580 | 3 | 22540 | Revenue Business |

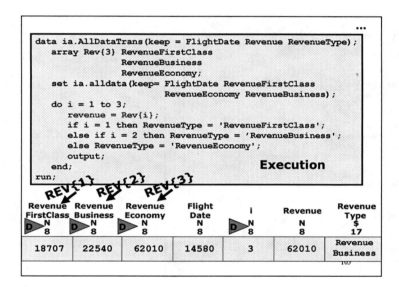

104

...

```
data ia.AllDataTrans(keep = FlightDate Revenue RevenueType);
   array Rev{3} RevenueFirstClass
                RevenueBusiness
                RevenueEconomy;
   set ia.alldata(keep= FlightDate RevenueFirstClass
                        RevenueEconomy RevenueBusiness);
   do i = 1 to 3;
      revenue = Rev{i};
      if i = 1 then RevenueType = 'RevenueFirstClass';
      else if i = 2 then RevenueType = 'RevenueBusiness';
      else RevenueType = 'RevenueEconomy';
      output;
   end;
run;
```

**Execution**

REV{1} REV{2} REV{3}

| Revenue FirstClass D N 8 | Revenue Business D N 8 | Revenue Economy D N 8 | Flight Date N 8 | i D N 8 | Revenue N 8 | Revenue Type $ 17 |
|---|---|---|---|---|---|---|
| 18707 | 22540 | 62010 | 14580 | 3 | 62010 | Revenue Business |

105

...

```
data ia.AllDataTrans(keep = FlightDate Revenue RevenueType);
   array Rev{3} RevenueFirstClass
                RevenueBusiness
                RevenueEconomy;
   set ia.alldata(keep= FlightDate RevenueFirstClass
                        RevenueEconomy RevenueBusiness);
   do i = 1 to 3;
      revenue = Rev{i};
      if i = 1 then RevenueType = 'RevenueFirstClass';
      else if i = 2 then RevenueType = 'RevenueBusiness';
      else RevenueType = 'RevenueEconomy';
      output;
   end;
run;
```

**Execution**

REV{1} REV{2} REV{3}

| Revenue FirstClass D N 8 | Revenue Business D N 8 | Revenue Economy D N 8 | Flight Date N 8 | i D N 8 | Revenue N 8 | Revenue Type $ 17 |
|---|---|---|---|---|---|---|
| 18707 | 22540 | 62010 | 14580 | 3 | 62010 | Revenue Economy |

107

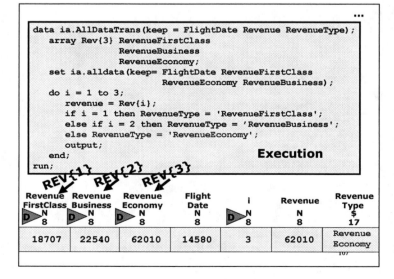

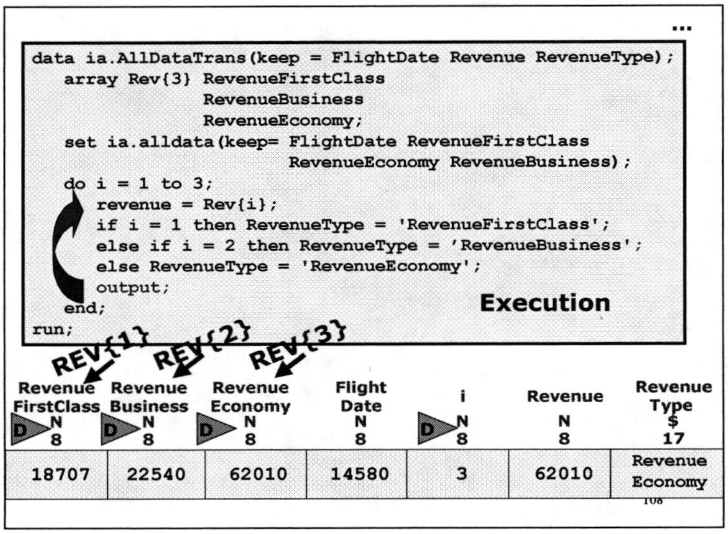
...
data ia.AllDataTrans(keep = FlightDate Revenue RevenueType);
array Rev{3} RevenueFirstClass
RevenueBusiness
RevenueEconomy;
set ia.alldata(keep= FlightDate RevenueFirstClass
RevenueEconomy RevenueBusiness);
do i = 1 to 3;
revenue = Rev{i};
if i = 1 then RevenueType = 'RevenueFirstClass';
else if i = 2 then RevenueType = 'RevenueBusiness';
else RevenueType = 'RevenueEconomy';
output;
end;
run;
Execution
REV{1}
REV{2}
REV{3}
Revenue FirstClass N 8
Revenue Business N 8
Revenue Economy N 8
Flight Date N 8
i N 8
Revenue N 8
Revenue Type $ 17
D
18707
22540
62010
14580
3
62010
Revenue Economy

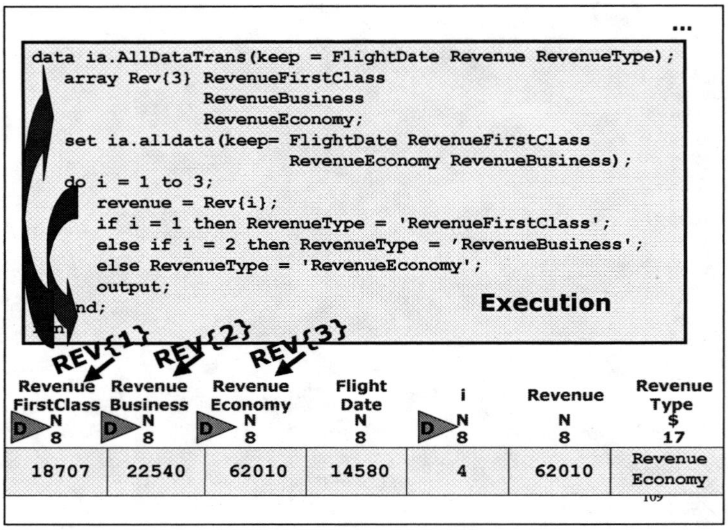
...
data ia.AllDataTrans(keep = FlightDate Revenue RevenueType);
array Rev{3} RevenueFirstClass
RevenueBusiness
RevenueEconomy;
set ia.alldata(keep= FlightDate RevenueFirstClass
RevenueEconomy RevenueBusiness);
i = 1 to 3;
revenue = Rev{i};
if i = 1 then RevenueType = 'RevenueFirstClass';
else if i = 2 then RevenueType = 'RevenueBusiness';
else RevenueType = 'RevenueEconomy';
output;
Execution
REV{1}
REV{2}
REV{3}
Revenue FirstClass N 8
Revenue Business N 8
Revenue Economy N 8
Flight Date N 8
i N 8
Revenue N 8
Revenue Type $ 17
D
18707
22540
62010
14580
4
62010
Revenue Economy

## Using an ARRAY to Rotate Data

c04s5d2

```
data ia.AllDataRotate
                  (keep = FlightDate Revenue RevenueType);
   array Rev{3} RevenueFirstClass
                RevenueBusiness
                RevenueEconomy;
   set ia.alldata(keep = FlightDate RevenueFirstClass
                         RevenueEconomy RevenueBusiness);
   do i = 1 to 3;
      revenue = Rev{i};
      if i = 1 then RevenueType = 'RevenueFirstClass';
      else if i = 2 then RevenueType = 'RevenueBusiness';
      else RevenueType = 'RevenueEconomy';
      output;
   end;
run;

proc print data = ia.AllDataRotate(obs = 10);
   title 'Rotated Data';
run;
```

Output

Rotated Data

| Obs | Flight Date | revenue | RevenueType |
|---|---|---|---|
| 1 | 14580 | 19200 | RevenueFirstClass |
| 2 | 14580 | 31610 | RevenueBusiness |
| 3 | 14580 | 79650 | RevenueEconomy |
| 4 | 14581 | 17600 | RevenueFirstClass |
| 5 | 14581 | 25070 | RevenueBusiness |
| 6 | 14581 | 80181 | RevenueEconomy |
| 7 | 14582 | 17600 | RevenueFirstClass |
| 8 | 14582 | 28340 | RevenueBusiness |
| 9 | 14582 | 84960 | RevenueEconomy |
| 10 | 14583 | 17600 | RevenueFirstClass |

The program that created the graph needed by International Airlines is

```
ods html body = 'report.html';
goptions hsize = 6 vsize = 5 device = gif;

proc gchart data = ia.AllDataTrans
   title 'Revenue Figures';
   format flightdate mmddyy10.;
   where flightdate between '01dec1999'd and '07dec1999'd;
   label RevenueTypes = 'Revenue Types';
   hbar FlightDate / sumvar=revenue
                     subgroup = RevenueTypes
                     nostats discrete;
run;
ods html close;
```

## Output

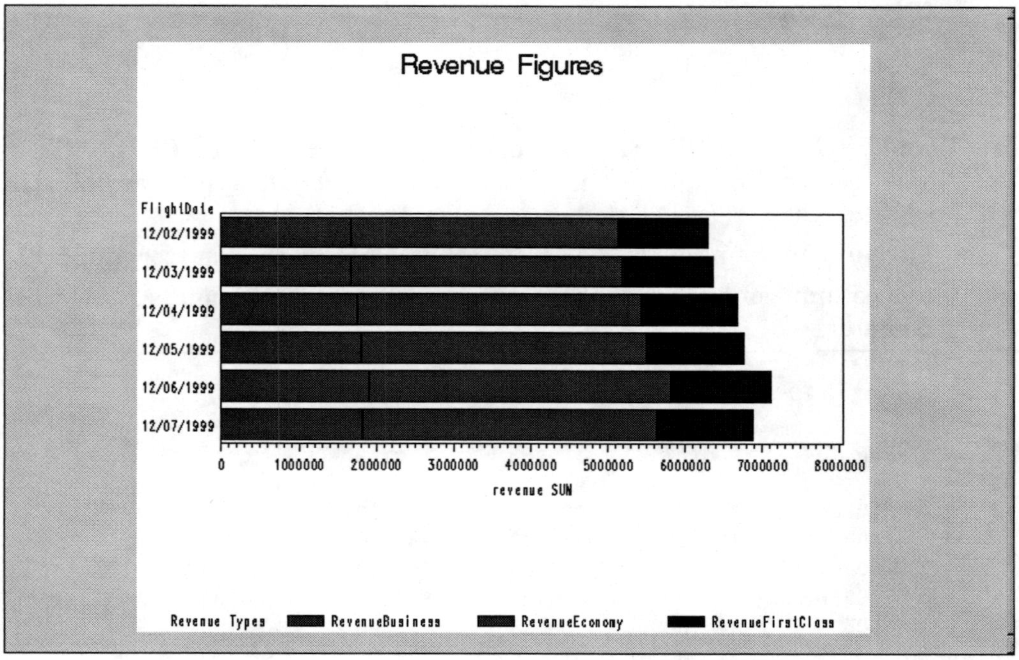
Revenue Figures
FlightDate
12/02/1999
12/03/1999
12/04/1999
12/05/1999
12/06/1999
12/07/1999
0 1000000 2000000 3000000 4000000 5000000 6000000 7000000 8000000
revenue SUM
Revenue Types RevenueBusiness RevenueEconomy RevenueFirstClass

## Exercises

5. Using PROC TRANSPOSE, transpose the data set IA.EMP_CONTRIB. Name the new SAS data set IA.NewContrib. It should appear as below in structure with :
   - QtrNum as the name of the column that contains the quarter number.
   - one column containing each unique employee contribution named Amount.

IA.EMP_CONTRIB

| EMP_ID | qtr1 | qtr2 | qtr3 | qtr4 |
|---|---|---|---|---|
| E00224 | $12.00 | $33.00 | $22.00 | . |
| E00367 | $35.00 | $48.00 | $40.00 | $30.00 |
| E00441 | . | $63.00 | $89.00 | $90.00 |
| E00587 | $16.00 | $19.00 | $30.00 | $29.00 |
| E00598 | $4.00 | $8.00 | $6.00 | $1.00 |
| E00621 | $10.00 | $12.00 | $15.00 | $25.00 |
| E00630 | $67.00 | $86.00 | $52.00 | $84.00 |
| E00705 | $9.00 | $7.00 | $49.00 | $2.00 |
| E00727 | $8.00 | $27.00 | $25.00 | $14.00 |
| E00860 | $10.00 | $15.00 | $6.00 | $20.00 |
| E00901 | $19.00 | $21.00 | $3.00 | $24.00 |
| E00907 | $18.00 | $26.00 | $46.00 | $65.00 |
| E00947 | $8.00 | $10.00 | $13.00 | $16.00 |
| E00955 | $55.00 | $66.00 | $11.00 | $14.00 |
| E00960 | $13.00 | $29.00 | $40.00 | $20.00 |
| E00997 | $6.00 | $9.00 | $12.00 | $18.00 |
| E01022 | $15.00 | . | $20.00 | $25.00 |
| E01442 | $50.00 | $72.00 | $54.00 | $52.00 |

Partial ia.NewContrib Output

| EMP_ID | Qtr Num | Amount |
|---|---|---|
| E00224 | qtr1 | $12.00 |
| E00224 | qtr2 | $33.00 |
| E00224 | qtr3 | $22.00 |
| E00224 | qtr4 | . |
| E00367 | qtr1 | $35.00 |
| E00367 | qtr2 | $48.00 |
| E00367 | qtr3 | $40.00 |
| E00367 | qtr4 | $30.00 |
| E00441 | qtr1 | . |
| E00441 | qtr2 | $63.00 |
| E00441 | qtr3 | $89.00 |
| E00441 | qtr4 | $90.00 |
| E00587 | qtr1 | $16.00 |
| E00587 | qtr2 | $19.00 |
| E00587 | qtr3 | $30.00 |
| E00587 | qtr4 | $29.00 |

**6.** Using arrays, rotate the data set IA.EMP_CONTRIB. Name the new SAS data set IA.ROTATE and place it in the permanent SAS data library. It should appear in the same structure as IA.NEWCONTRIB.

## 4.6 Chapter Summary

Raw data files in hierarchical structure consist of a header record and one or more detail records. The header type identifier, the trailing @ and the RETAIN statement can be used to read hierarchical files.

The RETAIN statement is used to give an initial value to a retained variable and prevents the initialization of variables to missing each time the DATA step executes.

General form of the RETAIN statement

```
RETAIN variables initial-value...;
```

The trailing @ can be used to read a single data line with multiple INPUT statements and for conditional execution of INPUT statements.

To read a raw data file containing repeated fields, you can use the double trailing @@. The @@ can be used to hold the

- current data line in the input buffer for another INPUT statement to process
- current data line in the input buffer across executions of the DATA step
- column pointer at its present location in that data line.

You can match-merge two or more SAS data sets when each named data set contains a common BY variable specified in a BY statement. The data values read from the data sets are automatically retained for all variables until the values of the BY variables change in all the data sets.

General form of the merge statement in a DATA step.

```
DATA SAS-data-set;
  MERGE SAS-data-set-1 ... SAS-data-set-n;
  BY common-by-variables;
RUN;
```

You can also use a PROC SQL join to perform a match-merge on two or more SAS data sets.

General form of the PROC SQL join

```
PROC SQL;
  CREATE TABLE SAS-data-set AS
    SELECT column-1, column-2,... ,column-n
      FROM table-1, table-2,...,table-n
      WHERE joining criteria;
```

The DATA step merge and the PROC SQL join have similar results for

- one-to-one matches
- one-to-many matches.

The DATA step merge and the PROC SQL join have different results for

- many-to-many matches
- nonmatches.

You can use PROC TRANSPOSE to transpose a SAS data set.

The general form for PROC TRANSPOSE

```
PROC TRANSPOSE <DATA=input-data-set>
                 <OUT=output-data-set>
                 <NAME = variable-name>;
   BY <DESCENDING> variable-1
      <...<DESCENDING> variable-n>;
   ID variable;
   IDLABEL variable;
   VAR variable(s);
RUN;
```

You can also use a DATA step with an ARRAY statement to rotate the data and achieve similar results.

The general form of the DATA step with an ARRAY statement to rotate data

```
DATA SAS-data-set;
  ARRAY array-name{dimensions}
        <$ length> elements;
  SET SAS-data-set;
  DO index = 1 to dimensions;
    newvariable = array-name{index};
    OUTPUT;
  END;
RUN;
```

Entire Program

```
/********* c04s2d1 ******************/

/************************************/
/*    Create a SAS data set         */
/*    from a heirarchical file.     */
/************************************/

data ia.revenue(drop = type);
   retain Origin Destination FlightIDNumber FlightDate;
   infile 'hiery.dat';
   input type $2. @;
   if type = 'ID' then
     input  @4 Origin $3.
            @8 Destination $3.
           @11 FlightIDNumber $7.;
   else do;
     input  @3 FlightDate date9.
           @13 RevenueFirstClass 6.
           @25 RevenueBusiness 6.
           @35 RevenueEconomy 6. ;
     output;
   end;
run;

proc print data = ia.revenue(obs = 10) noobs;
   title 'Revenue Data';
run;
```

```
/********* c04s3d1 *******************/

/*************************************/
/*    Create a SAS data set          */
/*    from a raw data file containing */
/*    repeated fields.               */
/*************************************/

data ia.Expenses;
   infile 'repeat.dat';
   input FlightIDNumber $
         FlightDate : date9.
         TotalExpenses @@;
run;

proc print data = ia.Expenses(obs = 10);
   title 'Expenses Data';
run;
```

```
/********* c04s4d1 ******************/

/**************************************/
/*    Create a SAS data set          */
/*    by merging three SAS data sets */
/*    that do not have a common BY   */
/*    variable.                      */
/**************************************/

proc sort data = ia.expenses out = work.expenses;
   by FlightIDNumber FlightDate;
run;

proc sort data = ia.revenue out = work.revenue;
   by FlightIDNumber FlightDate;
run;

data work.expenses_revenue;
   merge work.expenses(in = e) work.revenue(in = r);
   by FlightIDNumber FlightDate;
   if e and r;
   Profit = sum(RevenueFirstClass, RevenueBusiness,
                RevenueEconomy, - TotalExpenses);
run;

proc sort data = work.expenses_revenue;
      by Destination;
run;

data ia.AllData;
   merge work.expenses_revenue(in = exp) ia.AirportData
         (rename = (AirportCode = Destination)
          keep = AirportCity AirportName AirportCode);
   by Destination;
   if exp;
run;

proc print data = ia.AllData(obs = 10);
   title 'Result of Merging Three Data Sets';
   format FlightDate date9.;
run;
```

```
/********* c04s4d2 ******************/

/************************************/
/*    Create a SAS data set        */
/*    by joining three SAS data sets */
/*    that do not have a common BY   */
/*    variable.                      */
/************************************/

proc sql;
   create table ia.AllDataSQL as
      select revenue.FlightIDNumber, revenue.FlightDate,
             expenses.TotalExpenses, revenue.Origin,
             revenue.Destination,
             revenue.revenueFirstClass,
             revenue.revenueBusiness,
             revenue.revenueEconomy,
             sum(revenue.RevenueFirstClass,
                 revenue.RevenueBusiness,
                 revenue.RevenueEconomy,
                 - TotalExpenses) as profit,
             AirportData.AirportCity,
             AirportData.AirportName
      from work.expenses, work.revenue, ia.AirportData
      where
           expenses.FlightIDNumber = revenue.FlightIDNumber
       and expenses.FlightDate = revenue.FlightDate
       and AirportData.AirportCode = revenue.Destination
       order by revenue.Destination,
                revenue.FlightIDNumber,
                revenue.FlightDate;

proc print data = ia.AllDataSQL(obs = 10);
   title 'Result of Joining Three Data Sets';
   format FlightDate date9.;
run;
```

```
/********* c04s5d1 ******************/

/*************************************/
/*     Use PROC TRANSPOSE to         */
/*     transpose a SAS data set.     */
/*************************************/

proc sort data = ia.AllData;
   by FlightIDNumber FlightDate ;
run;

proc transpose data = ia.AllData
                           (keep = FlightDate
                                   FlightIDNumber
                                   RevenueFirstClass
                                   RevenueEconomy
                                   RevenueBusiness)
               out = ia.AllDataTrans
                     (rename = (col1 = Revenue))
               name = RevenueType;
   by FlightIDNumber FlightDate;
   var RevenueFirstClass RevenueEconomy RevenueBusiness;
run;

proc print data = ia.AllDataTrans(obs = 10);
   title 'Data Transposed';
   format FlightDate mmddyy10.;
run;
```

```
/********* c04s5d2 ******************/

/************************************/
/*    Use the DATA step and an array  */
/*    to rotate a SAS data set.       */
/************************************/

data ia.AllDataRotate(keep = FlightDate Revenue Name);
   array Rev{3} RevenueFirstClass
                RevenueBusiness
                RevenueEconomy;
   set ia.alldata(keep = FlightDate RevenueFirstClass
                         RevenueEconomy RevenueBusiness);
   do i = 1 to 3;
      revenue = Rev{i};
      if i = 1 then Name = 'RevenueFirstClass';
      else if i = 2 then Name = 'RevenueBusiness';
      else Name = 'RevenueEconomy';
      output;
   end;
run;

proc print data = ia.AllDataRotate(obs = 10);
   title 'Rotated Data';
run;
```

# 4.7 Solutions to Exercises

1. Create a SAS data set named work.Dependents from the hierarchical file Dependnt. The employee's ID number serves as the header record. All employee ID numbers start with E followed by a digit.

   One to many records follow with the information about the employee's dependents. The dependent record is free-formatted with the dependent's last name, first name, and dependent type (S = Spouse C = Child).

   A sample of the file is as follows:

```
E00179
ROBERTS SANDRA S
E00356
FULKERSON DAVID C
FULKERSON MICHAEL C
FULKERSON ALICE C
FULKERSON AMY C
FULKERSON JORN C
E00533
MILLS DINA C
MILLS GREG C
```

   Work.Dependents should have the following structure.

   Partial output

| Obs | EmpID | LastName | FirstName | relation |
|---|---|---|---|---|
| 1 | E00179 | ROBERTS | SANDRA | S |
| 2 | E00356 | FULKERSON | DAVID | C |
| 3 | E00356 | FULKERSON | MICHAEL | C |
| 4 | E00356 | FULKERSON | ALICE | C |
| 5 | E00356 | FULKERSON | AMY | C |
| 6 | E00356 | FULKERSON | JORN | C |
| 7 | E00533 | MILLS | DINA | C |
| 8 | E00533 | MILLS | GREG | C |

```
data work.Dependents(drop = FirstField);
   infile 'Dependnt.dat';
   retain EmpID;
   length FirstField LastName FirstName $ 20;
   input FirstField $ @;
   if FirstField =: "E" and
      substr(FirstField,2,1) in
            ('1' '2' '3' '4' '5' '6' '7' '8' '9' '0') then
                  EmpID = FirstField;
   else
      do;
         LastName = FirstField;
         input firstname $ relation $;
         output;
      end;
run;
```

2. Create a SAS data set named work.Commissions from the commissn raw data file. From one row of data create several SAS observations.

   Here is a sample of the raw data:

```
E00002   2704.07 E00002   2705.43 E00002   2706.78 E00002   2708.14
E00002   2709.50 E00002   2710.85 E00002   2712.21 E00003   2030.15
E00003   12036.18 E00003  12042.21 E00003  12048.24 E00003  12054.27
E00004   4218.99 E00005   1900.95 E00005   1901.91 E00005   1902.86
E00005   1903.82 E00005   1904.77 E00005   1905.73 E00005   1906.68
E00005   1907.64 E00005   1908.59 E00007   2904.37 E00007   2905.83
```

   Here is a sample of the resulting SAS data set:

| Obs | EmpID | amount1 |
|---|---|---|
| 1 | E00002 | 2704.07 |
| 2 | E00002 | 2705.43 |
| 3 | E00002 | 2706.78 |
| 4 | E00002 | 2708.14 |
| 5 | E00002 | 2709.50 |
| 6 | E00002 | 2710.85 |
| 7 | E00002 | 2712.21 |
| 8 | E00003 | 12030.15 |
| 9 | E00003 | 12036.18 |
| 10 | E00003 | 12042.21 |

```
data Commissions;
   infile 'commissns.dat';
   input EmpID $ amount @@;
run;
```

3. Using PROC SQL, join IA.Employee_Data, IA.Job_Code_Data, and IA.NewSals to create a report that displays:

```
Employee ID
Employee Job Code
Job Code Description
Current Salary
New Salary
```

There is not a common variable to all 3 SAS data sets. Use PROC CONTENTS or PROC DATASETS to determine the columns on which to join the rows.

```
proc datasets lib = ia;
   contents data = NewSals;
   contents data = Job_Code_Data;
    contents data = Employee_Data;
run;
quit;

proc sql;
select e.emp_id , j.job_code, j.job_description
        format=$40.,e.emp_salary, n.NewSalary
      from ia.NewSals n, ia.Job_Code_Data j,
      ia.Employee_Data e
      where e.emp_id = n.emp_id and
            j.job_code = e.job_code;
quit;
```

4. Repeat the same task using the DATA step MERGE statement to merge all three data sets.

```
proc sort data = ia.NewSals;
   by emp_id;
run;

proc sort data = ia.Employee_Data;
   by emp_id;
run;

data temp1;
   merge ia.NewSals(in = n) ia.Employee_Data(in = e);
   by emp_id;
   if n and e;
run;

proc sort data=temp1;
   by job_code;
run;

proc sort data=ia.Job_Code_Data;
   by job_code;
run;

data final;
   merge temp1(in = t) ia.Job_Code_Data(in = j);
   by Job_Code;
   if t and j;
run;
```

5. Using PROC TRANSPOSE, transpose the data set IA.EMP_CONTRIB. Name the new SAS data set IA.NewContrib. It should appear as below in structure with :
   - QtrNum as the name of the column that contains the quarter number.
   - one column containing each unique employee contribution named Amount.

IA.EMP_CONTRIB

| EMP_ID | qtr1 | qtr2 | qtr3 | qtr4 |
|---|---|---|---|---|
| E00224 | $12.00 | $33.00 | $22.00 | . |
| E00367 | $35.00 | $48.00 | $40.00 | $30.00 |
| E00441 | . | $63.00 | $89.00 | $90.00 |
| E00587 | $16.00 | $19.00 | $30.00 | $29.00 |
| E00598 | $4.00 | $8.00 | $6.00 | $1.00 |
| E00621 | $10.00 | $12.00 | $15.00 | $25.00 |
| E00630 | $67.00 | $86.00 | $52.00 | $84.00 |
| E00705 | $9.00 | $7.00 | $49.00 | $2.00 |
| E00727 | $8.00 | $27.00 | $25.00 | $14.00 |
| E00860 | $10.00 | $15.00 | $6.00 | $20.00 |
| E00901 | $19.00 | $21.00 | $3.00 | $24.00 |
| E00907 | $18.00 | $26.00 | $46.00 | $65.00 |
| E00947 | $8.00 | $10.00 | $13.00 | $16.00 |
| E00955 | $55.00 | $66.00 | $11.00 | $14.00 |
| E00960 | $13.00 | $29.00 | $40.00 | $20.00 |
| E00997 | $6.00 | $9.00 | $12.00 | $18.00 |
| E01022 | $15.00 | . | $20.00 | $25.00 |
| E01442 | $50.00 | $72.00 | $54.00 | $52.00 |

Partial ia.NewContrib Output

| EMP_ID | Qtr Num | Amount |
|---|---|---|
| E00224 | qtr1 | $12.00 |
| E00224 | qtr2 | $33.00 |
| E00224 | qtr3 | $22.00 |
| E00224 | qtr4 | . |
| E00367 | qtr1 | $35.00 |
| E00367 | qtr2 | $48.00 |
| E00367 | qtr3 | $40.00 |
| E00367 | qtr4 | $30.00 |
| E00441 | qtr1 | . |
| E00441 | qtr2 | $63.00 |
| E00441 | qtr3 | $89.00 |
| E00441 | qtr4 | $90.00 |
| E00587 | qtr1 | $16.00 |
| E00587 | qtr2 | $19.00 |
| E00587 | qtr3 | $30.00 |
| E00587 | qtr4 | $29.00 |

```
proc transpose data = ia.emp_contrib
               out = ia.NewContrib
              (rename = (col1 = Amount))
   name = QtrNum;
   by emp_id;
run;

options ls=72;
proc print data = ia.NewContrib noobs;
run;
```

6. Using arrays, rotate the data set IA.EMP_CONTRIB. Name the new SAS data set IA.ROTATE and place it in the permanent SAS data library. It should appear in the same structure as IA.NEWCONTRIB.

```
data ia.Rotate(drop = i qtr1-qtr4);
   set ia.Emp_Contrib;
   array qtrno{4} $ _temporary_
                   ('qtr1','qtr2','qtr3','qtr4');
   array contrib{4} qtr1 - qtr4;
   do i = 1 to 4;
      QtrNum = qtrno{i};
      Amount = contrib{i};
      output;
   end;
run;
```

# Chapter 5

# 5.1 Introduction

## General Business Scenario

International Airlines has

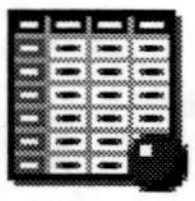

- a SAS data set containing the cargo revenue figures for each month from 1997 to 1999

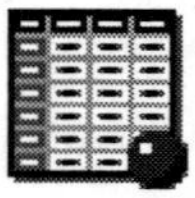

- a SAS data set containing the target amounts for those months.

3

## General Business Scenario

Using IA.MonthlySummary1997_1999, we must calculate

∑ the total cargo revenue for the year

% the percent of monthly total to yearly total.

4

## General Business Scenario

Since there are several techniques that we can use to perform this task, we need to try two and compare the results.

5

## General Business Scenario

The second SAS data set, IA.TARGET, contains the target cargo and passenger revenue figures for each month from 1997 to 1999.

We need to look up the target based on the month and year.

6

## Organize the Tasks

- Create a summary data set.
- Combine the summary data set with the detail data set and create percentages using two different techniques.
- Compare the two resulting SAS data sets.
- Lookup the target revenues.

7

# 5.2 Creating a Summary Data Set

## Objectives

- Define the Output Delivery System.
- Explore ODS objects generated by procedure output.
- Define the ODS statement to determine the names of ODS objects.
- Create output SAS data sets from procedure output.

9

## Business Scenario

The data set, IA.MONTHLYSUMMARY1997_1999 has one row for every FlightMonth (month and year) from 1997 to 1999.

```
        Flight                                  RevenueFirst
 Obs     Month          RevenueCargo                   Class

   1    JAN1997      $171,520,869.10          $51,136,353.00
   2    JAN1998      $238,786,807.60          $71,197,270.00
   3    JAN1999      $280,350,393.00          $83,667,651.00


 Obs    RevenueBusiness        RevenueEconomy      month

   1     $34,897,844.00       $169,193,900.00        1
   2     $48,749,365.00       $235,462,316.00        1
   3     $57,385,822.00       $278,553,207.00        1
```

## Business Scenario

First, we need to summarize the data to get the total revenue for cargo for the three year period.

| Revenue Cargo_Sum |
|---|
| 8,593,432,002.40 |

11

## Organize the Tasks:

- Create a summary data set.
- Combine the summary data set with the detail data set and create percentages using two different techniques.
- Compare the two resulting SAS data sets.
- Lookup the target revenues.

12

...

## Creating a Summary Data Set

There are several ways to create a summary data set

- Output Delivery System (ODS)
- the MEANS procedure with an OUTPUT statement
- the DATA step.

13

...

## ODS Objects

Procedure output is divided into components or *output objects.*

Output objects can consist of

- data components
- template components.

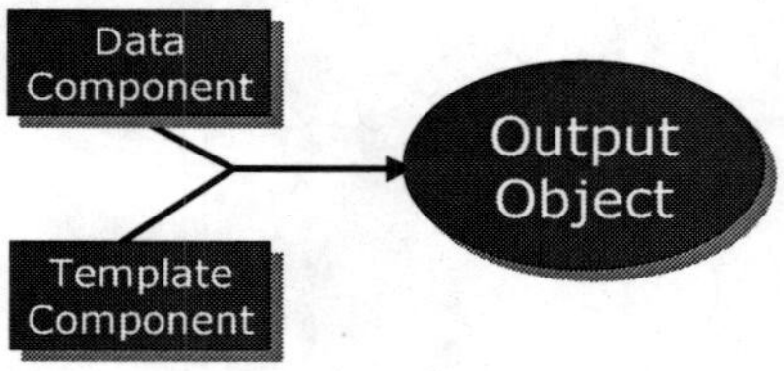


14

Each output object may be broken down into two component parts:

| | |
|---|---|
| *data component* | collection of raw numbers and characters comprising the contents of the output. The data component retains full numeric precision. |
| *template component* | description of what the output is supposed to look like when the data is formatted and arranged. |

Some documentation may refer to the template component as the table definition.

## ODS Objects

- Some procedures may only have a single output object while others have multiple output objects.
- Each output object has a set of attributes, which includes a name and a label.
- ODS stores a link to each output object in the Results folder in the Results window.

15

Any procedure that uses ODS produces multiple output objects when you use BY-group processing.

Procedure options may increase the number of output objects created by the procedure.

## Creating Procedure Objects

c05s2d1

Program

```
proc print data = ia.MonthlySummary1997_1999(obs = 10);
   title 'Objects from PROC PRINT';
run;


proc univariate data = ia.MonthlySummary1997_1999;
   var RevenueFirstClass;
   title 'Objects from PROC UNIVARIATE';
run;
```

PROC PRINT has one object.

The PRINT object

Objects from PROC PRINT

| Obs | Flight Month | RevenueCargo | RevenueFirst Class |
|---|---|---|---|
| 1 | JAN1997 | $171,520,869.10 | $51,136,353.00 |
| 2 | JAN1998 | $238,786,807.60 | $71,197,270.00 |
| 3 | JAN1999 | $280,350,393.00 | $83,667,651.00 |
| 4 | FEB1997 | $177,671,530.40 | $52,867,177.00 |
| 5 | FEB1998 | $215,959,695.50 | $64,092,727.00 |
| 6 | FEB1999 | $253,999,924.00 | $75,811,358.00 |
| 7 | MAR1997 | $196,591,378.20 | $58,562,490.00 |
| 8 | MAR1998 | $239,056,025.55 | $71,173,645.00 |
| 9 | MAR1999 | $281,433,310.00 | $83,864,006.00 |
| 10 | APR1997 | $380,804,120.20 | $113,826,330.00 |

| Obs | RevenueBusiness | RevenueEconomy | month |
|---|---|---|---|
| 1 | $34,897,844.00 | $169,193,900.00 | 1 |
| 2 | $48,749,365.00 | $235,462,316.00 | 1 |
| 3 | $57,385,822.00 | $278,553,207.00 | 1 |
| 4 | $36,397,032.00 | $175,250,984.00 | 2 |
| 5 | $44,111,168.00 | $212,667,536.00 | 2 |
| 6 | $51,871,453.00 | $251,355,652.00 | 2 |
| 7 | $40,116,649.00 | $193,982,585.00 | 3 |
| 8 | $48,767,636.00 | $235,501,953.00 | 3 |
| 9 | $57,546,222.00 | $278,491,696.00 | 3 |
| 10 | $77,817,068.00 | $375,598,996.00 | 4 |

By default PROC UNIVARIATE creates five objects.

The MOMENTS object

```
                    Objects from PROC UNIVARIATE

                      The UNIVARIATE Procedure
                    Variable:  RevenueFirstClass

                              Moments

N                          36    Sum Weights                  36
Mean               71154621.5    Sum Observations     2561566373
Std Deviation      12734798.1    Variance             1.62175E14
Skewness           0.86994156    Kurtosis             1.97859477
Uncorrected SS     1.87943E17    Corrected SS         5.67613E15
Coeff Variation    17.8973591    Std Error Mean       2122466.35
```

The BASIC STATISTICAL MEASURES object

```
                 Basic Statistical Measures

       Location                    Variability

   Mean     71154621     Std Deviation            12734798
   Median   71136554     Variance               1.62175E14
   Mode            .     Range                    62689977
                         Interquartile Range      22488256
```

The TEST FOR LOCATION object

```
                 Tests for Location: Mu0=0

     Test           -Statistic-    -----p Value------

     Student's t    t   33.5245    Pr > |t|    <.0001
     Sign           M        18    Pr >= |M|   <.0001
     Signed Rank    S       333    Pr >= |S|   <.0001
```

The QUANTILES object

```
                 Quantiles (Definition 5)

                 Quantile        Estimate

                 100% Max       113826330
                 99%            113826330
                 95%             83864513
                 90%             83816720
                 75% Q3          81093654
                 50% Median      71136554
                 25% Q1          58605398
                 10%             56702750
                 5%              52867177
                 1%              51136353
                 0% Min          51136353
```

The EXTREME OBSERVATIONS object

```
               Objects from PROC UNIVARIATE

                 The UNIVARIATE Procedure
               Variable:  RevenueFirstClass

                  Extreme Observations

      ------Lowest------          ------Highest------

         Value      Obs             Value       Obs

      51136353        1          83811034        30
      52867177        4          83816720        21
      56626819       31          83864006         9
      56702750       25          83864513        15
      56741721       16         113826330        10
```

The Results window contains links to each of the objects created by the procedures.

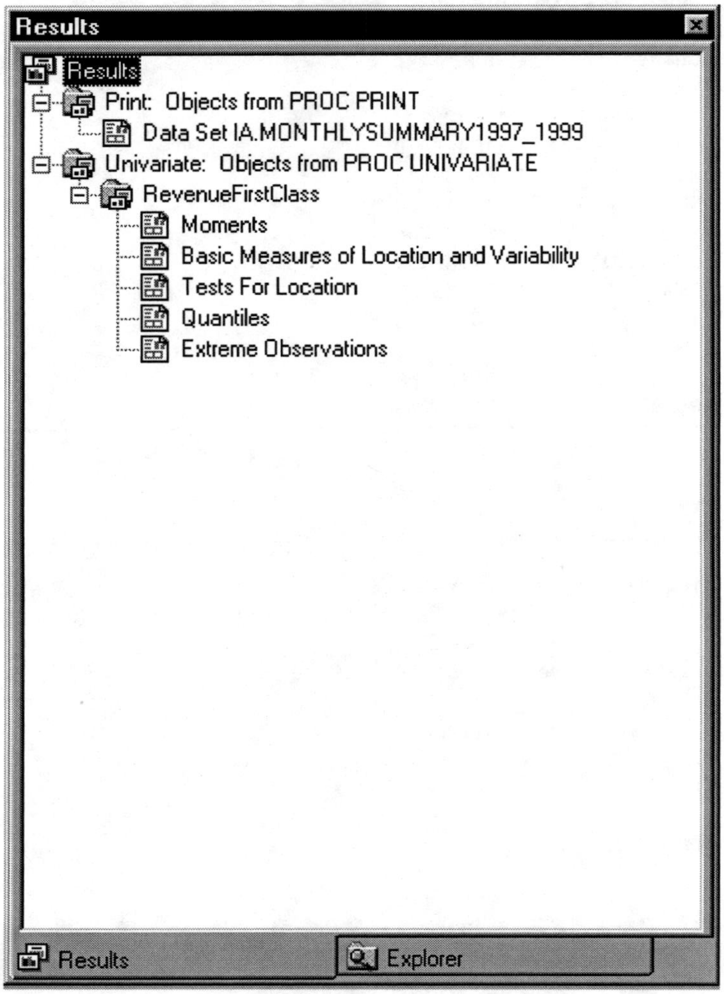


The icons above represent the LISTING destination for ODS. By default, the LISTING destination is the

- Output window for text reports (if you are using the SAS windowing environment)
- Graph1 window for graphics reports.

You can double click on a listing icon to activate the Output window to the appropriate report.

## Using ODS

Using ODS statements, you can

- **produce output data sets from most procedures**
- create HTML reports
- determine the attributes of an object
- organize and manage output in the Results folder of the Results window.

17

The attributes of an object include the name of the

- object
- data contained in the report created by the procedure
- template that determines the structure of the report created by the procedure.

## ODS TRACE Statement

To determine the names of the output objects, use the ODS TRACE statement.

The ODS TRACE statement writes a record to the SAS log for each output object that is created.

General form of the ODS TRACE statement

```
ODS TRACE ON </option(s)>;
ODS TRACE OFF;
```

18

By default, ODS TRACE is turned off.

When you turn on ODS TRACE, it stays on until you turn it off.

ODS TRACE statement options:

| | |
|---|---|
| LABEL | includes the label path for the output object in the record. |
| LISTING | writes the trace record to the LISTING destination (the Output window if you are using the SAS windowing environment) so that each part of the trace record immediately precedes the output object that it describes. |

### Default Contents of Trace Record

- **Name**
  is the name of the output object.
- **Label**
  briefly describes the contents of the output object.
- **Data name**
  is the name of the data component that was used to create this output object. The data name appears only if it is different from the name of the output object.

19

### Default Contents of Trace Record

- **Data label**
  describes the content of the data.
- **Template**
  is the name of the template component that ODS used to format the output object.
- **Path**
  is the path of the output object.

20

The object name is the last part of the path.

There is no template component for procedures such as REPORT and PRINT that use statements to control the format of the report.

## Using the TRACE Statement

c05s2d2

```
ods trace on;

proc print data = ia.monthlySummary1997_1999;
run;

proc univariate data = ia.MonthlySummary1997_1999;
   var RevenueFirstClass;
run;

ods trace off;
```

Log

```
322  ods trace on;
323
324  proc print data = ia.monthlysummary1997_1999;
325  run;

Output Added:
-------------
Name:       Print
Label:      Data Set IA.MONTHLYSUMMARY1997_1999
Data Name:
Path:       Print.Print
-------------
NOTE: PROCEDURE PRINT used:
      real time          0.15 seconds
      cpu time           0.01 seconds
```

```
330
331  proc univariate data = ia.monthlysummary1997_1999;
332     var RevenueFirstClass;
333  run;

Output Added:
-------------
Name:       Moments
Label:      Moments
Template:   base.univariate.Moments
Path:       Univariate.RevenueFirstClass.Moments
-------------

Output Added:
-------------
Name:       BasicMeasures
Label:      Basic Measures of Location and Variability
Template:   base.univariate.Measures
Path:       Univariate.RevenueFirstClass.BasicMeasures
-------------

Output Added:
-------------
Name:       TestsForLocation
Label:      Tests For Location
Template:   base.univariate.Location
Path:       Univariate.RevenueFirstClass.TestsForLocation
-------------

Output Added:
-------------
Name:       Quantiles
Label:      Quantiles
Template:   base.univariate.Quantiles
Path:       Univariate.RevenueFirstClass.Quantiles
-------------

Output Added:
-------------
Name:       ExtremeObs
Label:      Extreme Observations
Template:   base.univariate.ExtObs
Path:       Univariate.RevenueFirstClass.ExtremeObs
-------------
NOTE: There were 36 observations read from the data set
      IA.MONTHLYSUMMARY1997_1999.
NOTE: PROCEDURE UNIVARIATE used:
      real time           1.20 seconds
      cpu time            0.15 seconds
```

## Creating Output SAS Data Sets Using ODS

With ODS, you can create an output table containing **every** statistic in **every** report of **every** procedure by using the ODS OUTPUT statement.

General form of the ODS OUTPUT statement:

> **ODS OUTPUT**
> *output-object-specification = SAS-table;*

22

You can specify an output object as a

- full path or partial path
- label
- label path or partial label path
- mixture of labels and paths.

For example, when you submit the following program, you can refer to the MOMENTS object as

- Univariate.RevenueFirstClass.moments
- RevenueFirstClass.moments
- Moments.

```
proc univariate data = ia.MonthlySummary1997_1999;
   var RevenueFirstClass;
   title 'Objects from PROC UNIVARIATE';
run;
```

If you want to create output data sets from multiple procedure steps, by default, you must repeat the ODS OUTPUT statement.

The ODS OUTPUT statement is in effect only for the procedure immediately following it. SAS automatically clears the ODS OUTPUT object-list after a RUN statement, whether implicit or explicit, or after a QUIT statement.

SAS does not create an ODS output table unless you use the ODS OUTPUT statement.

The PRINT procedure and the REPORT procedure do not create an output table using ODS OUTPUT.

To create an output table using ODS with procedures such as MEANS, do **not** use the NOPRINT option. The NOPRINT option prevents SAS from producing a report, thus there is no output object produced. Instead, to prevent the report from being sent to the Output window, use

```
ODS listing close;
```

## Creating Data Sets Using ODS

c05s2d3

```
ods output basicmeasures = work.statistics
           Extremeobs = work.extremeobs;

proc univariate data = ia.MonthlySummary1997_1999;
   var RevenueFirstClass;
run;

proc print data = work.statistics;
   title  'The statistics from the BasicMeasures object';
   title2 'of PROC UNIVARIATE';
run;
```

Output from the PROC PRINT

```
             The statistics from the BasicMeasures object
                          of PROC UNIVARIATE

                              Loc
Obs        VarName          Measure  LocValue  VarMeasure               VarValue

  1   RevenueFirstClass  Mean     71154621  Std Deviation           12734798
  2   RevenueFirstClass  Median   71136554  Variance              1.62175E14
  3   RevenueFirstClass  Mode            .  Range                   62689977
  4   RevenueFirstClass                  _  Interquartile Range     22488256
```

BasicMeasures report from PROC UNIVARIATE

```
                       The UNIVARIATE Procedure
                    Variable:  RevenueFirstClass

                      Basic Statistical Measures

         Location                       Variability

      Mean      71154621      Std Deviation             12734798
      Median    71136554      Variance                1.62175E14
      Mode             .      Range                     62689977
                              Interquartile Range       22488256
```

```
proc print data = work.extremeobs;
   title  'The statistics from the ExtremeObs object';
   title2 'of PROC UNIVARIATE';
run;
```

Output from PROC PRINT

```
                The statistics from the ExtremeObs object
                           of PROC UNIVARIATE

                                                                    High
Obs         VarName                 Low    LowObs          High      Obs

 1      RevenueFirstClass      51136353         1      83811034       30
 2      RevenueFirstClass      52867177         4      83816720       21
 3      RevenueFirstClass      56626819        31      83864006        9
 4      RevenueFirstClass      56702750        25      83864513       15
 5      RevenueFirstClass      56741721        16     113826330       10
```

ExtremeObs report from PROC UNIVARIATE

```
                          Extreme Observations

              ------Lowest------          ------Highest------

                  Value      Obs               Value       Obs

               51136353        1            83811034        30
               52867177        4            83816720        21
               56626819       31            83864006         9
               56702750       25            83864513        15
               56741721       16           113826330        10
```

## Reference Information

Some procedures can create multiple output objects with the same output object name.

You can use the ODS OUTPUT statement to

- create one table containing information from all occurrences of the output object name (default)
- create a separate table for each occurrence of the output object name using the MATCH_ALL option.

Multiple output objects with the same output object name are created when you

- use BY-group processing
- perform the same analysis or report on multiple variables.

General form of the ODS OUTPUT statement with the MATCH_ALL option:

> **ODS OUTPUT** *output-object*(MATCH_ALL) =
> *SAS-table;*

If you are creating multiple tables with the MATCH_ALL option, ODS appends digits to the table name specified in the ODS OUTPUT statement.

The multiple SAS tables produced are named

*SAS-table*

*SAS-table1*

*SAS-table2*

...*SAS-tablen*

Example of Naming Multiple Tables with the MATCH_ALL Option

```
ods output extremeobs(match_all) =
           work.test;

proc univariate data=airline.SalesData2000;
   var RevenueFirstClass RevenueBusiness
       RevenueEconomy;
run;
```

The SAS output tables:

| | |
|---|---|
| WORK.TEST | is the name of the ExtremeObs table for RevenueFirstClass. |
| WORK.TEST1 | is the name of the ExtremeObs table for RevenueBusiness. |
| WORK.TEST2 | is the name of the ExtremeObs table for RevenueEconomy. |

✎ The columns present in the first output object with the given name determine the columns in the output table if you create only one table.

Example 1:

```
ods output quantiles = work.statistics;

proc univariate data = ia.SalesData2000;
   var RevenueFirstClass RevenueBusiness RevenueEconomy;
run;


proc print data = work.statistics;
   title 'The Quantiles Object of PROC UNIVARIATE';
   title2 'Data for RevenueFirstClass RevenueBusiness
           RevenueEconomy';
run;
```

✎ The data for all analysis variables are in the same data set.

Output

The Quantiles Object of PROC UNIVARIATE
Data for RevenueFirstClass RevenueBusiness RevenueEconomy

| Obs | VarName | Quantile | Estimate |
|---|---|---|---|
| 1 | RevenueFirstClass | 100% Max | 45752 |
| 2 | RevenueFirstClass | 99% | 36091 |
| 3 | RevenueFirstClass | 95% | 20800 |
| 4 | RevenueFirstClass | 90% | 16346 |
| 5 | RevenueFirstClass | 75% Q3 | 4428 |
| 6 | RevenueFirstClass | 50% Median | 3157 |
| 7 | RevenueFirstClass | 25% Q1 | 2060 |
| 8 | RevenueFirstClass | 10% | 1170 |
| 9 | RevenueFirstClass | 5% | 1001 |
| 10 | RevenueFirstClass | 1% | 704 |
| 11 | RevenueFirstClass | 0% Min | 640 |
| 12 | RevenueBusiness | 100% Max | 91896 |
| 13 | RevenueBusiness | 99% | 85332 |
| 14 | RevenueBusiness | 95% | 49198 |
| 15 | RevenueBusiness | 90% | 45150 |
| 16 | RevenueBusiness | 75% Q3 | 38180 |
| 17 | RevenueBusiness | 50% Median | 26696 |
| 18 | RevenueBusiness | 25% Q1 | 21164 |
| 19 | RevenueBusiness | 10% | 18278 |
| 20 | RevenueBusiness | 5% | 16872 |
| 21 | RevenueBusiness | 1% | 16152 |
| 22 | RevenueBusiness | 0% Min | 15479 |
| 23 | RevenueEconomy | 100% Max | 141705 |
| 24 | RevenueEconomy | 99% | 118252 |
| 25 | RevenueEconomy | 95% | 74910 |
| 26 | RevenueEconomy | 90% | 62016 |
| 27 | RevenueEconomy | 75% Q3 | 15252 |
| 28 | RevenueEconomy | 50% Median | 10560 |
| 29 | RevenueEconomy | 25% Q1 | 6480 |
| 30 | RevenueEconomy | 10% | 3510 |
| 31 | RevenueEconomy | 5% | 2987 |
| 32 | RevenueEconomy | 1% | 2436 |
| 33 | RevenueEconomy | 0% Min | 2184 |

Example 2

```
ods output quantiles(match_all) = work.stats;

proc univariate data = ia.SalesData2000;
   var RevenueFirstClass RevenueBusiness RevenueEconomy;
run;
```

The data for each analysis variable are in the separate data sets.

```
proc print data = work.stats;
   title 'The Quantiles Object of PROC UNIVARIATE';
   title2 'Data for RevenueFirstClass';
run;
```

Output

The Quantiles Object of PROC UNIVARIATE
Data for RevenueFirstClass

| Obs | VarName | Quantile | Estimate |
|---|---|---|---|
| 1 | RevenueFirstClass | 100% Max | 45752 |
| 2 | RevenueFirstClass | 99% | 36091 |
| 3 | RevenueFirstClass | 95% | 20800 |
| 4 | RevenueFirstClass | 90% | 16346 |
| 5 | RevenueFirstClass | 75% Q3 | 4428 |
| 6 | RevenueFirstClass | 50% Median | 3157 |
| 7 | RevenueFirstClass | 25% Q1 | 2060 |
| 8 | RevenueFirstClass | 10% | 1170 |
| 9 | RevenueFirstClass | 5% | 1001 |
| 10 | RevenueFirstClass | 1% | 704 |
| 11 | RevenueFirstClass | 0% Min | 640 |

```
proc print data = work.stats1;
   title 'The Quantiles Object of PROC UNIVARIATE';
   title2 'Data for RevenueBusiness';
run;
```

Output

```
              The Quantiles Object of PROC UNIVARIATE
                      Data for RevenueBusiness

        Obs          VarName           Quantile       Estimate

          1     RevenueBusiness    100% Max          91896
          2     RevenueBusiness    99%               85332
          3     RevenueBusiness    95%               49198
          4     RevenueBusiness    90%               45150
          5     RevenueBusiness    75% Q3            38180
          6     RevenueBusiness    50% Median        26696
          7     RevenueBusiness    25% Q1            21164
          8     RevenueBusiness    10%               18278
          9     RevenueBusiness    5%                16872
         10     RevenueBusiness    1%                16152
         11     RevenueBusiness    0% Min            15479
```

```
proc print data = work.stats2;
   title 'The Quantiles Object of PROC UNIVARIATE';
   title2 'Data for RevenueEconomy';
run;
```

Output

```
              The Quantiles Object of PROC UNIVARIATE
                      Data for RevenueEconomy

        Obs         VarName          Quantile       Estimate

          1     RevenueEconomy    100% Max          141705
          2     RevenueEconomy    99%               118252
          3     RevenueEconomy    95%                74910
          4     RevenueEconomy    90%                62016
          5     RevenueEconomy    75% Q3             15252
          6     RevenueEconomy    50% Median         10560
          7     RevenueEconomy    25% Q1              6480
          8     RevenueEconomy    10%                 3510
          9     RevenueEconomy    5%                  2987
         10     RevenueEconomy    1%                  2436
         11     RevenueEconomy    0% Min              2184
```

The OUTPUT destination is automatically cleared after a RUN or QUIT statement. You can use the PERSIST= option to capture tables over step boundaries.

| | |
|---|---|
| PERSIST=RUN | maintains specified selections between RUN groups within a specific procedure. |
| PERSIST=PROC | maintains specified selections between procedures. |

The PERSIST=RUN and the MATCH_ALL options can both be used.

When you use PERSIST=PROC, you

- must use the MATCH_ALL option
- can use the CLEAR option on the ODS OUTPUT statement to clear the list of output destinations.

## Exercises

1. Using ODS and PROC MEANS, create a SAS data set named ia.Mean that contains the overall average employee contribution stored in IA.Rotate that was created in a previous exercise.

    **a.** Use the ODS TRACE statement to determine the name of the output objects.

    **b.** Use the MEAN option on the PROC MEANS statement to limit the output to the mean statistic.

# 5.3 Combining Summary and Detail Data in the DATA Step

## Objectives

- Use ODS to create a summary data set containing a sum statistic.
- Combine the summary data with the detail data.
- Calculate a percentage.
- Create the summary data, combine it with the detail data, and calculate percentages in one DATA step.

30

...

## Business Scenario

We can

- use PROC MEANS with the Output Delivery System to create the summary statistic
- combine the summary information with the detail rows
- calculate the percentages.

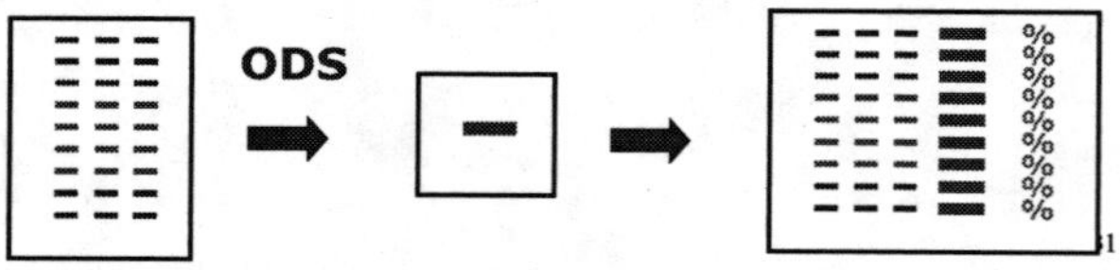


31

## Business Scenario

First we need to create the summary data.

IA.Summary

| Revenue Cargo_Sum |
|---|
| 8,593,432,002.4 |

32

## Business Scenario

Then we need to combine the summary data with the detail data so that we can calculate percentages.

Resulting SAS data set

| Obs | RevenueCargo | Flight Month | Percent Revenue |
|---|---|---|---|
| 1 | $171,520,869.10 | JAN1997 | 0.019960 |
| 2 | $238,786,807.60 | JAN1998 | 0.027787 |
| 3 | $280,350,393.00 | JAN1999 | 0.032624 |
| 4 | $177,671,530.40 | FEB1997 | 0.020675 |

33

## Organize the Tasks

- **Create a summary data set.**
- **Combine the summary data set with the detail data set and create percentages using two different techniques.**
- Compare the two resulting SAS data sets.
- Lookup the target revenues.

34

## Combining the Summary Data with the Detail Data

You can use multiple SET statements to combine observations from several SAS data sets.

When you use multiple SET statements

- processing stops when SAS encounters the end-of-file marker on any data set
- the variables in the PDV are not reinitialized when a second SET statement is executed.

35

## Combining the Summary Data with the Detail Data

```
ods output summary = work.summary;

proc means data = ia.MonthlySummary1997_1999 sum;
   var RevenueCargo;
run;

data ia.percentages;
   if _n_ = 1 then set ia.summary(keep = RevenueCargo_sum);
   set ia.MonthlySummary1997_1999
                    (keep = FlightMonth RevenueCargo);
   PercentRevenue = RevenueCargo / RevenueCargo_sum;
run;
```

36

## Using _N_

During execution of a DATA step, the automatic variable **_N_**

- is initially set to 1
- is incremented by 1 as the DATA step loops past the DATA statement
- is automatically dropped from the data set created
- can be used in the DATA step to control when statement are executed.

37

## Compilation

**Ia.Summary**

| Revenue Cargo_Sum |
|---|
| 8,593,432,002.4 |

**ia.MonthlySummary1997_1999**

| Flight Month | RevenueCargo |
|---|---|
| JAN1997 | 171520869.10 |
| JAN1998 | 238786807.60 |
| JAN1999 | 280350393.00 |
| FEB1997 | 177671530.40 |

```
data ia.percentages;
   if _n_ = 1 then set ia.summary(keep = RevenueCargo_sum);
   set ia.MonthlySummary1997_1999
                  (keep = FlightMonth RevenueCargo);
   PercentRevenue = RevenueCargo / RevenueCargo_sum;
run;
```

**PDV**

| _N_ | Revenue Cargo_sum | Flight Month | Revenue Cargo | Percent Revenue |
|---|---|---|---|---|
| | | | | |

38

## Execution

...

**Ia.Summary**

| Revenue Cargo_Sum |
|---|
| 8,593,432,002.4 |

**ia.MonthlySummary1997_1999**

| Flight Month | RevenueCargo |
|---|---|
| JAN1997 | 171520869.10 |
| JAN1998 | 238786807.60 |
| JAN1999 | 280350393.00 |
| FEB1997 | 177671530.40 |

```
data ia.percentages;
   if _n_ = 1 then set ia.summary(keep = RevenueCargo_sum);
   set ia.MonthlySummary1997_1999
                  (keep = FlightMonth RevenueCargo);
   PercentRevenue = RevenueCargo / RevenueCargo_sum;
run;
```

T

**PDV**

| _N_ | Revenue Cargo_sum | Flight Month | Revenue Cargo | Percent Revenue |
|---|---|---|---|---|
| 1 | . | | . | . |

39

## Execution

...

**Ia.Summary**

| Revenue Cargo_Sum |
|---|
| 8,593,432,002.4 |

**ia.MonthlySummary1997_1999**

| Flight Month | RevenueCargo |
|---|---|
| JAN1997 | 171520869.10 |
| JAN1998 | 238786807.60 |
| JAN1999 | 280350393.00 |
| FEB1997 | 177671530.40 |

```
data ia.percentages;
   if _n_ = 1 then set ia.summary(keep = RevenueCargo_sum);
   set ia.MonthlySummary1997_1999
                  (keep = FlightMonth RevenueCargo);
   PercentRevenue = RevenueCargo / RevenueCargo_sum;
run;
```

**PDV**

| _N_ | Revenue Cargo_sum | Flight Month | Revenue Cargo | Percent Revenue |
|---|---|---|---|---|
| 1 | 8593432002.4 | | . | . |

40

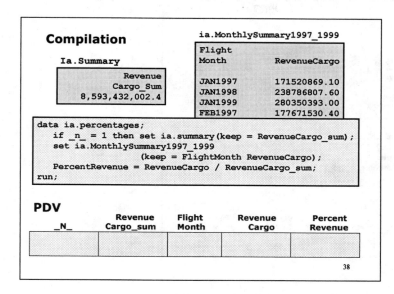

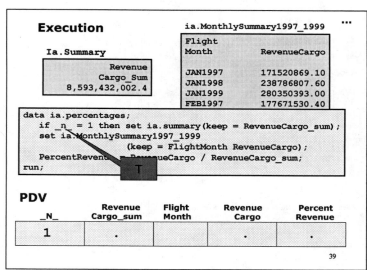

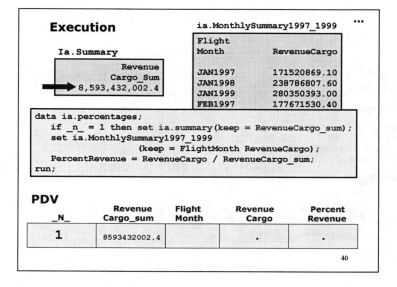

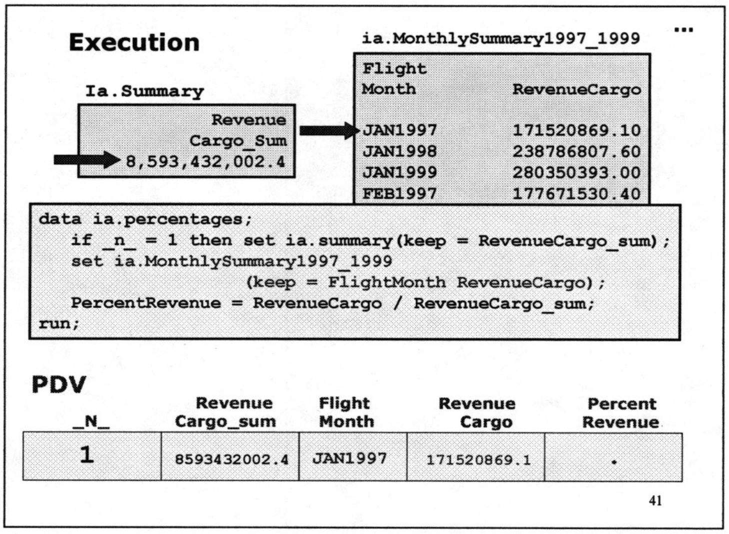
Execution
ia.MonthlySummary1997_1999
Ia.Summary
Revenue
Cargo_Sum
8,593,432,002.4
Flight
Month RevenueCargo
JAN1997 171520869.10
JAN1998 238786807.60
JAN1999 280350393.00
FEB1997 177671530.40
data ia.percentages;
if _n_ = 1 then set ia.summary(keep = RevenueCargo_sum);
set ia.MonthlySummary1997_1999
(keep = FlightMonth RevenueCargo);
PercentRevenue = RevenueCargo / RevenueCargo_sum;
run;
PDV
_N_ | Revenue Cargo_sum | Flight Month | Revenue Cargo | Percent Revenue
1 | 8593432002.4 | JAN1997 | 171520869.1 | .
41

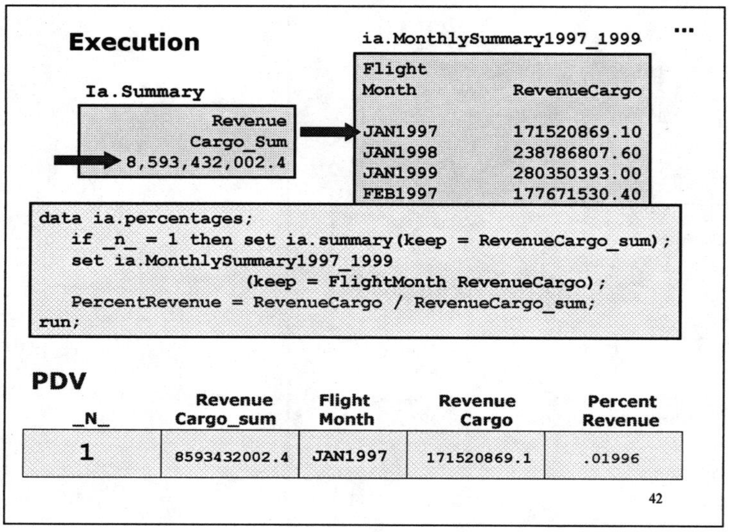
Execution
ia.MonthlySummary1997_1999
Ia.Summary
Revenue
Cargo_Sum
8,593,432,002.4
Flight
Month RevenueCargo
JAN1997 171520869.10
JAN1998 238786807.60
JAN1999 280350393.00
FEB1997 177671530.40
data ia.percentages;
if _n_ = 1 then set ia.summary(keep = RevenueCargo_sum);
set ia.MonthlySummary1997_1999
(keep = FlightMonth RevenueCargo);
PercentRevenue = RevenueCargo / RevenueCargo_sum;
run;
PDV
_N_ | Revenue Cargo_sum | Flight Month | Revenue Cargo | Percent Revenue
1 | 8593432002.4 | JAN1997 | 171520869.1 | .01996
42

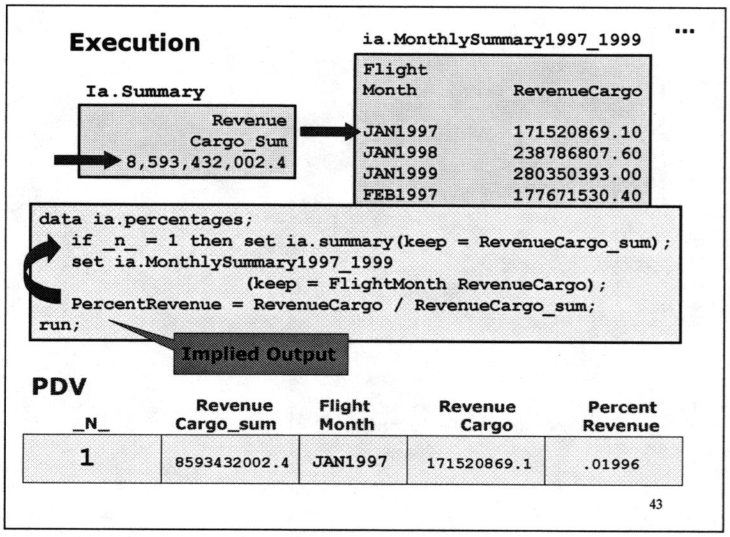
Execution
ia.MonthlySummary1997_1999
Ia.Summary
Revenue
Cargo_Sum
8,593,432,002.4
Flight
Month RevenueCargo
JAN1997 171520869.10
JAN1998 238786807.60
JAN1999 280350393.00
FEB1997 177671530.40
data ia.percentages;
if _n_ = 1 then set ia.summary(keep = RevenueCargo_sum);
set ia.MonthlySummary1997_1999
(keep = FlightMonth RevenueCargo);
PercentRevenue = RevenueCargo / RevenueCargo_sum;
run;
Implied Output
PDV
_N_ | Revenue Cargo_sum | Flight Month | Revenue Cargo | Percent Revenue
1 | 8593432002.4 | JAN1997 | 171520869.1 | .01996
43

**Execution** ...

Ia.Summary

| Revenue Cargo_Sum |
|---|
| 8,593,432,002.4 |

ia.MonthlySummary1997_1999

| Flight Month | RevenueCargo |
|---|---|
| JAN1997 | 171520869.10 |
| JAN1998 | 238786807.60 |
| JAN1999 | 280350393.00 |
| FEB1997 | 177671530.40 |

```
data ia.percentages;
   if _n_ = 1 then set ia.summary(keep = RevenueCargo_sum);
   set ia.MonthlySummary1997_1999
              (keep = FlightMonth RevenueCargo);
   Percent   F   e = RevenueCargo / RevenueCargo_sum;
run;
```

**PDV**

| _N_ | Revenue Cargo_sum | Flight Month | Revenue Cargo | Percent Revenue |
|---|---|---|---|---|
| 2 | 8593432002.4 | JAN1997 | 171520869.1 | . |

44

**Execution** ...

Ia.Summary

| Revenue Cargo_Sum |
|---|
| 8,593,432,002.4 |

ia.MonthlySummary1997_1999

| Flight Month | RevenueCargo |
|---|---|
| JAN1997 | 171520869.10 |
| JAN1998 | 238786807.60 |
| JAN1999 | 280350393.00 |
| FEB1997 | 177671530.40 |

```
data ia.percentages;
   if _n_ = 1 then set ia.summary(keep = RevenueCargo_sum);
   set ia.MonthlySummary1997_1999
              (keep = FlightMonth RevenueCargo);
   PercentRevenue = RevenueCargo / RevenueCargo_sum;
run;
```

**PDV**

| _N_ | Revenue Cargo_sum | Flight Month | Revenue Cargo | Percent Revenue |
|---|---|---|---|---|
| 2 | 8593432002.4 | JAN1998 | 238786869.1 | . |

45

**Execution** ...

Ia.Summary

| Revenue Cargo_Sum |
|---|
| 8,593,432,002.4 |

ia.MonthlySummary1997_1999

| Flight Month | RevenueCargo |
|---|---|
| JAN1997 | 171520869.10 |
| JAN1998 | 238786807.60 |
| JAN1999 | 280350393.00 |
| FEB1997 | 177671530.40 |

```
data ia.percentages;
   if _n_ = 1 then set ia.summary(keep = RevenueCargo_sum);
   set ia.MonthlySummary1997_1999
              (keep = FlightMonth RevenueCargo);
   PercentRevenue = RevenueCargo / RevenueCargo_sum;
run;
```

**PDV**

| _N_ | Revenue Cargo_sum | Flight Month | Revenue Cargo | Percent Revenue |
|---|---|---|---|---|
| 2 | 8593432002.4 | JAN1998 | 238786869.1 | .027787 |

46

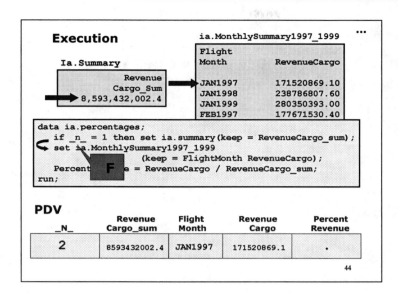

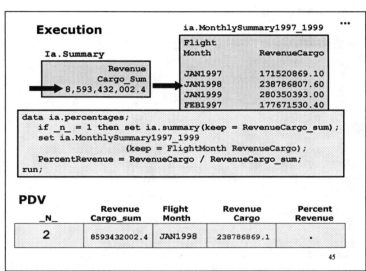

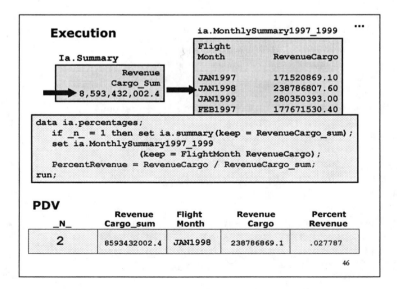

## Combining a Summary Data Set with a Detail Data Set

c05s3d1

Program

```
ods trace on;

proc means data = ia.MonthlySummary1997_1999;
   var RevenueCargo;
run;

ods trace off;


ods output summary = work.summary;

proc means data = ia.MonthlySummary1997_1999 sum;
   var RevenueCargo;
run;


data ia.percentages;
   if _n_ = 1 then set work.summary
                        (keep = RevenueCargo_sum);
   set ia.MonthlySummary1997_1999
                   (keep = FlightMonth RevenueCargo);
   PercentRevenue = RevenueCargo / RevenueCargo_sum;
run;

proc print data = ia.percentages(obs = 10);
   title 'Summary and Detailed Data Combined Using';
   title2 'ODS to Create the Summary';
run;
```

Output

Summary and Detailed Data Combined Using
ODS to Create the Summary

| Obs | Revenue Cargo_Sum | Flight Month | RevenueCargo | Percent Revenue |
|---|---|---|---|---|
| 1 | 8593432002.4 | JAN1997 | $171,520,869.10 | 0.019960 |
| 2 | 8593432002.4 | JAN1998 | $238,786,807.60 | 0.027787 |
| 3 | 8593432002.4 | JAN1999 | $280,350,393.00 | 0.032624 |
| 4 | 8593432002.4 | FEB1997 | $177,671,530.40 | 0.020675 |
| 5 | 8593432002.4 | FEB1998 | $215,959,695.50 | 0.025131 |
| 6 | 8593432002.4 | FEB1999 | $253,999,924.00 | 0.029557 |
| 7 | 8593432002.4 | MAR1997 | $196,591,378.20 | 0.022877 |
| 8 | 8593432002.4 | MAR1998 | $239,056,025.55 | 0.027818 |
| 9 | 8593432002.4 | MAR1999 | $281,433,310.00 | 0.032750 |
| 10 | 8593432002.4 | APR1997 | $380,804,120.20 | 0.044313 |

## Combining Detail and Summary in the DATA Step

To create the summary statistic in the DATA step and combine it with the detail data, we need to

- read the data once and calculate the summary statistic
- re-read the data to combine the summary statistic with the detail data and calculate the percentages.

48

## Combining Detail and Summary in the DATA Step

```
data ia.percentages_1(drop = TotalRevenue);
   if _n_ = 1 then do until(last);
      set ia.MonthlySummary1997_1999(keep = RevenueCargo)
                        end = last;
      TotalRevenue + RevenueCargo;
   end;
   set ia.MonthlySummary1997_1999
                 (keep = FlightMonth RevenueCargo);
   PercentRevenue = RevenueCargo / TotalRevenue;
run;
```

49

## Sum Statement Syntax

```
Variable + expression;
```

*variable* ASSUMED RETAINED

specifies the name of the accumulator variable, which contains a numeric value.

*expression*

is any SAS expression.

50

You can use the SUM statement to

- accumulate totals
- retain the accumulator variable
- initialize the accumulator variable to 0
- ignore missing values.

**Compilation**

ia.MonthlySummary1997_1999

| Flight Month | RevenueCargo |
|---|---|
| JAN1997 | 171520869.10 |
| JAN1998 | 238786807.60 |
| JAN1999 | 280350393.00 |

```
data ia.percentages_1(drop = TotalRevenue);
   if _n_ = 1 then do until(last);
      set ia.MonthlySummary1997_1999(keep = RevenueCargo)
                                end = last;
      TotalRevenue + RevenueCargo;
   end;
   set ia.MonthlySummary1997_1999
                (keep = FlightMonth RevenueCargo);
   PercentRevenue = RevenueCargo / TotalRevenue;
run;
```

**PDV**

| D _N_ | D last | Revenue Cargo | D Total Revenue | Flight Month | Percent Revenue |
|---|---|---|---|---|---|
| | | | | | |

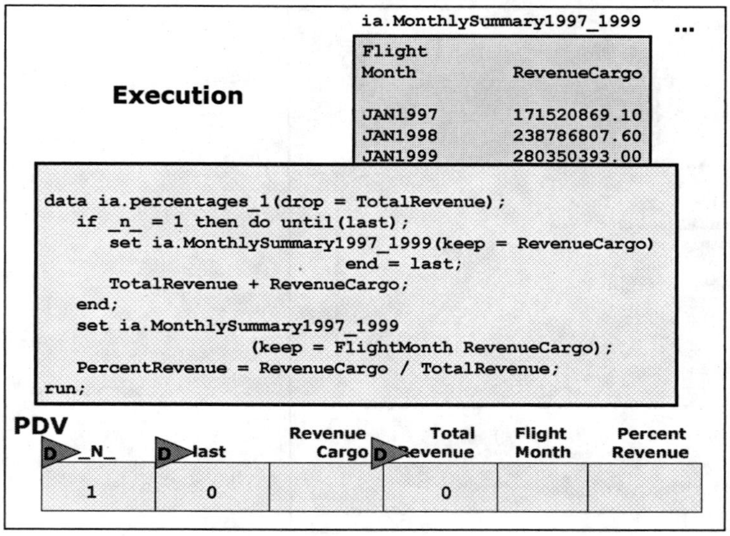
ia.MonthlySummary1997_1999
...
Execution
Flight Month RevenueCargo
JAN1997 171520869.10
JAN1998 238786807.60
JAN1999 280350393.00
data ia.percentages_1(drop = TotalRevenue);
if _n_ = 1 then do until(last);
set ia.MonthlySummary1997_1999(keep = RevenueCargo)
end = last;
TotalRevenue + RevenueCargo;
end;
set ia.MonthlySummary1997_1999
(keep = FlightMonth RevenueCargo);
PercentRevenue = RevenueCargo / TotalRevenue;
run;
PDV
D _N_
D last
Revenue Cargo
D Total Revenue
Flight Month
Percent Revenue
1
0
0

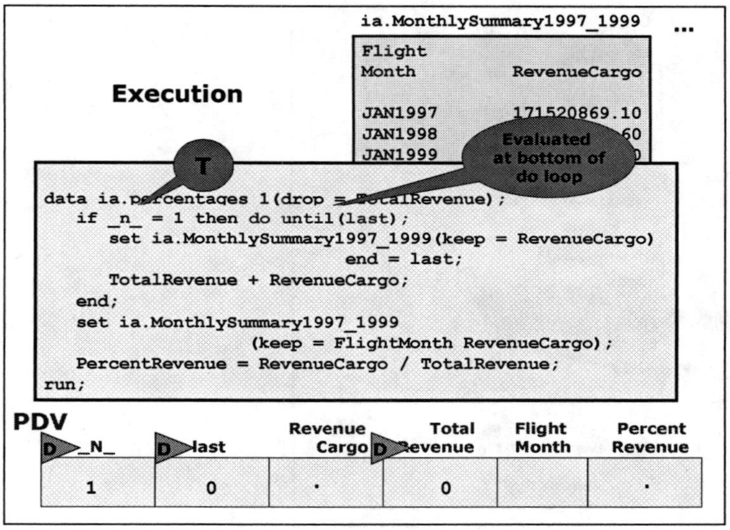
ia.MonthlySummary1997_1999
...
Execution
Flight Month RevenueCargo
JAN1997 171520869.10
JAN1998
JAN1999
T
Evaluated at bottom of do loop
data ia.percentages_1(drop = TotalRevenue);
if _n_ = 1 then do until(last);
set ia.MonthlySummary1997_1999(keep = RevenueCargo)
end = last;
TotalRevenue + RevenueCargo;
end;
set ia.MonthlySummary1997_1999
(keep = FlightMonth RevenueCargo);
PercentRevenue = RevenueCargo / TotalRevenue;
run;
PDV
D _N_
D last
Revenue Cargo
D Total Revenue
Flight Month
Percent Revenue
1
0
.
0
.

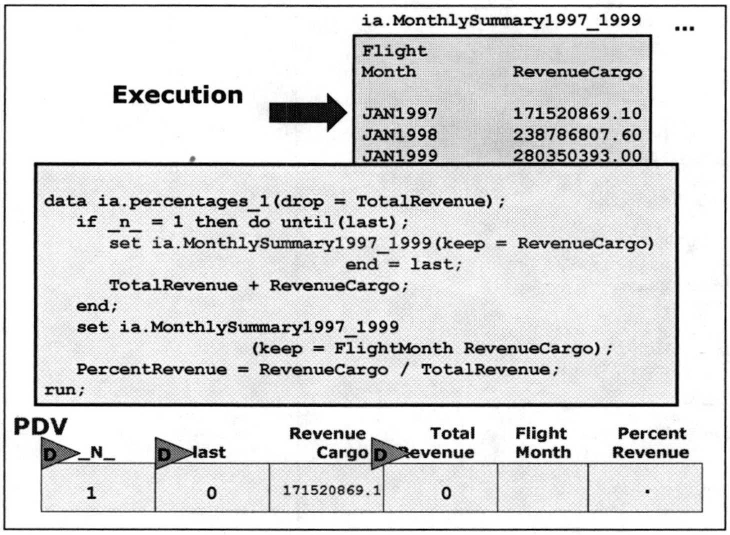
ia.MonthlySummary1997_1999
...
Execution
Flight Month RevenueCargo
JAN1997 171520869.10
JAN1998 238786807.60
JAN1999 280350393.00
data ia.percentages_1(drop = TotalRevenue);
if _n_ = 1 then do until(last);
set ia.MonthlySummary1997_1999(keep = RevenueCargo)
end = last;
TotalRevenue + RevenueCargo;
end;
set ia.MonthlySummary1997_1999
(keep = FlightMonth RevenueCargo);
PercentRevenue = RevenueCargo / TotalRevenue;
run;
PDV
D _N_
D last
Revenue Cargo
D Total Revenue
Flight Month
Percent Revenue
1
0
171520869.1
0
.

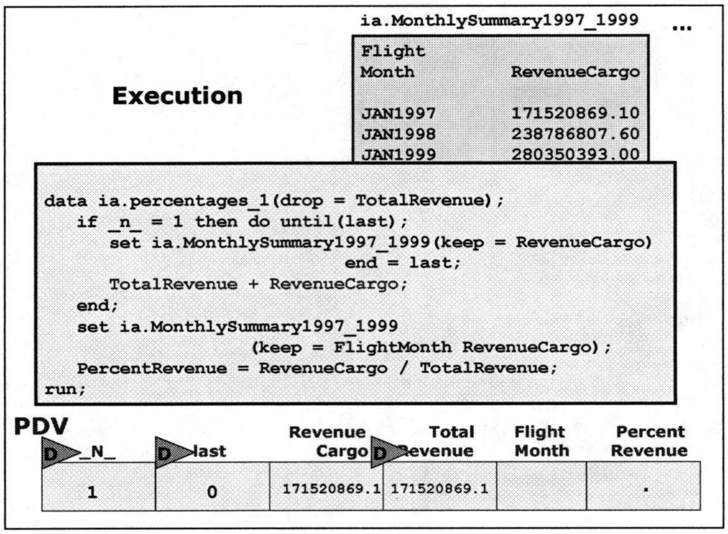
Execution
ia.MonthlySummary1997_1999
Flight Month RevenueCargo
JAN1997 171520869.10
JAN1998 238786807.60
JAN1999 280350393.00
data ia.percentages_1(drop = TotalRevenue);
if _n_ = 1 then do until(last);
set ia.MonthlySummary1997_1999(keep = RevenueCargo)
end = last;
TotalRevenue + RevenueCargo;
end;
set ia.MonthlySummary1997_1999
(keep = FlightMonth RevenueCargo);
PercentRevenue = RevenueCargo / TotalRevenue;
run;
PDV
D _N_
D last
Revenue Cargo
D Total Revenue
Flight Month
Percent Revenue
1
0
171520869.1
171520869.1
.

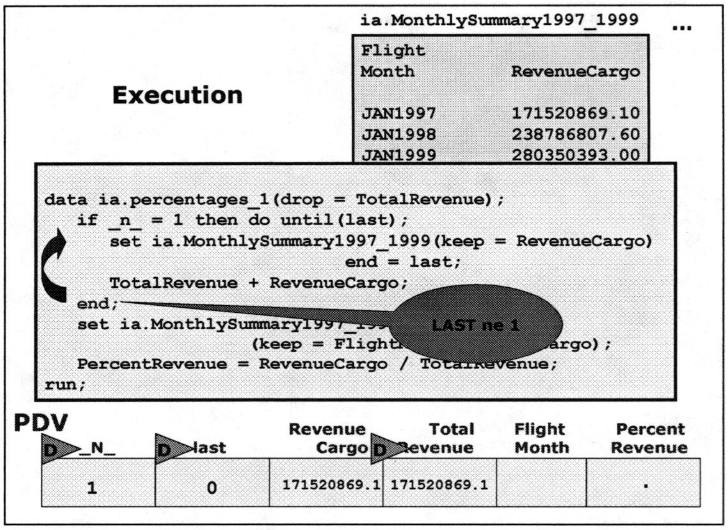
Execution
ia.MonthlySummary1997_1999
Flight Month RevenueCargo
JAN1997 171520869.10
JAN1998 238786807.60
JAN1999 280350393.00
data ia.percentages_1(drop = TotalRevenue);
if _n_ = 1 then do until(last);
set ia.MonthlySummary1997_1999(keep = RevenueCargo)
end = last;
TotalRevenue + RevenueCargo;
end;
LAST ne 1
PercentRevenue = RevenueCargo / TotalRevenue;
run;
PDV
D _N_
D last
Revenue Cargo
D Total Revenue
Flight Month
Percent Revenue
1
0
171520869.1
171520869.1
.

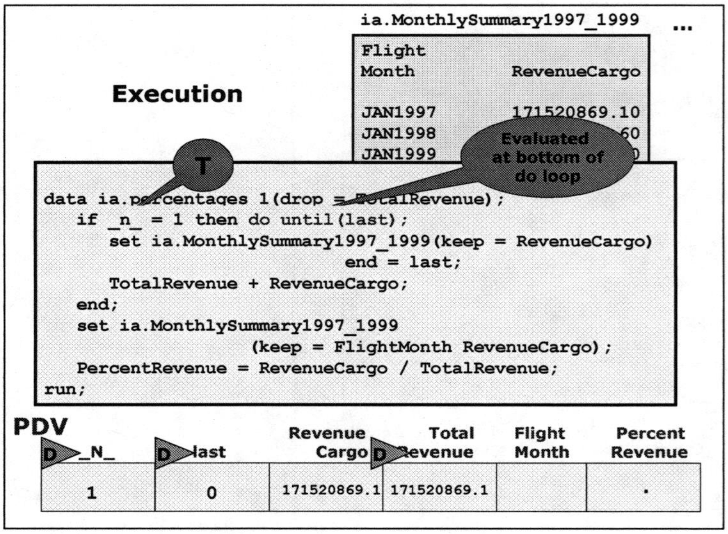
Execution
ia.MonthlySummary1997_1999
Flight Month RevenueCargo
JAN1997 171520869.10
JAN1998
JAN1999
T
Evaluated at bottom of do loop
if _n_ = 1 then do until(last);
set ia.MonthlySummary1997_1999(keep = RevenueCargo)
end = last;
TotalRevenue + RevenueCargo;
end;
set ia.MonthlySummary1997_1999
(keep = FlightMonth RevenueCargo);
PercentRevenue = RevenueCargo / TotalRevenue;
run;
PDV
D _N_
D last
Revenue Cargo
D Total Revenue
Flight Month
Percent Revenue
1
0
171520869.1
171520869.1
.

**Execution**

ia.MonthlySummary1997_1999 ...

| Flight Month | RevenueCargo |
|---|---|
| JAN1997 | 171520869.10 |
| JAN1998 | 238786807.60 |
| JAN1999 | 280350393.00 |

```
data ia.percentages_1(drop = TotalRevenue);
   if _n_ = 1 then do until(last);
      set ia.MonthlySummary1997_1999(keep = RevenueCargo)
                                   end = last;
      TotalRevenue + RevenueCargo;
   end;
   set ia.MonthlySummary1997_1999
                      (keep = FlightMonth RevenueCargo);
   PercentRevenue = RevenueCargo / TotalRevenue;
run;
```

**PDV**

| _N_ | last | Revenue Cargo | Total Revenue | Flight Month | Percent Revenue |
|---|---|---|---|---|---|
| 1 | 0 | 238786807.6 | 171520869.1 | | . |

**Execution**

ia.MonthlySummary1997_1999 ...

| Flight Month | RevenueCargo |
|---|---|
| JAN1997 | 171520869.10 |
| JAN1998 | 238786807.60 |
| JAN1999 | 280350393.00 |

```
data ia.percentages_1(drop = TotalRevenue);
   if _n_ = 1 then do until(last);
      set ia.MonthlySummary1997_1999(keep = RevenueCargo)
                                   end = last;
      TotalRevenue + RevenueCargo;
   end;
   set ia.MonthlySummary1997_1999
                      (keep = FlightMonth RevenueCargo);
   PercentRevenue = RevenueCargo / TotalRevenue;
run;
```

**PDV**

| _N_ | last | Revenue Cargo | Total Revenue | Flight Month | Percent Revenue |
|---|---|---|---|---|---|
| 1 | 0 | 238786807.6 | 410307676.7 | | . |

**Execution**

ia.MonthlySummary1997_1999 ...

| Flight Month | RevenueCargo |
|---|---|
| JAN1997 | 171520869.10 |
| JAN1998 | 238786807.60 |
| JAN1999 | 280350393.00 |

```
data ia.percentages_1(drop = TotalRevenue);
   if _n_ = 1 then do until(last);
      set ia.MonthlySummary1997_1999(keep = RevenueCargo)
                                   end = last;
      TotalRevenue + RevenueCargo;
   end;
   set ia.MonthlySummary1997_1999
                      (keep = FlightMonth RevenueCargo);
   PercentRevenue = RevenueCargo / TotalRevenue;
run;
```

LAST ne 1

**PDV**

| _N_ | last | Revenue Cargo | Total Revenue | Flight Month | Percent Revenue |
|---|---|---|---|---|---|
| 1 | 0 | 238786807.6 | 410307676.7 | | . |

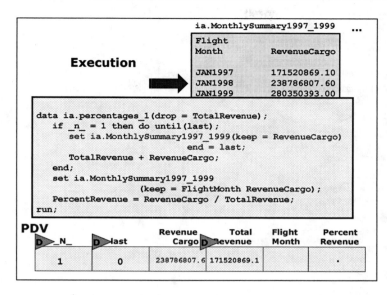

ia.MonthlySummary1997_1999 ...

Exec

Continuing until the last observation ...

```
data ia.percenta
   if _n_ = 1 t          til(last);
      set ia.          ySummary1997_1999(keep = RevenueCargo)
                                   end = last;
      TotalRevenue + RevenueCargo;
   end;
   set ia.MonthlySummary1997_1999
                     (keep = FlightMonth RevenueCargo);
   PercentRevenue = RevenueCargo / TotalRevenue;
run;
```

PDV

| _N_ | last | Revenue Cargo | Total Revenue | Flight Month | Percent Revenue |
|---|---|---|---|---|---|
| 1 | 0 | 238786807.6 | 410307676.7 | | . |

ia.MonthlySummary1997_1999 ...

**Execution**

| Flight Month | RevenueCargo |
|---|---|
| JAN1997 | 171520869.10 |
| JAN1998 | 238786807.60 |
| JAN1999 | 280350393.00 |

```
data ia.percentages_1(drop = TotalRevenue);
   if _n_ = 1 then do until(last);
      set ia.MonthlySummary1997_1999(keep = RevenueCargo)
                                   end = last;
      TotalRevenue + RevenueCargo;
   end;
   set ia.MonthlySummary1997_1999
                     (keep = FlightMonth RevenueCargo);
   PercentRevenue = RevenueCargo / TotalRevenue;
run;
```

PDV

| _N_ | last | Revenue Cargo | Total Revenue | Flight Month | Percent Revenue |
|---|---|---|---|---|---|
| 1 | 1 | 272149940.0 | 8321282062.4 | | . |

ia.MonthlySummary1997_1999 ...

**Execution**

| Flight Month | RevenueCargo |
|---|---|
| JAN1997 | 171520869.10 |
| JAN1998 | 238786807.60 |
| JAN1999 | 280350393.00 |

```
data ia.percentages_1(drop = TotalRevenue);
   if _n_ = 1 then do until(last);
      set ia.MonthlySummary1997_1999(keep = RevenueCargo)
                                   end = last;
      TotalRevenue + RevenueCargo;
   end;
   set ia.MonthlySummary1997_1999
                     (keep = FlightMonth RevenueCargo);
   PercentRevenue = RevenueCargo / TotalRevenue;
run;
```

PDV

| _N_ | last | Revenue Cargo | Total Revenue | Flight Month | Percent Revenue |
|---|---|---|---|---|---|
| 1 | 1 | 272149940.0 | 8593432002.4 | | . |

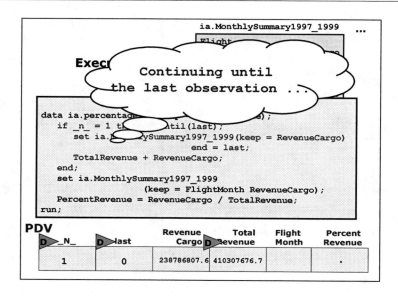

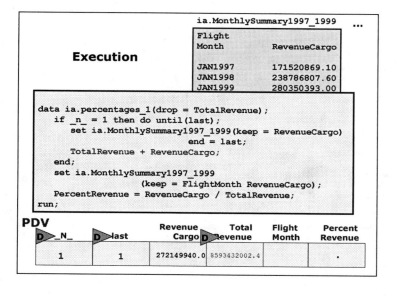

**Execution**

ia.MonthlySummary1997_1999 ...

| Flight Month | RevenueCargo |
|---|---|
| JAN1997 | 171520869.10 |
| JAN1998 | 238786807.60 |
| JAN1999 | 280350393.00 |

```
data ia.percentages_1(drop = TotalRevenue);
   if _n_ = 1 then do until(last);
      set ia.MonthlySummary1997_1999(keep = RevenueCargo)
                          end = last;
      TotalRevenue + RevenueCargo;
   end;
   set ia.MonthlySummary1997_1999
                (keep = FlightMonth RevenueCargo);
   PercentRevenue = RevenueCargo / TotalRevenue;
run;
```

LAST = 1

PDV

| D _N_ | D last | Revenue Cargo | D Total Revenue | Flight Month | Percent Revenue |
|---|---|---|---|---|---|
| 1 | 1 | 272149940.0 | 8593432002.4 | | . |

**Execution**

ia.MonthlySummary1997_1999 ...

| Flight Month | RevenueCargo |
|---|---|
| JAN1997 | 171520869.10 |
| JAN1998 | 238786807.60 |
| JAN1999 | 280350393.00 |

```
data ia.percentages_1(drop = TotalRevenue);
   if _n_ = 1 then do until(last);
      set ia.MonthlySummary1997_1999(keep = RevenueCargo)
                          end = last;
      TotalRevenue + RevenueCargo;
   end;
   set ia.MonthlySummary1997_1999
                (keep = FlightMonth RevenueCargo);
   PercentRevenue = RevenueCargo / TotalRevenue;
run;
```

PDV

| D _N_ | D last | Revenue Cargo | D Total Revenue | Flight Month | Percent Revenue |
|---|---|---|---|---|---|
| 1 | 1 | 171520869.1 | 8593432002.4 | JAN1997 | . |

**Execution**

ia.MonthlySummary1997_1999 ...

| Flight Month | RevenueCargo |
|---|---|
| JAN1997 | 171520869.10 |
| JAN1998 | 238786807.60 |
| JAN1999 | 280350393.00 |

```
data ia.percentages_1(drop = TotalRevenue);
   if _n_ = 1 then do until(last);
      set ia.MonthlySummary1997_1999(keep = RevenueCargo)
                          end = last;
      TotalRevenue + RevenueCargo;
   end;
   set ia.MonthlySummary1997_1999
                (keep = FlightMonth RevenueCargo);
   PercentRevenue = RevenueCargo / TotalRevenue;
run;
```

PDV

| D _N_ | D last | Revenue Cargo | D Total Revenue | Flight Month | Percent Revenue |
|---|---|---|---|---|---|
| 1 | 1 | 171520869.1 | 8593432002.4 | JAN1997 | .019960 |

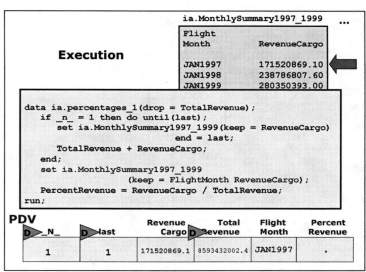

**Execution** ...

ia.MonthlySummary1997_1999

| Flight Month | RevenueCargo |
|---|---|
| JAN1997 | 171520869.10 |
| JAN1998 | 238786807.60 |
| JAN1999 | 280350393.00 |

```
data ia.percentages_1(drop = TotalRevenue);
   if _n_ = 1 then do until(last);
      set ia.MonthlySummary1997_1999(keep = RevenueCargo)
                    end = last;
      TotalRevenue + RevenueCargo;
   end;
   set ia.MonthlySummary1997_1999
                (keep = FlightMonth RevenueCargo);
   PercentRevenue = RevenueCargo / TotalRevenue;
run;
```

Implied Output

PDV

| D _N_ | D last | Revenue Cargo | D Total Revenue | Flight Month | Percent Revenue |
|---|---|---|---|---|---|
| 1 | 1 | 171520869.1 | 8593432002.4 | JAN1997 | .019960 |

**Execution** ...

ia.MonthlySummary1997_1999

| Flight Month | RevenueCargo |
|---|---|
| JAN1997 | 171520869.10 |
| JAN1998 | 238786807.60 |
| JAN1999 | 280350393.00 |

```
data ia.percentages_1(drop = TotalRevenue);
   if _n_ = 1 then do until(last);
      set ia.MonthlySummary1997_1999(keep = RevenueCargo)
                    end = last;
      TotalRevenue + RevenueCargo;
   end;
   set ia.MonthlySummary1997_1999
                (keep = FlightMonth RevenueCargo);
   PercentRevenue = RevenueCargo / TotalRevenue;
run;
```

PDV

| D _N_ | D last | Revenue Cargo | D Total Revenue | Flight Month | Percent Revenue |
|---|---|---|---|---|---|
| 2 | 1 | 171520869.1 | 8593432002.4 | JAN1997 | . |

**Execution** ...

ia.MonthlySummary1997_1999

| Flight Month | RevenueCargo |
|---|---|
| JAN1997 | 171520869.10 |
| JAN1998 | 238786807.60 |
| JAN1999 | 280350393.00 |

F

```
data ia.percentages_1(drop = TotalRevenue);
   if _n_ = 1 then do until(last);
      set ia.MonthlySummary1997_1999(keep = RevenueCargo)
                    end = last;
      TotalRevenue + RevenueCargo;
   end;
   set ia.MonthlySummary1997_1999
                (keep = FlightMonth RevenueCargo);
   PercentRevenue = RevenueCargo / TotalRevenue;
run;
```

PDV

| D _N_ | D last | Revenue Cargo | D Total Revenue | Flight Month | Percent Revenue |
|---|---|---|---|---|---|
| 2 | 1 | 171520869.1 | 8593432002.4 | JAN1997 | . |

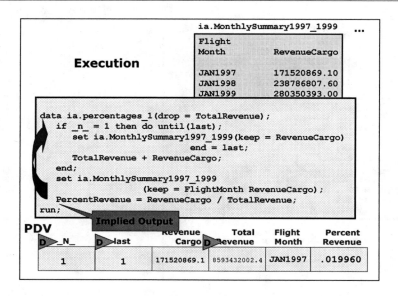

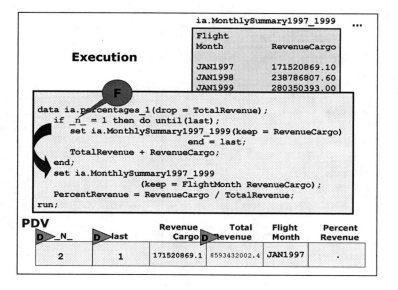

**Execution**

ia.MonthlySummary1997_1999 ...

| Flight Month | RevenueCargo |
|---|---|
| JAN1997 | 171520869.10 |
| JAN1998 | 238786807.60 |
| JAN1999 | 280350393.00 |

```
data ia.percentages_1(drop = TotalRevenue);
   if _n_ = 1 then do until(last);
      set ia.MonthlySummary1997_1999(keep = RevenueCargo)
                            end = last;
      TotalRevenue + RevenueCargo;
   end;
   set ia.MonthlySummary1997_1999
                (keep = FlightMonth RevenueCargo);
   PercentRevenue = RevenueCargo / TotalRevenue;
run;
```

**PDV**

| D _N_ | D last | Revenue Cargo | D Total Revenue | Flight Month | Percent Revenue |
|---|---|---|---|---|---|
| 2 | 1 | 238786807.1 | 8593432002.4 | JAN1998 | . |

**Execution**

ia.MonthlySummary1997_1999 ...

| Flight Month | RevenueCargo |
|---|---|
| JAN1997 | 171520869.10 |
| JAN1998 | 238786807.60 |
| JAN1999 | 280350393.00 |

```
data ia.percentages_1(drop = TotalRevenue);
   if _n_ = 1 then do until(last);
      set ia.MonthlySummary1997_1999(keep = RevenueCargo)
                            end = last;
      TotalRevenue + RevenueCargo;
   end;
   set ia.MonthlySummary1997_1999
                (keep = FlightMonth RevenueCargo);
   PercentRevenue = RevenueCargo / TotalRevenue;
run;
```

**PDV**

| D _N_ | D last | Revenue Cargo | D Total Revenue | Flight Month | Percent Revenue |
|---|---|---|---|---|---|
| 2 | 1 | 238786807.1 | 8593432002.4 | JAN1998 | .027787 |

**Execution**

ia.MonthlySummary1997_1999 ...

| Flight Month | RevenueCargo |
|---|---|
| JAN1997 | 171520869.10 |
| JAN1998 | 238786807.60 |
| JAN1999 | 280350393.00 |

```
data ia.percentages_1(drop = TotalRevenue);
   if _n_ = 1 then do until(last);
      set ia.MonthlySummary1997_1999(keep = RevenueCargo)
                            end = last;
      TotalRevenue + RevenueCargo;
   end;
   set ia.MonthlySummary1997_1999
                (keep = FlightMonth RevenueCargo);
   PercentRevenue = RevenueCargo / TotalRevenue;
run;
```

Implied Output

**PDV**

| D _N_ | D last | Revenue Cargo | D Total Revenue | Flight Month | Percent Revenue |
|---|---|---|---|---|---|
| 2 | 1 | 238786807.1 | 8593432002.4 | JAN1998 | .027787 |

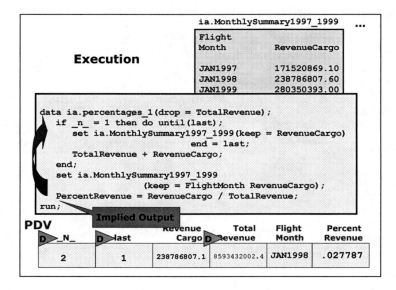

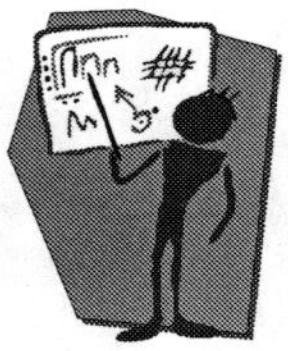


## Reading SAS Data Sets

c05s3d2

Program

```
data ia.percentages_1 ;
   if _n_ = 1 then do until (last);
      set ia.MonthlySummary1997_1999(keep = RevenueCargo)
                             end = last;
      TotalRevenue + RevenueCargo;
   end;
   set ia.MonthlySummary1997_1999
        (keep = FlightMonth RevenueCargo );
   PercentRevenue = RevenueCargo / TotalRevenue;
run;




proc print data = ia.percentages_1(obs = 10);
   title 'Creating Summary Statistics and Percentages';
   title2 'In the DATA Step';
   format PercentRevenue percent8.2
run;
```

Output

```
              Creating Summary Statistics and Percentages
                            In the DATA Step

                                                  Flight      Percent
 Obs       RevenueCargo       TotalRevenue        Month       Revenue

   1    $171,520,869.10      8593432002.4       JAN1997        2.00%
   2    $238,786,807.60      8593432002.4       JAN1998        2.78%
   3    $280,350,393.00      8593432002.4       JAN1999        3.26%
   4    $177,671,530.40      8593432002.4       FEB1997        2.07%
   5    $215,959,695.50      8593432002.4       FEB1998        2.51%
   6    $253,999,924.00      8593432002.4       FEB1999        2.96%
   7    $196,591,378.20      8593432002.4       MAR1997        2.29%
   8    $239,056,025.55      8593432002.4       MAR1998        2.78%
   9    $281,433,310.00      8593432002.4       MAR1999        3.27%
  10    $380,804,120.20      8593432002.4       APR1997        4.43%
```

## Exercises

2. Combine ia.Mean, from the previous exercise, with ia.Emp_Contrib to determine the difference between the overall average contribution and each individual employee contribution.
   - Create a new SAS data set containing the differences named ia.Diffs.
   - Round the difference to the nearest cent.

3. Create a data set named ia.Diffs2 with the same values as ia.Diffs by reading ia.Rotate twice with SET statements.
   - Calculate the overall average employee contribution.
   - Do not output observations from ia.Rotate where the contribution is missing and do not include the observation in the calculation of the mean.
   - Compare the average to each individual employee contribution.

# 5.4 Comparing Two Data Sets

## Objectives

- Compare the data created by two different techniques.

78

## Business Scenario

Now that we have created SAS data sets combining summary and detail data by using two techniques, we need to determine if the techniques produced the same results.

79

## Organize the Tasks

- Create a summary data set.
- Combine the summary data set with the detail data set and create percentages using two different techniques.
- **Compare the two resulting SAS data sets.**
- Lookup the target revenues.

80

## Comparing SAS Data Sets

You can use the COMPARE procedure to compare

- data set attributes of TYPE and LABEL
- variable names to determine common variables
- attributes of common variables
- data values in each observation.

81

By default you get four summary reports:

- data set
- variables
- observation
- values comparison.

## Comparing SAS Data Sets

General syntax for PROC COMPARE:

```
PROC COMPARE DATA = base-data-set
             COMPARE = comparison-data-set
             <options>;
RUN;
```

82

DATA= names the data set to be used as the base data set. If you omit this option, the COMPARE procedure uses the most recently created SAS data set. This option can also be written as BASE=.

COMPARE= names the data set to be used as the comparison data set. If you omit this option, the comparison data set is the same as the DATA= data set, and you must use a WITH statement to specify comparison variables.

### Reference Information

General form for PROC COMPARE:

```
PROC COMPARE DATA = base-data-set
             COMPARE = comparison-data-set
             <options>;
  ID variable-list <notsorted>;
  VAR variable-list;
  WITH variable-list;
RUN;
```

| To Do This | Use This Statement |
|---|---|
| Produce a separate comparison for each BY group | BY |
| Identify variables to use to match observations | ID |
| Restrict the comparison to values of specific variables | VAR |
| Compare variables of different names | WITH and VAR |
| Compare two variables in the same data set | WITH and VAR |

- The VAR statement identifies the variables to be compared.
- Without the VAR statement, PROC COMPARE compares the values of all variables except those on the ID or BY statements.
- The WITH statement is used to compare variables with different names in the BASE and COMPARE data sets.
- You must use a VAR statement when using a WITH statement.
- Variable names on the VAR and WITH statements are used in corresponding order. If the WITH statement variable list is shorter than the VAR statement list, PROC COMPARE assumes the variables in the COMPARE data set have the same names as those in the BASE data set. If the WITH statement variable list is longer than the VAR statement variable list, PROC COMPARE ignores the extra variables.
- If you omit the COMPARE= option, you must use the WITH statement.

## Comparing Data Sets

c05s4d1

Program

```
proc compare data = work.percentages
             compare = work.percentages_1;
   title 'Comparing Two Techniques';
run;
```

Output

```
                          Comparing Two Techniques

                             COMPARE Procedure
           Comparison of WORK.PERCENTAGES with WORK.PERCENTAGES_1
                              (Method=EXACT)

                             Data Set Summary

  Dataset                     Created          Modified  NVar    NObs

  WORK.PERCENTAGES     02JUN00:15:57:09  02JUN00:15:57:09     4      36
  WORK.PERCENTAGES_1   02JUN00:16:03:38  02JUN00:16:03:38     4      36


                             Variables Summary

Number of Variables in Common: 3.
Number of Variables in WORK.PERCENTAGES but not in WORK.PERCENTAGES_1:
1.
Number of Variables in WORK.PERCENTAGES_1 but not in WORK.PERCENTAGES:
1.


                            Observation Summary

                      Observation      Base  Compare

                      First Obs           1        1
                      Last  Obs          36       36

    Number of Observations in Common: 36.
    Total Number of Observations Read from WORK.PERCENTAGES: 36.
    Total Number of Observations Read from WORK.PERCENTAGES_1: 36.

    Number of Observations with Some Compared Variables Unequal: 0.
    Number of Observations with All Compared Variables Equal: 36.

    NOTE: No unequal values were found. All values compared are exactly
          equal.
```

## Exercises

4. Using PROC COMPARE, compare the two permanent SAS data sets Diffs and Diffs2 that were created in previous exercises.

   Compare only the amounts and differences by each employee id number and quarter number. (Hint: Sort both data sets by employee id number and quarter number prior to the comparison.)

# 5.5 Using Arrays for Table Lookups

## Objectives

- Write an ARRAY statement for a multidimensional array.
- Process a multidimensional array.
- Load a multidimensional array from a SAS data set.
- Use a multidimensional array to compare values.

86

## General Business Scenario

International Airlines needs to combine SAS data sets containing

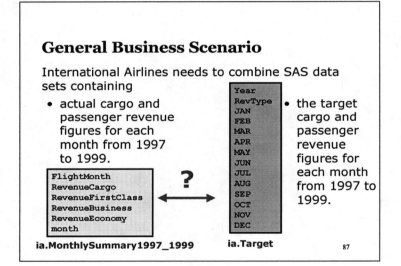

- actual cargo and passenger revenue figures for each month from 1997 to 1999.
- the target cargo and passenger revenue figures for each month from 1997 to 1999.

```
FlightMonth
RevenueCargo
RevenueFirstClass
RevenueBusiness
RevenueEconomy
month
```

**ia.MonthlySummary1997_1999**

?

```
Year
RevType
JAN
FEB
MAR
APR
MAY
JUN
JUL
AUG
SEP
OCT
NOV
DEC
```

**ia.Target**

87

## General Business Scenario

The SAS data sets ia.Target and ia.MonthlySummary1997_1999 cannot be merged because of different data set structures.

However, the data sets have three common factors:

- month
- year
- revenue type.

88

## Organize the Tasks

- Create a summary data set.
- Combine the summary data set with the detail data set and create percentages using two different techniques.
- Compare the two resulting SAS data sets.
- **Lookup the target revenues.**

89

## Using Multidimensional Arrays

When the lookup operation depends on more than one factor, you can use a multidimensional array.

90

In the scenario, the factors that define the table look up are

- year
- month
- revenue type.

## Using Multidimensional Arrays

General form for the multidimensional ARRAY statement:

**ARRAY** *array-name* {...,*rows, cols*} $ *length*
*elements* (*initial values*);

91

## Using Multidimensional Arrays

For example, we know the number of flights in the morning and in the afternoon for each day of a week.

We can use a two dimensional array to calculate the total number of flights for the week.

| AM | PM |
|---|---|
| 18 | 16 |
| 29 | 32 |
| 31 | 35 |
| 45 | 38 |
| 25 | 29 |
| 36 | 30 |
| 27 | 18 |

**406**

92

## Using Multidimensional Arrays

```
array NF{7,2}
        (18,16,29,32,31,35,42,38,25,29,36,30,27,18);
```

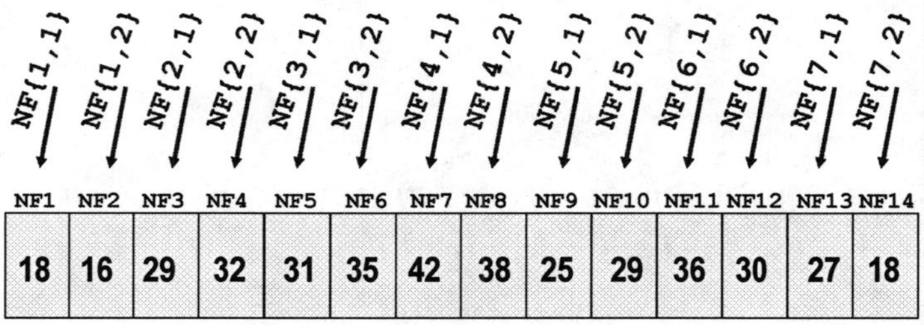


93

When you use a multidimensional array, you

- must supply an index value for each dimension to process a specific array element
- can use a DO loop to process elements in a given dimension
- use nested DO loops to process elements in more than one dimension.

## Using Multidimensional Arrays

If you wanted to know the total number of passengers for the week, you can submit

```
data work.AllWeek (drop = ampm day);
  array NF{7,2} _temporary_
        (18,16,29,32,31,35,42,
         38,25,29,36,30,27,18);
  do ampm = 1 to 2;
     do day = 1 to 7;
        totalpassengers + NF{day,ampm};
     end;
  end;
run;
```

94

The _TEMPORARY_ does not create variables in the data set work.AllWeek from the array NF.

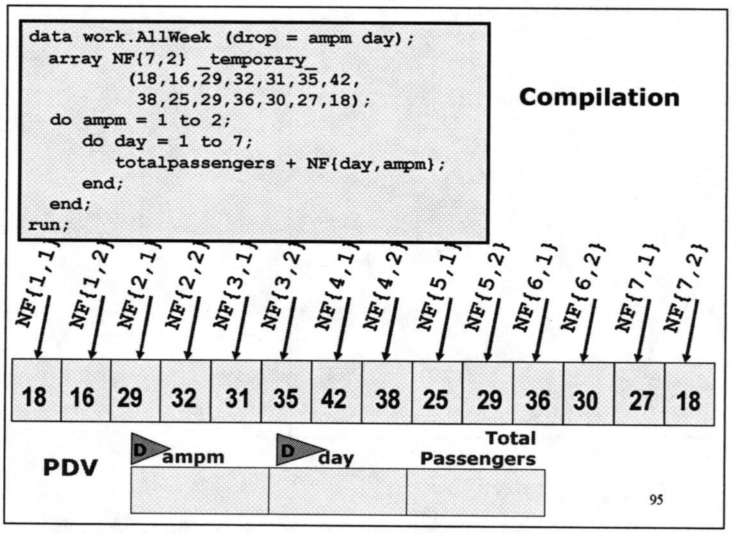

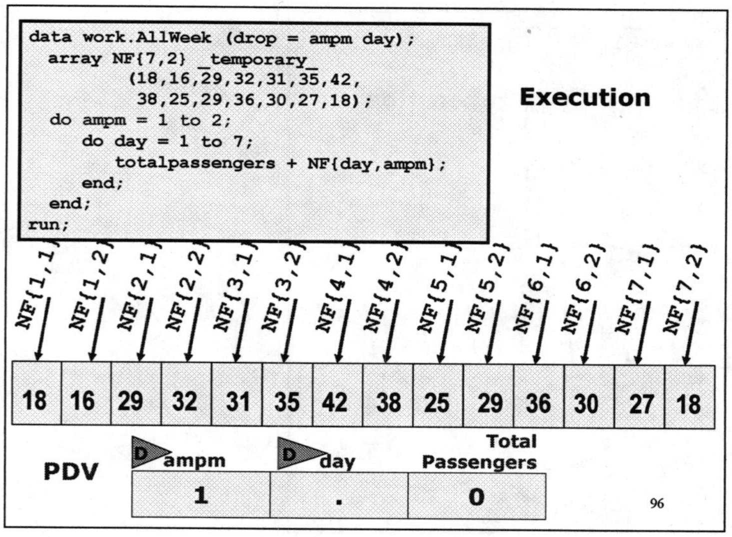
data work.AllWeek (drop = ampm day);
array NF{7,2} _temporary_
(18,16,29,32,31,35,42,
38,25,29,36,30,27,18);
do ampm = 1 to 2;
do day = 1 to 7;
totalpassengers + NF{day,ampm};
end;
end;
run;
Execution
NF{1,1} NF{1,2} NF{2,1} NF{2,2} NF{3,1} NF{3,2} NF{4,1} NF{4,2} NF{5,1} NF{5,2} NF{6,1} NF{6,2} NF{7,1} NF{7,2}
18 16 29 32 31 35 42 38 25 29 36 30 27 18
PDV
D ampm
D day
Total Passengers
1
.
0
96

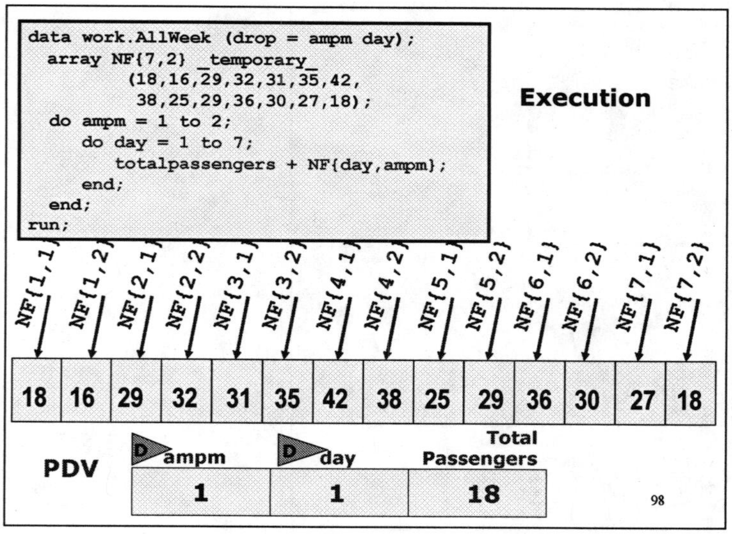
data work.AllWeek (drop = ampm day);
array NF{7,2} _temporary_
(18,16,29,32,31,35,42,
38,25,29,36,30,27,18);
do ampm = 1 to 2;
do day = 1 to 7;
totalpassengers + NF{day,ampm};
end;
end;
run;
Execution
NF{1,1} NF{1,2} NF{2,1} NF{2,2} NF{3,1} NF{3,2} NF{4,1} NF{4,2} NF{5,1} NF{5,2} NF{6,1} NF{6,2} NF{7,1} NF{7,2}
18 16 29 32 31 35 42 38 25 29 36 30 27 18
PDV
D ampm
D day
Total Passengers
1
1
18
98

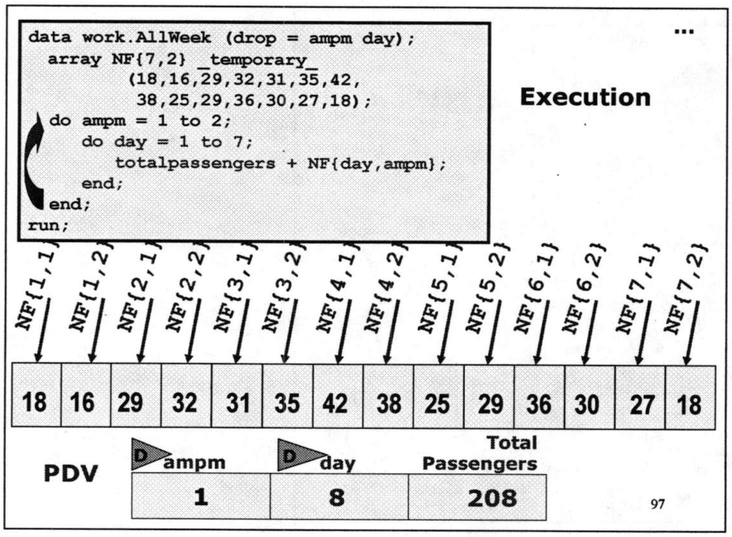
...
data work.AllWeek (drop = ampm day);
array NF{7,2} _temporary_
(18,16,29,32,31,35,42,
38,25,29,36,30,27,18);
do ampm = 1 to 2;
do day = 1 to 7;
totalpassengers + NF{day,ampm};
end;
end;
run;
Execution
NF{1,1} NF{1,2} NF{2,1} NF{2,2} NF{3,1} NF{3,2} NF{4,1} NF{4,2} NF{5,1} NF{5,2} NF{6,1} NF{6,2} NF{7,1} NF{7,2}
18 16 29 32 31 35 42 38 25 29 36 30 27 18
PDV
D ampm
D day
Total Passengers
1
8
208
97

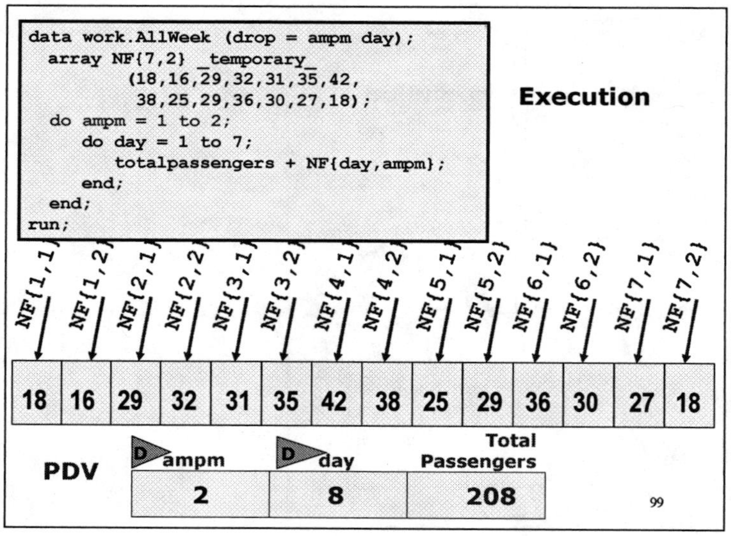
data work.AllWeek (drop = ampm day);
array NF{7,2} _temporary_
(18,16,29,32,31,35,42,
38,25,29,36,30,27,18);
do ampm = 1 to 2;
do day = 1 to 7;
totalpassengers + NF{day,ampm};
end;
end;
run;
Execution
NF{1,1} NF{1,2} NF{2,1} NF{2,2} NF{3,1} NF{3,2} NF{4,1} NF{4,2} NF{5,1} NF{5,2} NF{6,1} NF{6,2} NF{7,1} NF{7,2}
18 16 29 32 31 35 42 38 25 29 36 30 27 18
PDV
D ampm
D day
Total Passengers
2
8
208
99

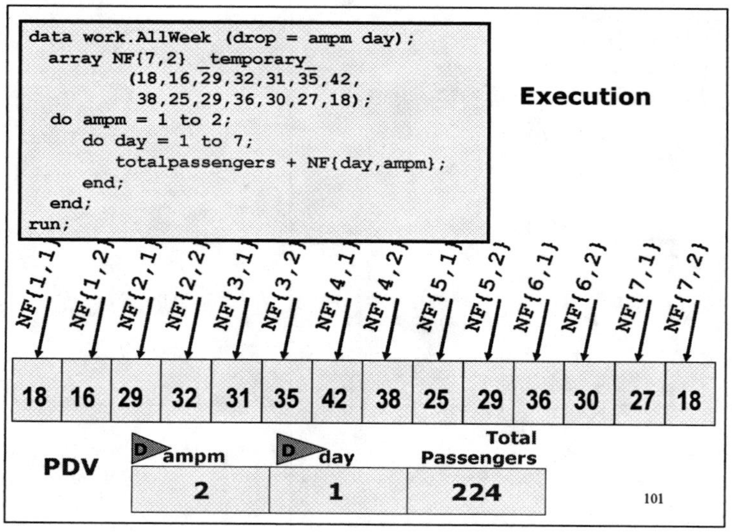
data work.AllWeek (drop = ampm day);
array NF{7,2} _temporary_
(18,16,29,32,31,35,42,
38,25,29,36,30,27,18);
do ampm = 1 to 2;
do day = 1 to 7;
totalpassengers + NF{day,ampm};
end;
end;
run;
Execution
NF{1,1} NF{1,2} NF{2,1} NF{2,2} NF{3,1} NF{3,2} NF{4,1} NF{4,2} NF{5,1} NF{5,2} NF{6,1} NF{6,2} NF{7,1} NF{7,2}
18 16 29 32 31 35 42 38 25 29 36 30 27 18
PDV
D ampm
D day
Total Passengers
2
1
224
101

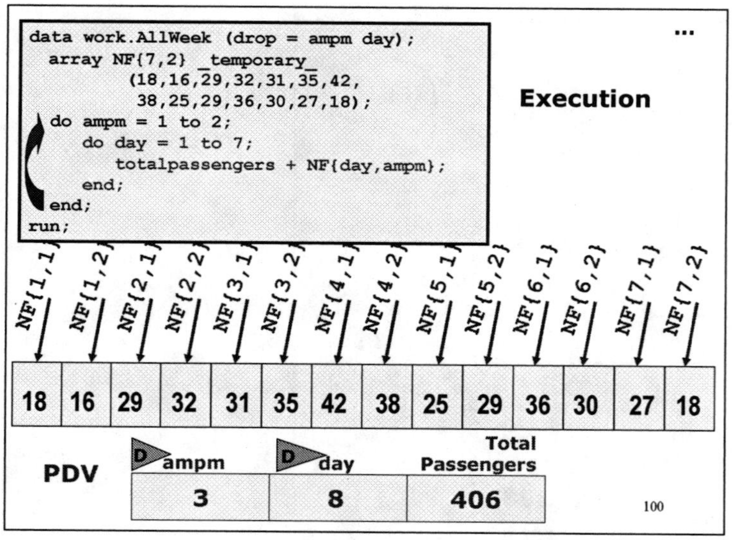
...
data work.AllWeek (drop = ampm day);
array NF{7,2} _temporary_
(18,16,29,32,31,35,42,
38,25,29,36,30,27,18);
do ampm = 1 to 2;
do day = 1 to 7;
totalpassengers + NF{day,ampm};
end;
end;
run;
Execution
NF{1,1} NF{1,2} NF{2,1} NF{2,2} NF{3,1} NF{3,2} NF{4,1} NF{4,2} NF{5,1} NF{5,2} NF{6,1} NF{6,2} NF{7,1} NF{7,2}
18 16 29 32 31 35 42 38 25 29 36 30 27 18
PDV
D ampm
D day
Total Passengers
3
8
406
100

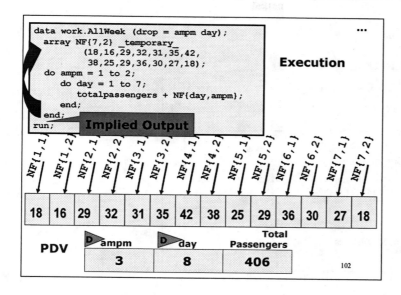

```
data work.AllWeek (drop = ampm day);
  array NF{7,2} _temporary_
        (18,16,29,32,31,35,42,
         38,25,29,36,30,27,18);
  do ampm = 1 to 2;
     do day = 1 to 7;
        totalpassengers + NF{day,ampm};
     end;
  end;
run;
```

**Execution** ...

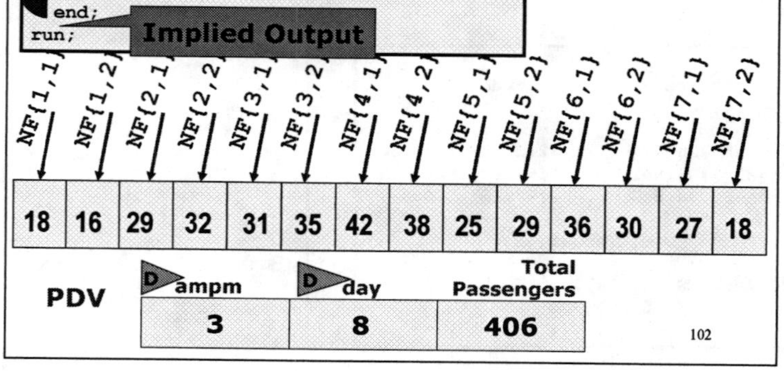


102

## General Business Scenario

The SAS data set ia.MonthlySummary1997_1999 contains the actual cargo and passenger revenue figures for each month from 1997 to 1999.

ia.MonthlySummary1997_1999
(first two observations)

| Flight Month | RevenueCargo | RevenueFirst Class |
|---|---|---|
| JAN1997 | $171,520,869.10 | $51,136,353.00 |
| JAN1998 | $238,786,807.60 | $71,197,270.00 |

| RevenueBusiness | RevenueEconomy | month |
|---|---|---|
| $34,897,844.00 | $169,193,900.00 | 1 |
| $48,749,365.00 | $235,462,316.00 | 1 |

104

## General Business Scenario

The SAS data set ia.Target contains the target cargo and passenger revenue figures for each month from 1997 to 1999.

ia.Target
(first two observations)

| Year | RevType | JAN | FEB | MAR |
|---|---|---|---|---|
| 1997 | cargo | 192284420 | 86376721 | 28526103 |
| 1997 | passenger | 211052672 | 309991890 | 123302226 |

| APR | MAY | JUN | JUL | AUG |
|---|---|---|---|---|
| 260386468 | 109975326 | 102833104 | 196728648 | 236996122 |
| 47862099 | 128810605 | 212378496 | 319499539 | 34004244 |

| SEP | OCT | NOV | DEC |
|---|---|---|---|
| 112413744 | 125401565 | 72551855 | 136042505 |
| 206472552 | 50706092 | 298545086 | 213838302 |

106

## General Business Scenario

We need to compare the actual values to the target values to create the following SAS data set.

| Flight Month | Total Passenger Revenue | Passenger Target |
|---|---|---|
| JAN1997 | $255,228,097 | $211,052,672 |
| JAN1998 | $355,408,951 | $167,270,825 |
| JAN1999 | $419,606,680 | $175,035,360 |

| RevenueCargo | CargoTarget |
|---|---|
| $171,520,869 | $192,284,420 |
| $238,786,808 | $108,645,734 |
| $280,350,393 | $85,730,444 |

107

## Using Multidimensional Arrays

```
data ia.lookup;
  array targets{1997:1999,2,12} _temporary_;
  array mon{12} JAN FEB MAR APR MAY JUN JUL AUG SEP OCT NOV DEC;
  if _n_ = 1 then do i = 1 to 6;
                    set ia.target;
                    if revtype = 'cargo' then t = 1;
                    else t = 2;
                    do j = 1 to 12;
                       targets{year,t,j} = mon{j};
                    end;
  end;
  set ia.MonthlySummary1997_1999;
  TotalPassengerRevenue = sum(RevenueFirstClass,RevenueBusiness,
     RevenueEconomy);
  year = input(substr(FlightMonth,4),4.);
  CargoTarget = targets{year,1,month};
  PassengerTarget = targets{year,2,month};
run;
```

Array values are stored in a SAS data set when

- there are too many values to easily initialize in the ARRAY statement
- values change frequently
- the same values are used in many programs.

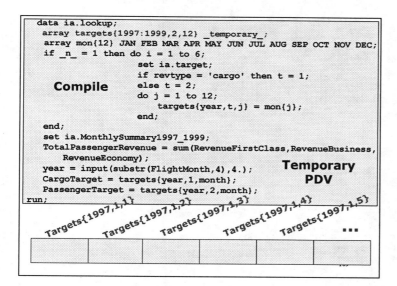

```
data ia.lookup;
  array targets{1997:1999,2,12} _temporary_;
  array mon{12} JAN FEB MAR APR MAY JUN JUL AUG SEP OCT NOV DEC;
  if _n_ = 1 then do i = 1 to 6;
                    set ia.target;
                    if revtype = 'cargo' then t = 1;
                    else t = 2;
                    do j = 1 to 12;
                       targets{year,t,j} = mon{j};
                    end;
  end;
  set ia.MonthlySummary1997_1999;
  TotalPassengerRevenue = sum(RevenueFirstClass,RevenueBusiness,
     RevenueEconomy);
  year = input(substr(FlightMonth,4),4.);
  CargoTarget = targets{year,1,month};
  PassengerTarget = targets{year,2,month};
run;
```

**Compile**

**Temporary PDV**

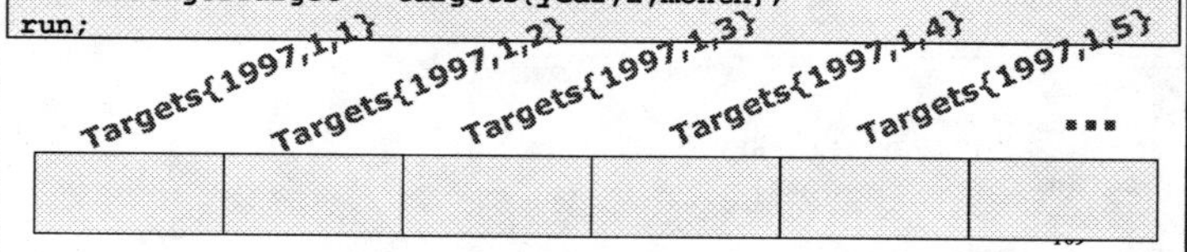

**Compile**

```
data ia.lookup;
  array targets{1997:1999,2,12} _temporary_;
  array mon{12} JAN FEB MAR APR MAY JUN JUL AUG SEP OCT NOV DEC;
  if _n_ = 1 then do i = 1 to 6;
                  set ia.target;
                  if revtype = 'cargo' then t = 1;
                  else t = 2;
                  do j = 1 to 12;
                     targets{year,t,j} = mon{j};
                  end;
  end;
  set ia.MonthlySummary1997_1999;
  TotalPassengerRevenue = sum(RevenueFirstClass,RevenueBusiness,
      RevenueEconomy);
  year = input(substr(FlightMonth,4),4.);
  CargoTarget = targets{year,1,month};
  PassengerTarget = targets{year,2,month};
run;
```

**Data Set PDV**

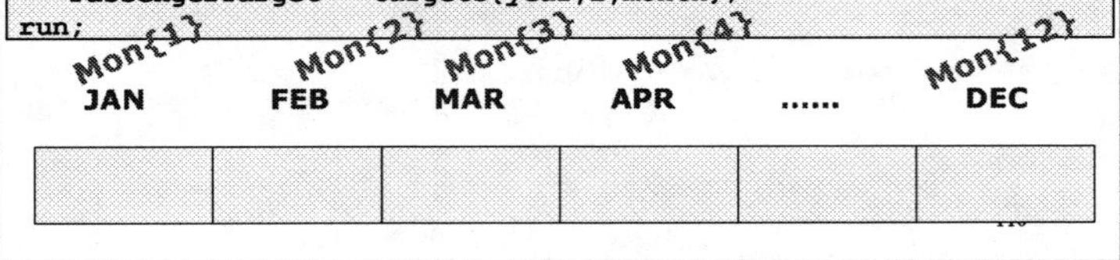


**Compile**

```
data ia.lookup;
  array targets{1997:1999,2,12} _temporary_;
  array mon{12} JAN FEB MAR APR MAY JUN JUL AUG SEP OCT NOV DEC;
  if _n_ = 1 then do i = 1 to 6;
                  set ia.target;
                  if revtype = 'cargo' then t = 1;
                  else t = 2;
                  do j = 1 to 12;
                     targets{year,t,j} = mon{j};
                  end;
  end;
  set ia.MonthlySummary1997_1999;
  TotalPassengerRevenue = sum(RevenueFirstClass,RevenueBusiness,
      RevenueEconomy);
  year = input(substr(FlightMonth,4),4.);
  CargoTarget = targets{year,1,month};
  PassengerTarget = targets{year,2,month};
run;
```

**Data Set PDV**

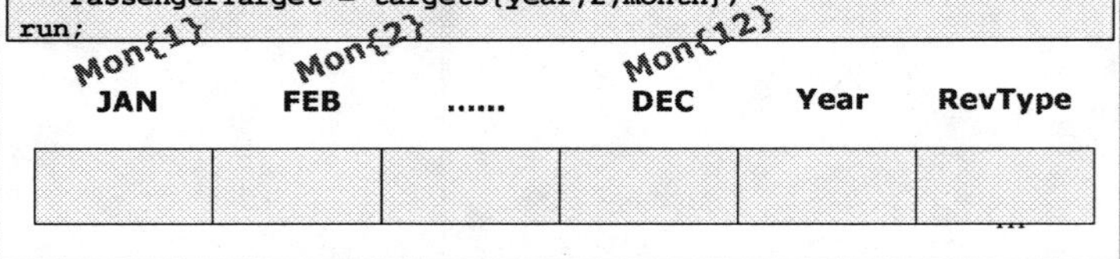


**Compile**

```
data ia.lookup;
  array targets{1997:1999,2,12} _temporary_;
  array mon{12} JAN FEB MAR APR MAY JUN JUL AUG SEP OCT NOV DEC;
  if _n_ = 1 then do i = 1 to 6;
                  set ia.target;
                  if revtype = 'cargo' then t = 1;
                  else t = 2;
                  do j = 1 to 12;
                     targets{year,t,j} = mon{j};
                  end;
  end;
  set ia.MonthlySummary1997_1999;
  TotalPassengerRevenue = sum(RevenueFirstClass,RevenueBusiness,
      RevenueEconomy);
  year = input(substr(FlightMonth,4),4.);
  CargoTarget = targets{year,1,month};
  PassengerTarget = targets{year,2,month};
run;
```

**Data Set PDV**

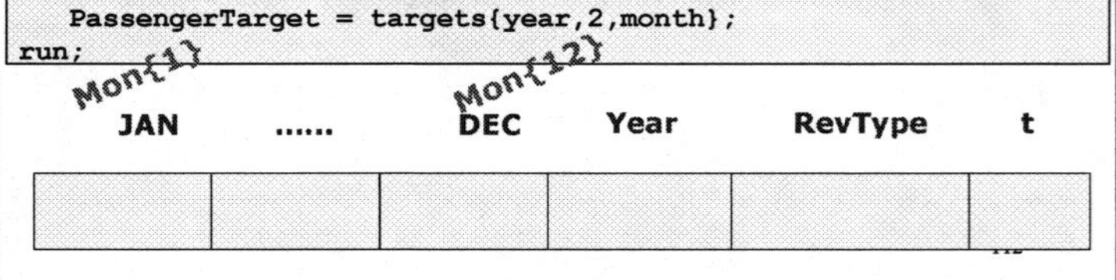

```
data ia.lookup;
 array targets{1997:1999,2,12} _temporary_;
 array mon{12} JAN FEB MAR APR MAY JUN JUL AUG SEP OCT NOV DEC;
 if _n_ = 1 then do i = 1 to 6;
                  set ia.target;
                  if revtype = 'cargo' then t = 1;
                  else t = 2;
                  do j = 1 to 12;
                     targets{year,t,j} = mon{j};
                  end;
 end;
 set ia.MonthlySummary1997_1999;
 TotalPassengerRevenue = sum(RevenueFirstClass,RevenueBusiness,
     RevenueEconomy);
 year = input(substr(FlightMonth,4),4.);
 CargoTarget = targets{year,1,month};
 PassengerTarget = targets{year,2,month};
run;
```

**Compile**

**Data Set PDV**

Mon{12}

| ...... | DEC | Year | RevType | t | j |
|---|---|---|---|---|---|
| | | | | | |

```
data ia.lookup;
 array targets{1997:1999,2,12} _temporary_;
 array mon{12} JAN FEB MAR APR MAY JUN JUL AUG SEP OCT NOV DEC;
 if _n_ = 1 then do i = 1 to 6;
                  set ia.target;
                  if revtype = 'cargo' then t = 1;
                  else t = 2;
                  do j = 1 to 12;
                     targets{year,t,j} = mon{j};
                  end;
 end;
 set ia.MonthlySummary1997_1999;
 TotalPassengerRevenue = sum(RevenueFirstClass,RevenueBusiness,
     RevenueEconomy);
 year = input(substr(FlightMonth,4),4.);
 CargoTarget = targets{year,1,month};
 PassengerTarget = targets{year,2,month};
run;
```

**Compile**

**Partial Data Set PDV**

| ... Year | RevType | t | j | Flight Month | month |
|---|---|---|---|---|---|
| | | | | | |

```
data ia.lookup;
 array targets{1997:1999,2,12} _temporary_;
 array mon{12} JAN FEB MAR APR MAY JUN JUL AUG SEP OCT NOV DEC;
 if _n_ = 1 then do i = 1 to 6;
                  set ia.target;
                  if revtype = 'cargo' then t = 1;
                  else t = 2;
                  do j = 1 to 12;
                     targets{year,t,j} = mon{j};
                  end;
 end;
 set ia.MonthlySummary1997_1999;
 TotalPassengerRevenue = sum(RevenueFirstClass,RevenueBusiness,
     RevenueEconomy);
 year = input(substr(FlightMonth,4),4.);
 CargoTarget = targets{year,1,month};
 PassengerTarget = targets{year,2,month};
run;
```

**Compile**

**Partial Data Set PDV**

| ... RevType | t | j | Flight Month | month | Total Passenger Revenue |
|---|---|---|---|---|---|
| | | | | | |

```
data ia.lookup;
  array targets{1997:1999,2,12} _temporary_;
  array mon{12} JAN FEB MAR APR MAY JUN JUL AUG SEP OCT NOV DEC;
  if _n_ = 1 then do i = 1 to 6;
                  set ia.target;
                  if revtype = 'cargo' then t = 1;
                  else t = 2;
                  do j = 1 to 12;
                     targets{year,t,j} = mon{j};
                  end;
  end;
  set ia.MonthlySummary1997_1999;
  TotalPassengerRevenue = sum(RevenueFirstClass,RevenueBusiness,
     RevenueEconomy);
  year = input(substr(FlightMonth,4),4.);
  CargoTarget = targets{year,1,month};
  PassengerTarget = targets{year,2,month};
run;
```

**Compile**

**Already exists**

**Partial Data Set PDV**

| ... Year | ... t | j | Flight Month | month | Total Passenger Revenue |
|---|---|---|---|---|---|
| | | | | | |

```
data ia.lookup;
  array targets{1997:1999,2,12} _temporary_;
  array mon{12} JAN FEB MAR APR MAY JUN JUL AUG SEP OCT NOV DEC;
  if _n_ = 1 then do i = 1 to 6;
                  set ia.target;
                  if revtype = 'cargo' then t = 1;
                  else t = 2;
                  do j = 1 to 12;
                     targets{year,t,j} = mon{j};
                  end;
  end;
  set ia.MonthlySummary1997_1999;
  TotalPassengerRevenue = sum(RevenueFirstClass,RevenueBusiness,
     RevenueEconomy);
  year = input(substr(FlightMonth,4),4.);
  CargoTarget = targets{year,1,month};
  PassengerTarget = targets{year,2,month};
run;
```

**Compile**

**Partial Data Set PDV**

| ... t | j | Flight Month | month | Total Passenger Revenue | Cargo Target |
|---|---|---|---|---|---|
| | | | | | |

```
data ia.lookup;
  array targets{1997:1999,2,12} _temporary_;
  array mon{12} JAN FEB MAR APR MAY JUN JUL AUG SEP OCT NOV DEC;
  if _n_ = 1 then do i = 1 to 6;
                  set ia.target;
                  if revtype = 'cargo' then t = 1;
                  else t = 2;
                  do j = 1 to 12;
                     targets{year,t,j} = mon{j};
                  end;
  end;
  set ia.MonthlySummary1997_1999;
  TotalPassengerRevenue = sum(RevenueFirstClass,RevenueBusiness,
     RevenueEconomy);
  year = input(substr(FlightMonth,4),4.);
  CargoTarget = targets{year,1,month};
  PassengerTarget = targets{year,2,month};
run;
```

**Compile**

**Partial Data Set PDV**

| ... j | Flight Month | month | Total Passenger Revenue | Cargo Target | Passenger Target |
|---|---|---|---|---|---|
| | | | | | |

```
data ia.lookup;                                                          ...
  array targets{1997:1999,2,12} _temporary_;
  array mon{12} JAN FEB MAR APR MAY JUN JUL AUG SEP OCT NOV DEC;
  if _n_ = 1 then do i = 1 to 6;
                  set ia.target;
                  if revtype = 'cargo' then t = 1;
                  else t = 2;                          Execute
                  do j = 1 to 12;
                     targets{year,t,j} = mon{j};
                  end;
  end;
  set ia.MonthlySummary1997_1999;
  TotalPassengerRevenue = sum(RevenueFirstClass,RevenueBusiness,
     RevenueEconomy);
  year = input(substr(FlightMonth,4),4.);
  CargoTarget = targets{year,1,month};
  PassengerTarget = targets{year,2,month};
run;
```

True

Partial Data Set PDV

| JAN | ...... DEC | Year | RevType | t | j |
|---|---|---|---|---|---|
| | | | | | |

```
data ia.lookup;                                                          ...
  array targets{1997:1999,2,12} _temporary_;
  array mon{12} JAN FEB MAR APR MAY JUN JUL AUG SEP OCT NOV DEC;
  if _n_ = 1 then do i = 1 to 6;
                  set ia.target;
                  if revtype = 'cargo' then t = 1;     i = 1
                  else t = 2;
                  do j = 1 to 12;
                     targets{year,t,j} = mon{j};
                  end;
  end;
  set ia.MonthlySummary1997_1999;
  TotalPassengerRevenue = sum(RevenueFirstClass,RevenueBusiness,
     RevenueEconomy);
  year = input(substr(FlightMonth,4),4.);
  CargoTarget = targets{year,1,month};
  PassengerTarget = targets{year,2,month};
run;
```

Partial Data Set PDV

| JAN | ...... DEC | Year | RevType | t | j |
|---|---|---|---|---|---|
| | | | | | |

```
data ia.lookup;
  array targets{1997:1999,2,12} _temporary_;
  array mon{12} JAN FEB MAR APR MAY JUN JUL AUG SEP OCT NOV DEC;
  if _n_ = 1 then do i = 1 to 6;
                  set ia.target;
                  if revtype='cargo' then t = 1;       i = 1
                  else t = 2;
                  do j = 1 to 12;
                     targets{year,t,j} = mon{j};
                  end;
  end;
  set ia.MonthlySummary1997_1999;
  TotalPassengerRevenue = sum(RevenueFirstClass,RevenueBusiness,
     RevenueEconomy);
  year = input(substr(FlightMonth,4),4.);
  CargoTarget = targets{year,1,month};
  PassengerTarget = targets{year,2,month};
run;
```

Partial Data Set PDV

| JAN | ...... DEC | Year | RevType | t | j |
|---|---|---|---|---|---|
| 71065758 | 163496594 | 1997 | cargo | | |

```
data ia.lookup;
  array targets{1997:1999,2,12} _temporary_;
  array mon{12} JAN FEB MAR APR MAY JUN JUL AUG SEP OCT NOV DEC;
  if _n_ = 1 then do i = 1 to 6;
                 set ia.target;
                 if revtype = 'cargo' then t = 1;
                 else t = 2;
                 do j = 1 to 12;
                    targets{year,t,j} = mon{j};
                 end;
  end;
  set ia.MonthlySummary1997_1999;
  TotalPassengerRevenue = sum(RevenueFirstClass,RevenueBusiness,
      RevenueEconomy);
  year = input(substr(FlightMonth,4),4.);
  CargoTarget = targets{year,1,month};
  PassengerTarget = targets{year,2,month};
run;
```

**i = 1**

**Partial Data Set PDV**

| JAN | ...... DEC | Year | RevType | t | j |
|---|---|---|---|---|---|
| 71065758 | 163496594 | 1997 | cargo | 1 | |

```
data ia.lookup;
  array targets{1997:1999,2,12} _temporary_;
  array mon{12} JAN FEB MAR APR MAY JUN JUL AUG SEP OCT NOV DEC;
  if _n_ = 1 then do i = 1 to 6;
                 set ia.target;
                 if revtype = 'cargo' then t = 1;
                 else t = 2;
                 do j = 1 to 12;
                    targets{year,t,j} = mon{j};
                 end;
  end;
  set ia.MonthlySummary1997_1999;
  TotalPassengerRevenue = sum(RevenueFirstClass,RevenueBusiness,
      RevenueEconomy);
  year = input(substr(FlightMonth,4),4.);
  CargoTarget = targets{year,1,month};
  PassengerTarget = targets{year,2,month};
run;
```

**i = 1**

**Partial Data Set PDV**

| JAN | ...... DEC | Year | RevType | t | j |
|---|---|---|---|---|---|
| 71065758 | 163496594 | 1997 | cargo | 1 | 1 |

```
data ia.lookup;                                                    ...
  array targets{1997:1999,2,12} _temporary_;
  array mon{12} JAN FEB MAR APR MAY JUN JUL AUG SEP OCT NOV DEC;
  if _n_ = 1 then do i = 1 to 6;
                 set ia.target;
                 if revtype = 'cargo' then t = 1;
                 else t = 2;
                 do j = 1 to 12;
                    targets{1997,1,1} = 71065758;
                 end;
  end;
  set ia.MonthlySummary1997_1999;
  TotalPassengerRevenue = sum(RevenueFirstClass,RevenueBusiness,
      RevenueEconomy);
  year = input(substr(FlightMonth,4),4.);
  CargoTarget = targets{year,1,month};
  PassengerTarget = targets{year,2,month};
run;
```

**i = 1**

**Partial Data Set PDV**

| JAN | ...... DEC | Year | RevType | t | j |
|---|---|---|---|---|---|
| 71065758 | 163496594 | 1997 | cargo | 1 | 1 |

...

## Targets Array

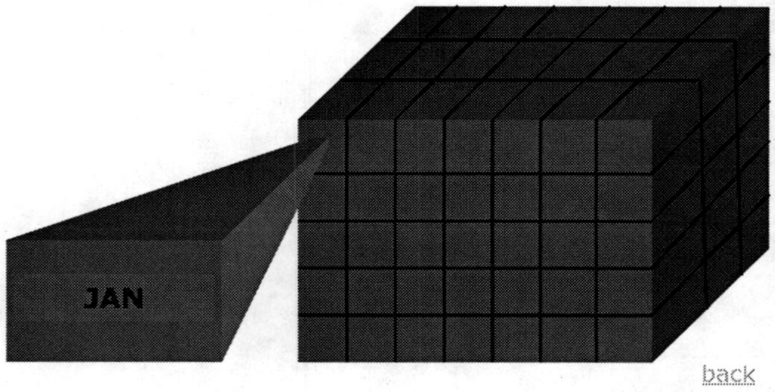


125

...

```
data ia.lookup;
  array targets{1997:1999,2,12} _temporary_;
  array mon{12} JAN FEB MAR APR MAY JUN JUL AUG SEP OCT NOV DEC;
  if _n_ = 1 then do i = 1 to 6;
                 set ia.target;
                 if revtype = 'cargo' then t = 1;
                 else t = 2;
                 do j = 1 to 12;
                    targets{year,t,j} = mon{j};
                 end;
  end;
  set ia.MonthlySummary1997_1999;
  TotalPassengerRevenue = sum(RevenueFirstClass,RevenueBusiness,
     RevenueEconomy);
  year = input(substr(FlightMonth,4),4.);
  CargoTarget = targets{year,1,month};
  PassengerTarget = targets{year,2,month};
run;
```

**i = 1**

**Partial Data Set PDV**

| JAN | ...... DEC | Year | RevType | t | j |
|---|---|---|---|---|---|
| 71065758 | 163496594 | 1997 | cargo | 1 | 1 |

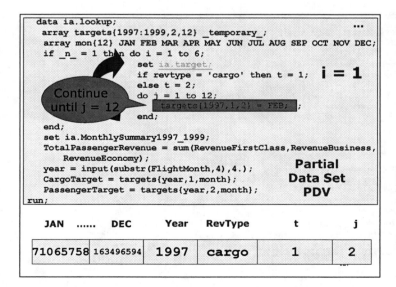

...

```
data ia.lookup;
  array targets{1997:1999,2,12} _temporary_;
  array mon{12} JAN FEB MAR APR MAY JUN JUL AUG SEP OCT NOV DEC;
  if _n_ = 1 then do i = 1 to 6;
                 set ia.target;
                 if revtype = 'cargo' then t = 1;
                 else t = 2;
                 do j = 1 to 12;
                    targets{1997,1,2} = FEB;
                 end;
  end;
  set ia.MonthlySummary1997_1999;
  TotalPassengerRevenue = sum(RevenueFirstClass,RevenueBusiness,
     RevenueEconomy);
  year = input(substr(FlightMonth,4),4.);
  CargoTarget = targets{year,1,month};
  PassengerTarget = targets{year,2,month};
run;
```

Continue until j = 12

**i = 1**

**Partial Data Set PDV**

| JAN | ...... DEC | Year | RevType | t | j |
|---|---|---|---|---|---|
| 71065758 | 163496594 | 1997 | cargo | 1 | 2 |

```
data ia.lookup;
  array targets{1997:1999,2,12} _temporary_;
  array mon{12} JAN FEB MAR APR MAY JUN JUL AUG SEP OCT NOV DEC;
  if _n_ = 1 then do i = 1 to 6;
                set ia.target;
                if revtype = 'cargo' then t = 1;
                else t = 2;
                do j = 1 to 12;
                   targets{year,t,j} = mon{j};
                end;
  end;
  set ia.MonthlySummary1997_1999;
  TotalPassengerRevenue = sum(RevenueFirstClass,RevenueBusiness,
     RevenueEconomy);
  year = input(substr(FlightMonth,4),4.);
  CargoTarget = targets{year,1,month};
  PassengerTarget = targets{year,2,month};
run;
```

i = 2

Partial Data Set PDV

| JAN | ...... | DEC | Year | RevType | t | j |
|---|---|---|---|---|---|---|
| 71065758 | | 163496594 | 1997 | cargo | 1 | 13 |

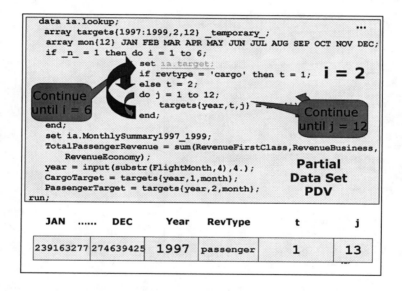

...

```
data ia.lookup;
  array targets{1997:1999,2,12} _temporary_;
  array mon{12} JAN FEB MAR APR MAY JUN JUL AUG SEP OCT NOV DEC;
  if _n_ = 1 then do i = 1 to 6;
                set ia.target;
                if revtype = 'cargo' then t = 1;
                else t = 2;
                do j = 1 to 12;
                   targets{year,t,j} = mon{j};
                end;
  end;
  set ia.MonthlySummary1997_1999;
  TotalPassengerRevenue = sum(RevenueFirstClass,RevenueBusiness,
     RevenueEconomy);
  year = input(substr(FlightMonth,4),4.);
  CargoTarget = targets{year,1,month};
  PassengerTarget = targets{year,2,month};
run;
```

i = 2

Continue until i = 6

Continue until j = 12

Partial Data Set PDV

| JAN | ...... | DEC | Year | RevType | t | j |
|---|---|---|---|---|---|---|
| 239163277 | | 274639425 | 1997 | passenger | 1 | 13 |

```
data ia.lookup;
  array targets{1997:1999,2,12} _temporary_;
  array mon{12} JAN FEB MAR APR MAY JUN JUL AUG SEP OCT NOV DEC;
  if _n_ = 1 then do i = 1 to 6;
                set ia.target;
                if revtype = 'cargo' then t = 1;
                else t = 2;
                do j = 1 to 12;
                   targets{year,t,j} = mon{j};
                end;
  end;
  set ia.MonthlySummary1997_1999;
  TotalPassengerRevenue = sum(RevenueFirstClass,RevenueBusiness,
     RevenueEconomy);
  year = input(substr(FlightMonth,4),4.);
  CargoTarget = targets{year,1,month};
  PassengerTarget = targets{year,2,month};
run;
```

Partial Data Set PDV

| Flight Month | Revenue FirstClass | Revenue Business | Revenue Economy | month | Total Passenger Revenue |
|---|---|---|---|---|---|
| JAN1997 | 51136353 | 34897844 | 169193900 | 1 | . |

```
data ia.lookup;
  array targets{1997:1999,2,12} _temporary_;
  array mon{12} JAN FEB MAR APR MAY JUN JUL AUG SEP OCT NOV DEC;
  if _n_ = 1 then do i = 1 to 6;
                  set ia.target;
                  if revtype = 'cargo' then t = 1;
                  else t = 2;
                  do j = 1 to 12;
                     targets{year,t,j} = mon{j};
                  end;
  end;
  set ia.MonthlySummary1997_1999;
  TotalPassengerRevenue = sum(RevenueFirstClass,RevenueBusiness,
      RevenueEconomy);
  year = input(substr(FlightMonth,4),4.);
  CargoTarget = targets{year,1,month};
  PassengerTarget = targets{year,2,month};
run;
```

**Partial Data Set PDV**

| Flight Month | Revenue FirstClass | Revenue Business | Revenue Economy | month | Total Passenger Revenue |
|---|---|---|---|---|---|
| JAN1997 | 51136353 | 34897844 | 169193900 | 1 | 255258097 |

```
data ia.lookup;
  array targets{1997:1999,2,12} _temporary_;
  array mon{12} JAN FEB MAR APR MAY JUN JUL AUG SEP OCT NOV DEC;
  if _n_ = 1 then do i = 1 to 6;
                  set ia.target;
                  if revtype = 'cargo' then t = 1;
                  else t = 2;
                  do j = 1 to 12;
                     targets{year,t,j} = mon{j};
                  end;
  end;
  set ia.MonthlySummary1997_1999;
  TotalPassengerRevenue = sum(RevenueFirstClass,RevenueBusiness,
      RevenueEconomy);
  year = input(substr(FlightMonth,4),4.);
  CargoTarget = targets{year,1,month};
  PassengerTarget = targets{year,2,month};
run;
```

**Partial Data Set PDV**

| year | Flight Month | Total Passenger Revenue | month | Cargo Target | Passenger Target |
|---|---|---|---|---|---|
| 1997 | JAN1997 | 255258097 | 1 | . | . |

...

```
data ia.lookup;
  array targets{1997:1999,2,12} _temporary_;
  array mon{12} JAN FEB MAR APR MAY JUN JUL AUG SEP OCT NOV DEC;
  if _n_ = 1 then do i = 1 to 6;
                  set ia.target;
                  if revtype = 'cargo' then t = 1;
                  else t = 2;
                  do j = 1 to 12;
                     targets{year,t,j} = mon{j};
                  end;
  end;
  set ia.MonthlySummary1997_1999;
  TotalPassengerRevenue = sum(RevenueFirstClass,RevenueBusiness,
      RevenueEconomy);
  year = input(substr(FlightMonth,4),4.);
  CargoTarget = targets{1997,1,1};
  PassengerTarget = targets{year,2,month};
run;
```

**Partial Data Set PDV**

| year | Flight Month | Total Passenger Revenue | month | Cargo Target | Passenger Target |
|---|---|---|---|---|---|
| 1997 | JAN1997 | 255258097 | 1 | 71065758 | . |

...

## Targets Array

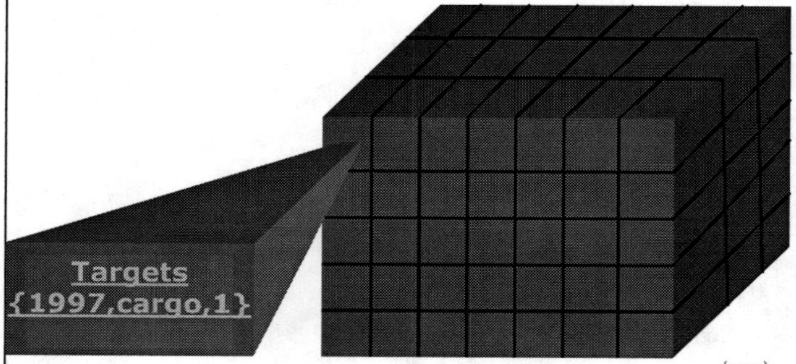


back

134

...

```
data ia.lookup;
  array targets{1997:1999,2,12} _temporary_;
  array mon{12} JAN FEB MAR APR MAY JUN JUL AUG SEP OCT NOV DEC;
  if _n_ = 1 then do i = 1 to 6;
                 set ia.target;
                 if revtype = 'cargo' then t = 1;
                 else t = 2;
                 do j = 1 to 12;
                    targets{year,t,j} = mon{j};
                 end;
  end;
  set ia.MonthlySummary1997_1999;
  TotalPassengerRevenue = sum(RevenueFirstClass,RevenueBusiness,
     RevenueEconomy);
  year = input(substr(FlightMonth,4),4.);
  CargoTarget = targets{year,1,month};
  PassengerTarget = targets{1997,2,1};
run;
```

**Partial Data Set PDV**

| year | Flight Month | Total Passenger Revenue | month | Cargo Target | Passenger Target |
|---|---|---|---|---|---|
| 1997 | JAN1997 | 255258097 | 1 | 71065758 | 239163277 |

...

## Targets Array

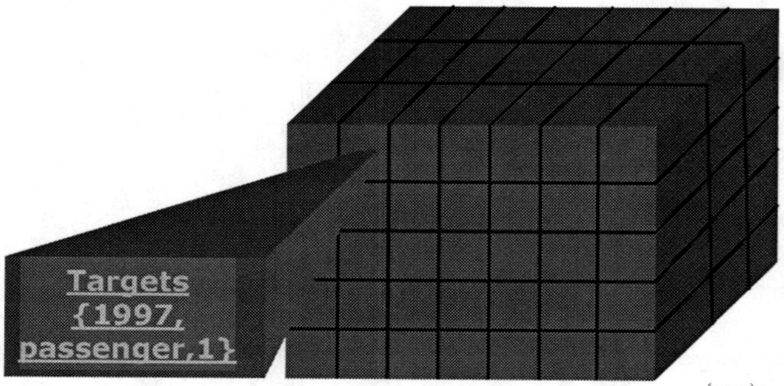


back

136

```
data ia.lookup;                                                    ...
  array targets{1997:1999,2,12} _temporary_;
  array mon{12} JAN FEB MAR APR MAY JUN JUL AUG SEP OCT NOV DEC;
  if _n_ = 1 then do i = 1 to 6;
                  set ia.target;
                  if revtype = 'cargo' then t = 1;
                  else t = 2;
                  do j = 1 to 12;
                     targets{year,t,j} = mon{j};
                  end;
  end;
  set ia.MonthlySummary1997_1999;
  TotalPassengerRevenue = sum(RevenueFirstClass,RevenueBusiness,
     RevenueEconomy);
  year = input(substr(FlightMonth,4),4.);
  CargoTarget = targets{year,1,month};
  PassengerTarget = targets{year,2,month};
run;
```

Implied Output

Partial Data Set PDV

| year | Flight Month | Passenger Revenue | month | Cargo Target | Passenger Target |
|---|---|---|---|---|---|
| 1997 | JAN1997 | 255258097 | 1 | 71065758 | 239163277 |

```
data ia.lookup;                                                    ...
  array targets{1997:1999,2,12} _temporary_;
  array mon{12} JAN FEB MAR APR MAY JUN JUL AUG SEP OCT NOV DEC;
  if _n_ = 1 then do i = 1 to 6;
                  set ia.target;
                  if revtype = 'cargo' then t = 1;
                  else t = 2;
                  do j = 1 to 12;
                     targets{year,t,j} = mon{j};
                  end;
  end;
  set ia.MonthlySummary1997_1999;
  TotalPassengerRevenue = sum(RevenueFirstClass,RevenueBusiness,
     RevenueEconomy);
  year = input(substr(FlightMonth,4),4.);
  CargoTarget = targets{year,1,month};
  PassengerTarget = targets{year,2,month};
run;
```

F

Partial Data Set PDV

| _N_ | Flight Month | Total Passenger Revenue | month | Cargo Target | Passenger Target |
|---|---|---|---|---|---|
| 2 | JAN1997 | 255258097 | 1 | 71065758 | 239163277 |

```
data ia.lookup;
  array targets{1997:1999,2,12} _temporary_;
  array mon{12} JAN FEB MAR APR MAY JUN JUL AUG SEP OCT NOV DEC;
  if _n_ = 1 then do i = 1 to 6;
                  set ia.target;
                  if revtype = 'cargo' then t = 1;
                  else t = 2;
                  do j = 1 to 12;
                     targets{year,t,j} = mon{j};
                  end;
  end;
  set ia.MonthlySummary1997_1999;
  TotalPassengerRevenue = sum(RevenueFirstClass,RevenueBusiness,
     RevenueEconomy);
  year = input(substr(FlightMonth,4),4.);
  CargoTarget = targets{year,1,month};
  PassengerTarget = targets{year,2,month};
run;
```

Partial Data Set PDV

| Flight Month | Revenue FirstClass | Revenue Business | Revenue Economy | month | Total Passenger Revenue |
|---|---|---|---|---|---|
| JAN1998 | 238786807.6 | 71197270 | 48749365 | 1 | . |

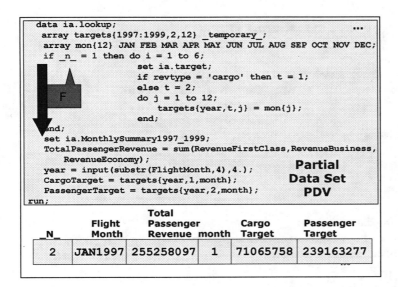

## Using Multidimensional Arrays for Table Lookup

c05s5d1

Program

```
data ia.lookup;
   array targets{1997:1999,2,12} _temporary_;
   array mon{12} JAN FEB MAR APR MAY JUN
                 JUL AUG SEP OCT NOV DEC;
   if _n_ = 1 then do i = 1 to 6;
      set ia.target;
      if revtype = 'cargo' then t = 1;
      else t = 2;
      do j = 1 to 12;
         targets{year,t,j} = mon{j};
      end;
   end;
   set ia.MonthlySummary1997_1999;
   TotalPassengerRevenue = sum(RevenueFirstClass,
                               RevenueBusiness,
                               RevenueEconomy);
   year = input(substr(FlightMonth,4),4.);
   CargoTarget = targets{year,1,month};
   PassengerTarget = targets{year,2,month};
run;

proc print data = ia.lookup;
   title 'Using a Multidimensional Array for Table Lookup';
   var FlightMonth TotalPassengerRevenue PassengerTarget
       RevenueCargo CargoTarget;
   format _numeric_ dollar14.;
run;
```

The keyword _NUMERIC_ refers to all the numeric variables.

Output

Using a Multidimensional Array for Table Lookup

| Obs | Flight Month | Total Passenger Revenue | Passenger Target | RevenueCargo | CargoTarget |
|---|---|---|---|---|---|
| 1 | JAN1997 | $255,228,097 | $211,052,672 | $171,520,869 | $192,284,420 |
| 2 | JAN1998 | $355,408,951 | $167,270,825 | $238,786,808 | $108,645,734 |
| 3 | JAN1999 | $419,606,680 | $175,035,360 | $280,350,393 | $85,730,444 |
| 4 | FEB1997 | $264,515,193 | $309,991,890 | $177,671,530 | $86,376,721 |
| 5 | FEB1998 | $320,871,431 | $105,489,944 | $215,959,696 | $147,656,369 |
| 6 | FEB1999 | $379,038,463 | $140,625,851 | $253,999,924 | $74,168,740 |
| 7 | MAR1997 | $292,661,724 | $123,302,226 | $196,591,378 | $28,526,103 |
| 8 | MAR1998 | $355,443,234 | $77,437,835 | $239,056,026 | $202,158,055 |
| 9 | MAR1999 | $419,901,924 | $66,436,824 | $281,433,310 | $39,955,768 |
| 10 | APR1997 | $567,242,394 | $47,862,099 | $380,804,120 | $260,386,468 |
| 11 | APR1998 | $344,270,933 | $333,474,626 | $231,609,634 | $41,160,707 |
| 12 | APR1999 | $406,393,250 | $442,134,756 | $272,049,319 | $312,654,811 |
| 13 | MAY1997 | $293,053,316 | $128,810,605 | $196,261,573 | $109,975,326 |
| 14 | MAY1998 | $355,539,235 | $92,904,623 | $238,245,243 | $264,294,440 |
| 15 | MAY1999 | $420,234,672 | $458,812,748 | $280,369,422 | $318,149,340 |
| 16 | JUN1997 | $283,288,496 | $212,378,496 | $190,560,829 | $102,833,104 |
| 17 | JUN1998 | $344,570,789 | $412,429,160 | $230,952,369 | $267,135,485 |
| 18 | JUN1999 | $406,557,215 | $184,286,073 | $271,894,927 | $187,270,927 |
| 19 | JUL1997 | $292,726,096 | $319,499,539 | $197,163,278 | $196,728,648 |
| 20 | JUL1998 | $355,598,014 | $240,654,274 | $239,396,212 | $208,694,865 |
| 21 | JUL1999 | $419,883,266 | $97,120,463 | $280,649,618 | $123,394,421 |
| 22 | AUG1997 | $292,339,489 | $34,004,244 | $196,639,501 | $236,996,122 |
| 23 | AUG1998 | $355,525,255 | $406,504,195 | $238,629,758 | $83,456,868 |
| 24 | AUG1999 | $419,240,506 | $438,102,259 | $281,582,229 | $34,273,985 |
| 25 | SEP1997 | $283,387,679 | $206,472,552 | $190,535,012 | $112,413,744 |
| 26 | SEP1998 | $344,299,612 | $226,480,968 | $231,186,018 | $286,846,554 |
| 27 | SEP1999 | $406,509,709 | $483,757,203 | $272,253,650 | $151,565,752 |
| 28 | OCT1997 | $292,979,274 | $50,706,092 | $196,957,153 | $125,401,565 |
| 29 | OCT1998 | $355,254,117 | $173,100,004 | $238,905,712 | $275,721,406 |
| 30 | OCT1999 | $420,009,172 | $436,676,381 | $280,100,981 | $141,528,519 |
| 31 | NOV1997 | $282,958,158 | $298,545,086 | $190,228,067 | $72,551,855 |
| 32 | NOV1998 | $344,234,146 | $377,287,496 | $231,314,163 | $230,488,351 |
| 33 | NOV1999 | $405,985,809 | $78,296,870 | $272,428,947 | $178,043,261 |
| 34 | DEC1997 | $293,489,962 | $213,838,302 | $196,504,413 | $136,042,505 |
| 35 | DEC1998 | $356,353,933 | $106,533,277 | $238,689,981 | $24,901,752 |
| 36 | DEC1999 | $406,894,881 | $14,306,308 | $272,149,940 | $181,668,256 |

## Exercises

5. The ia.MealPlan data set contains information on which meals, if any, will be served on flights. Meal service is based on the day of the week (1 to 7) and the hour of the day of the flight.

   **a.** Produce a SAS data set named ia.Meals that contains the meal service code for each flight.

   **b.** Use the ia.Schedule data set to obtain the flight information.

   **c.** Create a two-dimensional array from the ia.MealPlan data set.

   **d.** Look up the meal for each flight using the WEEKDAY function on the DATE and the HOUR function on DEPART.

## 5.6 Chapter Summary

The Output Delivery System (ODS) enables you to produce output sent to several different destinations:

- OUTPUT (tables)
- LISTING (window or file)

Procedures separate output into components or output objects. These objects consist of two parts: a data portion and a template portion (also called a table definition). Using ODS techniques, you can send all or some of the objects created by a procedure to the destinations listed above. Each object has a name and other characteristics.

To determine the name of the object, use

```
ODS TRACE ON;
```

The ODS TRACE statement lists the names of the objects, the template names, the data name, and several labels in the log. The ODS TRACE remains on until you turn it off using

```
ODS TRACE OFF;
```

To send objects to tables, use

```
ODS OUTPUT object-1-name=table-1-name
           object-2-name=table-2-name...;
```

If a procedure produces more than one object with the same name by using multiple analysis variables or a BY statement, ODS OUTPUT creates one table containing all of the information. By using the MATCH_ALL option, you can get separate data sets for each of the analysis variables or each BY value.

```
ODS OUTPUT object-1-name(MATCH_ALL)=table;
```

You can use multiple SET statements to combine observations from several SAS data sets.

When you use multiple SET statements

- processing stops when SAS encounters the end-of-file marker on any data set
- the variables in the PDV are not reinitialized when a second SET statement is executed.

You can use _N_ = 1 to control reading from one data set the first time through the DATA step.

To create the summary statistic in the DATA step and combine it with the detail data, we need to

- read the data once and calculate the summary statistic
- re-read the data to combine the summary statistic with the detail data and calculate the percentages.

You can use the SUM statement to

- accumulate totals
- retain the accumulator variable
- initialize the accumulator variable to 0
- ignore missing values.

General form of the SUM statement

```
accumulator-variable+expression;
```

You can use the COMPARE procedure to compare

- data set attributes of TYPE and LABEL
- variable names to determine common variables
- attributes of common variables
- data values in each observation.

```
PROC COMPARE DATA = base-data-set
   COMPARE = comparison-data-set
<options>;
  ID variable-list <notsorted>;
  VAR variable-list;
  WITH variable-list;
RUN;
```

You can use multidimensional arrays to perform table lookups when the forms of SAS data sets can not be merged.

General form for the multidimensional ARRAY statement:

```
ARRAY array-name {...,rows, cols} $ length
      elements (initial values);
```

Entire Program

```
/********* c05s2d1 ******************/

/*************************************/
/*    Investigate the objects        */
/*    created by PROC PRINT and      */
/*    PROC UNIVARIATE.               */
/*************************************/


proc print data = ia.MonthlySummary1997_1999(obs = 10);
   title 'Objects from PROC PRINT';
run;


proc univariate data = ia.MonthlySummary1997_1999;
   var RevenueFirstClass;
   title 'Objects from PROC UNIVARIATE';
run;



/********* c05s2d2 ******************/

/*************************************/
/*    Use the ODS TRACE statement    */
/*    to determine the names of the  */
/*    objects created by PROC PRINT  */
/*    and PROC UNIVARIATE.           */
/*************************************/


ods trace on;

proc print data = ia.monthlySummary1997_1999;
run;

proc univariate data = ia.MonthlySummary1997_1999;
   var RevenueFirstClass;
run;

ods trace off;
```

```
/********* c05s2d3 ******************/

/*************************************/
/*    Use the ODS OUTPUT statement   */
/*    to create data sets from       */
/*    objects PROC UNIVARIATE.       */
/*************************************/


ods output basicmeasures = work.statistics
              Extremeobs = work.extremeobs;
proc univariate data = ia.MonthlySummary1997_1999;
   var RevenueFirstClass;
run;

proc print data = work.statistics;
   title 'The statistics from the BasicMeasures object';
   title2 'Of PROC UNIVARIATE';
run;


proc print data = work.extremeobs;
   title 'The statistics from the ExtremeObs object';
   title2 'Of PROC UNIVARIATE';
run;




/********* c05s2d4 ******************/
/********* Example 1 ****************/

/*************************************/
/*    Use the ODS OUTPUT statement   */
/*    to create data sets from       */
/*    objects PROC UNIVARIATE.       */
/*************************************/


ods output quantiles = work.statistics;
proc univariate data = ia.SalesData2000;
   var RevenueFirstClass RevenueBusiness RevenueEconomy;
run;


proc print data = work.statistics;
   title 'The Quantiles object of PROC UNIVARIATE';
   title2 'Data for RevenueFirstClass RevenueBusiness
          RevenueEconomy';
run;
```

```
/********* Example 2 *****************/

ods output quantiles(match_all) = work.stats;
proc univariate data = ia.SalesData2000;
   var RevenueFirstClass RevenueBusiness RevenueEconomy;
run;


proc print data = work.stats;
   title 'The Quantiles object of PROC UNIVARIATE';
   title2 'Data for RevenueFirstClass';
run;


proc print data = work.stats1;
   title 'The Quantiles object of PROC UNIVARIATE';
   title2 'Data for RevenueBusiness';
run;

proc print data = work.stats2;
   title 'The Quantiles object of PROC UNIVARIATE';
   title2 'Data for RevenueEconomy';
run;




/********* c05s3d1 ******************/

/*************************************/
/*    Create a SAS data set using    */
/*    ODS and PROC MEANS.            */
/*    Combine this data set with     */
/*    the detail data.               */
/*************************************/


ods trace on;
proc means data = ia.MonthlySummary1997_1999;
   var RevenueCargo;
run;
ods trace off;


ods output summary = work.summary;
proc means data = ia.MonthlySummary1997_1999 sum;
   var RevenueCargo;
run;


data ia.percentages;
   if _n_ = 1 then set work.summary
                    (keep = RevenueCargo_sum);
```

```
    set ia.MonthlySummary1997_1999
        (keep = FlightMonth RevenueCargo);
    PercentRevenue = RevenueCargo / RevenueCargo_sum;
run;

proc print data = ia.percentages(obs = 10);
    title 'Summary and Detailed Data Combined Using';
    title2 'ODS to Create the Summary';
run;
```

```
/********* c05s3d2 ******************/

/*************************************/
/*    Create the summary data and    */
/*    combine it with the detail data */
/*    in the DATA step.              */
/*************************************/


data ia.percentages_1 ;
   if _n_ = 1 then do until(last);
      set ia.MonthlySummary1997_1999(keep = RevenueCargo)
                              end = last;
      TotalRevenue + RevenueCargo;
   end;
   set ia.MonthlySummary1997_1999
       (keep = FlightMonth RevenueCargo );
   PercentRevenue = RevenueCargo / TotalRevenue;
run;


proc print data = ia.percentages_1(obs = 10);
   title 'Creating Summary Statistics and Percentages';
   title2 'In the DATA Step';
run;
```

```
/********* c05s4d1 ******************/

/*************************************/
/*    Compare the data created by    */
/*    two different techniques       */
/*************************************/


proc compare data = work.percentages
             compare = work.percentages_1;
   title 'Comparing Two Techniques';
run;




/********* c05s5d1 ******************/

/*************************************/
/*    Use an array to compare values */
/*    in one data set to those       */
/*    in another.                    */
/*************************************/



data ia.lookup;
   array targets{1997:1999,2,12} _temporary_;
   array mon{12} JAN FEB MAR APR MAY JUN
                 JUL AUG SEP OCT NOV DEC;
   if _n_ = 1 then do i = 1 to 6;
      set ia.target;
        if revtype = 'cargo' then t = 1;
        else t = 2;
        do j = 1 to 12;
           targets{year,t,j} = mon{j};
        end;
   end;
   set ia.MonthlySummary1997_1999;
   TotalPassengerRevenue = sum(RevenueFirstClass,
                               RevenueBusiness,
                               RevenueEconomy);
   year = input(substr(FlightMonth,4),4.);
   CargoTarget = targets{year,1,month};
   PassengerTarget = targets{year,2,month};
run;

proc print data = ia.lookup;
   title 'Using a Multidimensional Array for Table Lookup';
   var FlightMonth TotalPassengerRevenue PassengerTarget
       RevenueCargo CargoTarget;
   format _numeric_ dollar14.;
run;
```

## 5.7 Solutions to Exercises

1. Using ODS and PROC MEANS, create a SAS data set named ia.Mean that contains only one observation - the overall average employee contribution.

   a. Use the ODS TRACE statement to determine the name of the ouput objects.

   b. Use the MEAN option on the PROC MEANS statement to limit the output to the mean statistic.

   c. The name of the data set on which to calculate statistics in the PROC MEANS step is IA.Rotate which was created in a previous exercise.

```
ods trace on;

proc means data = ia.rotate;
   var amount;
run;

ods trace off;

ods output summary = ia.mean;

proc means data = ia.rotate mean;
   var amount;
run;

proc print data = ia.mean;
run;
```

2. Combine ia.Mean, from the previous exercise, with ia.Emp_Contrib to determine the difference between the overall average contribution and each individual employee contribution.
   - Create a new SAS data set containing the differences named ia.Diffs
   - Round the difference to the nearest cent.

```
data ia.diffs;
   if _n_ = 1 then set ia.mean;
   set ia.rotate;
   diff= round(amount - amount_mean,.01);
run;
```

**3.** Create a data setnamed ia.Diffs2 with the same values as ia.Diffs by reading ia.Rotate twice with SET statements.

- Calculate the overall average employee contribution.
- Do not output observations from ia.Rotate where the contribution is missing and do not include the observation in the calculation of the mean.
- Compare the average to each individual employee contribution.

```
data ia.diffs2(drop = TotalContrib n);
   retain avg diff;
   if _n_ = 1 then do;
      do until(last);
         set ia.rotate end = last;
         TotalContrib + Amount;
         if amount ne . then n + 1;
      end;
      avg=totalContrib / n;
   end;
   set ia.rotate;
   if amount ne .;
   Diff = round(Amount - Avg,.01);
run;
```

Diffs2 Partial Output

| Obs | avg | diff | EMP_ID | Qtr Num | Amount |
|---|---|---|---|---|---|
| 1 | 28.9667 | -16.97 | E00224 | qtr1 | 12 |
| 2 | 28.9667 | 4.03 | E00224 | qtr2 | 33 |
| 3 | 28.9667 | -6.97 | E00224 | qtr3 | 22 |
| 4 | 28.9667 | 6.03 | E00367 | qtr1 | 35 |
| 5 | 28.9667 | 19.03 | E00367 | qtr2 | 48 |
| 6 | 28.9667 | 11.03 | E00367 | qtr3 | 40 |
| 7 | 28.9667 | 1.03 | E00367 | qtr4 | 30 |
| 8 | 28.9667 | 34.03 | E00441 | qtr2 | 63 |
| 9 | 28.9667 | 60.03 | E00441 | qtr3 | 89 |
| 10 | 28.9667 | 61.03 | E00441 | qtr4 | 90 |
| 11 | 28.9667 | -12.97 | E00587 | qtr1 | 16 |
| 12 | 28.9667 | -9.97 | E00587 | qtr2 | 19 |
| 13 | 28.9667 | 1.03 | E00587 | qtr3 | 30 |
| 14 | 28.9667 | 0.03 | E00587 | qtr4 | 29 |
| 15 | 28.9667 | -24.97 | E00598 | qtr1 | 4 |

4. Using PROC COMPARE, compare the two permanent SAS data sets Diffs and Diffs2 which were created in previous exercises.

   Compare only the amounts and differences by each employee id number and quarter number.

   **Hint:** Sort both data sets by employee id number and quarter number prior to the comparison.

```
proc sort data = ia.diffs;
   by emp_id qtrnum;
run;

proc sort data = ia.diffs2;
   by emp_id qtrnum;
run;

proc compare data = ia.diffs compare = ia.diffs2;
   id emp_id qtrnum;
   var amount diff;
run;
```

5. The ia.MealPlan data set contains information on which meals, if any, will be served on flights. Meal service is based on the day of the week (1 to 7) and the hour of the day of the flight.

   a. Produce a SAS data set named Meals that contains the meal service code for each flight.

   b. Use the ia.Schedule data set to obtain the flight information.

   c. Create a two-dimensional array from the ia.MealPlan data set.

   d. Look up the meal for each flight using the WEEKDAY function on the DATE and the HOUR function on DEPART.

```
data ia.meal;
   array food{7,24} $ 10 _temporary_;
   if _n_ = 1 then do i = 1 to all;
      set ia.mealplan nobs = all;
      food{dow,hour} = meal;
   end;
   set ia.schedule;
   service = food{weekday(date),hour(depart)};
   keep flight date depart service;
run;
```

# Chapter 6

# 6.1 Introduction

## General Business Scenario

International Airlines has two SAS data sets. One is a very large detail data set and the other a small data set. We must combine the two data sets to return the matches.

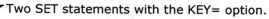

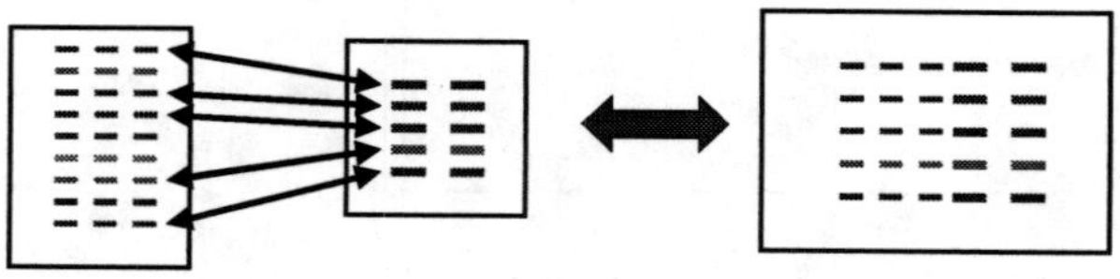

3

## Available Techniques

- DATA step with a MERGE statement
- PROC SQL join
- Two SET statements with the KEY= option.

4

## Organize the Tasks

- Create an index on the large data set.
- Combine the small data set with the large data set using the KEY= option on the SET statement.

5

# 6.2 Creating and Maintaining an Index

## Objectives

- Define indexes.
- List the uses of indexes.
- Use the DATA step to create indexes.
- Use PROC DATASETS to create and maintain indexes.
- Use PROC SQL to create and maintain indexes.

7

## Business Scenario

We must create an index on IA.SALESDATA2000.

| Obs | Flight IDNumber | Route IDNumber | Origin | Destination | ... | Flight ... Date ... |
|---|---|---|---|---|---|---|
| 1 | IA00100 | 0000001 | RDU | LHR | ... | 01JAN2000 ... |
| 2 | IA00101 | 0000001 | RDU | LHR | ... | 01JAN2000 ... |
| 3 | IA00100 | 0000001 | RDU | LHR | ... | 02JAN2000 ... |
| | : | : | : | : | : | : |
| Obs | Flight IDNumber | Route IDNumber | Origin | Destination | ... | Flight ... Date ... |
| 164629 | IA11200 | 0000112 | SFO | HND | ... | 30DEC2000 ... |
| 164630 | IA11201 | 0000112 | SFO | HND | ... | 30DEC2000 ... |
| 164631 | IA11200 | 0000112 | SFO | HND | ... | 31DEC2000 ... |
| 164632 | IA11201 | 0000112 | SFO | HND | ... | 31DEC2000 ... |

8

## Organize the Tasks:

- Create an index on the large data set.
- Combine the small data set with the large data set using the KEY= option on the SET statement.

9

## The Purpose of Indexes

10

```
where origin = 'LHR';
```

Without an index on the variable ORIGIN, a WHERE statement processes the data set ia.SalesData2000 sequentially. SAS reads all the data in ia.SalesData2000.

## The Purpose of Indexes

11

```
where origin = 'LHR';
```

With an index on the variable ORIGIN, a WHERE statement processes the data set ia.SalesData2000 directly. SAS reads only the data in ia.SalesData2000, satisfying the WHERE expression.

## Using Indexes

An *index* is an auxiliary data structure that specifies the location of observations based on the values of one or more *key variables.*

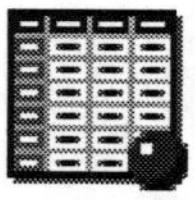

`FlightIDNumber`
`FlightDate`
`Origin`

**Key Variables in ia.SalesData2000**

`Origin`
`DateFlight`

**Indexes in the index file for ia.SalesData2000**

12

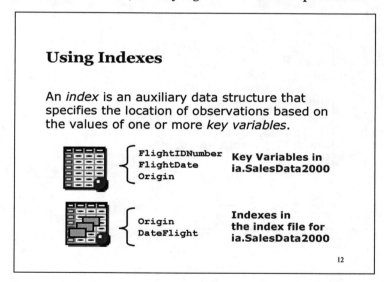

An index can be created on a SAS data file, not a SAS data view.

## The Purpose of Indexes

Indexes can provide direct access to observations in SAS data sets to

- yield faster access to small subsets
- return observations in sorted order
- perform table lookup operations
- join observations
- modify observations.

13

## Index Terminology

There are two types of indexes.

| Simple | Composite |
|---|---|
| Based on the values of only one variable. | Based on the values of more than one variable concatenated to form a single value. |
| Automatically given the same name as its key variable. | **Must** be given a name that is not the same as that of any variable or existing index. |

14

## Index Terminology

Index options include:

**UNIQUE** values of the key variable(s) must be unique. Prevents an observation with a duplicate value for the key variable from being added to the data set.

15

If the variable(s) on which you attempt to create a unique index have duplicate values, the index is not created.

### Creating Indexes

To create indexes in the same step during which you create a data set, use the INDEX= data set option on the output data set.

To create or delete indexes in existing data sets, use the

- DATASETS procedure
- SQL procedure.

16

### Creating Indexes

When creating the index, you

- designate the key variable(s)
- select a valid SAS name for the index (composite index only)
- specify an index option.

A data set can have

- multiple simple and composite indexes
- character and numeric key variables.

17

Though you can have multiple indexes on a SAS data set, for efficient usage, only create indexes on variables that are

- commonly used in a WHERE condition
- used to combine SAS data sets.

## Viewing Information about Indexes

To display information in the log concerning index creation or index usage, change the value of the MSGLEVEL= system option from its default value of N to I.

General form of the MSGLEVEL= system option:

```
OPTIONS MSGLEVEL=N | I;
```

18

I Information

N Notes

## Creating Indexes with the DATA Step

When creating a data set in a DATA step, use the INDEX= data set option to create an index at the same time.

General form of the INDEX= data set option:

```
DATA SAS-data-file-name(INDEX=
        (index-specification-1</option>
    ...<index-specification-n</option>>));
```

19

*index-specification* for a

| | |
|---|---|
| simple index | is the name of the key variable. |
| composite index | is *index-name* = (list of key variables). |

## Creating Indexes with the DATA Step

c06s2d1

Program

```
options mslevel = i;

data ia.SalesData2000 (index = (Origin DateFlight =
                        (FlightIDNumber FlightDate)/unique));
   set ia.SalesData2000;
run;
```

Log

```
7     options msglevel = i;

8     data ia.SalesData2000 (index = (Origin DateFlight =
9                           (FlightIDNumber FlightDate)/unique));

10      set ia.SalesData2000;
11    run;

NOTE: There were 164632 observations read from the data set IA.SALESDATA2000.
NOTE: The data set IA.SALESDATA2000 has 164632 observations and 20 variables.
NOTE: Composite index DateFlight has been defined.
NOTE: Simple index Origin has been defined.
```

For increased efficiency, use the INDEX= option to create indexes when you initially create a SAS data set.

## Managing Indexes with PROC DATASETS

You can use PROC DATASETS on existing data sets to create or delete indexes.

General form of the PROC DATASETS step to delete or create indexes:

```
PROC DATASETS LIBRARY=libref;
    MODIFY SAS-data-set-name;
        INDEX DELETE index-name;
        INDEX CREATE index-specification
                          < / options>;
QUIT;
```

21

PROC DATASETS cannot be used if the index to be created already exists.

## Managing Indexes with PROC DATASETS

c06s2d2

Program

```
options msglevel = i;

proc datasets library = ia nolist;
   modify SalesData2000;
   index delete Origin;
   index delete DateFlight;

   index create Origin;
   index create DateFlight =
               (FlightIDNumber FlightDate) / unique;
quit;
```

The NOLIST option prevents a list of library members from being printed in the LOG.

Log

```
21   options msglevel = i;
22
23   proc datasets library = ia nolist;
24      modify SalesData2000;
25      index delete Origin;
NOTE: Index Origin deleted.
26      index delete id;
NOTE: All indexes defined on IA.SALESDATA2000.DATA have been deleted.
27
28      index create Origin;
NOTE: Simple index Origin has been defined.
29      index create id = (FlightIDNumber FlightDate) / unique;
NOTE: Composite index id has been defined.
30   quit;
```

## Managing Indexes with PROC SQL

You can use PROC SQL on existing data sets to create or delete indexes.

General form of the PROC SQL step to create or delete indexes:

```
PROC SQL;
   CREATE <option> INDEX index-name
      ON table-name(column-name-1,...
                    column-name-n);
   DROP INDEX index-name
      FROM table-name;
```

23

PROC SQL cannot be used if the index to be created already exists.

## Managing Indexes with PROC SQL

c06s2d3

Program

```
options msglevel = i;

proc sql;
   drop index Origin
      from ia.SalesData2000;
   drop index DateFlight
      from ia.SalesData2000;

   create index Origin
         on ia.SalesData2000(Origin);
   create unique index DateFlight
         on ia.SalesData2000(FlightIDNumber,FlightDate);
quit;
```

Log

```
44   options msglevel = i;
45
46   proc sql;
47      drop index Origin
48         from ia.SalesData2000;
NOTE: Index Origin has been dropped.
49      drop index DateFlight
50         from ia.SalesData2000;
NOTE: Index DateFlight has been dropped.
51
52      create index Origin
53            on ia.SalesData2000(Origin);
NOTE: Simple index Origin has been defined.
54      create unique index DateFlight
55            on ia.SalesData2000(FlightIDNumber,FlightDate);
NOTE: Composite index DateFlight has been defined.
56   quit;
```

## How Indexes Are Stored

Indexes are stored in

- the same SAS data library as the data set they index
- a separate SAS file from the data set.

An index file

- may contain multiple indexes for an individual data set
- does not appear as a separate file in OS/390 operating system file lists.

25

## Index Documentation

- PROC CONTENTS
- PROC DATASETS
- SAS Explorer
- Columns Window.

26

## Documenting Indexes

c06s2d4

Program

```
proc contents data = ia.SalesData2000;
run;
```

Log

```
The CONTENTS Procedure

Data Set Name: IA.SALESDATA2000              Observations:          164632
Member Type:   DATA                          Variables:             20
Engine:        V8                            Indexes:               2
Created:       10:35 Saturday,               Observation Length:    152
               June 3, 2000
Last Modified: 10:48 Saturday,               Deleted Observations: 0
               June 3, 2000
Protection:                                  Compressed:            NO
Data Set Type:                               Sorted:                NO
Label:


              -----Engine/Host Dependent Information-----

Data Set Page Size:          12288
Number of Data Set Pages:    2060
First Data Page:             1
Max Obs per Page:            80
Obs in First Data Page:      56
Index File Page Size:        4096
Number of Index File Pages: 1294
Number of Data Set Repairs: 0
File Name:                   C:\workshop\winsas\prog3\salesdata2000.sas7bdat
Release Created:             8.0101M0
Host Created:                WIN_NT


         -----Alphabetic List of Variables and Attributes-----

 # Variable       Type Len Pos Format     Informat Label
___________________________________________________________________________
12 Business       Num    8  56                     Number of Business
   Passengers                                      Passengers
 6 Capacity       Num    8   8 8.         8.       Aircraft Capacity
   Business                                        - Business Class
                                                   Passengers
 9 CapacityCargo Num     8  32 8.         8.       Aircraft Capacity -
                                                   Total Payload
                                                   in Pounds
 7 Capacity       Num    8  16 8.         8.       Aircraft Capacity
   Economy                                         - Economy Class
                                                   Passengers
```

```
 5 Capacity      Num    8   0 8.        8.        Aircraft Capacity -
   FirstClass                                     First Class
                                                  Passengers
 8 CapacityTotal Num    8  24 8.        8.        Aircraft Capacity
                                                  - Total Passengers
18 CargoWeight   Num    8  96                     Weight of Cargo
                                                  in Pounds
 4 Destination   Char   3 137                     Destination
13 Economy       Num    8  64                     Number of Economy
   Passengers                                     Passengers
11 FirstClass    Num    8  48                     Number of First
   Passengers                                     Class Passengers
10 FlightDate    Num    8  40 DATE9.              Scheduled Date
                                                  of Flight
 1 Flight        Char   7 120                     Flight Number
   IDNumber
20 FlightMonth   Num    8 112
17 Month         Char   7 140                     Sales Month
 3 Origin        Char   3 134                     Start Point
15 RevBusiness   Num    8  80 DOLLAR15.2          Revenue from Business
                                                  Passengers
19 RevCargo      Num    8 104 DOLLAR15.2          Revenue from Cargo
16 RevEconomy    Num    8  88 DOLLAR15.2          Revenue from Economy
                                                  Passengers
14 RevFirstClass Num    8  72 DOLLAR15.2          Revenue from First
                                                  Class Passengers
 2 RouteIDNumber Char   7 127                     Route Number


           -----Alphabetic List of Indexes and Attributes-----

                                       # of
                            Unique    Unique
      #    Index            Option    Values     Variables
      ____________________________________________________________
      1    DateFlight         YES      164632    FlightIDNumber FlightDate
      2    Origin                          52
```

## Maintaining Indexes

| Data Management Tasks | Index Action Taken |
|---|---|
| Copy data set with PROC COPY or PROC DATASETS | Index file constructed for new data file |
| Move the data set with the MOVE option in PROC COPY | Index file deleted from IN= library, rebuilt in OUT= library |

28

If you use PROC UPLOAD or PROC DOWNLOAD, the index is re-created by default when you upload or download a single data set and omit the OUT= option, or when you upload or download a SAS data library. Use the INDEX=NO data set option to upload or download without re-creating the index.

## Maintaining Indexes

| Data Management Tasks | Index Action Taken |
|---|---|
| Rename data set | Index file renamed |
| Rename variable | Variable renamed to new name in index file |
| Add observations | Value/identifier pairs added |
| Delete observations | Value/identifier pairs deleted; space recovered for reuse |
| Update observations | Value/identifier pairs updated if values change |

29

## Maintaining Indexes

| Data Management Tasks | Index Action Taken |
|---|---|
| Delete data set | Index file deleted |
| Rebuild data set with a DATA step | Index file deleted |
| Sort data set with the FORCE option in PROC SORT | Index file deleted |

30

If the data set A has an index file, these programs would delete the index file.

```
proc datasets lib = work;
   delete A;
run;

data A;
   set A;
run;


proc sort data = A force;
   by X;
run;
```

## Exercises

1. Create two indexes for the ia.Schedule data set using PROC DATASETS.
   - A simple index Flight, based on the Flight variable
   - A unique composite index FltDte, based on the Flight and Date variables.
2. Delete the indexes for the ia.Schedule data set using PROC SQL.
3. Re-create the indexes for the ia.Schedule data set using the DATA step and the INDEX= option.
4. Use PROC CONTENTS to look at the index information.

# 6.3 Combining SAS Data Sets Using an Index

## Objectives

- Use an index to combine two data sets.

33

## Business Scenario

The index on IA.SALESDATA2000 enables us to merge it with a small SAS data set, IA.DOWNUNDER, that contains information about New Zealand and Australia.

ia.DownUnder

| Obs | Flight IDNumber | Route IDNumber | Flight Date | Fare Expenses |
|---|---|---|---|---|
| 1 | IA10200 | 0000102 | 01DEC2000 | 38587 |
| 2 | IA10201 | 0000102 | 01DEC2000 | 16622 |
| 3 | IA10200 | 0000102 | 02DEC2000 | 160433 |
| 4 | IA10201 | 0000102 | 02DEC2000 | 19987 |
| 5 | IA10200 | 0000102 | 03DEC2000 | 64585 |
| | : | : | : | : |

34

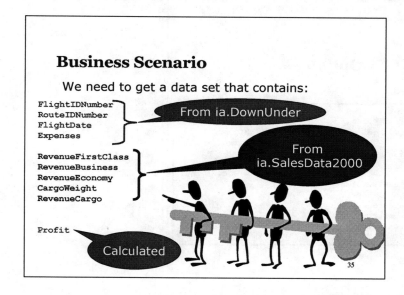

## Business Scenario

We need to get a data set that contains:

```
FlightIDNumber
RouteIDNumber
FlightDate
Expenses
```

From ia.DownUnder

```
RevenueFirstClass
RevenueBusiness
RevenueEconomy
CargoWeight
RevenueCargo
```

From ia.SalesData2000

```
Profit
```

Calculated

35

## Using the KEY= Option

An index is used when a SET or MODIFY statement contains the KEY= option.

Specify the KEY= option in the SET statement to use an index to retrieve observations having key values equal to the current value of the key variable(s).

General form of the KEY= option:

**SET** *SAS-data-file-name* KEY= *index-name*;

36

To use this feature, assign a value to the index key variable(s) before the SET statement is executed. The index is then used to retrieve an observation with the key value.

WHERE processing is not allowed for a data set read with the KEY= option.

## Using the KEY= Option

```
data work.DownUnderProfit;
   set ia.DownUnder;
   set ia.SalesData2000(keep = RouteIDNumber FlightIDNumber
                               FlightDate RevenueFirstClass
                               RevenueBusiness
                               RevenueEconomy
                               RevenueCargo) key = DateFlight;
   Profit = sum(RevenueFirstClass,
                RevenueBusiness,
                RevenueEconomy
                RevenueCargo,
                - Expenses);
run;
```

37

```
data work.DownUnderProfit;
   set ia.DownUnder;
   set ia.SalesData2000(keep = RouteIDNumber FlightIDNumber
                               FlightDate RevenueFirstClass
                               RevenueBusiness RevenueEconomy
                               RevenueCargo) key = DateFlight;
   Profit = sum(RevenueFirstClass,
                RevenueBusiness,
                RevenueEconomy,
                RevenueCargo,
                - Expenses);
run;
```

**Compilation**

| RouteID Number | FlightID Number | Flight Date | Expenses | Revenue FirstClass |
|---|---|---|---|---|
| | | | | |

| Revenue Business | Revenue Economy | Revenue Cargo | Profit | D _N_ |
|---|---|---|---|---|
| | | | | |

38

```
data work.DownUnderProfit;
   set ia.DownUnder;
   set ia.SalesData2000(keep = RouteIDNumber FlightIDNumber
                               FlightDate RevenueFirstClass
                               RevenueBusiness RevenueEconomy
                               RevenueCargo) key = DateFlight;
   Profit = sum(RevenueFirstClass
                RevenueBusiness,
                RevenueEconomy,
                RevenueCargo,
                - Expenses);
run;
```

**Execution**

| RouteID Number | FlightID Number | Flight Date | Expenses | Revenue FirstClass |
|---|---|---|---|---|
| IA10200 | 0000102 | 01DEC2000 | 38587 | |

| Revenue Business | Revenue Economy | Revenue Cargo | Profit | D _N_ |
|---|---|---|---|---|
| | | | | 1 |

39

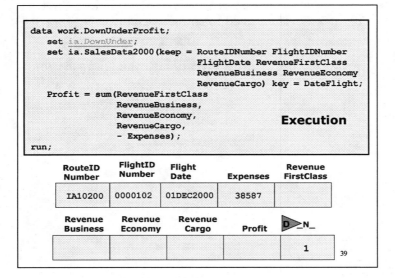

An observation is read from ia.DownUnder sequentially by the first SET statement.

```
data work.DownUnderProfit;
   set ia.DownUnder;
   set ia.SalesData2000(keep = RouteIDNumber FlightIDNumber
                               FlightDate RevenueFirstClass
                               RevenueBusiness RevenueEconomy
                               RevenueCargo) key = DateFlight;
   Profit = sum(RevenueFirstClass,
                RevenueBusiness,
                RevenueEconomy,
                RevenueCargo,
                - Expenses);
run;
```

**Execution**

| RouteID Number | FlightID Number | Flight Date | Expenses | Revenue FirstClass |
|---|---|---|---|---|
| IA10200 | 0000102 | 01DEC2000 | 38587 | 35967 |

| Revenue Business | Revenue Economy | Revenue Cargo | Profit | D _N_ |
|---|---|---|---|---|
| 37410 | 98124 | 188277 | | 1 |

40

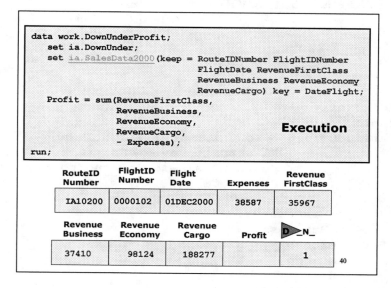

The KEY= causes the second SET to use the values in FLIGHTIDNUMBER and FLIGHTDATE to access an observation through the DATEFLIGHT index.

```
data work.DownUnderProfit;
   set ia.DownUnder;
   set ia.SalesData2000(keep = RouteIDNumber FlightIDNumber
                               FlightDate RevenueFirstClass
                               RevenueBusiness RevenueEconomy
                               RevenueCargo) key = DateFlight;
   Profit = sum(RevenueFirstClass,
                RevenueBusiness,
                RevenueEconomy,
                RevenueCargo,
                - Expenses);
run;
```

**Execution**

**Implied Output**

| RouteID Number | FlightID Number | Flight Date | Expenses | Revenue FirstClass |
|---|---|---|---|---|
| IA10200 | 0000102 | 01DEC2000 | 38587 | 35967 |

| Revenue Business | Revenue Economy | Revenue Cargo | Profit | D _N_ |
|---|---|---|---|---|
| 37410 | 98124 | 188277 | 321191 | 1 |

41

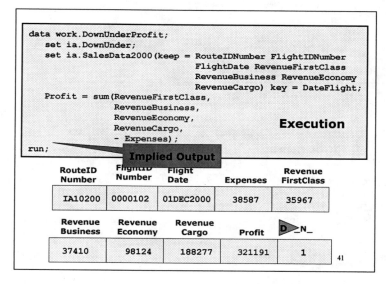

The assignment statement calculates values for PROFIT.

The updated observation is written to work.DownUnderFareProfit.

## Using Two SET Statements with the KEY= Option

c06s3d1

Program

```
data work.DownUnderProfit;
   set ia.DownUnder;
   set ia.SalesData2000(keep = RouteIDNumber FlightIDNumber
                               FlightDate RevenueFirstClass
                               RevenueBusiness RevenueEconomy
                               RevenueCargo)  key =
DateFlight;
   Profit = sum(RevenueFirstClass,
                RevenueBusiness,
                RevenueEconomy,
                RevenueCargo,
                - Expenses);
run;

proc print data = work.DownUnderProfit;
   title1 'Profit for the Flights';
   title2 'to Australia and New Zealand';
run;
```

Partial Output (First Four Observations)

```
                        Profit for the Flights
                      to Australia and New Zealand

    Flight   Route       Flight              RevenueFirst
Obs IDNumber IDNumber      Date Expenses            Class RevenueBusiness

  1 IA10200  0000102  01DEC2000    71655       $35,967.00      $37,410.00
  2 IA10201  0000102  01DEC2000    57640       $34,074.00      $42,570.00
  3 IA10200  0000102  02DEC2000   127371       $30,288.00      $41,280.00
  4 IA10201  0000102  02DEC2000    22012       $28,395.00      $43,860.00


Obs  Revenueeconomy       RevenueCargo    Profit

  1      $98,124.00        $188,277.00    288123
  2     $106,301.00        $178,965.00    304270
  3      $96,237.00        $190,023.00    230457
  4      $97,495.00        $188,277.00    336015
```

Last Four Observations

```
                          Profit for the Flights
                       to Australia and New Zealand

     Flight   Route      Flight                  RevenueFirst
Obs IDNumber IDNumber      Date Expenses                Class RevenueBusiness

897 IA10802  0000108  30DEC2000    5673             $1,397.00               .
898 IA10803  0000108  30DEC2000    1192             $1,270.00               .
899 IA10804  0000108  30DEC2000    1336             $1,397.00               .
900 IA11805  0000108  30DEC2000    2413             $1,397.00               .


Obs  Revenueeconomy         RevenueCargo     Profit

897       $5,292.00            $1,900.00       2916
898       $5,376.00            $1,860.00       7314
899       $4,872.00            $2,300.00       7233
900       $4,872.00            $2,300.00       6156
```

Observation 899 is correct, but because the data values are retained when SAS reads observation 900 from ia.DownUnder, observation 900 is incorrect.

Log

```
252  options msglevel=i;
253  data work.DownUnderProfit;
254     set ia.DownUnder;
255     set ia.SalesData2000(keep = RouteIDNumber FlightIDNumber
256                               FlightDate RevenueFirstClass
257                               RevenueBusiness RevenueEconomy
258                               RevenueCargo)  key = DateFlight;
259     Profit = sum(RevenueFirstClass,
260                  RevenueBusiness,
261                  RevenueEconomy,
262                  RevenueCargo,
263                  - Expenses);
264  run;

FlightIDNumber=IA11805 RouteIDNumber=0000108 FlightDate=30DEC2000
Expenses=2413 RevenueFirstClass=$1,397.00 RevenueBusiness=.
Revenueeconomy=$4,872.00 RevenueCargo=$2,300.00 Profit=6156 _ERROR_=1
_IORC_=1230015 _N_=900
NOTE: There were 900 observations read from the data set IA.DOWNUNDER.
NOTE: There were 899 observations read from the data set
      IA.SALESDATA2000.
NOTE: The data set WORK.DOWNUNDERPROFIT has 900 observations and 9
      variables.
NOTE: DATA statement used:
      real time           0.42 seconds
      cpu time            0.39 seconds
```

The observation appearing in the log is the result of having an observation in ia.DownUnder that does not match an observation in ia.SalesData2000.

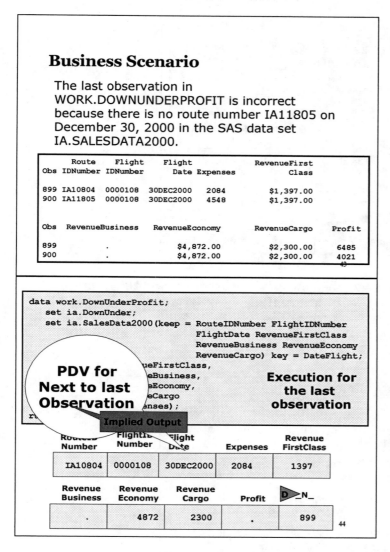

## Business Scenario

The last observation in WORK.DOWNUNDERPROFIT is incorrect because there is no route number IA11805 on December 30, 2000 in the SAS data set IA.SALESDATA2000.

| Obs | Route IDNumber | Flight IDNumber | Flight Date | Expenses | RevenueFirst Class |
|---|---|---|---|---|---|
| 899 | IA10804 | 0000108 | 30DEC2000 | 2084 | $1,397.00 |
| 900 | IA11805 | 0000108 | 30DEC2000 | 4548 | $1,397.00 |

| Obs | RevenueBusiness | RevenueEconomy | RevenueCargo | Profit |
|---|---|---|---|---|
| 899 | . | $4,872.00 | $2,300.00 | 6485 |
| 900 | . | $4,872.00 | $2,300.00 | 4021 |

43

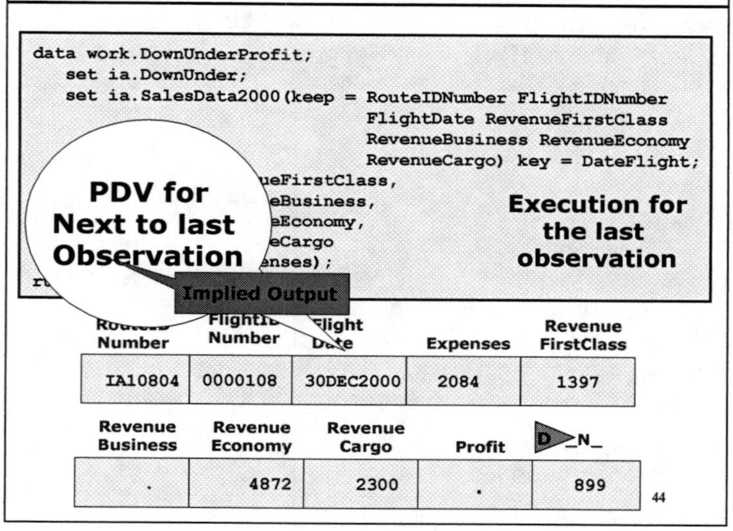


At the next iteration of the DATA step, only PROFIT is reinitialized to missing.

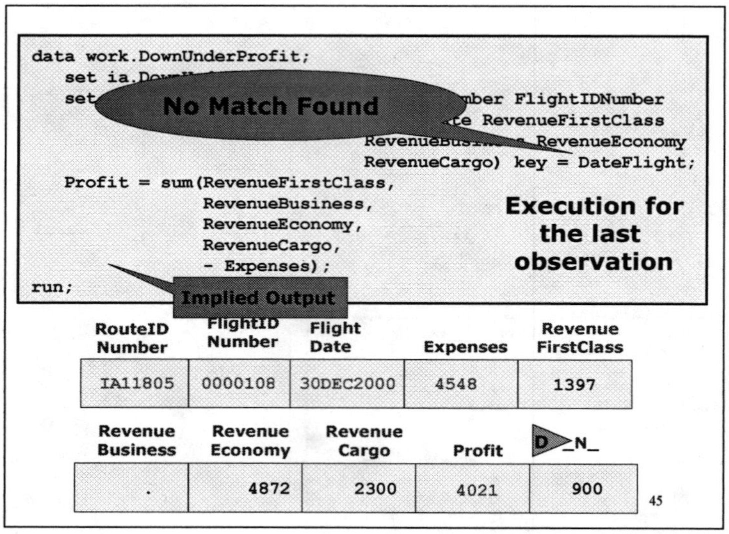


Profit is recalculated using the new value of Expenses and the retained values of RevenueFirstClass, RevenueBusiness, RevenueEconomy, and RevenueCargo.

## Using the KEY= Option

When you use the KEY= option, SAS creates an automatic variable named _IORC_.

You can use _IORC_ to determine whether the index search was successful.

| | |
|---|---|
| _IORC_=0 | indicates that SAS found a matching observation. |
| _IORC_ ne 0 | indicates that SAS did not find a matching observation. |

46

## Using _IORC_

To prevent writing the data error to the log,

- check the value of _IORC_
- set _ERROR_ to 0, if there is no match
- delete the non-matching data or write the non-matching data to an errors data set.

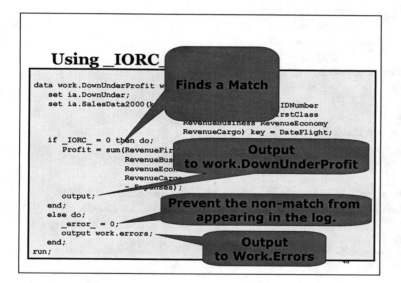

47

## Using _IORC_

```
data work.DownUnderProfit w
   set ia.DownUnder;
   set ia.SalesData2000(k                       IDNumber
                                                rstClass
                              RevenueBusiness RevenueEconomy
                              RevenueCargo) key = DateFlight;

   if _IORC_ = 0 then do;
      Profit = sum(RevenueFir
                   RevenueBus
                   RevenueEco
                   RevenueCarg
                   - Expenses);
      output;
   end;
   else do;
      _error_ = 0;
      output work.errors;
   end;
run;
```

Finds a Match

Output to work.DownUnderProfit

Prevent the non-match from appearing in the log.

Output to Work.Errors

## Using Two SET Statements with the KEY= Option and _IORC_

c06s3d2

Program

```
data work.DownUnderProfit work.errors;
   set ia.DownUnder;
   set ia.SalesData2000(keep = RouteIDNumber FlightIDNumber
                        FlightDate RevenueFirstClass
                        RevenueBusiness RevenueEconomy
                        RevenueCargo)  key = DateFlight;
   if _IORC_ = 0 then do;
       Profit = sum(RevenueFirstClass,
                    RevenueBusiness,
                    RevenueEconomy,
                    RevenueCargo,
                    - Expenses);
      output work.DownUnderProfit;
   end;
   else do;
      _error_ = 0;
        output work.errors;
   end;
run;

proc print data = work.DownUnderProfit (firstobs = 895);
   title 'Combining Data Sets and Eliminating Non-matches';
run;
```

Output

```
          Combining Data Sets and Eliminating Non-matches


      Flight     Route        Flight
Obs  IDNumber   IDNumber        Date   Expenses   Origin   Destination

895  IA10800    0000108    30DEC2000     2934      AKL         WLG
896  IA10801    0000108    30DEC2000     5488      AKL         WLG
897  IA10802    0000108    30DEC2000     3720      AKL         WLG
898  IA10803    0000108    30DEC2000     1204      AKL         WLG
899  IA10804    0000108    30DEC2000     2084      AKL         WLG

     Capacity                                                  First
      First    Capacity   Capacity   Capacity   Capacity       Class
Obs   Class    Business   Economy     Total      Cargo      Passengers

895       12          .        138        150      36900        12
896       12          .        138        150      36900        12
897       12          .        138        150      36900        11
898       12          .        138        150      36900        10
899       12          .        138        150      36900        11


      Business        Economy        RevenueFirst
Obs  Passengers     Passengers              Class    RevenueBusiness

895         .            112           $1,524.00                   .
896         .            133           $1,524.00                   .
897         .            126           $1,397.00                   .
898         .            128           $1,270.00                   .
899         .            116           $1,397.00                   .


                                   Cargo                       Flight
Obs   RevenueEconomy    Month     Weight     RevenueCargo     Month   Profit

895        $4,704.00   DEC2000     12100        $2,420.00       12     5714
896        $5,586.00   DEC2000      7900        $1,580.00       12     3202
897        $5,292.00   DEC2000      9500        $1,900.00       12     4869
898        $5,376.00   DEC2000      9300        $1,860.00       12     7302
899        $4,872.00   DEC2000     11500        $2,300.00       12     6485
```

Log

```
68  data work.DownUnderProfit work.errors;
369     set ia.DownUnder;
370     set ia.SalesData2000 (keep = RouteIDNumber FlightIDNumber
371                               FlightDate RevenueFirstClass
372                               RevenueBusiness RevenueEconomy
373                               RevenueCargo)  key = DateFlight;
374     if _IORC_ = 0 then do;
375         Profit = sum(RevenueFirstClass,
376                      RevenueBusiness,
377                      RevenueEconomy,
378                      RevenueCargo,
379                      - Expenses);
380        output work.DownUnderProfit;
381     end;
382     else do;
383        _error_ = 0;
384        output work.errors;
385     end;
386  run;

NOTE: There were 900 observations read from the data set IA.DOWNUNDER.
NOTE: There were 899 observations read from the data set
      IA.SALESDATA2000.
NOTE: The data set WORK.DOWNUNDERPROFIT has 899 observations and 9
      variables.
NOTE: The data set WORK.ERRORS has 1 observations and 9 variables.
NOTE: DATA statement used:
      real time           0.56 seconds
      cpu time            0.50 seconds


387
388  proc print data = work.DownUnderProfit (firstobs = 895);
389     title 'Combining Data Sets and Eliminating Non-matches';
390  run;

NOTE: There were 5 observations read from the data set
      WORK.DOWNUNDERPROFIT.
NOTE: PROCEDURE PRINT used:
      real time           0.05 seconds
      cpu time            0.05 seconds


391
392  proc print data = work.errors;
393     title 'Errors data';
394  run;

NOTE: There were 1 observations read from the data set WORK.ERRORS.
NOTE: PROCEDURE PRINT used:
      real time           0.04 seconds
      cpu time            0.04 seconds
```

The non-matching record does not appear in the log.

```
proc print data = work.errors;
   title 'Errors data';
run;
```

```
                              Errors data

     Flight   Route       Flight                 RevenueFirst
Obs IDNumber IDNumber       Date Expenses               Class RevenueBusiness

 1  IA11805  0000108  30DEC2000    2413           $1,397.00               .


Obs  Revenueeconomy       RevenueCargo     Profit

 1        $4,872.00          $2,300.00        .
```

## Exercises

5. Combine the ia.NewTimes data set with the ia.Schedule data set using the ID index.

   a. Ia.NewTimes contains a column named TimeDiff that has the number of minutes later that the flight will depart starting 26Jun2000.

   b. Locate the flight using the ID index in the ia.Schedule data set.

   c. Create the variable NewDepart that will be the new departure time for the flights.

   d. The flight times are stored as a SAS time (the number of seconds since midnight).

## 6.4 Chapter Summary

An index is an auxiliary data structure that specifies the location of observations based on the values of one or more key variables. SAS uses an index

- for faster access to subsets
- to return observations in sorted order
- to perform table lookup operations
- to join observations
- to modify observations.

An index can have the UNIQUE option if the indexed variable values have unique values.

You can use the system option MSGLEVEL=I to have index usage notes display in the SAS log.

General form of the MSGLEVEL= option

```
OPTIONS MSGLEVEL = N | I;
```

You can create or delete indexes with the INDEX= data set option in

- a DATA statement
- PROC DATASETS
- PROC SQL.

The index is stored in the same library as the data set but as a separate SAS file.

General form of the INDEX= data set option

```
DATA SAS-data-file-name(INDEX=
        (index-specification-1/option/option ...
        index-specification-n/option/option));
```

General form of PROC DATASETS to delete or create indexes

```
PROC DATASETS LIBRARY=libref;
        MODIFY SAS-data-set-name;
                INDEX DELETE index-name;
                INDEX CREATE index-specification
                        < / options>;
QUIT;
```

General form of PROC SQL to delete or create indexes

```
PROC SQL;
      CREATE <option> INDEX index-name
            ON table-name(column-name-1,...
                          column-name-n);
      DROP INDEX index-name
            FROM table-name;
```

You can combine two SAS data sets, one of which has an index, by using the KEY= SET statement option.

General form of the KEY= option

```
SET SAS-data-file-name KEY = index-name;
```

Entire Program

```
/********* c06s2d1 ******************/

/*************************************/
/*    Use a DATA step to create a    */
/*    simple index and a composite   */
/*    index.                         */
/*************************************/


options mslevel = i;

data ia.SalesData2000 (index = (Origin
                       DateFlight =
                       (FlightIDNumber FlightDate)));
   set ia.SalesData2000;
run;
```

```
/********* c06s2d2 ******************/

/*************************************/
/*    Use a DATA step to create a    */
/*    simple index and a composite   */
/*    index.                         */
/*************************************/


options msglevel = i;

proc datasets library = ia nolist;
   modify SalesData2000;
   index delete Origin;
   index delete DateFlight;

   index create Origin;
   index create DateFlight =
               (FlightIDNumber FlightDate) / unique;
quit;
```

```
/********* c06s2d3 ******************/

/*************************************/
/*    Use a DATA step to create a    */
/*    simple index and a composite   */
/*    index.                         */
/*************************************/


options msglevel = i;

proc sql;
   drop index Origin
      from ia.SalesData2000;
   drop index DateFlight
      from ia.SalesData2000;

   create index Origin
        on ia.SalesData2000(Origin);
   create unique index DateFlight
        on ia.SalesData2000(FlightIDNumber,FlightDate);
quit;





/********* c06s2d4 ******************/

/*************************************/
/*    View information about the     */
/*    indexes.                       */
/*************************************/


proc contents data = ia.SalesData2000;
run;



/********* c06s3d1 ******************/

/*************************************/
/*    Use a DATA step to combine two */
/*    data sets, one having an index. */
/*************************************/


data work.DownUnderProfit;
   set ia.DownUnder;
   set SalesData2000 key = DateFlight;
   Profit = sum(RevenueFirstClass,
                RevenueBusiness,
```

```
                  RevenueEconomy,
                  RevenueCargo,
                  - Expenses);
run;

proc print data = work.DownUnderProfit;
   title1 'Profit for the Flights';
   title2 'to Australia and New Zealand';
run;



/********* c06s3d2 ******************/

/*************************************/
/*    Use a DATA step to combine two  */
/*    data sets, one having an index. */
/*    Use the _IORC_ variable to      */
/*    eliminate non-matches.          */
/*************************************/


data work.DownUnderProfit work.errors;
   set ia.DownUnder;
   set ia.SalesData2000 (keep = RouteIDNumber
                                FlightIDNumber
                                FlightDate
                                RevenueFirstClass
                                RevenueBusiness
                                RevenueEconomy
                                RevenueCargo)
                         key = DateFlight;
   if _IORC_ = 0 then do;
      Profit = sum(RevenueFirstClass,
                   RevenueBusiness,
                   RevenueEconomy,
                   RevenueCargo,
                   - Expenses);
     output work.DownUnderProfit;
   end;
   else do;
       _error_ = 0;
       output work.errors;
   end;
run;

proc print data = work.DownUnderProfit (firstobs = 895);
   title 'Combining Data Sets and Eliminating Non-matches';
run;

proc print data = work.errors;
   title 'Errors data';
run;
```

## 6.5 Solutions to Exercises

1. Create two indexes for the ia.Schedule data set using PROC DATASETS.
   - A simple index Flight, based on the Flight variable
   - A unique composite index FltDte, based on the Flight and Date variables.

```
proc datasets library = ia nolist;
   modify schedule;
   index create flight;
   index create id = (Flight Date) / unique;
quit;
```

2. Delete the indexes for the ia.Schedule data set using PROC SQL.

```
proc sql;
   drop index Flight
      from ia.schedule;
   drop index ID
      from ia.schedule;
quit;
```

3. Recreate the indexes for the ia.Schedule data set using the DATA step and the INDEX= option.

```
data ia.schedule (index = (Flight
                           ID = (Flight Date)));
   set ia.schedule;
run;
```

4. Use PROC CONTENTS to look at the index information.

```
proc contents data=ia.schedule;
run;
```

5. Combine the ia.NewTimes data set with the ia.Schedule data set using the ID index.

   a. Ia.NewTimes contains a column named TimeDiff that has the number of minutes later that the flight will depart starting 26Jun2000.

   b. Locate the flight using the ID index in the ia.Schedule data set.

   c. Create the variable NewDepart that will be the new departure time for the flights.

   d. The flight times are stored as a SAS time (the number of seconds since midnight).

```
data work.NewSched;
   set ia.NewTimes;
   set ia.Schedule key = id;
   if _IORC_ = 0 then do;
      newdepart = sum(TimeDiff*60,depart);
      output;
   end;
   else do;
      _error_ = 0;
   end;
   format newdepart time5.;
run;
```

# Chapter 7

# 7.1 Introduction

## General Business Scenario

We must create a library of formats for the report writers of International Airlines to use for their report writing tasks.

They asked us to create formats to ...

3

## General Business Scenario

Group routes into zones

Route 1 → **Zone 1**

Route 2
Route 3 } **Zone 2**
Route 4

Route 5
Route 6 } **Zone 3**
Route 7

Missing

Other Values

4

## General Business Scenario

Group destinations into

International Flights

```
'AKL','AMS','ARN',
'ATH','BKK','BRU',
'CBR','CCU','CDG',
'CPH','CPT','DEL',
'DXB','FBU','FCO',
'FRA','GLA','GVA',
'HEL','HKG','HND',
'JED','JNB','JRS',
'LHR','LIS','MAD',
'NBO','PEK','PRG',
'SIN','SYD','VIE',
'WLG'
```

Domestic Flights

```
'ANC','BHM','BNA',
'BOS','DFW','HNL',
'IAD','IND','JFK',
'LAX','MCI','MIA',
'MSY','ORD','PWM',
'RDU','SEA','SFO'
```

5

## General Business Scenario

Group revenue figures according to this chart:

```
Less than or Equal to $10,000
From $10,000 to $20,000
From $20,000 to $30,000
From $30,000 to $40,000
From $40,000 to $50,000
More than $50,000
```

6

## General Business Scenario

Group dates into overlapping categories

| | |
|---|---|
| Jan - Mar → | First Quarter |
| Apr - Jun → | Second Quarter |
| Jul - Sep → | Third Quarter |
| Oct - Dec → | Fourth Quarter |
| Jan - Jun → | First Half of Year |
| Jul - Dec → | Second Half of Year |

7

## General Business Scenario

In addition, the report writers have a data set containing airport codes and airport cities. From this data set we can create a format.

| Airport Code | Airport City | Airport Name | Airport Country |
|---|---|---|---|
| AKL | Auckland | International | New Zealand |
| AMS | Amsterdam | Schiphol | Netherlands |
| ANC | Anchorage, AK | Anchorage International | USA |
| ARN | Stockholm | Arlanda | Sweden |
| ATH | Athens | Hellinikon International | Greece |
| BHM | Birmingham, AL | Birmingham International | USA |
| BKK | Bangkok | Don Muang International | Thailand |

8

## General Business Scenario

Finally, we need to add new airports to a format that already exists.

| New Airport Code | City |
|---|---|
| YYC | Calgary, AB |
| YYZ | Toronto, ON |
| YQB | Quebec, QC |
| YMX | Montreal, QC |

9

## Organize the Tasks

- Create formats with PROC FORMAT and store them permanently.
- Create a format with overlapping ranges.
- Create a format from a SAS data set.
- Add new routes to the existing formats.

10

# 7.2 Creating Permanent Formats

## Objectives

- Create permanent formats.
- Access permanent formats.
- Create and use overlapping formats.

12

## Business Scenario

We must create formats to group

- airline routes into three zones and account for missing data and unknown routes.
- destinations into International Flights and Domestic Flights
- dates into quarters and half years
- revenue figures.

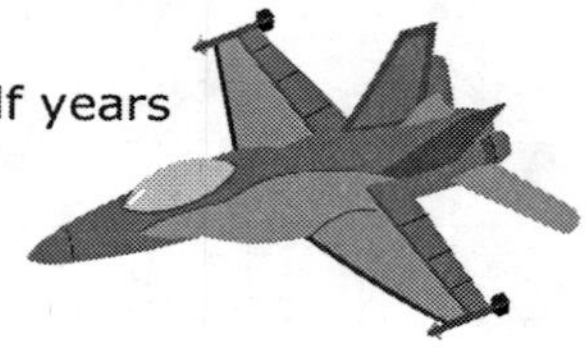

13

## The FORMAT Procedure

You can

- use PROC FORMAT to define
  - VALUES
  - PICTURES
  - INFORMATS
- code missing values using
  - ' ' (missing character)
  - . (missing numeric)

14

| | |
|---|---|
| value formats | establish descriptive labels for coded numeric or character values. |
| picture formats | create patterns (templates) for printing numeric values, such as (999)999-9999 for phone numbers. |
| informats | control the reading and storing of values. |

This course covers only value formats.

## The FORMAT Procedure

- use the key words
  - OTHER
  - HIGH
  - LOW
- code non-inclusive ranges
  - <

15

| | |
|---|---|
| OTHER | handles values not specifically stated in a previous range. Missing values are considered to be OTHER unless handled separately. |
| HIGH | specifies the highest possible numeric value. |
| LOW | specifies the lowest possible numeric value. LOW does not include missing values. |

The low and high values are dependent on platform sort order.

## Organize the Tasks:

- **Create formats with PROC FORMAT and store them permanently.**
- **Create a format with overlapping ranges.**
- Create a format from a SAS data set.
- Add new routes to the existing formats.

16

## General Form of a PROC FORMAT Step

```
PROC FORMAT LIBRARY = libref.catalog;
  VALUE $charfmt 'value1' = 'formatted-value-1'
                 'value2' = 'formatted-value-2'
                 'valuen' = 'formatted-value-n';
  VALUE numfmt  value1  = 'formatted-value-1'
                value2  = 'formatted-value-2'
                valuen  = 'formatted-value-n';
RUN;
```

17

A VALUE statement is required for each format.

User defined formats are stored in a catalog in a SAS data library.

- Without the LIBRARY= option, formats are stored in the WORK.FORMATS catalog and exist for the duration of the SAS session.
- If the LIBRARY= option specifies only a *libref*, formats are permanently stored in *libref*.FORMATS.
- If the LIBRARY= option specifies *libref.catalog*, formats are permanently stored in that catalog.

Format names cannot duplicate SAS format names (such as DOLLAR and SSN).

For character formats:

- Format names must begin with a $ and must be 8 characters or less including the $, and they cannot end in a number.
- Input values are quoted.

For numeric formats

- Format names must be 8 characters or less and they cannot end in a number.
- Input values are not quoted.

## Using Permanent Formats

You can reference formats in

- FORMAT statements
- PUT statements
- PUT functions in assignment, WHERE, or IF statements.

18

When a user-defined format is referenced in a step, SAS

- loads the format from the catalog entry into memory
- performs a binary search on values in the table to execute a lookup
- returns a single result for each lookup.

General form of the FORMAT statement:

**FORMAT** *variable(s) format;*

General form of the PUT statement:

**PUT** *<@n1>variable1 format1 ...*
*<@nn>variablen formatn;*

General form of the PUT function:

**PUT** *(argument, format)*

## Using the FMTSEARCH System Option

To use permanent formats or to search multiple catalogs, use the FMTSEARCH= system option to identify the catalog(s) to be searched for the format(s).

General form of the FMTSEARCH= system option

OPTIONS FMTSEARCH = (*item-1 item-2…item-n*);

19

By specifying multiple items in the FMTSEARCH option, you can concatenate format catalogs. This enables you to

- define personal format catalogs to be used in addition to corporate catalogs
- use test and production format catalogs without duplicating the production catalog
- control the order in which catalogs are searched.

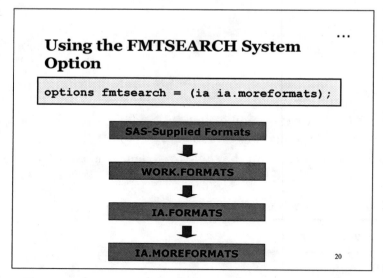

...

## Using the FMTSEARCH System Option

```
options fmtsearch = (ia ia.moreformats);
```

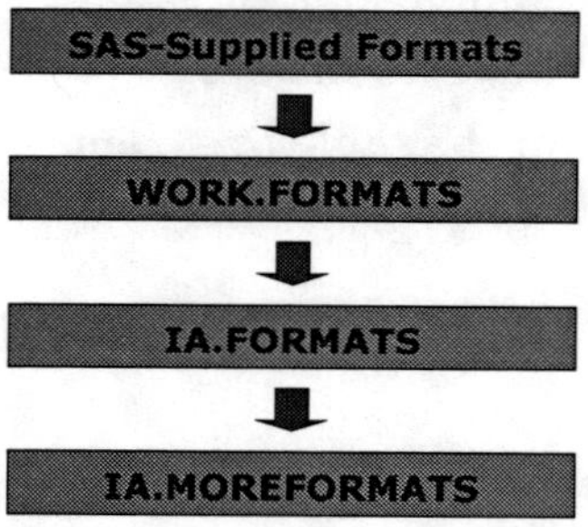


20

- Because IA is a libref with a catalog name, FORMATS is assumed as the catalog name.
- SAS-supplied formats are always searched first.
- The WORK.FORMATS catalog is always searched second, unless it appears in the FMTSEARCH list.

## Reference Information

If the LIBRARY libref is assigned, the LIBRARY.FORMATS catalog is searched after WORK.FORMATS and before anything else in the FMTSEARCH list, unless it appears in the list.

To assign the LIBRARY libref, use

```
libname library 'SAS-data-library-containing-formats';
```

### Using the NOFMTERR Option

By default, the FMTERR system option is in effect. If you use a format that SAS can not load, SAS issues an error message and stops processing.

To prevent the default action, change the system option FMTERR to NOFMTERR.

```
options FMTERR | NOFMTERR;
```

21

FMTERR specifies that when SAS cannot find a specified variable format, it generates an error message and does not allow default substitution to occur.

NOFMTERR replaces missing formats with the *w.* or *$w.* default format, issues a note, and continues processing.

## Creating Permanent Formats

c07s2d1

Example 1

Program

```
proc format library = ia;

   value $routes            'Route1' = 'Zone 1'
                 'Route2' - 'Route4' = 'Zone Two'
                 'Route5' - 'Route7' = 'Zone Three'
                                 ' ' = 'Missing'
                               other = 'Unknown';

   value $dest   'AKL','AMS','ARN',
                 'ATH','BKK','BRU',
                 'CBR','CCU','CDG',
                 'CPH','CPT','DEL',
                 'DXB','FBU','FCO',
                 'FRA','GLA','GVA',
                 'HEL','HKG','HND',
                 'JED','JNB','JRS',
                 'LHR','LIS','MAD',
                 'NBO','PEK','PRG',
                 'SIN','SYD','VIE','WLG' = 'International'
                 'ANC','BHM','BNA',
                 'BOS','DFW','HNL',
                 'IAD','IND','JFK',
                 'LAX','MCI','MIA',
                 'MSY','ORD','PWM',
                 'RDU','SEA','SFO' = 'Domestic';

   value revfmt                  . = 'Missing'
                     low - 10000 = 'Up to $10,000'
                  10000 <- 20000 = '$10,000 to $20000'
                  20000 <- 30000 = '$20,000 to $30000'
                  30000 <- 40000 = '$30,000 to $40000'
                  40000 <- 50000 = '$40,000 to $50000'
                   50000 <- high = 'More than $50,000';
run;
```

Example 2

Program

```
proc catalog data = ia.formats;
   contents;
   title 'IA.FORMATS Catalog Contents';
run;
```

Output

IA.FORMATS Catalog Contents

Contents of Catalog IA.FORMATS

| # | Name | Type | Create Date | Modified Date | Description |
|---|---|---|---|---|---|
| 1 | DATES | FORMAT | 03JUN2000:15:57:54 | 03JUN2000:15:57:54 | |
| 2 | REVFMT | FORMAT | 03JUN2000:16:06:25 | 03JUN2000:16:06:25 | |
| 3 | AIRPORT | FORMATC | 15MAY2000:11:51:40 | 15MAY2000:11:51:40 | |
| 4 | DEST | FORMATC | 03JUN2000:16:06:25 | 03JUN2000:16:06:25 | |
| 5 | ROUTES | FORMATC | 03JUN2000:16:06:25 | 03JUN2000:16:06:25 | |

Example 3

Program

```
proc sort data = ia.CargoRevenue;
   by FlightDate;
run;

options fmtsearch = (ia) nofmterr;

proc print data = ia.CargoRevenue(obs=10);
   where put(route,$routes.) = 'Zone Two';
   format RevenueCargo revfmt. FlightDate mmddyyb10.;
   var FlightDate Route RevenueCargo;
   title 'Revenue Cargo for Zone Two';
   title2 'First Ten Rows';
run;
```

Partial Output

```
                    Revenue Cargo for Zone Two
                          First Ten Rows

          Obs     FlightDate     Route         RevenueCargo

            1     01 01 2000     Route2    Up to $10,000
            2     01 01 2000     Route2    Up to $10,000
            3     01 01 2000     Route2    Up to $10,000
            4     01 01 2000     Route2    Up to $10,000
            5     01 01 2000     Route2    Up to $10,000
            6     01 01 2000     Route2    Up to $10,000
           23     01 01 2000     Route3    $20,000 to $30000
           24     01 01 2000     Route3    $20,000 to $30000
           31     01 01 2000     Route4    Up to $10,000
           32     01 01 2000     Route4    Up to $10,000
           49     01 01 2000     Route3    Up to $10,000
```

It is possible to use the WHERE statement when the OBS= option is in effect.

## Creating Overlapping Ranges

To create overlapping ranges, use the MULTILABEL option on the VALUE statement in PROC FORMAT

| |
|---|
| **VALUE** <$>*fmtname* <(MULTILABEL)> ... |

Create a report with any procedure that supports the MLF option

- PROC TABULATE
- PROC MEANS
- PROC SUMMARY.

23

## Using the MULTILABEL Option

c07s2d2

Program

```
proc format library = ia.moreformats;
   value dates (multilabel)
      '01jan2000'd - '31mar2000'd = 'First Quarter'
      '01apr2000'd - '30jun2000'd = 'Second Quarter'
      '01jul2000'd - '30sep2000'd = 'Third Quarter'
      '01oct2000'd - '31dec2000'd = 'Fourth Quarter'
      '01jan2000'd - '30jun2000'd = 'First Half of Year'
      '01jul2000'd - '31dec2000'd = 'Second Half of Year';
run;

options fmtsearch = (ia.moreformats);

proc tabulate data = ia.SalesData2000 format = dollar15.2;
   title 'Example using Multilabel Formats';
   format FlightDate dates.;
   class FlightDate / mlf;
   var RevenueCargo;
   table FlightDate, RevenueCargo*(mean median);
run;
```

Output

Example using Multilabel Formats

| | Revenue from Cargo | |
|---|---|---|
| | Mean | Median |
| Scheduled Date of Flight | | |
| First Half of Year | $20,034.66 | $5,075.00 |
| First Quarter | $20,041.36 | $5,075.00 |
| Fourth Quarter | $20,036.93 | $5,109.00 |
| Second Half of Year | $20,045.73 | $5,117.00 |
| Second Quarter | $20,028.03 | $5,109.00 |
| Third Quarter | $20,054.44 | $5,117.00 |

## Exercises

1. Create a format named TIMES that has mutilabels. The first is for the following labels:

| Data Value | Label |
|---|---|
| Midnight to 4:59 a.m. | Red Eye |
| 5 a.m. to 11:59 a.m. | Morning |
| noon to 5:59 p.m. | Afternoon |
| 6 p.m. to 11:59 p.m. | Evening |

The second is for AM (midnight to noon) and PM (noon to midnight) flights.

Use the format in the following program named **ch7ex1**:

```
proc tabulate data = ia.schedule;
   where date = '15jun2000'd;
   title 'Example using Multilabel Formats';
   format depart times.;
   class  depart / mlf order = data;
   table depart;
run;
```

# 7.3 Creating Formats from SAS Data Sets

## Objectives

- Create a format from a SAS data set.
- Document permanent formats.

27

## Business Scenario

The report writers have a data set containing airport codes and airport cities. From this data set we can create a format.

| Airport Code | Airport City | Airport Name | Airport Country |
|---|---|---|---|
| AKL | Auckland | International | New Zealand |
| AMS | Amsterdam | Schiphol | Netherlands |
| ANC | Anchorage, AK | Anchorage International | USA |
| ARN | Stockholm | Arlanda | Sweden |
| ATH | Athens | Hellinikon International | Greece |
| BHM | Birmingham, AL | Birmingham International | USA |
| BKK | Bangkok | Don Muang International | Thailand |

28

## Organize the Tasks

- Create formats with PROC FORMAT and store them permanently.
- Create a format with overlapping ranges.
- **Create a format from a SAS data set.**
- Add new routes to the existing formats.

29

## Using a Control Data Set to Create a Format

You can create a format from a SAS data set containing value information (called a *control data set*).

Use the CNTLIN= option to read the data and create the format.

General form of CNTLIN= option:

```
PROC FORMAT LIBRARY = libref.catalog
            CNTLIN = SAS-data-set;
RUN;
```

30

The CNTLIN data set

- must contain the variables FMTNAME, START, LABEL
- must contain the variable TYPE for character formats, unless the value for FMTNAME begins with a $
- does not require a TYPE variable for numeric formats
- assumes that the ending value of the format range is equal to the value of START if no variable named END is found
- does not require the other variables created by the CNTLOUT= option that specify optional attributes
- can be created by a DATA step, another PROC step, or an interactive application such as the Viewtable window
- can be used to create new formats, as well as re-create existing formats
- must be sorted by FMTNAME if multiple formats are specified.

## Documenting Formats

You can use the FMTLIB option in the PROC FORMAT statement to document the format.

General form of the FMTLIB option:

```
PROC FORMAT LIBRARY = libref.catalog
                    FMTLIB;
    other statement;
RUN;
```

3

other statements can include

SELECT *format-name format-name...;*

EXCLUDE *format-name format-name...;*

You can use either the SELECT or EXCLUDE statement to process specific formats rather than an entire catalog.

## Using a Control Data Set to Create a Format

c07s3d1

Program

```
data work.airports;
   keep start label fmtname;
   retain fmtname '$airport';
   set ia.AirportCities (rename = (AirportCode = start
                                   AirportCity = label));
run;

proc format library = ia cntlin = airports;
run;

options ls = 80;

proc print data=work.airports(obs=10) noobs;
   title 'Work.Airports';
run;
```

Output

```
                          Work.Airports

             fmtname     label                    start

             $airport    Auckland                  AKL
             $airport    Amsterdam                 AMS
             $airport    Anchorage, AK             ANC
             $airport    Stockholm                 ARN
             $airport    Athens (Athinai)          ATH
             $airport    Birmingham, AL            BHM
             $airport    Bangkok                   BKK
             $airport    Nashville, TN             BNA
             $airport    Boston, MA                BOS
             $airport    Brussels (Bruxelles)      BRU
```

```
proc format library = ia fmtlib;
   select $airport;
   title '$AIRPORT format';
run;
```

Output

```
                              $AIRPORT format

 ----------------------------------------------------------------------------
 |       FORMAT NAME: $AIRPORT LENGTH:   22   NUMBER OF VALUES:   52         |
 |   MIN LENGTH:   1  MAX LENGTH:  40  DEFAULT LENGTH  22  FUZZ:        0    |
 |--------------------------------------------------------------------------|
 |START           |END             |LABEL  (VER. 8.1     03JUN2000:17:00:03)|
 |----------------+----------------+----------------------------------------|
 |AKL             |AKL             |Auckland                                |
 |AMS             |AMS             |Amsterdam                               |
 |ANC             |ANC             |Anchorage, AK                           |
 |ARN             |ARN             |Stockholm                               |
 |ATH             |ATH             |Athens (Athinai)                        |
 |BHM             |BHM             |Birmingham, AL                          |
 |BKK             |BKK             |Bangkok                                 |
 |BNA             |BNA             |Nashville, TN                           |
 |BOS             |BOS             |Boston, MA                              |
 |BRU             |BRU             |Brussels (Bruxelles)                    |
 |CBR             |CBR             |Canberra, Australian C                  |
 |CCU             |CCU             |Calcutta                                |
 |CDG             |CDG             |Paris                                   |
 |CPH             |CPH             |Kobenhavn (Copenhagen)                  |
 |CPT             |CPT             |Cape Town                               |
 |DEL             |DEL             |Delhi                                   |
 |DFW             |DFW             |Dallas/Fort Worth, TX                   |
 |DXB             |DXB             |Dubai                                   |
 |FBU             |FBU             |Oslo                                    |
 |FCO             |FCO             |Roma (Rome)                             |
 |FRA             |FRA             |Frankfurt                               |
 |GLA             |GLA             |Glasgow, Scotland                       |
 |GVA             |GVA             |Geneva                                  |
 |HEL             |HEL             |Helsinki                                |
 |HKG             |HKG             |Hong Kong                               |
 |HND             |HND             |Tokyo                                   |
 |HNL             |HNL             |Honolulu, HI                            |
 |IAD             |IAD             |Washington, DC                          |
 |IND             |IND             |Indianapolis, IN                        |
 |JED             |JED             |Jeddah                                  |
 |JFK             |JFK             |New York, NY                            |
 |JNB             |JNB             |Johannesburg                            |
 |JRS             |JRS             |Jerusalem                               |
 |LAX             |LAX             |Los Angeles, CA                         |
 |LHR             |LHR             |London, England                         |
 |LIS             |LIS             |Lisboa (Lisbon)                         |
 |MAD             |MAD             |Madrid                                  |
 |MCI             |MCI             |Kansas City, MO                         |
 |MIA             |MIA             |Miami, FL                               |
 |MSY             |MSY             |New Orleans, LA                         |
 |NBO             |NBO             |Nairobi                                 |
```

| | | |
|---|---|---|
| ORD | ORD | Chicago, IL |
| PEK | PEK | Beijing (Peking) |
| PRG | PRG | Praha (Prague) |
| PWM | PWM | Portland, ME |
| RDU | RDU | Raleigh-Durham, NC |
| SEA | SEA | Seattle, WA |
| SFO | SFO | San Francisco, CA |
| SIN | SIN | Singapore |
| SYD | SYD | Sydney, New South Wale |
| VIE | VIE | Wien (Vienna) |
| WLG | WLG | Wellington |

## Exercises

2. Use the ia.Job_Code_Data data set to create a format named $JCodes. View the new format using the PROC FORMAT FMTLIB option.

# 7.4 Maintaining Permanent Formats

## Objectives

- Create a SAS data set from a permanent format.
- Edit the SAS data set to add observations.
- Create a format from the resulting SAS data set.

3

## Organize the Tasks

- Create formats with PROC FORMAT and store them permanently.
- Create a format with overlapping ranges.
- Create a format from a SAS data set.
- **Add new routes to the existing formats.**

36

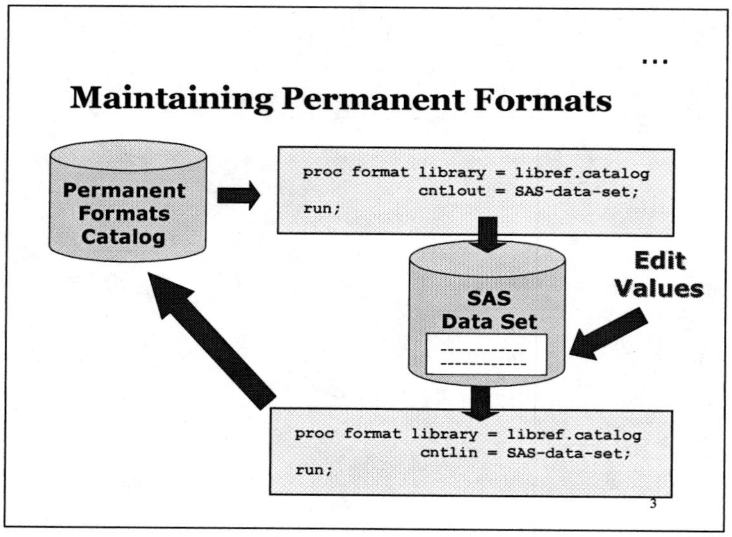


## Maintaining Permanent Formats

General form of PROC FORMAT with the CNTLOUT= option:

**PROC FORMAT** LIBRARY = *libref.catalog*
CNTLOUT = *SAS-data-set*;
*other statements*
**RUN**;

38

other statements can include

SELECT *format-name format-name...;*

EXCLUDE *format-name format-name...;*

You can use either the SELECT or EXCLUDE statement to process specific formats rather than an entire catalog.

The variables in the output control data set completely describe all aspects of each format or informat, including optional settings.

The output control data set contains one observation per range per format or informat in the specified catalog.

## Maintaining Permanent Formats

c07s4d1

Program

Example 1

```
proc format lib = ia cntlout = work.fmtdata;
   select $airport;
run;
```

Log

```
705  proc format lib = ia cntlout = work.fmtdata;
706     select $airport;
707  run;

NOTE: PROCEDURE FORMAT used:
      real time           0.09 seconds
      cpu time            0.08 seconds

NOTE: The data set WORK.FMTDATA has 52 observations and 21 variables.
```

Example 2:

Rather than using an interactive technique to add data, you can use procedures such as PROC SQL.

Program

```
proc sql;
   insert into work.fmtdata
      set fmtname = 'AIRPORT',
             start = 'YYC',
               end = 'YYC',
             label = 'Calgary, AB',
              type = 'C'
        set fmtname = 'AIRPORT',
             start = 'YYZ',
               end = 'YYZ',
             label = 'Toronto, ON',
              type = 'C'
        set fmtname = 'AIRPORT',
             start = 'YQB',
               end = 'YQB',
             label = 'Quebec, QC',
              type = 'C'
      set fmtname = 'AIRPORT',
             start = 'YMX',
               end = 'YMX',
             label = 'Montreal, QC',
              type = 'C' ;
quit;
```

Log

```
709  proc sql;
710     insert into work.fmtdata
711        set fmtname = 'AIRPORT',
712               start = 'YYC',
713                 end = 'YYC',
714               label = 'Calgary, AB',
715                type = 'C'
716        set fmtname = 'AIRPORT',
717               start = 'YYZ',
718                 end = 'YYZ',
719               label = 'Toronto, ON',
720                type = 'C'
721        set fmtname = 'AIRPORT',
722               start = 'YQB',
723                 end = 'YQB',
724               label = 'Quebec, QC',
725                type = 'C'
726        set fmtname = 'AIRPORT',
727               start = 'YMX',
728                 end = 'YMX',
729               label = 'Montreal, QC',
730                type = 'C' ;
NOTE: 4 rows were inserted into WORK.FMTDATA.
731  quit;
```

Example 3

```
proc format library = ia cntlin = work.fmtdata;
run;

proc format library = ia fmtlib;
   select $airport;
   title 'New values in the $AIRPORT Format';
run;
```

Output

New values in the $AIRPORT Format

FORMAT NAME: $AIRPORT LENGTH: 22 NUMBER OF VALUES: 56
MIN LENGTH: 1 MAX LENGTH: 40 DEFAULT LENGTH 22 FUZZ: 0

| START | END | LABEL (VER. 8.1 03JUN2000:17:20:27) |
|---|---|---|
| AKL | AKL | Auckland |
| AMS | AMS | Amsterdam |
| ANC | ANC | Anchorage, AK |
| ARN | ARN | Stockholm |
| ATH | ATH | Athens (Athinai) |
| BHM | BHM | Birmingham, AL |
| BKK | BKK | Bangkok |
| BNA | BNA | Nashville, TN |
| BOS | BOS | Boston, MA |
| BRU | BRU | Brussels (Bruxelles) |
| CBR | CBR | Canberra, Australian C |
| CCU | CCU | Calcutta |
| CDG | CDG | Paris |
| CPH | CPH | Kobenhavn (Copenhagen) |
| CPT | CPT | Cape Town |
| DEL | DEL | Delhi |
| DFW | DFW | Dallas/Fort Worth, TX |
| DXB | DXB | Dubai |
| FBU | FBU | Oslo |
| FCO | FCO | Roma (Rome) |
| FRA | FRA | Frankfurt |
| GLA | GLA | Glasgow, Scotland |
| GVA | GVA | Geneva |
| HEL | HEL | Helsinki |
| HKG | HKG | Hong Kong |
| HND | HND | Tokyo |
| HNL | HNL | Honolulu, HI |
| IAD | IAD | Washington, DC |
| IND | IND | Indianapolis, IN |
| JED | JED | Jeddah |
| JFK | JFK | New York, NY |
| JNB | JNB | Johannesburg |
| JRS | JRS | Jerusalem |
| LAX | LAX | Los Angeles, CA |
| LHR | LHR | London, England |
| LIS | LIS | Lisboa (Lisbon) |

| | | |
|---|---|---|
| MAD | MAD | Madrid |
| MCI | MCI | Kansas City, MO |
| MIA | MIA | Miami, FL |
| MSY | MSY | New Orleans, LA |
| NBO | NBO | Nairobi |
| ORD | ORD | Chicago, IL |
| PEK | PEK | Beijing (Peking) |
| PRG | PRG | Praha (Prague) |
| PWM | PWM | Portland, ME |
| RDU | RDU | Raleigh-Durham, NC |
| SEA | SEA | Seattle, WA |
| SFO | SFO | San Francisco, CA |
| SIN | SIN | Singapore |
| SYD | SYD | Sydney, New South Wale |
| VIE | VIE | Wien (Vienna) |
| WLG | WLG | Wellington |
| YMX | YMX | Montreal, QC |
| YQB | YQB | Quebec, QC |
| YYC | YYC | Calgary, AB |
| YYZ | YYZ | Toronto, ON |

## Exercises

3. Add to the $Jcodes format.

   a. Use the PROC FORMAT CNTLOUT= and CNTLIN= options. View the new format using the PROC FORMAT FMTLIB option.

   b. Add new data for ticket agents using PROC SQL INSERT statement:

| | |
|---|---|
| TKTAG1 | Ticket Agent Grade 1 |
| TKTAG2 | Ticket Agent Grade 2 |
| TKTAG3 | Ticket Agent Grade 3 |

## 7.5 Chapter Summary

You can use SAS formats to hold lookup values to use in DATA steps or in procedures.

Formats are created using PROC FORMAT and can be stored temporarily or permanently. Formats can be used in FORMAT statements or PUT functions.

General form of a PROC FORMAT step:

```
PROC FORMAT LIBRARY=libref.catalog;
  VALUE $charfmt 'value1'='formatted-value-1'
                 'value2'='formatted-value-2'
                 'valuen'='formatted-value-n';
  VALUE numfmt value1='formatted-value-1'
               value2='formatted-value-2'
               valuen='formatted-value-n';
RUN;
```

To create overlapping ranges, use the MULTILABEL option on the VALUE statement in PROC FORMAT

```
VALUE <$>fmtname <(MULTILABEL)>...
```

Create a report with any procedure that supports the MLF option such as PROC TABULATE, PROC MEANS, and PROC SUMMARY.

You can control where SAS searches for your formats by using the FMTSEARCH system option.

General form of the FMTSEARCH= system option:

```
OPTIONS FMTSEARCH= (item-1 item-2... item-n);
```

You can create a format from a SAS data set using the CNTLIN= options in the PROC FORMAT statement.

General form of a PROC FORMAT step with the CNTLIN= option:

```
PROC FORMAT LIBRARY = libref.catalog
         CNTLIN = SAS-data-set;
RUN;
```

You can maintain format tables by creating and reading control data sets using the CNTLOUT= and CNTLIN= options in the PROC FORMAT statement.

General form of a PROC FORMAT step with the CNTLOUT= option:

```
PROC FORMAT LIBRARY = libref.catalog
         CNTLOUT= SAS-data-set;
RUN;
```

You can document the content of your format catalogs by using the FMTLIB option in the PROC FORMAT statement.

General form for PROC FORMAT with the FMTLIB option:

> **PROC FORMAT** LIBRARY = *libref.catalog* FMTLIB;
> *other statements*;
> **RUN**;

Entire Program

```
/********* c07s2d1 ******************/
/******** Example 1 *****************/

/*************************************/
/*    Create permanent formats and   */
/*    store them in the IA.FORMATS   */
/*    catalog.                       */
/*************************************/


proc format library = ia;

   value $routes            'Route1' = 'Zone 1'
                 'Route2' - 'Route4' = 'Zone Two'
                 'Route5' - 'Route7' = 'Zone Three'
                                 ' ' = 'Missing'
                               other = 'Unknown';

   value $dest  'AKL','AMS','ARN',
                'ATH','BKK','BRU',
                'CBR','CCU','CDG',
                'CPH','CPT','DEL',
                'DXB','FBU','FCO',
                'FRA','GLA','GVA',
                'HEL','HKG','HND',
                'JED','JNB','JRS',
                'LHR','LIS','MAD',
                'NBO','PEK','PRG',
                'SIN','SYD','VIE','WLG' = 'International'
                'ANC','BHM','BNA',
                'BOS','DFW','HNL',
                'IAD','IND','JFK',
                'LAX','MCI','MIA',
                'MSY','ORD','PWM',
                'RDU','SEA','SFO' = 'Domestic';

value revfmt                     . = 'Missing'
                     low - 10000 = 'Up to $10,000'
                  10000 <- 20000 = '$10,000 to $20000'
                  20000 <- 30000 = '$20,000 to $30000'
                  30000 <- 40000 = '$30,000 to $40000'
                  40000 <- 50000 = '$40,000 to $50000'
                   50000 <- high = 'More than $50,000';
run;


/******** Example 2 *****************/

options fmtsearch = (ia);
```

```
proc catalog data = ia.formats;
   contents;
   title 'IA.FORMATS Catalog Contents';
run;


/******** Example 3 *****************/

proc sort data = ia.CargoRevenue;
   by FlightDate;
run;

proc print data = ia.CargoRevenue(obs = 10);
   where put(route,$routes.) = 'Zone Two';
   format RevenueCargo revfmt. FlightDate mmddyyb10.;
   var FlightDate Route RevenueCargo;
   title 'Revenue Cargo for Zone Two';
   title2 'First Ten Rows';
run;




/********* c07s2d2 ******************/

/*************************************/
/*    Create an overlapping format    */
/*    and store them in the           */
/*    IA.MOREFORMATS catalog.         */
/*************************************/


proc format library = ia.moreformats;
   value dates (multilabel)
      '01jan2000'd - '31mar2000'd = 'First Quarter'
      '01apr2000'd - '30jun2000'd = 'Second Quarter'
      '01jul2000'd - '30sep2000'd = 'Third Quarter'
      '01oct2000'd - '31dec2000'd = 'Fourth Quarter'
      '01jan2000'd - '30jun2000'd = 'First Half of Year'
      '01jul2000'd - '31dec2000'd = 'Second Half of Year';
run;

options fmtsearch = (ia.moreformats);

proc tabulate data = ia.SalesData2000 format = dollar15.2;
   title 'Example using Multilabel Formats';
   format FlightDate dates.;
   class FlightDate / mlf;
   var RevenueCargo;
   table FlightDate, RevenueCargo*(mean median);
run;
```

```
/********* c07s3d1 *******************/

/*************************************/
/*    Create a format from a SAS      */
/*    data set.                       */
/*    Document the format.            */
/*************************************/


data work.airports;
   keep start label fmtname;
   retain fmtname '$airport';
   set ia1.AirportCities (rename = (AirportCode = start
                                    AirportCity = label));
run;

proc format library = ia cntlin = airports;
run;

options ls = 80;

proc print data=work.airports(obs=10) noobs;
   title 'Work.Airports';
run;

proc format library = ia fmtlib;
   select $airport;
   title '$AIRPORT format';
run;




/*************************************/
/*    Create a CNTLOUT SAS data set,  */
/*    edit the data, and recreate     */
/*    the format.                     */
/*************************************/

/*********** Example 1 ***************/


proc format lib = ia cntlout = work.fmtdata;
   select $airport;
run;
```

```
/*********** Example 2 ****************/

proc sql;
   insert into work.fmtdata
      set fmtname = 'AIRPORT',
            start = 'YYC',
              end = 'YYC',
            label = 'Calgary, AB',
             type = 'C'
        set fmtname = 'AIRPORT',
            start = 'YYZ',
              end = 'YYZ',
            label = 'Toronto, ON',
             type = 'C'
        set fmtname = 'AIRPORT',
            start = 'YQB',
              end = 'YQB',
            label = 'Quebec, QC',
             type = 'C'
      set fmtname = 'AIRPORT',
            start = 'YMX',
              end = 'YMX',
            label = 'Montreal, QC',
             type = 'C' ;
quit;


/*********** Example 3 ****************/

proc format library = ia cntlin = work.fmtdata;
run;

proc format library = ia fmtlib;
   select $airport;
   title 'New values in the $AIRPORT Format';
run;
```

## 7.6 Solutions to Exercises

1. Create a format named TIMES that has mutilabels. The first is for the following labels:

| Data Value | Label |
|---|---|
| Midnight to 4:59 a.m. | Red Eye |
| 5 a.m. to 11:59 a.m. | Morning |
| noon to 5:59 p.m. | Afternoon |
| 6 p.m. to 11:59 p.m. | Evening |

The second is for AM (midnight to noon) and PM (noon to midnight) flights.

Use the format in the following program named **ch7ex1**:

```
proc tabulate data = ia.schedule;
   where date = '15jun2000'd;
   title 'Example using Multilabel Formats';
   format depart times.;
   class  depart / mlf order = data;
   table depart;
run;
```

```
proc format library = ia;
   value times (multilabel)
         '00:00't - '04:59't = 'Red Eye'
         '05:00't - '11:59't = 'Morning'
         '12:00't - '17:59't = 'Afternoon'
         '18:00't - '23:59't = 'Evening'
         '00:00't - '11:59't = 'AM'
         '12:00't - '23:59't = 'PM';
run;

options fmtsearch = (ia);

proc tabulate data = ia.schedule;
   where date = '15jun2000'd;
   title 'Example using Multilabel Formats';
   format depart times.;
   class  depart / mlf order = data;
   table depart;
run;
```

2. Use the ia.Job_Code_Data data set to create a format named $JCodes. View the new format using the PROC FORMAT FMTLIB option.

```
data work.JobCodes;
   keep start label fmtname;
   retain fmtname '$jcodes';
   set ia.Job_Code_Data(rename = (Job_Code = start
                                  Job_Description = label));
run;

proc format library = ia cntlin = JobCodes;
run;

options ls = 80;
proc format library = ia fmtlib;
   select $jcodes;
   title '$JbCodes Format';
run;
```

3. Add to the $Jcodes format.

   a. Use the PROC FORMAT CNTLOUT= and CNTLIN= options. View the new format using the PROC FORMAT FMTLIB option.

   b. Add new data for ticket agents using PROC SQL INSERT statement:

| | |
|---|---|
| TKTAG1 | Ticket Agent Grade 1 |
| TKTAG2 | Ticket Agent Grade 2 |
| TKTAG3 | Ticket Agent Grade 3 |

```
proc format lib = prog3 cntlout = work.fmtdata;
   select $jcodes;
run;

proc sql;
   insert into work.fmtdata
      set fmtname = 'JCODES',
            start = 'TKTAG1',
              end = 'TKTAG1',
            label = 'Ticket Agent Grade 1',
             type = 'C'
      set fmtname = 'JCODES',
            start = 'TKTAG2',
              end = 'TKTAG2',
            label = 'Ticket Agent Grade 2',
             type = 'C'
      set fmtname = 'JCODES',
            start = 'TKTAG3',
              end = 'TKTAG3',
```

```
            label = 'Ticket Agent Grade 3',
             type = 'C';
quit;

proc format library = ia cntlin = work.fmtdata;
run;

proc format library = ia fmtlib;
   select $jcodes;
   title 'New values in the $JCODES Format';
run;
```

# Chapter 8

# 8.1 Introduction

## General Business Scenario

Monthly cargo revenue figures are stored every quarter.

For the first quarter, the data is stored in a blank delimited raw data file.

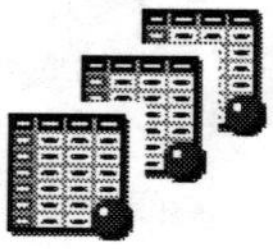

The data for the other three quarters are stored in SAS data sets.

3

## General Business Scenario

International Airlines needs to age a copy of these quarterly data sets so that each quarter a historic version is saved.

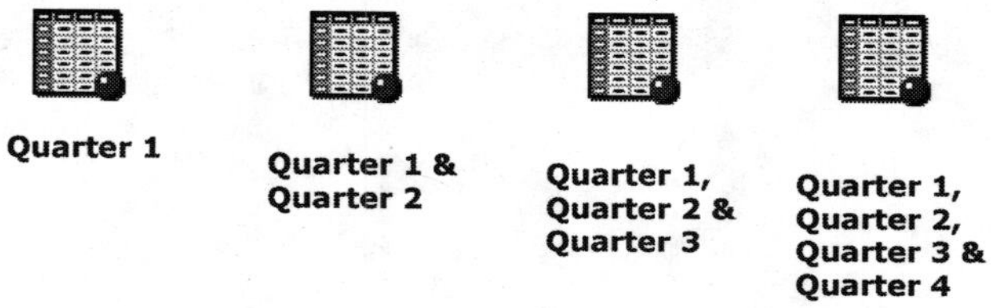


4

## Organize the Tasks

- Read the comma delimited file to create a SAS data set.
- Create four generations of the SAS data set.
- Each quarter, use the DATA step to append the new data onto the last generation.

5

# 8.2 Reading Free-formatted Data

## Objectives

- Create a SAS data set from a free-formatted raw data file.

7

## Business Scenario

The raw data file for the first quarter contains information in free-formatted style. We need to know the flight date and the cargo revenues.

Qtr1Carg Raw data file

```
01JAN2000    Lots of Cargo/Heavy Load   $3,280,638...
02JAN2000    Light Load   $3,275,164   $534,184...
03JAN2000    Medium Filled   $3,258,884   $552,088...
04JAN2000    Lots of Cargo/Heavy Load   $3,330,580...
05JAN2000    Lots of Cargo/Heavy Load   $3,301,534...
```

8

## Business Scenario

The file layout for this raw data file:

| Description | Type | Comments |
|---|---|---|
| Date of Flight | N | Date9. |
| Category of Cargo Load | C | 10 – 15 characters |
| Cargo Revenue | N | Maximum of 6 cargo revenues containing dollar signs and commas. |

9

## Organize the Tasks

- **Read the comma delimited file to create a SAS data set.**
- Create four generations of the SAS data set.
- Each quarter, use the DATA step to append the new data onto the last generation.

10

## What Happens If.....

- there are missing values?
- fields contain delimiters?
- the character values are longer than 8 characters?

For example,

**Raw data file**

```
Chicago    ORD    MDW
Washington    IAD    BWI    DCA
New York    LGA    JFK
```

11

```
Chicago    ORD    MDW
Washington    IAD    BWI    DCA
New York    LGA    JFK
```

**Compilation**

**Missing Values Long Values & Delimiters**

```
data work.TestData;
   infile rawdata;
   input City $
         (AirportCode1 -
          AirportCode3) ($);
   run;
```

**Input Buffer**

**PDV**

| City $ 8 | Airport Code1 $ 8 | Airport Code2 $ 8 | Airport Code3 $ 8 |
|---|---|---|---|
| | | | |

12

```
Chicago    ORD    MDW
Washington    IAD    BWI    DCA
New York    LGA    JFK
```

**Execution**

**Missing Values Long Values & Delimiters**

```
data work.TestData;
   infile rawdata;
   input City $
         (AirportCode1 -
          AirportCode3) ($);
   run;
```

**Input Buffer**

**PDV**

| City $ 8 | Airport Code1 $ 8 | Airport Code2 $ 8 | Airport Code3 $ 8 |
|---|---|---|---|
| | | | |

13

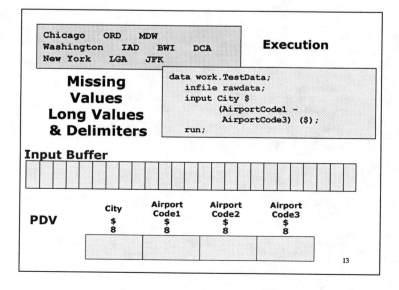

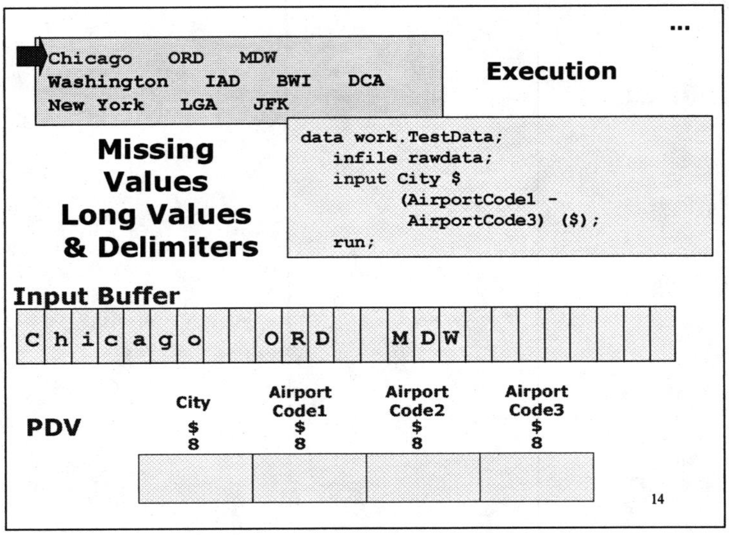
...
Chicago ORD MDW
Washington IAD BWI DCA
New York LGA JFK
Execution
Missing Values Long Values & Delimiters
data work.TestData;
infile rawdata;
input City $
(AirportCode1 -
AirportCode3) ($);
run;
Input Buffer
C h i c a g o O R D M D W
PDV
City $ 8
Airport Code1 $ 8
Airport Code2 $ 8
Airport Code3 $ 8
14

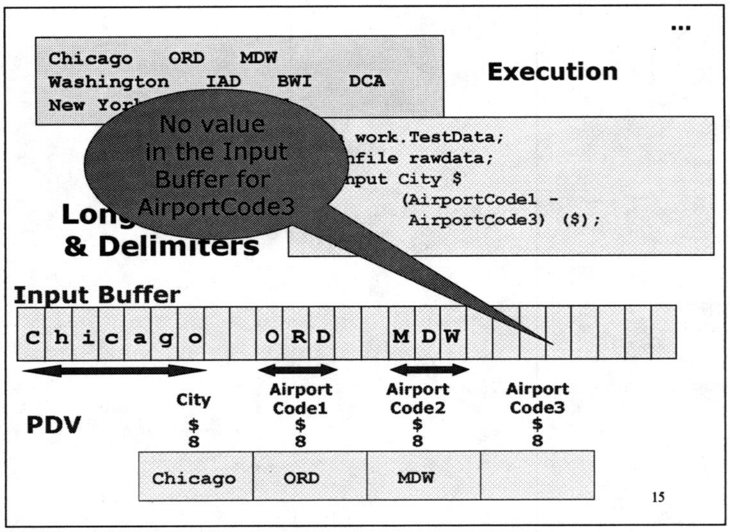
...
Chicago ORD MDW
Washington IAD BWI DCA
Execution
No value in the Input Buffer for AirportCode3
& Delimiters
work.TestData;
infile rawdata;
input City $
(AirportCode1 -
AirportCode3) ($);
Input Buffer
C h i c a g o O R D M D W
PDV
City $ 8
Airport Code1 $ 8
Airport Code2 $ 8
Airport Code3 $ 8
Chicago
ORD
MDW
15

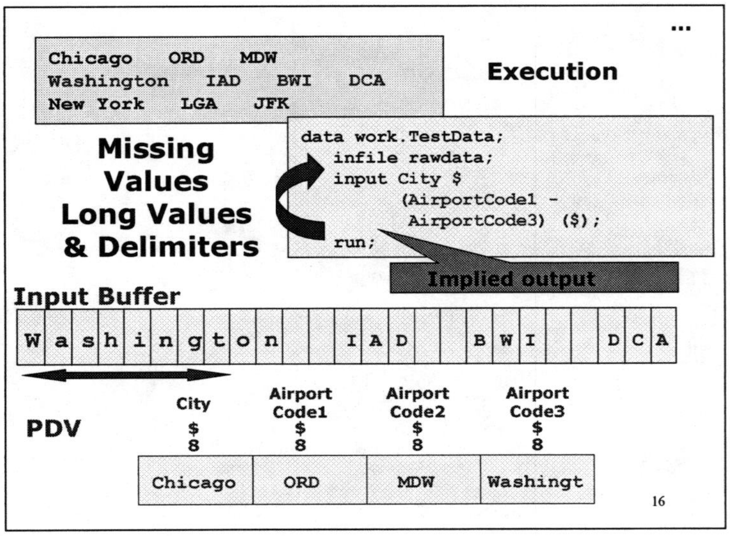
...
Chicago ORD MDW
Washington IAD BWI DCA
New York LGA JFK
Execution
Missing Values Long Values & Delimiters
data work.TestData;
infile rawdata;
input City $
(AirportCode1 -
AirportCode3) ($);
run;
Implied output
Input Buffer
W a s h i n g t o n I A D B W I D C A
PDV
City $ 8
Airport Code1 $ 8
Airport Code2 $ 8
Airport Code3 $ 8
Chicago
ORD
MDW
Washingt
16

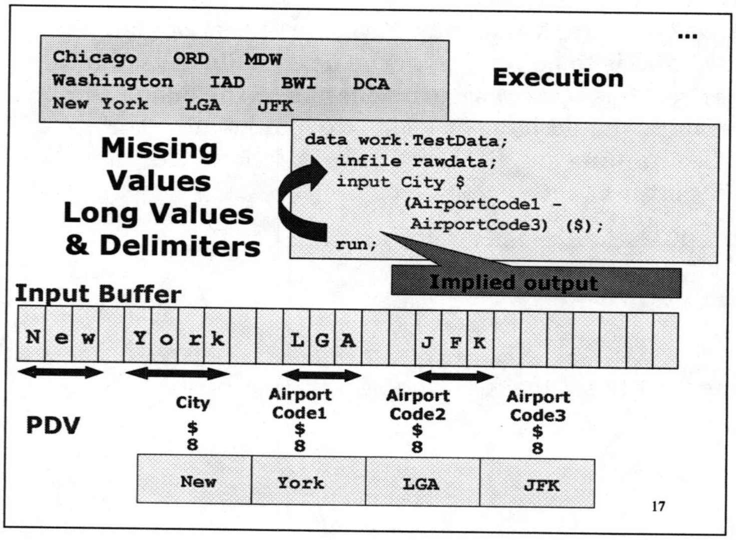


## Resulting SAS Data Set

| City | Airport Code1 | Airport Code2 | Airport Code3 |
|---|---|---|---|
| Chicago | ORD | MDW | Washingt |
| New | York | LGA | JFK |

18

## Tools to Use

- The MISSOVER option in the INFILE statement to
  - prevent loading another record
  - assign missing values to remaining variables.
- The & format modifier to read character values that contain a single embedded blank.

19

& indicates that the character value may have one or more single embedded blanks and is to be read from the next nonblank column until the pointer reaches two consecutive blanks or the end of the input line. Your data should have at least two blanks after the character value containing single blanks. The & follows the variable name *and* the $ that it affects.

## Tools to Use

- The ATTRIB statement to set the following attributes
  - length
  - informat
  - format.
- The DLM= option to specify delimiters other than blanks.
- The DSD option to specify that
  - the delimiter is a comma
  - data values containing commas are enclosed in quotation marks.

20

The general form for the ATTRIB statement.

**ATTRIB** *variable-list(s) attribute-list(*s);

*variable-list* names the variables that you want to associate with the attributes.

*attribute-list* specifies one or more attributes to assign to *variable-list*. Specify one or more of these attributes in the ATTRIB statement:

| | |
|---|---|
| FORMAT=*format* | associates a format with variables in *variable-list.* |
| INFORMAT=*informat* | associates an informat with variables in *variable-list.* |
| LABEL='*label*' | associates a label with variables in *variable-list.* |
| LENGTH=<$>*length* | specifies the length of variables in *variable-list.* |

The DLM= and DSD options are not necessary in our example.

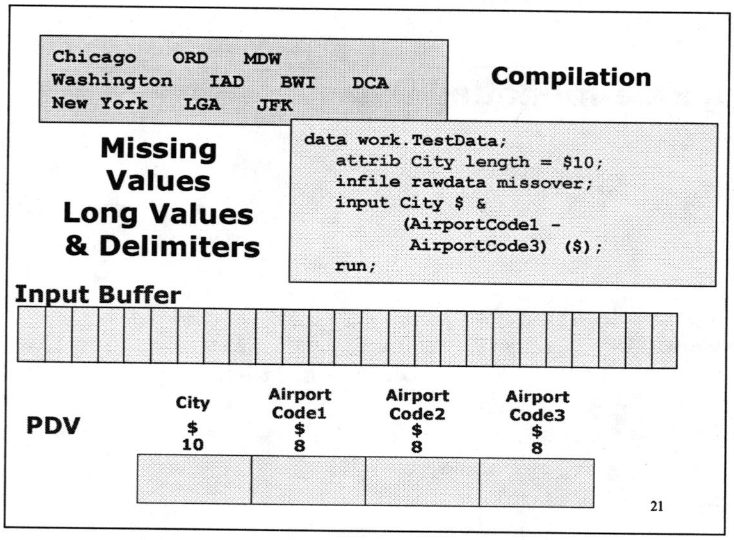


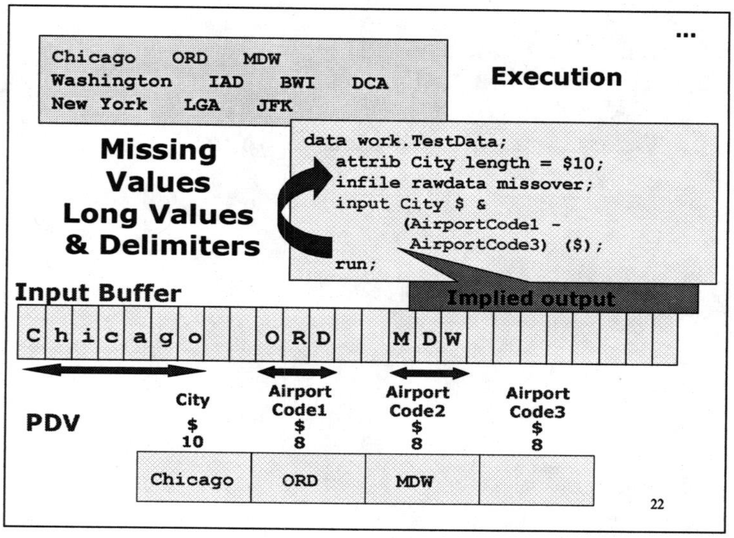


## What Are the Observations?

| City | Airport Code1 | Airport Code2 | Airport Code3 |
|---|---|---|---|
| Chicago | ORD | MDW | |
| Washington | IAD | BWI | DCA |
| New York | LGA | JFK | |

23

## Reading Free-formatted Data

c08s2d1

Program

```
data ia.Year2000;
   infile 'Qtr1Carg.dat' missover;
   attrib CargoRevenue1 - CargoRevenue6 informat = comma12.
                                          format = dollar12.
          FlightDate format = date9.
          comment length = $25;
   input FlightDate : date9. comment $ &
         CargoRevenue1 - CargoRevenue6;

run;

proc print data = ia.Year2000 (obs = 15);
   title 'Reading Free-Formatted Data with
   title2 Missing Values,';
   title3 'Long Data Values, and Embedded Blanks';
run;
```

## Output

Reading Free-Formatted Data with Missing Values,
Long Data Values, and Embedded Blanks

| Obs | Cargo Revenue1 | Cargo Revenue2 | Cargo Revenue3 | Cargo Revenue4 | Cargo Revenue5 |
|---|---|---|---|---|---|
| 1 | $3,280,638 | $561,692 | $2,128,545 | $1,817,984 | $223,134 |
| 2 | $3,275,164 | $534,184 | $1,878,010 | $1,860,242 | $214,236 |
| 3 | $3,258,884 | $552,088 | $2,123,491 | $1,840,034 | $213,864 |
| 4 | $3,330,580 | $552,294 | $2,357,934 | $1,812,278 | $226,276 |
| 5 | $3,301,534 | $564,340 | $2,145,639 | $1,819,898 | $227,258 |
| 6 | $3,326,138 | $576,790 | $2,131,639 | $1,833,088 | $220,462 |
| 7 | $3,246,350 | $533,278 | $2,377,156 | $1,844,822 | $222,436 |
| 8 | $3,298,714 | $547,340 | $2,156,809 | $1,820,122 | $220,312 |
| 9 | $3,285,232 | $544,116 | $1,952,562 | $1,807,724 | $218,156 |
| 10 | $3,280,508 | $555,252 | $2,142,039 | $1,804,266 | $217,604 |
| 11 | $3,302,822 | $555,976 | $2,345,564 | $1,754,802 | $217,096 |
| 12 | $3,296,096 | $538,238 | $2,179,523 | $1,853,246 | $233,602 |
| 13 | $3,277,750 | $545,314 | $2,138,169 | $1,829,864 | $233,022 |
| 14 | $3,251,002 | $575,892 | $2,394,990 | $1,804,538 | $212,506 |
| 15 | $3,174,884 | $531,338 | $2,133,343 | $1,819,038 | $216,170 |

| Obs | Cargo Revenue6 | Flight Date | comment |
|---|---|---|---|
| 1 | . | 01JAN2000 | Lots of Cargo/Heavy Load |
| 2 | $969,241 | 02JAN2000 | Light Load |
| 3 | $942,459 | 03JAN2000 | Medium Filled |
| 4 | $958,295 | 04JAN2000 | Lots of Cargo/Heavy Load |
| 5 | $982,329 | 05JAN2000 | Lots of Cargo/Heavy Load |
| 6 | $1,163,366 | 06JAN2000 | Lots of Cargo/Heavy Load |
| 7 | . | 07JAN2000 | Lots of Cargo/Heavy Load |
| 8 | $950,041 | 08JAN2000 | Medium Filled |
| 9 | $976,357 | 09JAN2000 | Light Load |
| 10 | $983,877 | 10JAN2000 | Medium Filled |
| 11 | $976,635 | 11JAN2000 | Lots of Cargo/Heavy Load |
| 12 | $992,769 | 12JAN2000 | Lots of Cargo/Heavy Load |
| 13 | $1,194,362 | 13JAN2000 | Lots of Cargo/Heavy Load |
| 14 | $1,002,203 | 14JAN2000 | Lots of Cargo/Heavy Load |
| 15 | $968,085 | 15JAN2000 | Medium Filled |

## Exercises

1. The following raw data file named JobHistory contains job history of a few employees. There are a variable number of jobs for each person.

```
MILLS FLTAT1 FLTAT2 FLTAT3
BOWER FINCLK
READING ITPROG ITMGR VICEPR
JUDD FACMNT
MASSENGILL MECH01
BADINE RECEPT OFFMGR
DEMENT ITPROG
FOSKEY GRCREW
POOLE FLTAT2 FLTAT3
```

Create a SAS data set named ia.JobHistory that contains the last name of the employee and variables Job1, Job2, and Job3.

# 8.3 Creating Generation Data Sets

## Objectives

- Introduce the terminology for generation data sets.
- Create generations of a SAS data set.
- Process generations of a SAS data set.

27

## Business Scenario

Since the data needs to be aged, we can rerun the previous program to create a maximum of four generations of the data.

**Quarter 1**

**Quarter 1 & Quarter 2**

**Quarter 1, Quarter 2 & Quarter 3**

**Quarter 1, Quarter 2, Quarter 3 & Quarter 4**

28

*Generation data sets* are historical versions of

- SAS data files
- SAS data views

✎ OpenVMS does not support generation data sets.

...

## Business Scenario

As we append data onto the data set IA.YEAR2000, the generations of the data are kept.

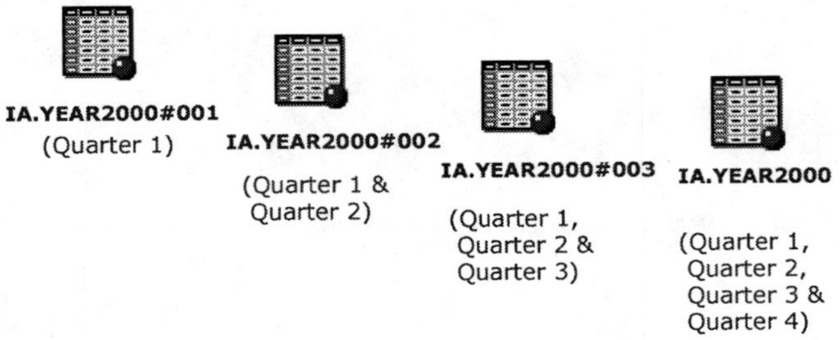


29

## Organize the Tasks

- Read the comma delimited file to create a SAS data set.
- **Create four generations of the SAS data set.**
- **Each quarter, use the data step to append the new data onto the last generation.**

30

## Uses of Generation Data Sets

You can use generation data sets to

- have multiple copies of either SAS data sets or SAS data views.
- archive data without having to age the data manually.

31

...

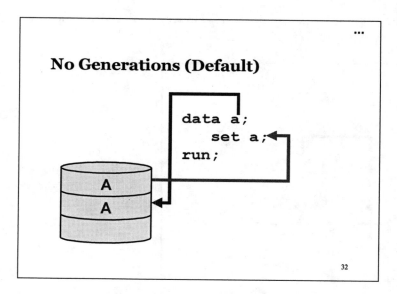

## No Generations (Default)

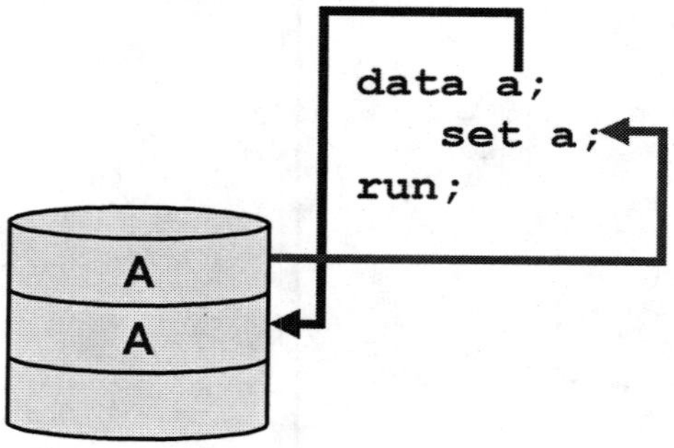


32

By default, as the SAS data set A is replaced, there are two copies of A in the SAS data library.

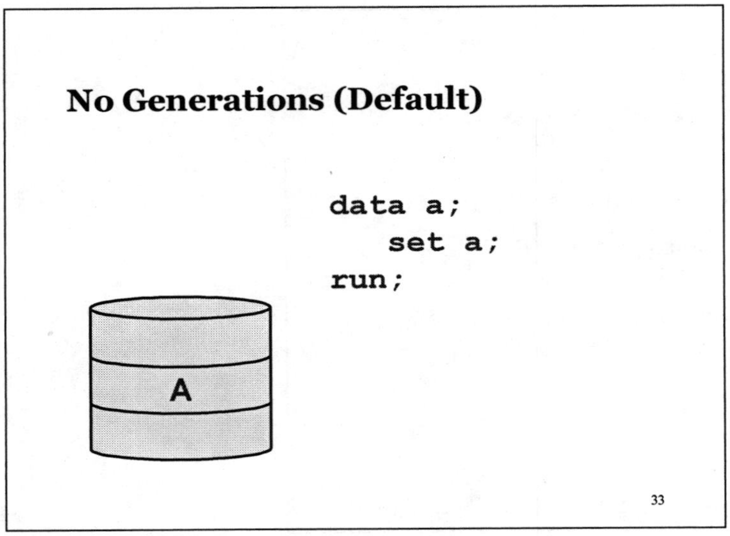


When the DATA step completes execution, SAS removes the original copy of the data set A from the data library.

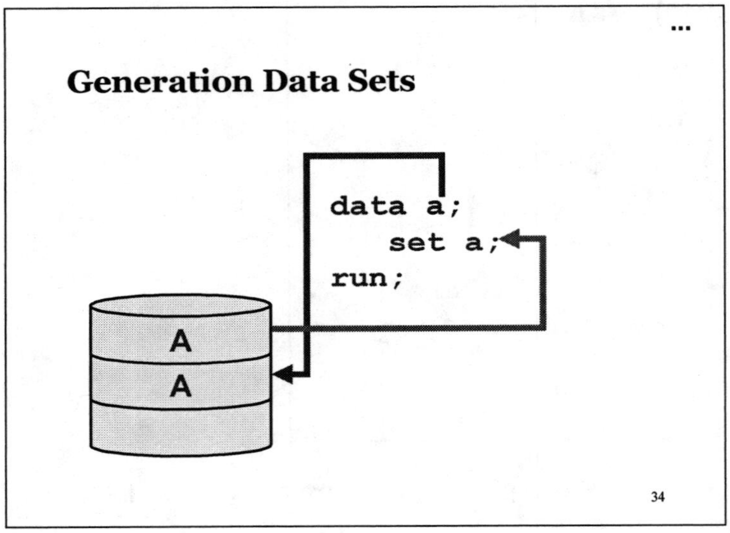


By default, as the SAS data set A is replaced, there are two copies of A in the SAS data library.

...

## Generation Data Sets

```
data a;
   set a;
run;
```

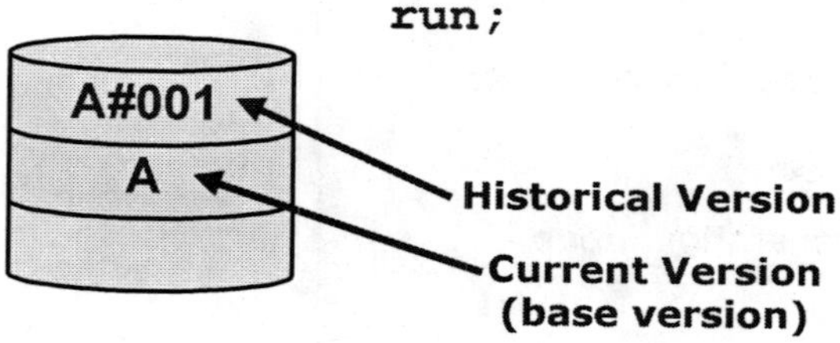


35

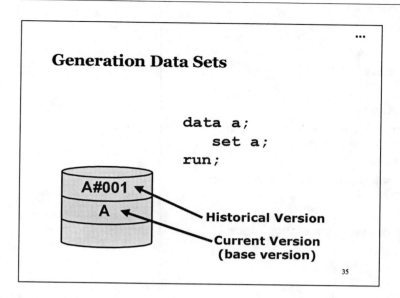

When the DATA step completes execution, SAS keeps the original copy of the SAS data set A in the data library and renames it. New versions are created only when a data set is replaced, not when it is modified in place.

## Terms to Know

**Generation group**

the group of files that represents a series of replacement data sets. The generation group consists of the base version and a set of historical versions of a file.

**Version**

any one of the files in a generation group.

**Base version**

the most recently created version of a file.

36

## Terms to Know

**Historical versions**

all the versions of a file in the generation group except the base version.

**Youngest version**

the version that is chronologically closest to the base version.

**Eldest version**

the oldest version in a generation group.

37

The eldest version is not necessarily the first version created.

## Names for Generation Data Sets

When generations are in effect, SAS file names are limited to 28 characters.

The last four characters are reserved for the version numbers.

38

## Documentation of Generation Data Sets

The Explorer window displays the base name followed by all of the historical names.

The CONTENTS and DATASETS procedures include generation information.

39

DICTIONARY.TABLES does not include information about generation data sets.

## Data Set Option to Create Generations

GENMAX=
: an output data set option that establishes how many generations to keep.

A GENMAX value

- =0 no historical versions are kept. (This is the default.)
- >0 how many versions of the file will be kept. For example, GENMAX=2 keeps the base version and 1 historical version.

40

## Example:

Create a SAS data set with a maximum of four versions.

```
data ia.Year2000(genmax = 4);
   infile 'Qtr1Carg.dat' missover;
   attrib CargoRevenue1 - CargoRevenue6
                informat = comma12.
                format = dollar12.
          FlightDate format = date9.
          comment length = $25;
   input FlightDate : date9. comment $ &
         CargoRevenue1  - CargoRevenue6;
run;
```

41

...

## Generation Data Sets: Time 1

| Data Set name | Absolute generation number | Relative generation number |
|---|---|---|
| ia.Year2000 | 1 | 0 |

42

## Creating New Generations

To create new generations, you use

- a DATA step with a SET statement
- a DATA step with a MERGE statement
- PROC SORT without the OUT= option
- PROC SQL with a CREATE TABLE statement.

43

These are all replacement techniques, not updating techniques.

## Generation Data Sets: Time 2

Replace the data set:

```
data ia.Year2000;
   set ia.Year2000
       ia.Quarter2;
run;
```

44

...

## Generation Data Sets: Time 2

| Data Set name | Absolute generation number | Relative generation number |
|---|---|---|
| ia.Year2000 | 2 | 0 |
| ia.Year2000#001 | 1 | -1 |

45

The original data set is renamed to ia.Year2000#001. The relative generation number is reassigned as –1.

## Generation Data Sets: Time 3

Replace the data set:

```
data ia.Year2000;
   set ia.Year2000
       ia.Quarter3;
run;
```

46

...

## Generation Data Sets: Time 3

| Data Set name | Absolute generation number | Relative generation number |
|---|---|---|
| ia.Year2000 | 3 | 0 |
| ia.Year2000#002 | 2 | -1 |
| ia.Year2000#001 | 1 | -2 |

47

The second version of ia.Year2000 is renamed to ia.Year2000#002 and is assigned a new relative generation number of –1.

The first version of ia.Year2000, named ia.Year2000#001, is reassigned a relative generation number of –2.

## Generation Data Sets: Time 4

Replace the data set:

```
data ia.Year2000;
   set ia.Year2000
       ia.Quarter4;
run;
```

48

...

## Generation Data Sets: Time 4

| Data Set name | Absolute generation number | Relative generation number |
|---|---|---|
| `ia.Year2000` | 4 | 0 |
| `ia.Year2000#003` | 3 | -1 |
| `ia.Year2000#002` | 2 | -2 |
| `ia.Year2000#001` | 1 | -3 |

49

The third copy of ia.Year2000# is renamed to ia.Year2000#003 and is assigned a relative generation number of –1.

The second version of ia.Year2000, named ia.Year2000#002, is assigned a new relative generation number of –1.

The first version of ia.Year2000, named ia.Year2000#001, is reassigned a relative generation number of –3.

## Generation Data Sets: Time 5

Sort the data set:

```
proc sort data = ia.Year2000;
   by FlightDate;
run;
```

50

...

**Generation Data Sets: Time 5**

| Data Set name | Absolute generation number | Relative generation number |
|---|---|---|
| ia.Year2000 | 5 | 0 |
| ia.Year2000#004 | 4 | -1 |
| ia.Year2000#003 | 3 | -2 |
| ia.Year2000#002 | 2 | -3 |
| ia.Year2000#001 | 1 | |

Deleted

51

The fourth copy of ia.Year2000 is renamed to ia.Year2000#004 and is assigned a relative generation number of –1.

The third copy of ia.Year2000, named ia.Year2000#003, is assigned a relative generation number of –2.

The second version of ia.Year2000, named ia.Year2000#002, is assigned a new relative generation number of –3.

The first version of ia.Year2000 is deleted.

## Generation Data Sets

c08s3d1

Program

```
data ia.Year2000(genmax = 4);
   infile 'Qtr1Carg.dat' missover;
   attrib CargoRevenue1 - CargoRevenue6 informat = comma12.
                                        format = dollar12.
          FlightDate format = date9.
          comment length = $25;
   input FlightDate : date9. comment $ &
         CargoRevenue1  - CargoRevenue6;
run;


/*************Self Study**************************/
/* Instead of submitting the previous program,   */
/*  you could use PROC DATASETS.                 */
/*                                               */
/*  proc datasets lib = ia;                      */
/*     modify Year2000 (genmax = 4);             */
/*  run;                                         */
/*************Self Study**************************/


data ia.Year2000;
   set ia.Year2000
       ia.Quarter2;
run;

data ia.Year2000;
   set ia.Year2000
       ia.Quarter3;
run;

data ia.Year2000;
   set ia.Year2000
       ia.Quarter4;
run;

proc sort data = ia.Year2000;
   by FlightDate;
run;
```

```
proc datasets library = ia;
   title 'All data sets in the IA library';
   contents data = _all_;
   title 'Contents of the Current Version of IA.YEAR2000';
   contents data = Year2000;
run;
quit;
```

Output

```
              Contents of the Current Version of IA.YEAR2000

                         The DATASETS Procedure

                          -----Directory-----

                Libref:         IA
                Engine:         V8
                Physical Name: c:\workshop\winsas\prog3
                File Name:      c:\workshop\winsas\prog3


 #  Name                    Gennum  Memtype   File Size  Last Modified
 ----------------------------------------------------------------------
 1  AIRPORTCITIES                   DATA          13312  03JUN2000:17:00:02
 2  AIRPORTDATA                     DATA        1364992  30MAY2000:15:32:17
 3  CAPACITY2000                    DATA        9307136  17MAY2000:08:41:40
    CAPACITY2000                    AUDIT          9216  04JUN2000:22:02:54
 4  CAPACITYINFORMATION             DATA           9216  17MAY2000:08:41:12
 5  CARGO1999                       DATA        9315328  17MAY2000:08:41:25
    CARGO1999                       INDEX       2110464  17MAY2000:08:41:25
 6  CARGOREVENUE                    DATA        5354496  15MAY2000:09:29:55
 7  DOWNUNDER                       DATA          33792  03JUN2000:14:09:02
 8  FORMATS                         CATALOG       17408  03JUN2000:15:52:49
 9  MONTHLYSUMMARY1997_             DATA           5120  16MAY2000:12:52:43
    1999
10  NEWCARGONUMBERS                 DATA           9216  17MAY2000:08:42:20
11  NEWFLIGHTNUMBERS                DATA           5120  24MAY2000:19:09:21
12  QUARTER2                        DATA           9216  03JUN2000:18:34:59
13  QUARTER3                        DATA           9216  03JUN2000:18:35:00
14  QUARTER4                        DATA           9216  03JUN2000:18:35:00
15  SALESDATA2000                   DATA       23815168  03JUN2000:15:16:40
16  TARGET                          DATA          13312  02JUN2000:20:35:50
17  YEAR2000                        DATA          33792  04JUN2000:22:02:51
18  YEAR2000                     2  DATA          17408  04JUN2000:22:02:50
19  YEAR2000                     3  DATA          25600  04JUN2000:22:02:50
20  YEAR2000                     4  DATA          33792  04JUN2000:22:02:50
```

```
                Contents of the Current Version of IA.YEAR2000

                          The DATASETS Procedure

Data Set Name:        IA.YEAR2000              Observations:          274
Member Type:          DATA                     Variables:             8
Engine:               V8                       Indexes:               0
Created:              22:02 Sunday,            Observation Length:    88
                      June 4, 2000
Last Modified:        22:02 Sunday,            Deleted Observations: 0
                      June 4, 2000
Protection:                                    Compressed:            NO
Data Set Type:                                 Sorted:                YES
Max Generations:      4
Next Generation Num: 5
Label:


              -----Engine/Host Dependent Information-----

   Data Set Page Size:          8192
   Number of Data Set Pages:    4
   First Data Page:             1
   Max Obs per Page:            92
   Obs in First Data Page:      70
   Number of Data Set Repairs: 0
   File Name:                   c:\workshop\winsas\prog3\year2000.sas7bdat
   Release Created:             8.0101M0
   Host Created:                WIN_NT


         -----Alphabetic List of Variables and Attributes-----

   #    Variable          Type    Len    Pos    Format        Informat
   ____________________________________________________________________
   1    CargoRevenue1     Num       8      0    DOLLAR12.     COMMA12.
   2    CargoRevenue2     Num       8      8    DOLLAR12.     COMMA12.
   3    CargoRevenue3     Num       8     16    DOLLAR12.     COMMA12.
   4    CargoRevenue4     Num       8     24    DOLLAR12.     COMMA12.
   5    CargoRevenue5     Num       8     32    DOLLAR12.     COMMA12.
   6    CargoRevenue6     Num       8     40    DOLLAR12.     COMMA12.
   7    FlightDate        Num       8     48    DATE9.
   8    comment           Char     25     56


                        -----Sort Information-----

                        Sortedby:       FlightDate
                        Validated:      YES
                        Character Set: ANSI
```

## Processing Generation Data Sets

GENNUM =
an input/update data set option that identifies which generation to open.

A GENNUM value

- >0 absolute reference to a historical version by its generation number.
- <0 relative reference to historical versions.
- =0 current version.

53

## GENNUM= Option

For example,

GENNUM = -1 refers to the youngest version.

GENNUM = 0 refers to the current version.

GENNUM = 1 refers to the first version created.

As new generations are created, the absolute generation number increases sequentially.

As older generations are deleted, their absolute generation numbers are retired.

54

## Processing Generation Data Sets

Examples:

Print the current version:

```
proc print data = ia.Year2000;
run;
```

Print the youngest version:

```
proc print data = ia.Year2000(gennum = 4);
run;
```

or

```
proc print data = ia.Year2000(gennum = -1);
run;
```

55

## Generation Data Sets

c08s3d2

Example 1

Program

```
proc print data = ia.Year2000(gennum = 4 obs = 5);
   title 'The Youngest Generation of IA.YEAR200';
run;
```

Output

The Youngest Generation of IA.YEAR200

| Obs | Cargo Revenue1 | Cargo Revenue2 | Cargo Revenue3 | Cargo Revenue4 | Cargo Revenue5 |
|---|---|---|---|---|---|
| 1 | $3,280,638 | $561,692 | $2,128,545 | $1,817,984 | $223,134 |
| 2 | $3,275,164 | $534,184 | $1,878,010 | $1,860,242 | $214,236 |
| 3 | $3,258,884 | $552,088 | $2,123,491 | $1,840,034 | $213,864 |
| 4 | $3,330,580 | $552,294 | $2,357,934 | $1,812,278 | $226,276 |
| 5 | $3,301,534 | $564,340 | $2,145,639 | $1,819,898 | $227,258 |

| Obs | Cargo Revenue6 | Flight Date | comment |
|---|---|---|---|
| 1 | . | 01JAN2000 | Lots of Cargo/Heavy Load |
| 2 | $969,241 | 02JAN2000 | Light Load |
| 3 | $942,459 | 03JAN2000 | Medium Filled |
| 4 | $958,295 | 04JAN2000 | Lots of Cargo/Heavy Load |
| 5 | $982,329 | 05JAN2000 | Lots of Cargo/Heavy Load |

Example 2

Program

```
proc print data=ia.Year2000(gennum = -1 obs = 5);
   title 'The Youngest Generation of IA.YEAR200';
run;
```

Output

```
                      The Youngest Generation of IA.YEAR200

              Cargo        Cargo        Cargo        Cargo        Cargo
 Obs       Revenue1     Revenue2     Revenue3     Revenue4     Revenue5

   1     $3,280,638     $561,692   $2,128,545   $1,817,984     $223,134
   2     $3,275,164     $534,184   $1,878,010   $1,860,242     $214,236
   3     $3,258,884     $552,088   $2,123,491   $1,840,034     $213,864
   4     $3,330,580     $552,294   $2,357,934   $1,812,278     $226,276
   5     $3,301,534     $564,340   $2,145,639   $1,819,898     $227,258

              Cargo       Flight
 Obs       Revenue6         Date    comment

   1              .    01JAN2000    Lots of Cargo/Heavy Load
   2       $969,241    02JAN2000    Light Load
   3       $942,459    03JAN2000    Medium Filled
   4       $958,295    04JAN2000    Lots of Cargo/Heavy Load
   5       $982,329    05JAN2000    Lots of Cargo/Heavy Load
```

# Reference Information

## Maintenance of Generation Data Sets

You can

- browse or update a historical version
- transfer generations with PROC COPY
- use PROC DATASETS to
- delete all or some of the generations
- rename an entire generation or any member of the group to a new base name.
- increase or decrease the GENMAX value.

You cannot

- retain the version number when renaming a member
- open a historical version for output.

Example

To change the number of generations created:

```
proc datasets library = ia;
   modify SalesData2000(genmax = 10);
run;
```

To rename all the generations:

```
proc datasets library = ia;
   change SalesData2000 = Sales;
run;
```

To rename only the second historical data set:

```
proc datasets library = ia;
   change Sales(gennum = 2) = NewSales;
run;
```

To delete one historic version. This may leave a hole in the generation group:

```
proc datasets library = ia;
   delete NewSales(gennum = -1);
run;
```

To delete all of the historic versions:

```
proc datasets library = ia;
   delete NewSales(gennum = HIST);
run;
```

HIST is a keyword for the GENNUM= option on the PROC DATASETS DELETE statement that refers to all generations (excludes the base name).

To delete all of the SAS data sets in a generation group:

```
proc datasets library = ia;
   delete NewSales(gennum = ALL);
run;
```

ALL is a keyword for the GENNUM= option on the PROC DATASETS DELETE statement that refers to the base name and all generations.

## Exercises

2. Create the same data set as the previous exercise, ia.JobHistory, with a maximum of three generations.

   a. Use the ia.Y200061 and ia.Y200062 data sets to concatenate to JobHistory and test your program.

   b. Use PROC DATASETS to look at the generation information for ia.JobHistory.

## 8.4 Chapter Summary

List input is appropriate for reading data that are not in fixed columns (free-format). List input is generally used to read standard data values that contain no embedded blanks that are separated by at least one blank, but can be combined with format modifiers to read data formatted otherwise.

To read data with embedded blanks, you can use the & modifier, provided that there are at least two blanks following the data values.

Use the DLM= or the DSD option to specify delimiters other than blanks. By default, the DSD option specifies that the delimiter is a comma and the data values containing commas are enclosed in quotation marks.

To prevent SAS from loading another record and assigning missing values to the remaining variables, you can use the MISSOVER option.

Use the ATTRIB statement to set the following attributes

length

informat

format.

The general form of the ATTRIB statement

**ATTRIB** *variable-list(s) attribute-list(s)* ;

Generation data sets are historical versions of SAS tables or SAS data views. They enable you to have multiple copies of a SAS table or data view without having to age the data manually.

To specify how many generations to keep, use the data set option

GENMAX=*n*

To reference a version of a generation group, use the data set option

GENNUM=*n*

A positive value for *n* refers to the absolute generation number and a negative value for *n* refers to the relative generation number. Absolute generation numbers specify the time at which the generation was created. Relative generation numbers specify the position of the historical version in relation to the current (base) version.

You can use PROC DATASETS to delete generations, rename generations, and increase the GENMAX= value.

Entire Program

```
/********* c08s2d1 ******************/

/************************************/
/*    Create a SAS data set from a    */
/*    free-formatted raw data file.   */
/************************************/


data ia.Year2000;
   infile 'Qtr1Carg.dat' missover;
   attrib CargoRevenue1 - CargoRevenue6 informat = comma12.
                                          format = dollar12.
          FlightDate format = date9.
          comment length = $25;
   input FlightDate : date9. comment $ &
         CargoRevenue1  - CargoRevenue6;

run;

proc print data = ia.Year2000 (obs = 15);
   title 'Reading Free-Formatted Data with
   title2 Missing Values,';
   title3 'Long Data Values, and Embedded Blanks';
run;


/********* c08s3d1 ******************/


/************************************/
/*    Create a SAS data set from a    */
/*    free-formatted raw data file.   */
/************************************/


data ia.Year2000 (genmax = 4);
   infile 'Qtr1Carg.dat' missover;
   attrib CargoRevenue1 - CargoRevenue6 informat = comma12.
                                          format = dollar12.
          FlightDate format = date9.
          comment length = $25;
   input FlightDate : date9. comment $ &
         CargoRevenue1  - CargoRevenue6;
run;
```

```
/*************Self Study**************************/
/* Instead of submitting the previous program    */
/*  you could use PROC DATASETS                  */
/*                                               */
/*  proc datasets lib = ia;                      */
/*     modify Year2000 (genmax = 4);             */
/*  run;                                         */
/*************Self Study**************************/


data ia.Year2000;
   set ia.Year2000
       ia.Quarter2;
run;

data ia.Year2000;
   set ia.Year2000
       ia.Quarter3;
run;

data ia.Year2000;
   set ia.Year2000
       ia.Quarter4;
run;

proc sort data = ia.Year2000;
   by FlightDate;
run;

proc datasets library = ia;
   title 'All data sets in the IA library';
   contents data = _all_;
   title 'Contents of the Current Version of IA.YEAR2000';
   contents data = Year2000;
run;
quit;


/********* c08s2d2 ******************/


/*************************************/
/*    Print the youngest version of  */
/*    a SAS data set.                */
/*************************************/

/*********** Example 1    *************/


proc print data = ia.Year2000(gennum = 3 obs = 5);
   title 'The Youngest Generation of IA.YEAR200';
run;
```

```
/*********** Example 2    *************/

proc print data=ia.Year2000(gennum = -1 obs = 5);
   title 'The Youngest Generation of IA.YEAR200';
run;
```

## 8.5 Solutions to Exercises

1. The following raw data file named JobHistory contains job history of a few employees. There are a variable number of jobs for each person.

```
MILLS FLTAT1 FLTAT2 FLTAT3
BOWER FINCLK
READING ITPROG ITMGR VICEPR
JUDD FACMNT
MASSENGILL MECH01
BADINE RECEPT OFFMGR
DEMENT ITPROG
FOSKEY GRCREW
POOLE FLTAT2 FLTAT3
```

Create a SAS data set named ia.JobHistory that contains the last name of the employee and variables Job1, Job2, and Job3.

```
data ia.JobHistory;
   infile 'history.dat' missover;
   attrib lastname length = $25
        Job1 - Job3 length = $6;
   input lastname $
         Job1  - Job3 $;

run;

proc print data = ia.JobHistory;
run;
```

2. Create the same data set as the previous exercise, ia.JobHistory, with a maximum of three generations.

   a. Use the ia.Y200061 and ia.Y200062 data sets to concatenate to JobHistory and test your program.

   b. Use PROC DATASETS to look at the generation information for ia.JobHistory.

```
data ia.JobHistory(genmax=3);
   infile 'history.dat' missover;
   attrib lastname length = $25
             Job1 - Job3 length=$6;
   input lastname $
         Job1  - Job3 $;

run;

data ia.JobHistory;
   set ia.JobHistory
       ia.Y200061;
run;
```

```
         data ia.JobHistory;
            set ia.JobHistory
               ia.Y200062;
run;

proc datasets library = ia;
   contents data = _all_;
   contents data = JobHistory;
run;
quit;
```

# Chapter 9 (Self-Study)

# 9.1 Introduction

## General Business Scenario

International Airlines needs a method of keeping their SAS data sets updated.

When the data set ia.CapacityInformation is updated, it often has data entry errors. We need to provide validity checks to the data.

3

## General Business Scenario

Managers need a technique to determine

- who is making the changes to ia.CapacityInformation
- what these changes are.

4

## General Business Scenario

The CEO of International Airlines wants to decrease the number of seats for the business and economy classes to give passengers more leg room.

5

## General Business Scenario

There are changes to some of the route ID numbers. We must apply these changes to ia.CapacityInformation.

| FlightID Number | RouteID Number | Origin | Destination |
|---|---|---|---|
| IA00500 | 0000035 | RDU | JFK |

6

## General Business Scenario

An accountant has discovered that some of the cargo figures for 1999 are incorrect.

7

## Organize the Tasks

- Create integrity constraints on ia.CapacityInformation and ia.Capacity2000.
- Create an audit trail file on ia.CapacityInformation.
- Modify ia.Capacity to decrease the number of seats.
- Modify ia.Capacity to change some of the route ID numbers.
- Modify ia.Cargo1999 to correct cargo revenues.

8

# 9.2 Creating Integrity Constraints

## Objectives

- Define integrity constraints.
- Determine the available types of integrity constraints.
- Describe the benefits of integrity constraints.
- Create integrity constraints.

10

## Business Scenario

The data set IA.CAPACITYINFORMATION is updated frequently, and data errors are prevalent.

12

## Organize the Tasks:

- **Create integrity constraints on ia.CapacityInformation and ia.Capacity2000.**
- Create an audit trail file on ia.CapacityInformation.
- Modify ia.CapacityInformation to decrease the number of seats.
- Modify ia.CapacityInformation to change some of the route ID numbers.
- Modify ia.Cargo1999 to correct cargo revenues.

13

## Integrity Constraints

We can create integrity constraints on the data to

- preserve the consistency and correctness of data
- validate data when inserting or updating the values of a column for which integrity constraints have been defined.

14

Integrity constraints are rules that SAS data set modifications must follow to guarantee validity of data.

Integrity constraints apply **only** when data values are modified in place **not** when the table is replaced.

Techniques for modifying data in place include

- Viewtable window
- FSVIEW window
- FSEDIT window
- DATA step with the MODIFY statement
- PROC SQL with the INSERT INTO statement or the SET statement
- PROC APPEND.

## Two Categories of Integrity Constraints

- ***General constraints***

  allow you to restrict the data values accepted for a column.

- ***Referential constraints***

  allow you to link the data values for a column in one table to the values of columns in another table.

15

General constraints:

- required data (non-missing data)
- validity checking (checks the values of a column against a list of acceptable values or against the data values in another column)
- uniqueness.

Referential constraints:

- primary key (both unique and non-missing)
- foreign keys link the column values in one table to the primary key values in another table.

### Five Integrity Constraints

**General**
- NOT NULL
- CHECK
- UNIQUE

**Referential**
- PRIMARY KEY
- FOREIGN KEY

16

You can create integrity constraints for tables containing no rows, one row, or many rows.

| | |
|---|---|
| NOT NULL | guarantees that corresponding columns have non-missing values in each row. |
| CHECK | insures that a specific set or range of values are the only values in a column. It can also check the validity of a value in one column based on another value in another column within the same row. |
| UNIQUE | enforces uniqueness for the value of a column. |
| PRIMARY KEY | uniquely defines a row within a table. There can be at most one primary key based on one column or a set of columns. The primary key combines the NOT NULL and UNIQUE attributes. |
| FOREIGN KEY | links one or more rows in a table to a specific row in another table by matching a column or set of columns in one table with the primary key in another table. This parent/child relationship limits modifications made to both primary and foreign keys. The only acceptable values for a foreign key are values of the primary key or missing values. |

If the table contains data, all data values are checked to determine whether they satisfy the constraint before the constraint is added.

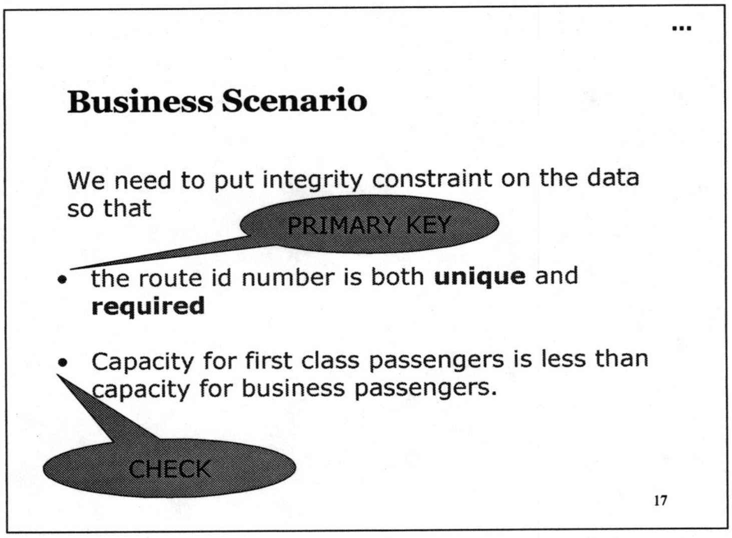


For the UNIQUE constraint and the PRIMARY KEY constraint, SAS builds unique indexes on the column(s) involved if an appropriate index does not already exist. Any index created by an integrity constraint can be used for other purposes such as WHERE processing or the KEY= option on a SET statement.

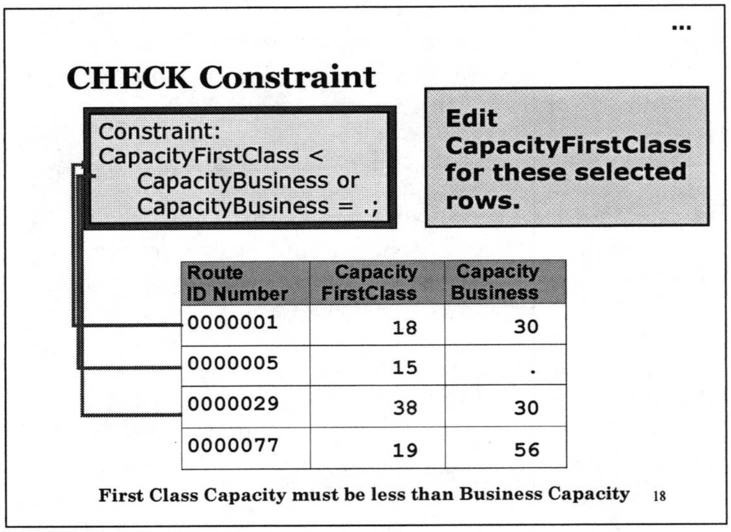


| Route ID Number | Capacity FirstClass | Capacity Business |
|---|---|---|
| 0000001 | 18 | 30 |
| 0000005 | 15 | . |
| 0000029 | 38 | 30 |
| 0000077 | 19 | 56 |

## Methods for Creating Integrity Constraints

- PROC SQL
- PROC DATASETS
- SCL (SAS Component Language) ICCREATE function

19

PROC SQL can assign constraints either as it creates a new table or as modifications to an existing table.

PROC DATASETS can only assign constraints to an existing table.

## Using PROC DATASETS to Create or Alter Integrity Constraints

```
PROC DATASETS LIB=libref;
    MODIFY member;
        INTEGRITY CONSTRAINT CREATE
            constraint-name=constraint
            message='New Error Message';
        INTEGRITY CONSTRAINT DELETE
            constraint-name;
```

20

You can abbreviate INTEGRITY CONSTRAINT as IC.

Required Arguments

<constraint-name=> is a name for the constraint. The name must be a valid SAS name. When you do not supply a constraint name, a default name is generated. This default constraint name has the following form.

| Default name | Constraint type |
|---|---|
| _NMxxxx_ | Not Null |
| _UNxxxx_ | Unique |
| _CKxxxx_ | Check |
| _PKxxxx_ | Primary key |
| _FKxxxx_ | Foreign key |

where ***xxxx*** is a counter beginning at 0001.

The names PRIMARY, FOREIGN, MESSAGE, UNIQUE, DISTINCT, CHECK, and NOT cannot be used as values for ***constraint-name***.

constraint — is the type of constraint. Valid values are

NOT NULL(variable)
: specifies that variable does not contain a SAS missing value, including special missing values.

UNIQUE(variables)
: specifies that the values of variables must be unique. This constraint is identical to DISTINCT.

DISTINCT(variables)
: specifies that the values of variables must be unique. This constraint is identical to UNIQUE.

CHECK(WHERE-clause)
: specifies validity checking with respect to lists and ranges. This is accomplished with a WHERE clause.

PRIMARY KEY(variable)
: specifies a primary key variable, that is, a variable that does not contain missing values and whose values are unique.

FOREIGN KEY(variable(s)) REFERENCES table-name
<ON DELETE referential-action>
<ON UPDATE referential-action>
: specifies a foreign key, that is, one or a set of variables whose values are linked to the values of the primary key variable in another data set. The referential actions are performed when updates are made to the values of a primary key variable that is referenced by a foreign key.

For a RESTRICT referential action,

*a delete operation*
: deletes the primary key row, but only if no foreign key values matches the deleted value.

*an update operation*
: updates the primary key value, but only if no foreign keys match the current value to be updated.

For a SET NULL referential action,

*a delete operation*
: deletes the primary key row and sets the corresponding foreign key values to NULL.

*an update operation*
: modifies the primary key value and sets all matching foreign key values to NULL.

MESSAGE='message-string'

"message-string" is the text of an error message that is written to the log when the data fail the constraint. The maximum length for a message is 256 characters.

Using the IC CREATE statement, you can specify all of the columns for an integrity constraint in a single statement except for NOT NULL. You must use a separate IC CREATE statement for each column that has the NOT NULL constraint defined.

## Using PROC SQL to Create Integrity Constraints on Existing Tables

```
PROC SQL;
     ALTER TABLE table-name
     <constraint-clause-1>,...
     <constraint-clause-n>;
```

21

| | |
|---|---|
| *table-name* | name of table containing primary key referenced by the foreign key. |

where each *constraint-clause* is one of the following

ADD <CONSTRAINT *constraint-name*> *constraint*

DROP CONSTRAINT *constraint-name*

| | |
|---|---|
| *constraint-name* | name for the constraint being specified. If you do not name the constraint, a default will be used. |

where *constraint* can be one of the following

NOT NULL (*column-name*)

CHECK (*WHERE clause*)

DISTINCT (*column-name*)

UNIQUE (*column-name*)

FOREIGN KEY(*column name*) REFERENCES *table-name* <ON DELETE *referential-action*><ON UPDATE *referential-action*>

| | |
|---|---|
| *column-name* | column name in current table. |

*referential-action*

| | |
|---|---|
| RESTRICT | occurs only if there are matching foreign key values (default). |
| SET NULL | sets all matching foreign key values to NULL. |

### Using PROC SQL to Create Integrity Constraints on New Tables

```
PROC SQL;
    CREATE TABLE table-name
        (column-definition  <column-attribute>,
         <CONSTRAINT constraint-name
                    constraint>);
```

22

*constraint-name* name for the constraint being specified. If you do not name the constraint, a default will be used.

*constraint* is one of the following

NOT NULL (*column-name*)

CHECK (*WHERE clause*)

DISTINCT (*column-name*)

UNIQUE (*column-name*)

FOREIGN KEY(*column name*) REFERENCES *table-name* <ON DELETE *referential-action*> <ON UPDATE *referential-action*>

| | |
|---|---|
| *column-name* | column name in current table. |
| *table-name* | name of table containing primary key referenced by the foreign key. |

*referential-action*

| | |
|---|---|
| RESTRICT | occurs only if there are matching foreign key values (default). |
| SET NULL | sets all matching foreign key values to NULL. |

## Documenting Integrity Constraints

General form of the PROC SQL with the DESCRIBE statement:

```
PROC SQL;
   DESCRIBE TABLE CONSTRAINTS table-name;
```

General form of the PROC CONTENTS statement:

```
PROC CONTENTS DATA=libref.dataname;
RUN;
```

23

The DESCRIBE statement in PROC SQL prints the report in the LOG window.

## Creating Integrity Constraints

c09s2d1

```
*Execute one PROC only.  They do the same thing.;

proc datasets lib = ia;
   modify CapacityInformation;
       ic create PK_idinfo = Primary Key (RouteIdNumber)
          message = 'You must supply a Route ID Number';
       ic create firstclass = check
                                (where = (CapacityFirstClass <
                                          CapacityBusiness or
                                          CapacityBusiness = .))
          Message = 'First Class Capacity must be less than
                     Business Capacity';
      contents data = CapacityInformation;
run;
quit;
```

PROC DATASETS uses a WHERE= data set option for the CHECK constraint.

Output:

```
                         The DATASETS Procedure

Data Set Name: IA.CAPACITYINFORMATION        Observations:            108
Member Type:   DATA                          Variables:               7
Engine:        V8                            Indexes:                 1
Created:       18:27 Saturday,               Integrity Constraints:   1
               May 27, 2000
Last Modified: 11:56 Sunday, May 28, 2000    Observation Length:      48
Protection:                                  Deleted Observations:    0
Data Set Type:                               Compressed:              NO
Label:                                       Sorted:                  NO


              -----Engine/Host Dependent Information-----

Data Set Page Size:          4096
Number of Data Set Pages:    3
First Data Page:             1
Max Obs per Page:            84
Obs in First Data Page:      44
Index File Page Size:        4096
Number of Index File Pages:  2
Number of Data Set Repairs:  0
File Name:                   C:\workshop\winsas\prog3\
                                capacityinformation.sas7bdat
Release Created:             8.0101M0
Host Created:                WIN_NT
```

```
        -----Alphabetic List of Variables and Attributes-----

# Variable      Type Len Pos Format Informat Label
----------------------------------------------------------------------
6 Capacity      Num    8   8 8.     8.       Aircraft Capacity -
  Business                                   Business Class Passengers
7 Capacity      Num    8  16 8.     8.       Aircraft Capacity -
  Economy                                    Economy Class Passengers
5 Capacity      Num    8   0 8.     8.       Aircraft Capacity - First
  FirstClass                                 Class Passengers
4 Destination   Char   3  41                 Destination
1 FlightId      Char   7  24                 Flight Number
  Number
3 Origin        Char   3  38                 Start Point
2 RouteIdNumber Char   7  31                 Route Number


         -----Alphabetic List of Integrity Constraints-----

  Integrity                        Where             User
# Constraint Type        Variables Clause            Message

-----------------------------------------------------------------------------
1 PK_idinfo  Primary Key RouteId                     You must supply a flight
                         Number                      ID Number and
                                                     Route ID Number and Date
                                                     of Flight
2 firstclass Check                 (CapacityFirst    First Class Capacity must
                                   Class<Capacity    be less than
                                   Business) or      Business Capacity
                                   (Capacity
                                   Business=.)

         -----Alphabetic List of Indexes and Attributes-----

                                                          # of
                           Unique     Built    Owned     Unique
      #    Index           Option     by IC    by IC     Values
      ---------------------------------------------------------
      1    RouteIdNumber   YES        YES      YES          108
```

```
proc sql;
   alter table ia.CapacityInformation
       add constraint PK_idinfo Primary Key (RouteIDNumber)
       add constraint firstclass check
                                        (CapacityFirstClass <
                                         CapacityBusiness or
                                         CapacityBusiness = .);
   describe table constraints ia.CapacityInformation;
quit;
```

PROC SQL uses a WHERE clause for a CHECK constraint.

Log

```
7    proc sql;
8    describe table constraints prog3.CapacityInformation;
NOTE: SQL table PROG3.CAPACITYINFORMATION ( bufsize=4096 ) has the
      following integrity constraint(s):



-----Alphabetic List of Integrity Constraints-----

   Integrity                         Where              User
 # Constraint Type         Variables Clause             Message

------------------------------------------------------------------------------
 1 PK_idinfo  Primary Key RouteId                      You must supply a flight
                          Number                       ID Number and
                                                       Route ID Number and Date
                                                       of Flight
 2 firstclass Check                 (CapacityFirst     First Class Capacity must
                                    Class<Capacity     be less than
                                    Business) or       Business Capacity
                                    (Capacity
                                    Business=.)
```

## Business Scenario

The data set IA.CAPACITY2000 contains information about every flight in 2000.

We need to ensure that an added route id number is valid and that it is one of the route id numbers in the data set IA.CAPACITYINFORMATION.

26

## Primary Keys and Foreign Keys

**ia.CapacityInformation (parent table)**

| Route ID Number |
|---|
| 0000001 |
| 0000045 |
| 0000077 |
| 0000112 |

RouteIDNumber is Primary Key

Linked

**ia.Capacity2000 (child table)**

| Route IDNumber | WeightOf Cargo | Revenue Cargo |
|---|---|---|
| 0000001 | 45600 | 111720 |
| 0000045 | 14500 | 3190 |
| 0000077 | 67500 | 128250 |
| 0000112 | 55700 | 181582 |

RouteIDNumber is Foreign Key

27

## Primary Keys and Foreign Keys

When you use the primary keys and foreign keys

- specify a primary key on a parent table
- specify a foreign key on the child tables and identify
  - what the parent table is
  - what happens when you add data to the child table
  - what happens when you delete data from the parent table.

28

When you define a foreign key, the following must be true:

- The primary key and foreign key must specify the columns in the same order.
- The columns must be the same type and length.
- If you are adding foreign key constraints to existing columns, the data values for the foreign key must exist in the primary key.
- When you define a foreign key, you can choose what action occurs when you attempt to update or delete the primary key data value:

  RESTRICT prevents the update or delete of a primary key value unless no matching foreign key data values exist. This is the default.

  SET NULL allows update or delete of a primary key value and changes any affected foreign key data value to a missing value.

- You cannot delete a primary key until all foreign key constraints that reference it have been deleted. There are no restrictions on deleting a foreign key.

You cannot delete a table having a referential integrity constraint to another table without first removing the constraint.

**Primary Keys and Foreign Keys**

If you add a new observation to the child table, you must specify the action you want to take.

- ON UPDATE RESTRICT
  force the user to delete the corresponding foreign key values from the children tables.

29

## Adding a Row to the Child Table

**ia.CapacityInformation (parent table)**

| Route ID Number |
|---|
| 0000001 |
| 0000045 |
| 0000077 |
| 0000112 |

**ia.Capacity2000 (child table)**

| Route IDNumber | WeightOf Cargo | Revenue Cargo |
|---|---|---|
| 0000001 | 45600 | 111720 |
| 0000045 | 14500 | 3190 |
| 0000077 | 67500 | 128250 |
| 0000112 | 55700 | 181582 |

30

...

## Adding a Row to the Child Table

**ia.CapacityInformation (parent table)**

| Route ID Number |
|---|
| 0000001 |
| 0000045 |
| 0000077 |
| 0000112 |

**ia.Capacity2000 (child table)**

| Route IDNumber | WeightOf Cargo | Revenue Cargo |
|---|---|---|
| 0000001 | 45600 | 111720 |
| 0000045 | 14500 | 3190 |
| 0000077 | 67500 | 128250 |
| 0000112 | 55700 | 181582 |
| 0000145 | 23987 | 176000 |

?

31

## Adding a Row to the Child Table

**ia.CapacityInformation (parent table)**

| Route ID Number |
|---|
| 0000001 |
| 0000045 |
| 0000077 |
| 0000112 |

**ia.Capacity2000 (child table)**

| Route IDNumber | WeightOf Cargo | Revenue Cargo |
|---|---|---|
| 0000001 | 45600 | 111720 |
| 0000045 | 14500 | 3190 |
| 0000077 | 67500 | 128250 |
| 0000112 | 55700 | 181582 |

32

## Adding a Row to the Child Table

**ia.CapacityInformation (parent table)**

| Route ID Number |
|---|
| 0000001 |
| 0000045 |
| 0000077 |
| 0000112 |
| 0000145 |

**ia.Capacity2000 (child table)**

| Route IDNumber | WeightOf Cargo | Revenue Cargo |
|---|---|---|
| 0000001 | 45600 | 111720 |
| 0000045 | 14500 | 3190 |
| 0000077 | 67500 | 128250 |
| 0000112 | 55700 | 181582 |

33

## Adding a Row to the Child Table

**ia.CapacityInformation (parent table)**

| Route ID Number |
|---|
| 0000001 |
| 0000045 |
| 0000077 |
| 0000112 |
| 0000145 |

**ia.Capacity2000 (child table)**

| Route IDNumber | WeightOf Cargo | Revenue Cargo |
|---|---|---|
| 0000001 | 45600 | 111720 |
| 0000045 | 14500 | 3190 |
| 0000077 | 67500 | 128250 |
| 0000112 | 55700 | 181582 |
| 0000145 | 23987 | 176000 |

34

## Primary Keys and Foreign Keys

If you delete primary key data from the parent table, which action do you want to take

- ON DELETE RESTRICT

  force the user to delete the corresponding foreign key values from the children tables before the user could delete the primary key value from the parent table.

*continued...*

35

## Primary Keys and Foreign Keys

- ON DELETE SET NULL

  set the foreign key values in the children tables to missing when a primary key value is deleted from the parent table.

36

## Creating Integrity Constraints

c09s2d2

Create the foreign key constraint on the 'child table'.

```
proc sql;
   alter table ia.Capacity2000
      add Constraint FKRoute Foreign Key (RouteIDNumber)
                    references ia.CapacityInformation
                              on update restrict
                              on delete restrict;
```

Add an invalid observation.

```
proc sql;
   insert into ia.Capacity2000
       set  FlightIDNumber = 'IA00101',
              RouteIDNumber = '0000145',
                Origin = 'RDU',
                Destination = 'LHR',
                CapacityFirstClass = 15,
                CapacityBusiness = 29,
                CapacityEconomy = 200;

quit;
```

Log

```
15    proc sql;
16       insert into ia.Capacity2000
17           set  FlightIDNumber = 'IA00101',
18                RouteIDNumber = '0000145',
19                Origin = 'RDU',
20                Destination = 'LHR',
21                CapacityFirstClass = 15,
22                CapacityBusiness = 29,
23                CapacityEconomy = 200;
ERROR: Observation was not added/updated because no match was found for
       the foreign key value.
NOTE: Deleting the successful inserts before error noted above to
      restore table to a consistent state.
24
25    quit;
NOTE: The SAS System stopped processing this step because of errors.
NOTE: PROCEDURE SQL used:
      real time           0.66 seconds
      cpu time            0.25 seconds
```

## Reference Information

To drop a constraint so that you can delete a SAS data set, use

```
proc sql;
   alter table ia.CapacityInformation
       drop constraint pk_idinfo;
   alter table ia.CapacityInformation
       drop constraint firstclass;
quit;
```

## Exercises

1. Create integrity constraints with PROC DATASETS for ia.Employee_Data.
   - Place a primary key on the variable EMP_ID and add a custom message.
   - Do not allow missing values for the LASTNAME variable and add a custom message.
2. Use PROC FSEDIT to test the constraints.
3. Create a foreign key on the data set IA.Pilots on the variable Emp_ID using PROC SQL. The parent table is IA.Employee_data.
   - Restrict the update and deletion of the Emp_id value.
4. Test the constraints by trying to add the employee number E01724 to the ia.Pilots data set using the PROC SQL INSERT statement.

# 9.3 Creating and Using Audit Trails

## Objectives

- Determine what an audit trail file is.
- Examine the columns in an audit trail file.
- Initiate an audit trail file.
- Add values to the audit trail file.
- Report on an audit trail file.
- Manage an audit trail file.

38

## Business Scenario

We need to monitor the updates for the data set IA.CAPACITYINFORMATION.

Creating an audit trail file allows us to document

- who
- why
- when

39

## Organize the Tasks:

- Create integrity constraints on ia.CapacityInformation and Capacity2000.
- **Create an audit trail file on ia.CapacityInformation.**
- Modify ia.CapacityInformation to decrease the number of seats.
- Modify ia.CapacityInformation to change some of the route ID numbers.
- Modify ia.Cargo1999 to correct cargo revenues.

40

## Audit Trail

- The audit trail is an optional SAS file that logs modifications to a SAS table.
- For each addition, deletion and update to the data, the audit file stores information about
  - who made the modification
  - what was modified
  - when the modification was made.

41

## The Audit Trail File is

- a SAS file with the same name as the data file it is monitoring, but with a member type of AUDIT
- created by PROC DATASETS
- read only
- read by any PROC that accepts the TYPE= data set option.

42

The audit trail file must reside in the same SAS data library as the data file associated with it.

A SAS table can have at most one audit file.

Procedures such as PRINT, TABULATE, and FREQ can read audit trail files using the TYPE= data set option.

Windows such as the Viewtable window, FSEDIT window, or FSVIEW window display the audit trail variables only if they are invoked in edit mode.

## Audit Trail File Variables

The audit trail file can contain three types of columns:

***data file variables***
copies of the columns in the audited SAS data file

***_AT*_ variables***
store information about the data modifications

***USER_VAR variables***
user defined special columns that enable you to enter information into the audit file.

43

For the _AT*_ variables, the asterisk is replaced by a specific string such as DATETIME.

USER_VAR variables are optional. They supplement the information automatically recorded in the **_AT*_** variables.

## _AT*_ Variables

| _AT* Variable_ | Description |
|---|---|
| _ATDATETIME_ | Date & time of a modification |
| _ATUSERID_ | Login user-id associated with a modification |
| _ATOBSNO_ | Observation number affected by the modification unless REUSE=YES |
| _ATRETURNCODE_ | Event return code |
| _ATMESSAGE_ | SAS log message at the time of the modification |
| _ATOPCODE_ | Code describing the type of operation |

44

By default SAS logs all _ATOPTCODE_ codes. You can change this behavior when you initiate an audit trail.

## _ATOPTCODE_ Values

| Code | Event |
|---|---|
| DA | Added data record image |
| DD | Deleted data record image |
| DR | Before-update record image |
| DW | After-update record image |
| EA | Observation add failed |
| ED | Observation delete failed |
| EU | Observation update failed |

45

An image can be

- an edited data value
- an added data value
- a deleted row.

## User Variables are

- defined as part of the audit trail specification
- displayed when the associated data file is opened for update
- edited as you would edit data values
- written to the audit trail as each row is saved
- not available when the associated data file is opened for browsing.

46

## Initiating an Audit Trail using PROC DATASETS

```
PROC DATASETS LIB=libname;
     AUDIT SAS-file <SAS-password>;
     INITIATE;
        <LOG <BEFORE_IMAGE=YES|NO>
        <DATA_IMAGE=YES|NO>
        <ERROR_MESSAGE=YES|NO>>;
        <USER_VAR=specification-1
                   <specification-n>>;
RUN;
```

47

| | |
|---|---|
| *libname* | the library where the table to be audited resides. |
| *SAS-file* | the name of the table to be audited. |
| *SAS-password* | the SAS data file password, if one exists. |
| **INITIATE** | creates the audit file. |
| **LOG** | specifies the images (events) to be logged on the audit file. If you omit the LOG statement, all images are recorded. |

**BEFORE_IMAGE=YES | NO**
controls storage of before-update record images (for example, the 'DR' operation).

**DATA_IMAGE=YES | NO**
controls storage of after-update record images (for example, other operations starting with 'D').

**ERROR_IMAGE=YES | NO**
controls storage of unsuccessful update record images (for example, operations starting with 'E').

The audit file uses the SAS password assigned to the parent data file; therefore, it is recommended that you use an alter password for the parent data file. An alter password can be assigned with the ALTER= data set option. You can use this option to assign an alter-password to a SAS file or to access a read-, write-, or alter-protected SAS file. If another password is used or no password is used, then the audit file is still created, but is not protected.

## PROC DATASETS USER_VAR Statement

```
USER_VAR=variable-name <$><length>
              <LABEL='variable-label'>
              <variable-name-n ...>;
```

48

USER_VAR variables are unique in SAS in that they are stored in one file (for example, the audit file) and opened for update in another (for example, the data file).

When the data file is opened for update, the USER_VAR variables display, and you can edit them as though they were part of the data file.

## Initiating an Audit Trail

```
proc datasets lib = ia;
   audit Capacity2000;
   initiate;
   user_var who $20 label = 'Who made the change'
            why $20 label = 'Why the change was made';
run;
```

49

## Controlling the Audit Trail

Once you initiate the audit trail, use PROC DATASETS to

- change which record images are logged
- suspend logging
- resume logging
- terminate (delete) the audit file.

50

## Terminating an Audit Trail

To terminate and delete an audit trail, use PROC DATASETS with the TERMINATE statement.

```
PROC DATASETS LIB=libname;
     AUDIT SAS-file <SAS-password>;
     TERMINATE;
RUN;
```

51

## Creating and Viewing an Audit Trail

c09d3d1

Create the Audit Trail

```
proc datasets library = ia nolist;
   audit Capacity2000;
   initiate;
   user_var who $20 label = 'Who made the change'
            why $20 label = 'Why the change was made';
run;


proc sql;
   insert into ia.Capacity2000
      set FlightIDNumber = 'IA00040',
          RouteIDNumber = '0000100',
          Origin = 'CDG',
          Destination = 'LHR',
          CapacityFirstClass = 12,
          CapacityBusiness = 20,
          CapacityEconomy = 120,
          FlightDate = '03JUN2000'd,
          who = 'Administrator',
          why = 'New Flight';

proc print data = ia.Capacity2000 (type=audit);
   title 'Audit Trail for IA.CAPACITY2000';
run;


/*  To terminate the audit trail */

proc datasets library = ia nolist;
   audit Capacity2000;
   terminate;
run;
quit;
```

### Output

```
                         Audit Trail for IA.CAPACITY2000

                 Route                         Capacity
       Flight     Id                            First    Capacity Capacity
 Obs IdNumber  Number  Origin Destination      Class    Business Economy

  1  IA00040   0000100  CDG        LHR             12         20      120


         Flight
 Obs       Date       who          why              _ATDATETIME_  _ATOBSNO_

  1  03JUN2000 Administrator New Flight  06JUN2000:20:44:14    164638



 Obs _ATRETURNCODE_    _ATUSERID_    _ATOPCODE_     _ATMESSAGE_

  1         .             sasjss         DA
```

## Exercises

5. Create an audit trail for the data set IA.Pilots.
   - Add user variables to track who edited the data set and why it was edited.
   - Use PROC FSEDIT to give a pilot a salary increase. Be sure to include who edited the data set and give a reason for the increase.
   - Use PROC PRINT to look at the audit trail.
   - Terminate the audit trail.

# 9.4 Modifying SAS Data Sets in Place

## Objectives

- Use the MODIFY statement in a DATA step to update a data set in place.
- Use a transaction data set to make modifications to a SAS data set.
- Use the KEY= option with the MODIFY statement.

55

...

## Business Scenario

International Airlines has decided to give passengers more leg room, so they want to decrease the number of seats for business and economy classes.

| First Class | Capacity Business | Capacity Economy |
|---|---|---|
| 14 | 27 | 155 |

56

## Organize the Tasks

- Create integrity constraints on ia.CapacityInformation and ia.Capacity2000.
- Create an audit trail file on ia.CapacityInformation.
- **Modify ia.Capacity to decrease the number of seats.**
- Modify ia.Capacity to change some of the route ID numbers.
- Modify ia.Cargo1999 to correct cargo revenues.

57

...

## Using the SET Statement

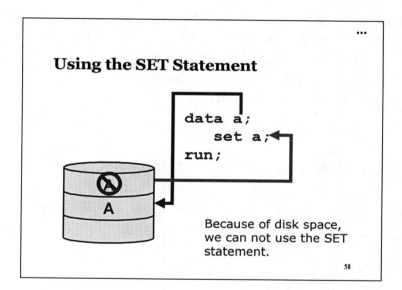

Because of disk space, we can not use the SET statement.

58

When you use the SET statement or the UPDATE statement to modify a SAS data set, SAS creates a second copy of the data until execution is completed. SAS then deletes the original copy of the data.

### Using the Modify Statement

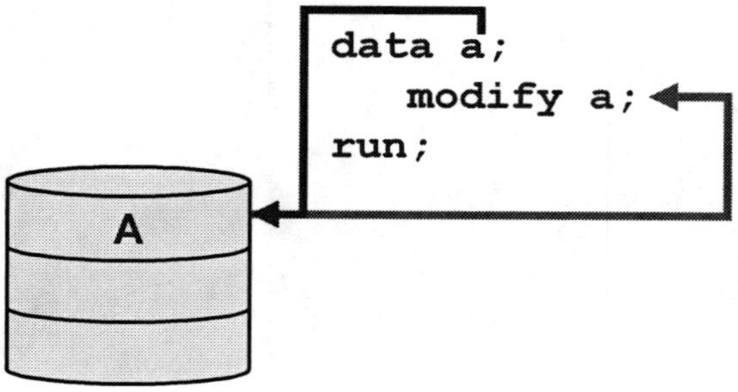


59

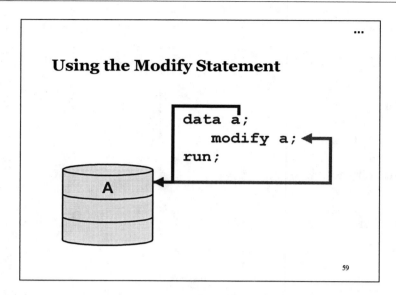

When you use the MODIFY statement to modify a SAS data set, SAS does not create a second copy of the data. The updated observation is written to the data set in the location of the original observation.

One advantage of using the MODIFY statement is that integrity constraints are checked and audits written to the audit trail.

### Using the MODIFY statement

Using the MODIFY statement, you can modify

- every observation in a data set
- observations using a transaction data set and a BY statement
- observations located using an index.

60

## How MODIFY Affects DATA Step Processing

- During compilation, new variables can be added to the PDV but are automatically dropped from the output.

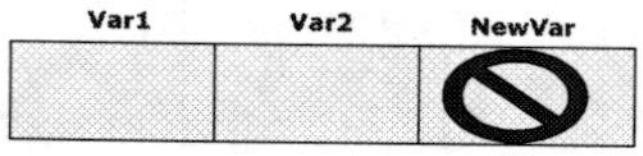


*continued...*

61

## How MODIFY Affects DATA Step Processing

- During execution, the new values in the PDV replace the original observation in the master SAS data set at the bottom of the DATA step (or when a REPLACE statement is executed) instead of being output to the SAS data set.

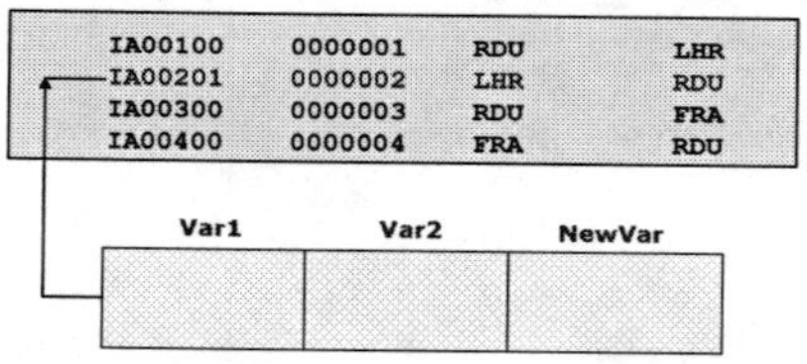


62

If the system terminates abnormally while a DATA step using the MODIFY statement is processing, you can lose data and possibly damage your master data set. You can recover from the failure by

- restoring the master file from a backup and restarting the step
- keeping an audit file and using this file to determine which master observations have been updated.

## Updating a Data Set in Place

If every observation in a SAS data set requires the same modification, you can specify the modification using an assignment statement.

**DATA** *SAS-data-set*;
    **MODIFY** *SAS-data-set*;
    *existing-variable* = *expression*;
  **run**;

63

## Updating a Data Set in Place

```
data ia.Capacity;
   modify ia.Capacity;
   CapacityEconomy = CapacityEconomy * .95;
   CapacityBusiness = CapacityBusiness * .90;
run;
```

64

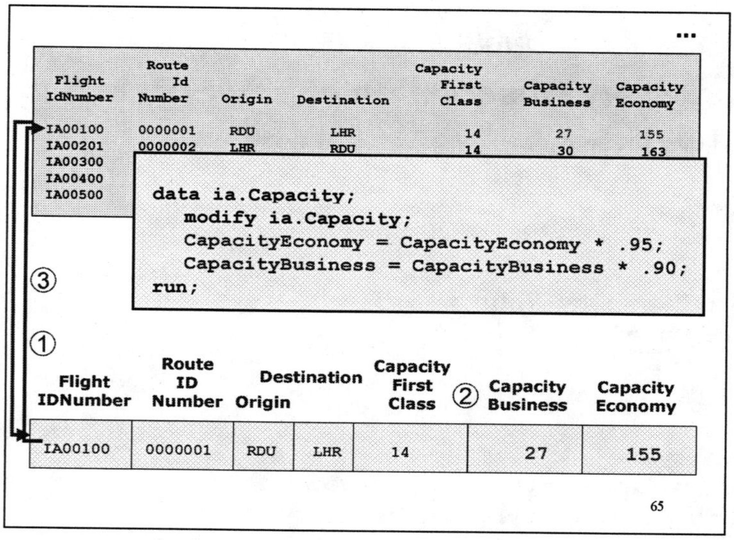

| Flight IdNumber | Route Id Number | Origin | Destination | Capacity First Class | Capacity Business | Capacity Economy |
|---|---|---|---|---|---|---|
| IA00100 | 0000001 | RDU | LHR | 14 | 27 | 155 |
| IA00201 | 0000002 | LHR | RDU | 14 | 30 | 163 |
| IA00300 | | | | | | |
| IA00400 | | | | | | |
| IA00500 | | | | | | |

```
data ia.Capacity;
   modify ia.Capacity;
   CapacityEconomy = CapacityEconomy * .95;
   CapacityBusiness = CapacityBusiness * .90;
run;
```

| Flight IDNumber | Route ID Number | Origin | Destination | Capacity First Class | Capacity Business | Capacity Economy |
|---|---|---|---|---|---|---|
| IA00100 | 0000001 | RDU | LHR | 14 | 27 | 155 |



❶ Reads an observation.

❷ Updates PDV using an assignment statement.

❸ Rewrites updated observation (same location).

## Updating Every Observation of a SAS Data Set (Self-Study)

c09s4d1

Program

```
proc print data=ia.Capacity (obs = 5);
   title 'Original Data';
run;

data ia.Capacity;
   modify ia.Capacity;
   CapacityEconomy = CapacityEconomy * .95;
   CapacityBusiness = CapacityBusiness * .90;
run;

proc print data=ia.Capacity (obs = 5);
   title 'Modified Data';
run;
```

Original Data

| Obs | Flight IdNumber | Route Id Number | Origin | Destination | Capacity First Class | Capacity Business | Capacity Economy |
|---|---|---|---|---|---|---|---|
| 1 | IA00100 | 0000001 | RDU | LHR | 14 | 30 | 163 |
| 2 | IA00201 | 0000002 | LHR | RDU | 14 | 30 | 163 |
| 3 | IA00300 | 0000003 | RDU | FRA | 14 | 30 | 163 |
| 4 | IA00400 | 0000004 | FRA | RDU | 14 | 30 | 163 |
| 5 | IA00500 | 0000005 | RDU | JFK | 16 | . | 251 |

Modified Data

| Obs | Flight IdNumber | Route Id Number | Origin | Destination | Capacity First Class | Capacity Business | Capacity Economy |
|---|---|---|---|---|---|---|---|
| 1 | IA00100 | 0000001 | RDU | LHR | 14 | 27 | 155 |
| 2 | IA00201 | 0000002 | LHR | RDU | 14 | 27 | 155 |
| 3 | IA00300 | 0000003 | RDU | FRA | 14 | 27 | 155 |
| 4 | IA00400 | 0000004 | FRA | RDU | 14 | 27 | 155 |
| 5 | IA00500 | 0000005 | RDU | JFK | 16 | . | 238 |

## Business Scenario

Some of the route ID numbers have changed. The changes are stored in a SAS data set.

Ia.NewRouteNumbers

| Flight IdNumber | Route Id Number | Origin | Destination |
|---|---|---|---|
| IA00500 | 0000035 | RDU | JFK |
| IA02000 | 0000080 | BOS | RDU |
| IA03500 | 0000045 | RDU | BNA |
| IA05000 | 0000120 | BRU | LHR |
| IA06700 | 0000067 | LHR | PRG |

67

## Business Scenario

We need to apply these changes to the large data set.

ia.Capacity

| Flight IdNumber | Route Id Number | Origin | Destination | Capacity First Class | Capacity Business | Capacity Economy |
|---|---|---|---|---|---|---|
| IA00100 | 0000001 | RDU | LHR | 14 | 30 | 163 |
| IA00201 | 0000002 | LHR | RDU | 14 | 30 | 163 |
| IA00300 | 0000003 | RDU | FRA | 14 | 30 | 163 |
| IA00400 | 0000004 | FRA | RDU | 14 | 30 | 163 |
| IA00500 | 0000005 | RDU | JFK | 16 | . | 251 |

68

## Organize the Tasks

- Create integrity constraints on ia.CapacityInformation and ia.Capacity2000.
- Create an audit trail file on ia.CapacityInformation.
- Modify ia.Capacity to decrease the number of seats.
- **Modify ia.Capacity to change some of the route ID numbers.**
- Modify ia.Cargo1999 to correct cargo revenues.

69

## Using a Transaction Data Set to Update

The MODIFY statement can be used with a BY statement to apply updates to a master data set from a transaction data set.

```
DATA SAS-data-set;
   MODIFY SAS-data-set;
            transaction data set;
   BY key-variable;
RUN;
```

70

When you use the MODIFY statement to update a data set, if

- a variable has a missing value in the transaction data set, the corresponding master value is not changed by default
- duplicate values of the BY variable exit in the master data set, only the first observation of the group is updated
- multiple transactions exist for one master observation, all transactions are applied in order.

The MODIFY statement locates the matching observation in the master data set by using dynamic WHERE processing.

Neither data set requires sorting.

## Using a Transaction Data Set to Update

```
data ia.Capacity;
   modify ia.Capacity
          ia.NewRouteNumbers;
   by FlightIdNumber;
run;
```

71

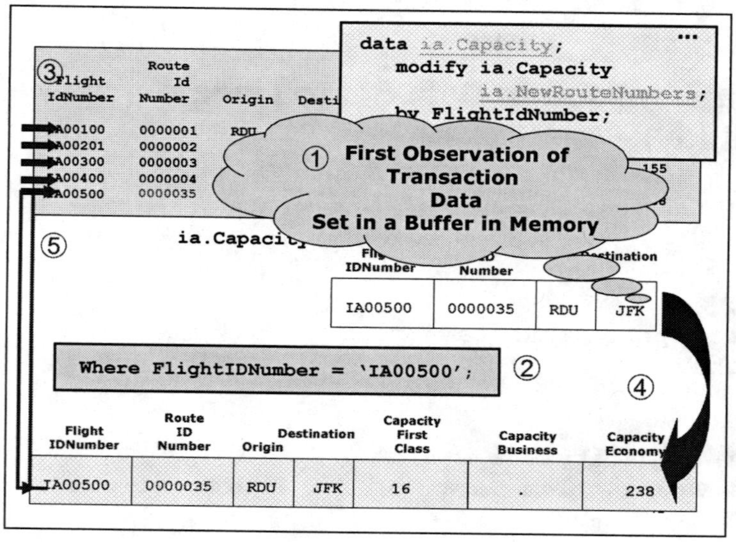


❶ Reads transaction observation into a memory buffer.

❷ Builds dynamic WHERE statement.

❸ Applies dynamic WHERE to the master data set. Reads an observation from the master data set into the PDV.

❹ Overlays common variables in the PDV.

❺ Rewrites the observation back to the master data set in the same location.

## Using a Transaction Data Set to Update (Self-Study)

c09s4d2

Program

```
data ia.Capacity;
   modify ia.Capacity ia.NewRouteNumbers;
   by FlightIdNumber;
run;

proc print data=ia.Capacity(obs = 5);
   title 'Using a Transaction Data Set for Modifications';
run;
```

Output

Using a Transaction Data Set for Modifications

| Obs | Flight IdNumber | Route Id Number | Origin | Destination | Capacity First Class | Capacity Business | Capacity Economy |
|---|---|---|---|---|---|---|---|
| 1 | IA00100 | 0000001 | RDU | LHR | 14 | 27 | 155 |
| 2 | IA00201 | 0000002 | LHR | RDU | 14 | 27 | 155 |
| 3 | IA00300 | 0000003 | RDU | FRA | 14 | 27 | 155 |
| 4 | IA00400 | 0000004 | FRA | RDU | 14 | 27 | 155 |
| 5 | IA00500 | 0000035 | RDU | JFK | 16 | . | 238 |

## Business Scenario

The cargo figures for 1999 are stored in IA.CARGO1999, which has a composite index, ROUTE, on FlightIDNumber and FlightDate.

IA.CARGO1999

| Flight IDNumber | Route IDNumber | Flight Date | Origin | |
|---|---|---|---|---|
| IA00100 | 0000001 | 01JAN1999 | RDU | ... |
| IA00101 | 0000001 | 01JAN1999 | RDU | ... |
| IA00100 | 0000001 | 02JAN1999 | RDU | ... |
| IA00101 | 0000001 | 02JAN1999 | RDU | ... |
| IA00100 | 0000001 | 03JAN1999 | RDU | ... |

74

## Business Scenario

An accountant has discovered that some of the figures are incorrect.

75

## Business Scenario

We must modify the cargo data to correct the figures. The correct cargo numbers are stored in IA.NEWCARGONUMBERS.

IA.NEWCARGONUMBERS

| Flight IDNumber | Route IDNumber | Origin | Destination | Capacity Cargo | |
|---|---|---|---|---|---|
| IA01102 | 0000011 | RDU | ORD | 35055 | ... |
| IA01400 | 0000014 | IAD | RDU | 35055 | ... |
| IA01503 | 0000015 | RDU | SEA | 73530 | ... |
| IA01700 | 0000017 | SEA | SFO | 35055 | ... |
| IA01704 | 0000017 | SEA | SFO | 35055 | ... |

76

## Organize the Tasks:

- Create integrity constraints on ia.CapacityInformation and ia.Capacity2000.
- Create an audit trail file on ia.CapacityInformation.
- Modify ia.Capacity to decrease the number of seats.
- Modify ia.Capacity to change some of the route ID numbers.
- **Modify ia.Cargo1999 to correct cargo revenues.**

77

## Updating Selected Observations

When you have an indexed data set, you can use

- a SET statement to read a transaction data set
- the MODIFY statement with the KEY= option to locate the observations for updating.

78

## Updating Selected Observations

```
DATA SAS-data-set;
   SET transaction data set;
   MODIFY SAS-data-set
         KEY=key-variable;
   old-variable = new-variable;
RUN;
```

79

When you use an index with the MODIFY statement,

- the index named in the KEY= option can be a simple or composite index.
- you must explicitly specify the update you want to occur. No automatic overlay of non-missing transaction values occurs as it does with the MODIFY/BY method.
- the data set you are updating must support indexes (data sets in Version 5 or sequential libraries, for example, cannot be processed).
- each transaction must have a matching observation in the master data set. If you have multiple transactions for one master observation, only the first transaction is applied. The others generate runtime errors and terminate the DATA step (unless you use the UNIQUE option, which is discussed later in this section).

## Using a Transaction Data Set to Update

```
data ia.cargo1999;
   set ia.NewCargoNumbers (rename =
                 (CapacityCargo = newCargoCapacity
                  CargoWeight = newCargoWeight
                  CargoRevenue = newCargoRevenue));
   modify ia.cargo1999 key = DateFlight;
   CapacityCargo = newCargoCapacity;
   CargoWeight = newCargoWeight;
   CargoRevenue = newCargoRevenue;
run;
```

80

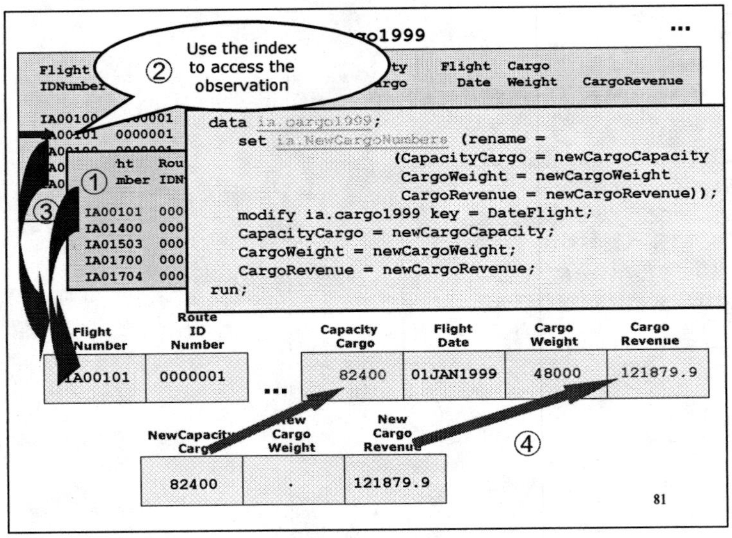


❶ SET statement reads an observation from the transaction data set.

❷ KEY= causes MODIFY to use the value in Flight Number to access an observation in the master data set using the index.

❸ Assignment statements update CapacityCargo, CargoWeight, and CargoRevenue.

❹ Updated observation is written back to the master data set.

## Using a Transaction Data Set to Update (Self-Study)

c09s4d3

Program

```
data ia.cargo1999;
   set ia.NewCargoNumbers (rename =
                        (CapacityCargo = newCargoCapacity
                           CargoWeight = newCargoWeight
                          CargoRevenue = newCargoRevenue));
   modify ia.cargo1999 key = DateFlight;
   CapacityCargo = newCargoCapacity;
   CargoWeight = newCargoWeight;
   CargoRevenue = newCargoRevenue;
run;

proc print data=ia.cargo1999 (obs = 5) heading = h;
   title 'Updated Cargo Numbers';
run;
```

Output

```
Updated Cargo Numbers

          Flight      Route                                    Capacity
   Obs    IDNumber    IDNumber    Origin    Destination        Cargo

    1     IA00100     0000001      RDU         LHR              82400
    2     IA00101     0000001      RDU         LHR              82400
    3     IA00100     0000001      RDU         LHR              82400
    4     IA00101     0000001      RDU         LHR              82400
    5     IA00100     0000001      RDU         LHR              82400

             Flight    Cargo
   Obs        Date     Weight      CargoRevenue

    1     01JAN1999       .        $121,879.90
    2     01JAN1999     48000      $117,600.00
    3     02JAN1999     46800      $114,660.00
    4     02JAN1999     46800      $114,660.00
    5     03JAN1999     46600      $114,170.00
```

## Exercises

6. Copy the IA.Employee_data SAS data set into the WORK library using PROC COPY:

```
proc copy in=ia out=work;
   select Employee_Data;
run;
```

7. Give all the employees in the IA.Employee_Data SAS data set a 5% salary increase using the MODIFY statement. Print the data before and after the increase.

8. Use the transaction data set IA.Employee_Data_Updates to modify the IA.Employee_Data SAS data set by the employee ID. Do not use an index.

9. Use the transaction data set IA.Employee_Data_Updates2 to modify the IA.Employee_Data SAS data set by the employee ID. Use the index on the IA.Employee_Data SAS data set. Only the variables emp_salary, emp_location, and lastname will be modified.

## Reference Information

### Missing Values

The MODIFY statement with a BY statement enables you to specify how missing values in the transaction data set are handled by using the UPDATEMODE= option on the MODIFY statement.

> **MODIFY** *SAS-data-set1 SAS-data-set2*
> <UPDATEMODE=
> MISSINGCHECK |
> NOMISSINGCHECK>;
> BY *by-expression*;

The default is MISSINGCHECK. When MISSINGCHECK is in effect, SAS checks for missing data in the transaction data set and does not replace the data in the master data set with missing values unless they are special missing values.

NOMISSINGCHECK does not check for missing values in the transaction data set and allows missing values in the transaction data set to replace the values in the master data set. Special missing values in the transaction data set still replace values in the master data set.

Example:

```
modify sasdata.payroll sasdata.update1
   updatemode=nomissingcheck;
```

### Duplicate Values

If there are duplicates in either MASTER or TRANSACTION:

```
data MASTER;
   set TRANSACTION;
   modify MASTER key=id;
   x=y;
run;
```

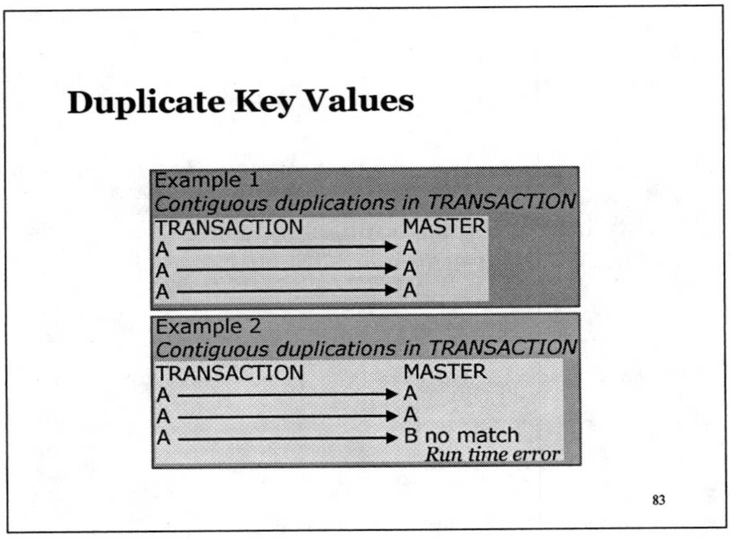


EXAMPLE 1: If there are contiguous duplications in TRANSACTION, each of which has a match in MASTER, then SAS performs one-to-one update.

EXAMPLE 2: If there are contiguous duplications in TRANSACTION, some of which do not have a match in MASTER, then SAS performs one-to-one update until it finds a non-match. At that time, SAS encounters a runtime error.

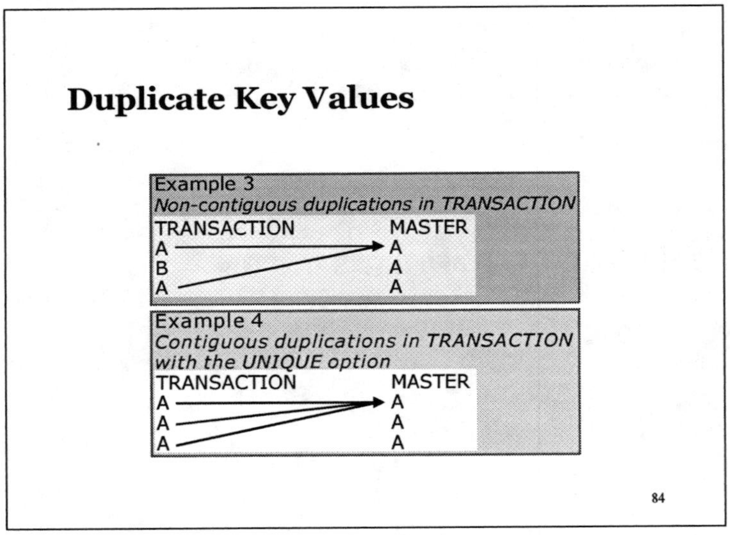


You can specify the UNIQUE argument with the KEY= option in the MODIFY statement to

- apply multiple transactions to one master observation
- identify that each observation in the master data set contains a unique value of the index variable(s).

For example:

```
data MASTER;
   set TRANSACTION;
   modify MASTER key=id/unique;
   x=y;
run;
```

EXAMPLE 3: If there are non-contiguous duplications in TRANSACTION, then SAS updates the first observation in MASTER. This is the same action as if the UNIQUE option had been used.

EXAMPLE 4: If there are contiguous duplications in TRANSACTION and the UNIQUE option is used, then SAS updates the first observation in MASTER.

#### Controlling the Update Process

You can further control processing.

REPLACE specifies that the current observation is rewritten to the master data set. A REPLACE statement is added to the end of the DATA step by default if a REPLACE, OUTPUT or REMOVE statement is not specified.

REMOVE specifies that the current observation is deleted from the master data set.

OUTPUT specifies that the current observation is written to the end of the master data set.

If you use an OUTPUT statement in conjunction with a REMOVE or REPLACE statement, be sure the OUTPUT statement is executed after any REMOVE or REPLACE statements to ensure the integrity of the index position.

If the SAS data set TRANSACTION has a variable named y having values of 'yes', 'no', and 'new', you can submit the following program to

- delete the rows for the y value of 'no'
- update the rows with the y value of 'yes'
- append the rows for the y value of 'new'.

```
data MASTER;
   set TRANSACTION;
   modify MASTER key=id;
   a = b;
   if y = 'no' then remove;
   else if y = 'yes' then replace;
   else if y = 'new' then output;
run;
```

If you do not have a variable indicating how to process the data, you can use the automatic variable _IORC_, which is assigned a value after a MODIFY statement is executed, indicating abnormal I/O conditions.

An _IORC_ = 0 indicates that the MODIFY statement was successful, and that the observation was located in the data set.

For example,

```
data MASTER;
   set TRANSACTION;
   modify MASTER key=id;
   a = b;
   if _IORC_ = 0 then replace;
   else do;
      output;
      _ERROR_ = 0; /* prevents PDV being printed */
                   /* when there is no match.    */
   end;
run;
```

#### Monitoring I/O Error Conditions

You can use the automatic variable _IORC_ with the %SYSRC autocall macro to test for specific I/O error conditions created when you use the KEY= option in the MODIFY or SET statements or use the BY statement with the MODIFY statement.

General form for using %SYSRC with _IORC_:

> IF _IORC_ = %SYSRC(*mnemonic*) THEN...

| MNEMONIC | MEANING |
|---|---|
| _DSENMR | The observation in the transaction data set does not exist in the master data set. Used with MODIFY with a BY. |
| _DSEMTR | Multiple transaction data set observations do not exist on the master data set. Used with MODIFY with a BY. |
| _DSENOM | No matching observation. Used with the KEY=. |
| _SOK | The observation was located. _SOK has a value of 0. |

To test for error conditions, use the mnemonics above.

The %SYSRC macro is in the AUTOCALL library. You must have the MACRO system option in effect to use this macro. You can view the source code for the %SYSRC macro in sas/core/sasmacro.

For example,

```
data MASTER;
   set TRANSACTION;
   modify MASTER key=id;
   select (_IORC_);
      when (%sysrc(_sok)) do;
         a = b;
         replace;
      end;
      when (%sysrc(_dsenom)) do;
         output;
         _ERROR_ = 0;
      end;
      otherwise;
   end;
run;
```

## 9.5 Chapter Summary

You can create integrity constraints on tables that you update in place. Integrity constraints are rules that table modifications must follow to guarantee consistency of data.

There are five integrity constraints available.

| General Constraints | |
|---|---|
| NOT NULL | Non-missing |
| CHECK | Where clause |
| UNIQUE | Non-duplication |
| **Referential Constraints** | |
| PRIMARY KEY | Both NOT NULL and UNIQUE |
| FOREIGN KEY | Links column in one table to a PRIMARY KEY in another. |

To create a constraint, use either PROC SQL or PROC DATASETS.

```
PROC SQL;
      CREATE TABLE table
            (column-specification,...
             <constraint-specification,...>);
where
column-specification: column-name data-type width
                            <column-attribute>
constraint-specification:
                            CONSTRAINT
                            constraint-name constraint
constraint:
                  NOT NULL (column-name)
                  CHECK (WHERE clause)
                  UNIQUE (column-name)
                  PRIMARY KEY(column name)
                  FOREIGN KEY(column name)
                     REFERENCES table-name
                            <(reference-list)>
                  <ON DELETE referential-action>
                  <ON UPDATE referential-action>
```

```
PROC SQL;
      ALTER TABLE table
            DROP CONSTRAINT constraint-name
            DROP FOREIGN KEY constraint-name
            DROP PRIMARY KEY
            ADD CONSTRAINT constraint-name
                                  constraint;
```

```
PROC DATASETS LIB=libref;
      MODIFY member;
            INTEGRITY CONSTRAINT CREATE
                  constraint-name=constraint
                  message='New Error Message';
            INTEGRITY CONSTRAINT DELETE
                  constraint-name;
RUN;
```

To document constraints, use

```
PROC SQL;
      DESCRIBE TABLE CONSTRAINTS table-name;
```

```
PROC CONTENTS DATA=libref.dataname;
RUN;
```

An audit trail is an optional SAS file that logs modifications to a SAS table. The audit trail contains information about

- who made a modification
- what was modified
- when the modification was made.

There are three types of variables in an audit trail file:

| | |
|---|---|
| Data file | copies of the columns in the audited SAS data file |
| _AT*_ | store information about the data modifications |
| USER_VAR | user defined special variables that allow you to enter information into the audit file. |

| _AT* Variable_ | Description |
|---|---|
| _ATDATETIME_ | Date and time of a modification |
| _ATUSERID_ | Login user-id associated with a modification |
| _ATOBSNO_ | Observation number affected by the modification unless REUSE=YES (SAS system option) |
| _ATRETURNCODE_ | Event return code |
| _ATMESSAGE_ | SAS log message at the time of the modification |
| _ATOPCODE_ | Code describing the type of operation |

**_ATOPCODE_ Values**

| Code | Event |
|---|---|
| DA | Added data record image |
| DD | Deleted data record image |
| DR | Before-update record image |
| DW | After-update record image |
| EA | Observation add failed |
| ED | Observation delete failed |
| EU | Observation update failed |

To create an audit trail, use

```
PROC DATASETS LIB=libname;
     AUDIT SAS-file <SAS-password>;
     INITIATE;
        <LOG <BEFORE_IMAGE=YES | NO>
        <DATA_IMAGE=YES | NO>
        <ERROR_MESSAGE=YES | NO>>;
        <USER_VAR=specification-1
        <specification-n>>;
RUN;
```

To terminate collecting information about data edits, use

```
PROC DATASETS LIB=libname;
     AUDIT SAS-file <SAS-password>;
     TERMINATE;
RUN;
```

You can use a MODIFY statement in the DATA step to modify a SAS data set in place. You can use the MODIFY statement to

- modify every observation in a data set
- observations using a transaction data set and a BY statement
- observations located using an index
- observations located using an observation number.

The MODIFY statement is best used when the master data set is indexed based on the variable(s) used for matching transactions and/or when conserving disk space is an important issue (because the MODIFY statement performs its update in place).

General forms of the MODIFY statement:

**MODIFY** *SAS-data set;*

**MODIFY** *SAS-data-set1 SAS-data-set2;*
**BY** *by-expression;*

**MODIFY** *SAS-data-set* KEY=*index-name;*

Entire Program

```
/*********** c09s2d1 *****************/

/*********** Example 1    *************/

/*************************************/
/*    Create a check constraint and   */
/*    a primary key constraint.       */
/*************************************/

/*********** Example 1    *************/


proc datasets lib = ia;
   modify CapacityInformation;
       ic create PK_idinfo = Primary Key (RouteIdNumber)
          message = 'You must supply a Route ID Number';
       ic create firstclass = check
                             (where= (CapacityFirstClass <
                                      CapacityBusiness or
                                      CapacityBusiness = .))
          Message = 'First Class Capacity must be less than
                     Business Capacity';
     contents data = CapacityInformation;
run;
quit;



/*********** Example 2    *************/
/********* DO NOT SUBMIT IF ***********/
/********* EXAMPLE 1 SUBMITTED ********/

proc sql;
   alter table ia.CapacityInformation
       add constraint PK_idinfo Primary Key (RouteIDNumber)
       add constraint firstclass check
                                 (CapacityFirstClass <
                                  CapacityBusiness or
                                  CapacityBusiness = .);
   describe table constraints ia.CapacityInformation;
quit;
```

```
/*********** c09s2d2 *****************/

/**************************************/
/*    Create foreign key constraint   */
/*    on the 'child table'.           */
/**************************************/

proc sql;
   alter table ia.Capacity2000
      add Constraint FKRoute Foreign Key (RouteIDNumber)
                   references ia.CapacityInformation
                            on update restrict
                            on delete restrict;

/**************************************/
/*    Add an invalid observation.     */
/**************************************/

proc sql;
   insert into ia.Capacity2000
        set  FlightIDNumber = 'IA00101',
                RouteIDNumber = '0000145',
                  Origin = 'RDU',
                  Destination = 'LHR',
                  CapacityFirstClass = 15,
                  CapacityBusiness = 29,
                  CapacityEconomy = 200;

quit;



/*********** c09s3d1 *****************/

/**************************************/
/*    Create an audit trail, modify   */
/*    the data, and report the audits.*/
/**************************************/



proc datasets library = ia nolist;
   audit Capacity2000;
   initiate;
   user_var who $20 label = 'Who made the change'
            why $20 label = 'Why the change was made';
run;


proc sql;
   insert into ia.Capacity2000
      set FlightIDNumber = 'IA00040',
          RouteIDNumber = '0000100',
```

```
          Origin = 'CDG',
          Destination = 'LHR',
          CapacityFirstClass = 12,
          CapacityBusiness = 20,
          CapacityEconomy = 120,
          FlightDate = '03JUN2000'd,
          who = 'Administrator',
          why = 'New Flight';

proc print data = ia.Capacity2000 (type=audit);
   title 'Audit Trail for IA.CAPACITY2000';
run;


/*  To terminate the audit trail */

proc datasets library = ia nolist;
   audit Capacity2000;
   terminate;
run;
quit;




/*********** c09s4d1 *****************/

/*************************************/
/*    Modify all observations of a    */
/*    SAS data set.                   */
/*************************************/


proc print data=ia.Capacity (obs = 5);
   title 'Original Data';
run;

data ia.Capacity;
   modify ia.Capacity;
   CapacityEconomy = CapacityEconomy * .95;
   CapacityBusiness = CapacityBusiness * .90;
run;

proc print data=ia.Capacity (obs = 5);
   title 'Modified Data';
run;
```

```
/*********** c09s4d2 *****************/

/**************************************/
/*    Modify the observations of a    */
/*    SAS data set using a            */
/*    transaction data set.           */
/**************************************/

data ia.Capacity;
   modify ia.Capacity ia.NewRouteNumbers;
   by FlightIdNumber;
run;

proc print data=ia.Capacity (obs = 5);
   title 'Using a Transaction Data Set for Modifications';
run;
```

```
/*********** c09s4d3 *****************/

/**************************************/
/*    Modify the observations of a    */
/*    SAS data set using a            */
/*    transaction data set.           */
/**************************************/

data ia.cargo1999;
   set ia.NewCargoNumbers (rename =
                     (CapacityCargo = newCargoCapacity
                        CargoWeight = newCargoWeight
                       CargoRevenue = newCargoRevenue));
   modify ia.cargo1999 key = DateFlight;
   CapacityCargo = newCargoCapacity;
   CargoWeight = newCargoWeight;
   CargoRevenue = newCargoRevenue;
run;

proc print data=ia.cargo1999 (obs = 5) heading = h;
   title 'Updated Cargo Numbers';
run;
```

## 9.6 Solutions to Exercises

1. Create integrity constraints with PROC DATASETS for ia.Employee_Data.
   - Place a primary key on the variable EMP_ID and add a custom message.
   - Do not allow missing values for the LASTNAME variable and add a custom message.
2. Use a PROC FSEDIT to test the constraints.

```
proc datasets lib=ia;
   modify Employee_Data;
   ic create PK_empid = Primary Key (Emp_ID)
      message = 'You must supply an employee ID number';
   ic create lname = Not Null (lastname)
      message = 'You must supply a last name for the
                employee';
   contents data = Employee_Data;
run;
quit;

proc fsedit data = ia.Employee_Data;
run;
```

3. Create a foreign key on the data set IA.Pilots on the variable EMP_ID using PROC SQL. The parent table is ia.Employee_Data.

   Restrict the update and deletion of the EMP_ID value.

4. Test the constraints by trying to add the employee number E01724 to the ia.Pilots data set using the PROC SQL INSERT statement.

```
proc sql;
   alter table ia.Pilots
      add constraint FK_empid Foreign Key (Emp_ID)
         references ia.Employee_Data
            on update restrict
            on delete restrict;
   describe table constraints ia.Pilots;
quit;

proc sql;
   insert into ia.Pilot
      set Emp_ID = 'E01724';
quit;
```

5. Create an audit trail on the data set IA.Pilots.
   - Add user variables to track who edited the data set and why it was edited.
   - Use PROC FSEDIT to give a pilot a salary increase. Be sure to include who edited the data set and give a reason for the increase.
   - Use PROC PRINT to look at the audit trail.
   - Terminate the audit trail.

```
proc datasets library = ia nolist;
   audit Pilots;
   initiate;
   user_var who $20 label = 'Who made the change'
            why $20 label = 'Why the change was made';
run;

proc fsedit data = ia.Pilots;
run;

proc print data = ia.Pilots(type = audit);
   title 'Audit Trail for IA.PILOTS';
run;

proc datasets library = ia nolist;
   audit Pilots;
   terminate;
run;
quit;
```

6. Give all the employees in the IA.Employee_Data SAS data set a 5% salary increase using the MODIFY statement. Print the data set before and after the increase.

```
proc print data = ia.Employee_Data (obs = 5);
   title 'Original Data';
run;

data ia.Employee_Data;
   modify ia.Employee_Data;
   emp_salary = emp_salary * 1.05;
run;

proc print data = ia.Employee_Data (obs = 5);
   title 'Modified Data';
run;
```

7. Use the transaction data set IA.Employee_Data_Updates to modify the IA.Employee_Data SAS data set by the employee ID number. Do not use an index.

```
data ia.Employee_Data;
   modify ia.Employee_Data ia.Employee_Data_Updates;
   by Emp_ID;
run;
```

8. Use the transaction data set IA.Employee_Data_Updates2 to modify the IA.Employee_Data SAS dataset the employee ID number. Use the index on the IA.Employee_Data SAS data set. Only the variables Emp_Salary, Emp_Location, and LastName will be modified.

```
data ia.Employee_Data;
   set ia.Employee_Data_Updates2 (rename =
                                  (LastName = NewLastName
                              Emp_Location = NewLocation
                                Emp_Salary = NewSalary));
   modify ia.Employee_Data key = Emp_ID;
   LastName = NewLastName;
   Emp_Location = NewLocation;
   Emp_Salary = NewSalary;
run;
```

# Index